ZÜRICH

NORTHERN
SWITZERLAND

**NORTHERN
SWITZERLAND**
Pages 134–157

ZÜRICH
Pages 158–175

CENTRAL
SWITZERLAND
AND TICINO

EASTERN
SWITZERLAND AND
GRAUBÜNDEN

**EASTERN
SWITZERLAND
AND GRAUBÜNDEN**
Pages 176–205

0 km   50

0 miles   50

**CENTRAL
SWITZERLAND
AND TICINO**
Pages 206–239

EYEWITNESS TRAVEL GUIDES
SWITZERLAND

EYEWITNESS TRAVEL GUIDES

SWITZERLAND

ADRIANA CZUPRYN
MAŁGORZATA OMILANOWSKA
ULRICH SCHWENDIMANN

DK

LONDON, NEW YORK,
MELBOURNE, MUNICH AND DELHI
www.dk.com

Produced by Hachette Livre Polska sp. z o.o., Warsaw, Poland

EDITORS Teresa Czerniewicz-Umer, Joanna Egert-Romanowska
DESIGNER Paweł Pasternak
CARTOGRAPHERS Magdalena Polak, Olaf Rodowald
PHOTOGRAPHERS Wojciech and Katarzyna Mędrzakowie,
Oldrich Karasek
ILLUSTRATORS Michał Burkiewicz, Paweł Marczak

CONTRIBUTORS
Małgorzata Omilanowska, Ulrich Schwendimann,
Adriana Czupryn, Marek Pernal, Marianna Dudek

FOR DORLING KINDERSLEY
EDITOR Lucilla Watson
CONSULTANTS Gerhard Brüschke, Matthew Teller
TRANSLATOR Magda Hannay
PRODUCTION CONTROLLER Louise Minihane

Reproduced by Colourscan, Singapore.
Printed and bound by South China Printing Co. Ltd., China.

First published in Great Britain in 2005
by Dorling Kindersley Limited
80 Strand, London WC2R 0RL

Copyright © 2005 Dorling Kindersley Limited, London
A Penguin Company

A CIP CATALOGUE RECORD IS AVAILABLE FROM THE BRITISH LIBRARY
ISBN-13: 978-1-4053-0292-0
ISBN-10: 1-4053-0292-5

**The information in every
Dorling Kindersley Travel Guide is checked regularly.**
Every effort has been made to ensure that this book is as
up-to-date as possible at the time of going to press. Some details,
however, such as telephone numbers, opening hours, prices,
gallery hanging arrangements and travel information are liable
to change. The publishers cannot accept responsibility for any
consequences arising from the use of this book, nor for
any material on third party websites, and cannot guarantee
that any website address in this book will be a suitable
source of travel infomation.

We value the views and suggestions of our readers very highly.
Please write to: Publisher, DK Eyewitness Travel Guides,
Dorling Kindersley, 80 Strand, London WC2R 0RL, Great Britain.

◁ **The Matterhorn, Zermatt**

CONTENTS

**The massive towers of the
Grossmünster, Zürich**

INTRODUCING
SWITZERLAND

**Emblem of Zürich, Schweizer-
isches Landesmuseum, Zürich**

Lake Lucerne, at the geographical and historical heart of Switzerland

Panel from the 1513 altarpiece in
the Église des Cordeliers, Fribourg

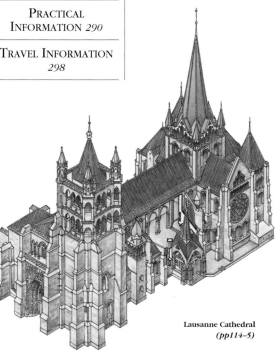

Lausanne Cathedral
(pp114–5)

How to Use this Guide

THIS GUIDE HELPS you to get the most from your visit to Switzerland. *Introducing Switzerland* maps the country and sets it in its historical and cultural context. Features cover topics from wildlife to geology. The eight sections comprising *Switzerland Region by Region*, three of which focus on Bern, Geneva and Zürich, describe the main sights, with photographs, maps and illustrations. Restaurant and hotel listings, and information about winter sports and many other outdoor activities can be found in *Travellers' Needs*. The *Survival Guide* contains practical tips on everything from using the Swiss rail network to choosing the best times of year to visit Switzerland.

Bern
A separate section is devoted to Switzerland's capital city. Each of Bern's main sights is shown on the map of the city centre and described in numerical order.

Sights at a Glance lists key places of interest.

A locator map shows where you are in relation to other areas of the city.

1 City Map
For easy reference, sights are numbered and located on a map. The main streets, bus stations, railway stations and tourist offices are also shown.

A suggested route for a walk is marked by a broken red line.

2 Street-by-Street Map
This gives a bird's-eye view of the key areas described in each section.

3 Detailed Information
All the sights in each city are described individually. Addresses, telephone numbers, opening hours and admission charges are given for each sight. The key to symbols is on the back flap.

1 Introduction
An overview of the history and character of a major city or region of Switzerland is given here.

SWITZERLAND REGION BY REGION
In this book, the country is described in eight chapters, three of which focus on Switzerland's major cities and five on its distinctive regions. The map on the inside front cover shows this regional division. The sights listed are shown and numbered on the *Pictorial Map* at the beginning of each chapter.

2 Pictorial Map
This shows the main road network and gives an illustrated overview of the whole region. All sights covered in the chapter are numbered and there are useful tips on getting around.

Each area of Switzerland is identified by colour-coded thumb tabs corresponding to the map on the inside front cover.

3 Detailed Information
All towns, villages and other places to visit are described individually and listed in order, following the numbering given on the Pictorial Map. Each entry also contains practical information such as museum opening times.

Story boxes explore some of the region's historical and cultural subjects in detail.

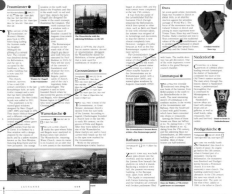

A Visitors' Checklist provides a summary of the practical information you need to plan your visit.

4 Switzerland's Top Sights
These are given two or more full pages. Historic buildings are often dissected so as to reveal their interiors. Stars indicate sights that visitors should not miss.

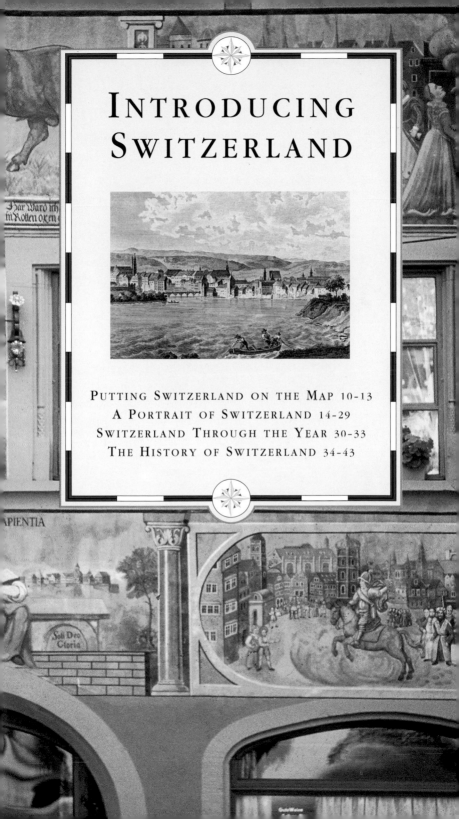

INTRODUCING
SWITZERLAND

Putting Switzerland on the Map

Located in the Alpine region of central Europe, Switzerland is a landlocked country covering some 41,300 sq km (15,950 sq miles) and inhabited by 7 million people. It borders Germany to the north, Austria and Liechtenstein to the east, Italy to the south, and France to the west and northwest. Switzerland consists of three distinct geographical regions, which stretch across the country southwest to northeast: the Jura mountains, covering a small area in the northwest; the Mittelland, a central plateau, and the Alps, the largest area of the country, in the south and east. The capital city is Bern.

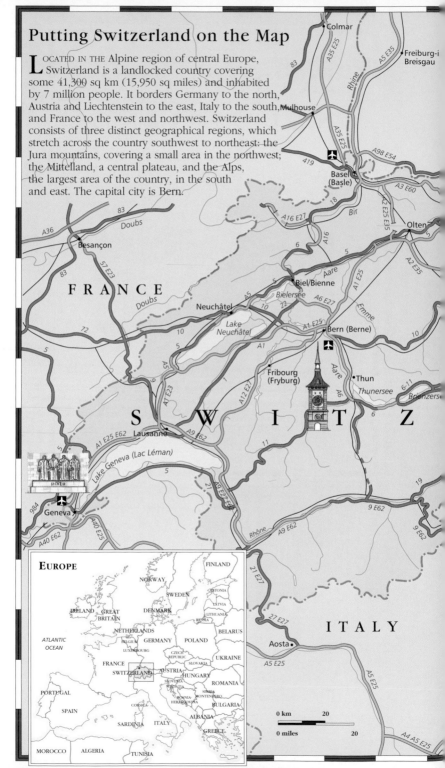

⊲ Painted façade of the Roter Ochsen, a house on the Rathausplatz in Stein am Rhein

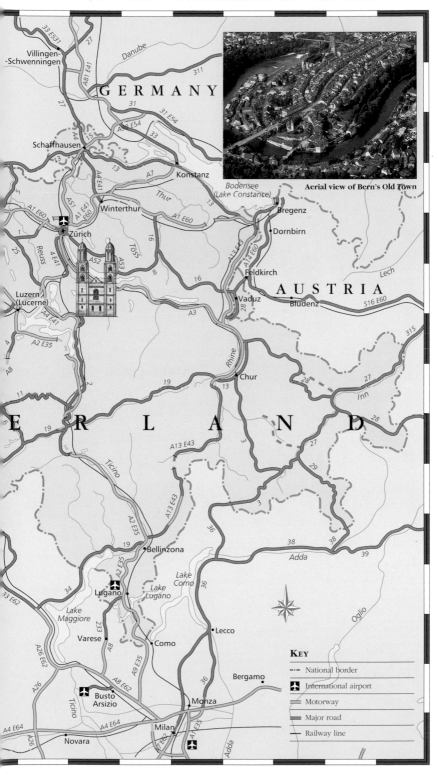

GERMANY

Villingen-
-Schwenningen

Danube

33 E531

27

A81 E41

A98 E54

31 E54

31

311

Schaffhausen

A4

15

13

13

33

A7

Konstanz

Thur

13

A1 E60

A51

A1 E60

Winterthur

Töss

16

Zürich

Reuss

A4 E41

A52

A53

8

Luzern
(Lucerne)

A4 E41

A2 E35

2

A8

4

11

19

ERLAND

19

Bodensee
(Lake Constance)

Bregenz

Dornbirn

Feldkirch

Vaduz

Bludeno

AUSTRIA

A3.E43

A14 E60

Lech

S16 E60

A3

Rhine

28

19

Chur

13

3

315

28

27

Inn

28

Aerial view of Bern's Old Town

A13 E43

A2 E35

Ticino

A13 E43

27

29

Bellinzona

36

38

38

39

Adda

Lugano

Lake
Lugano

Lake
Como

9C

Lake
Maggiore

34

233

Varese

Como

Lecco

Bergamo

33 E62

A26 E62

9V

A8 E62

A26

Busto
Arsizio

A8 E62

9C

9V

A8

36

Monza

A4 E64

Ticino

A4 E64

Milan

A4 E35

Novara

A26

Adda

Oglio

Switzerland's Cantons and Linguistic Regions

SWITZERLAND IS divided into 26 cantons, six of which (Appenzell-Ausserrhoden, Appenzell-Innerrhoden, Basel-Landschaft, Basel-Stadt, Nidwalden and Obwalden) are known as half-cantons but which operate as full cantons. Each canton has its own constitution, legislation and financial autonomy. The country is divided into three main linguistic regions. While German predominates in northern, eastern and central Switzerland, French is spoken in the west, and Italian in the south. Both French and German are spoken in Valais. Romansh is the language of a small minority of people in Graubünden, where German and Italian predominate.

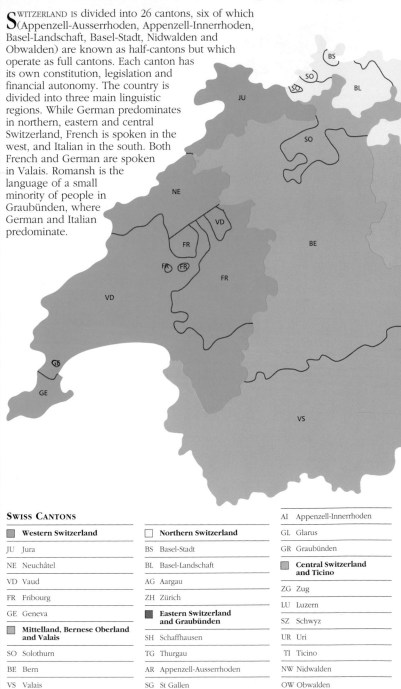

Swiss Cantons

▨ Western Switzerland	▢ Northern Switzerland
JU Jura	BS Basel-Stadt
NE Neuchâtel	BL Basel-Landschaft
VD Vaud	AG Aargau
FR Fribourg	ZH Zürich
GE Geneva	▨ Eastern Switzerland and Graubünden
▨ Mittelland, Bernese Oberland and Valais	SH Schaffhausen
SO Solothurn	TG Thurgau
BE Bern	AR Appenzell-Ausserrhoden
VS Valais	SG St Gallen

AI Appenzell-Innerrhoden
GL Glarus
GR Graubünden
▨ Central Switzerland and Ticino
ZG Zug
LU Luzern
SZ Schwyz
UR Uri
TI Ticino
NW Nidwalden
OW Obwalden

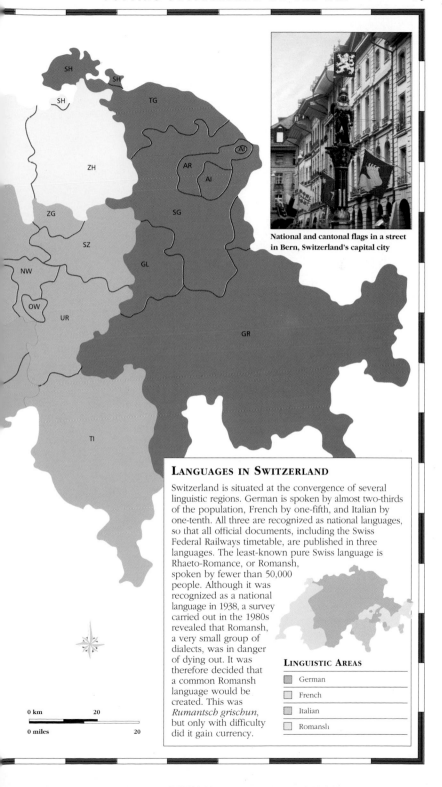

SH

SH

SH

TG

ZH

AR

AI

AI

ZG

SZ

SG

GL

NW

OW

UR

GR

TI

National and cantonal flags in a street in Bern, Switzerland's capital city

LANGUAGES IN SWITZERLAND

Switzerland is situated at the convergence of several linguistic regions. German is spoken by almost two-thirds of the population, French by one-fifth, and Italian by one-tenth. All three are recognized as national languages, so that all official documents, including the Swiss Federal Railways timetable, are published in three languages. The least-known pure Swiss language is Rhaeto-Romance, or Romansh, spoken by fewer than 50,000 people. Although it was recognized as a national language in 1938, a survey carried out in the 1980s revealed that Romansh, a very small group of dialects, was in danger of dying out. It was therefore decided that a common Romansh language would be created. This was *Rumantsch grischun*, but only with difficulty did it gain currency.

LINGUISTIC AREAS

▮	German
▯	French
▮	Italian
▯	Romansh

0 km   20

0 miles   20

A PORTRAIT OF SWITZERLAND

A LANDLOCKED COUNTRY *in the cultural and geographical heart of Europe, Switzerland has a distinct character and dynamism. While the country is admired for the beauty of its Alpine environment, its people are respected for their industry and technical ingenuity, as well as their social responsibility and radically democratic system of government. It is also one of the world's richest countries.*

Switzerland has virtually no natural borders. The Alpine mass of which it mostly consists extends eastwards into Austria, westwards into France, and southwards to form valleys that run down to Lombardy, where the border straddles several lakes. Although Switzerland's northern border follows the course of the Rhine, even here it crosses this natural feature, bulging out around Basel and taking in a mosaic of German and Swiss enclaves around Schaffhausen.

This mountainous country has engendered a robust spirit of independence and enterprise and a zealous work ethic in its population. Though divided by religion,

"Welcome to the Swiss Alps"

and with diverse cultural roots, the Swiss are remarkable for their strong sense of unified nationhood. Switzerland's national character has also been moulded by its neutrality. Having avoided many of the major conflicts that shaped the culture of other European nations, Switzerland stands at a slight remove from the wider world.

Switzerland today is a prosperous and highly industrialized nation with a cosmopolitan lifestyle. On the one hand, it is forward-looking and innovative. On the other, it is traditional and conservative, valuing stability above change, with a keenness to maintain cultural continuity and links with the past.

The Aletsch Glacier seen from the Eggishorn, whose peak reaches 2,927 m (9,603 ft)

◁ The Église St-Jean and Fontaine St-Jean in Fribourg

Biel/Bienne, the Bielersee and St Petersinsel, seen from Boezingenberg, in the Jura mountains

POPULATION, LANGUAGE AND RELIGION

While the Jura mountains, in the north, and the Alpine region, to the south, are sparsely populated, the highest population density, and most of the country's industrial activity, is in the central Mittelland, concentrated in and around the capital Bern, and the lakeside cities of Geneva, Lausanne, Luzern and Zürich.

Switzerland's linguistic and religious divisions are also distinctive. The German-speaking population inhabits the northern slopes and valleys of the Alps and a large section of the Mittelland plateau. The northern shores of Lake Geneva, the gentle slopes of the Jura mountains and the western Alps are inhabited by French-speaking Swiss.

Italian is spoken south of the main Alpine ridge, while the Romansh-speaking minority inhabits a few isolated high mountain valleys in the east. German is spoken by two-thirds of the population, French by one fifth, Italian by one tenth and Romansh by no more than about 1 per cent. Switzerland is almost equally divided between Protestant and Catholic, these religions crossing linguistic divides. The population also includes a small number of Jews and Muslims.

Divisions between French- and German-speakers, and between Protestants and Catholics, which have dogged the unity of the Confederation throughout its history, are still tangible today.

Traditional folk costume of the Fribourg region

DEMOCRACY IN ACTION

Switzerland is a federal republic consisting of 26 cantons. With its own tax, legal, fiscal and educational systems, each canton is virtually an independent state, enjoying considerable autonomy within the Swiss Confederation.

The country is governed by a Federal Assembly, a bicameral parliament consisting of a directly elected Federal Council and a Council of States, whose delegates represent the individual cantons. The most important parties are the

Regatta on Lej da Silvaplana in Graubünden

Liberal Democrats, Social Democrats and Christian Democrats, and the Swiss People's Party. Certain major issues are decided directly by the people, by referendum. Voting, on matters ranging from the national speed limit to concerns of strictly local relevance, takes place at national, cantonal and communal level.

Alpine festival in Beatenberg, on the Thunersee

THE ECONOMY

The Swiss economy is based on banking and international trade, the service industries, manufacturing industry, agriculture, winter sports and tourism. Standards of living are high, unemployment is low and the country's per capita income is one of the highest in the world.

The country's major exports are precision machinery, clocks and watches, textiles, chemicals and pharmaceuticals. Chocolate and dairy products, including cheese, are also major exports.

Although only 4 per cent of the population is engaged in agriculture, this sector of the economy enjoys a privileged status. The subsidies that it receives are the highest in the world. This is not only of benefit to farmers but, since it contributes to the preservation of Switzerland's picturesque landscape, it also supports the country's hugely important tourist industry.

Livestock accounts for almost three-quarters of Swiss farming, and dairy farming and agriculture for one quarter. Half of the country's cheese production is exported, chiefly in the form of Emmental and Gruyère.

ARTS AND SCIENCES

A highly cultured country, Switzerland plays a leading role in the arts, hosting such important events as the Lucerne Music Festival, the Montreux Jazz Festival and the Rose d'Or television awards in Montreux. Art Basel is the world's largest contemporary art fair, and the Kunsthaus in Zürich is a national art gallery of international importance.

The best-known of all Swiss intellectuals is perhaps the philosopher Jean-Jacques Rousseau (1712–78), who was born in Geneva but who spent most of his life in France. Other important Swiss writers include the German-born dramatists Max Frisch (1911–91) and Friedrich Dürrenmatt (1921–90). Herman Hesse (1877–1962),

Cattle returning from mountain pastures, in the Schwarzenburg region

who was born in Germany, became a Swiss citizen and wrote many of his greatest works in Switzerland. Many Swiss artists and architects have also won international recognition. Among the most prominent is the architect Le Corbusier (1887–1965), who was born and grew up in La-Chaux-de-Fonds, but who is more closely associated with France, and the sculptor and painter Alberto Giacometti (1901–66), a native of Graubünden, who spent nearly all his adult life in Paris. Although he retained his German citizenship, the artist Paul Klee (1879–1940), who was born near Bern, is treated as Swiss. Other notable Swiss artists include the painter Ferdinand Hodler (1853–1918), the sculptor Jean Tinguely (1925–91) and the graphic artist Max Bill (1908–94).

Since the 1930s, Switzerland has produced several architects of international renown. Mario Botta (b. 1943) designed the Museum of Modern of Art in San Francisco, and Jacques Herzog and Pierre de Meuron were the architects who converted London's Bankside power station into the prestigious Tate Modern gallery (1999).

Switzerland also has a tradition of excellence in the sciences. It was in Bern that Albert Einstein developed his theory of relativity, and to date no fewer than eleven Swiss chemists have

Clearing, an installation by Gillian White, depicting the links between art and nature

been awarded the Nobel Prize. The Federal Institute of Technology in Zürich and the ground-breaking European Centre for Nuclear Research near Geneva have put Switzerland at the forefront of scientific research.

TRADITIONAL ACTIVITIES

A sport-loving nation, the Swiss make the most of their Alpine country. Both cross-country and downhill skiing are popular winter sports. Kayaking, rafting, hiking and a host of other active summer sports have a large following among the Swiss.

Certain rural areas have distinctive types of sport. These include *Schwingen*, an Alpine form of wrestling, *Hornussen*, a ball game played with long, curved bats, and cow fights *(combats des reines)*, staged in the canton of Valais. Yodelling and alphorn-playing are also an integral

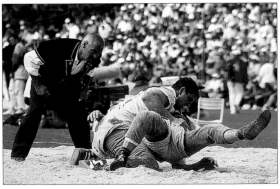

Contestants in a *Schwingen* match, a Swiss form of wrestling

A PORTRAIT OF SWITZERLAND

part of the Alpine way of life. However, many young town folk, regardless of region, are deeply indifferent to these traditional activities, as they are to the *Waffenlauf*, a long-distance race run by competitors dressed in uniforms and carrying rucksacks and rifles on their backs.

Swiss Guards at a ceremony at the Vatican in Rome

ENVIRONMENTAL ISSUES

The Swiss have a punctilious approach to preserving their natural environment. Two examples of this are a remarkably developed and well coordinated public transport system, and a scrupulous approach to recycling waste.

Switzerland is also the first country to have made compulsory the fitting of catalytic converters to cars, and national regulations concerning the emission of toxic gases and other substances are among the most stringent in the world. Such consideration towards the environment has had a measurable effect on the quality of life in Switzerland. Even in towns or cities the size of Luzern, Bern or Zürich, the rivers and lakes are so clean that it is perfectly safe to swim in them.

Most Alpine plants and many wild animals are protected by law, and certain animals, such as the ibex, have been reintroduced. Forests, which cover about a third of the country, are also

Kayaking on the Valser Rhine in Graubünden

protected. Forestry is tightly regulated and deforestation, which heightens the risk of landslides and avalanches, is forbidden. Naturally, Switzerland is a signatory to the Alpine Convention, which was drawn up together with France, Germany, Austria and Italy to protect the Alpine environment from the harmful effects of tourism and motorized transport.

SWITZERLAND ON THE WORLD STAGE

Although it is a neutral country, Switzerland maintains an army to defend its borders. National service is compulsory. However, except in time of war, the Swiss army has no active units and no top general, although regular training takes place. The last mobilization occurred during World War II. Today, the only Swiss mercenaries are the Swiss Guards, who defend the Vatican and act as the papal bodyguard in Rome.

Switzerland has both the European headquarters of the UN and the International Red Cross based in the country, and sees its role in international affairs as a humanitarian one.

The Swiss Alps

A BOUT TWO-THIRDS OF Swiss territory consists of Alpine and sub-Alpine areas. At lower elevations up to 1,500 m (5,000 ft) agricultural land and deciduous trees predominate. These give way to coniferous forest, which above 2,200 m (7,200 ft) in turn gives way to scrub and alpine pastures. At altitudes above 3,000 m (9,800 ft) mosses and lichens cover a desolate rocky landscape, above which are snowfields, glaciers and permanently snow-covered peaks. While snow and rainfall increase with altitude, the Alpine climate is affected by two seasonal winds, the cold, dry easterly *bise* and the warm southerly *Föhn*, which brings clear, sunny skies then rainfall to the western Alps.

Meadow and pasture *cover almost half of Switzerland. Wild clover and campanula grow abundantly in the high meadows of the Bernese Oberland.*

Mosses and lichens cling to the surface of rugged crests and precipitous scree-filled gorges.

Glacial lakes*, formed by the melting of glaciers, are a common sight in Alpine valleys. The Bachalpsee, near which rises the Wetterhorn, lies at the heart of a particularly scenic part of the Swiss Alps.*

Scrub, including dwarf mountain pine, as well as rhododendron and alder, cover the transitional zone between the forests and the high mountain peaks. At this altitude the growing season, from June to August, is brief.

Lush vegetation thrives on sheltered slopes and along gulleys cut by mountain streams.

High alpine meadows provide lush summer grazing for cattle.

MOUNTAIN LANDSCAPE

The Alps are cut through by deep valleys, terraces, cols and gorges. To the south of the Alps lies the canton of Ticino, which enjoys a Mediterranean climate. To their north are the long limestone sub-Alpine ranges, whose sheer rockfaces merge into the flatter Mittelland, central Switzerland's relatively low-lying plateau.

Forests *in Switzerland are continuously being degraded by environmental pollution. Deforestation, which increases the danger of avalanches, is forbidden.*

Alpine streams *flowing through dense pine forests are a part of the extraordinarily beautiful scenery in the Parc Naziunal Svizzer, Switzerland's national park.*

Spruce predominates in forests at higher altitudes.

ALPINE PLANTS AND ANIMALS

In spring Switzerland's high Alpine meadows are covered with a carpet of flowers, including aster, edelweiss, campion, and several species of gentian. Most Alpine flowers are protected and it is forbidden to pick them. Alpine wildlife includes ibex and chamois, marmot, Alpine hare, golden eagle, bearded vulture, and the rarely seen European lynx. Several species of these animals, including those that have been reintroduced, are also protected.

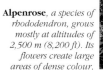

Edelweiss, *the symbol of Switzerland, grows among rocks at altitudes up to 3,500 m (11,500 ft). It has star-shaped flowers and woolly leaves.*

Alpenrose, *a species of rhododendron, grows mostly at altitudes of 2,500 m (8,200 ft). Its flowers create large areas of dense colour.*

Gentian *grows mainly in rock crevices and in woodlands. Its roots are used in the pharmaceutical industry.*

The Alpine ibex *lives above the tree line for most of the year. A species of wild goat, it is extremely agile over mountainous terrain.*

The chamois, *a goat antelope, frequents regions between wooded mountainsides and the snow line. Agile and shy, it is seldom seen at close range.*

The marmot *lives in burrows in Alpine meadows. When disturbed, it emits a piercing, high-pitched whistle.*

Areas of grassland, *like this one around the Schwarzsee, a lake at the foot of the Matterhorn, provide summer grazing for sheep. Thick snow covers these pastures during winter.*

Formation of the Alps

ABOUT 70 MILLION YEARS ago, the Adriatic Microplate began to drift northward, colliding with the rigid European Plate. While the oceanic floor that lay between them was forced downwards, the Adriatic Microplate was thrust upwards, creating the Alps. This upheaval, which continued until 2 million years ago, caused the upper strata of rock to fold over on themselves. The older metamorphic rocks, thrust up from the substratum, thus form the highest part of the Alps, while the more recent sedimentary and igneous rocks make up the lower levels. The action of glaciers during successive ice ages then scoured and sculpted the Alps, giving them their present appearance.

The Matterhorn, carved by the action of ice, is the most distinctive and best-known of Switzerland's peaks. Lofty and awe-inspiring, it rises to a height of 4,478 m (14,672 ft).

The Aletsch Glacier, in the Pennine Alps, covers about 120 sq km (45 sq miles) and is about 800 m (2,600 ft) deep. It is the largest glacier in Europe.

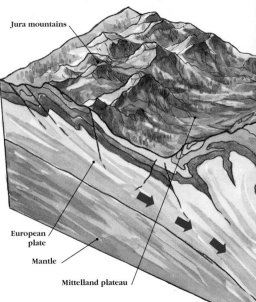

Jura mountains

European plate

Mantle

Mittelland plateau

ALPINE GLACIERS

Vestiges of the Ice Age, Alpine glaciers continue their erosive action. As they advance, they scour valley floors and sides, carrying away rocks which are ground and then deposited as lateral and terminal moraines. While glacial lakes fill basins scooped out by glaciers, hanging valleys were created when glaciers deepened the main valley.

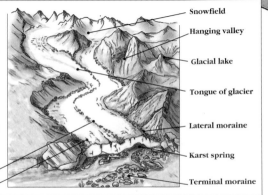

Snowfield

Hanging valley

Glacial lake

Tongue of glacier

Lateral moraine

Karst spring

Terminal moraine

Medial moraine

Crevasses

The Jura mountains, consisting of fossil-rich marl and limestone, are relatively low. They feature caves, sinkholes and underground streams. Because of their exceptionally well-preserved strata, the mountains gave their name to a geological period, the Jurassic.

THE SWISS ALPS

Apart from those in the eastern part of the canton of Graubünden, the Swiss Alps, like the French Alps, belong to the Western Alpine Group, which in turn consists of several separate ranges. This part of the Alpine range has the highest and steepest peaks and most contorted geological formations. It is also where Switzerland's landscapes of snow and ice are at their most breathtaking. The Valais Alps contain many of Switzerland's most impressive peaks, including the Matterhorn and Dufourspitze, which at 4,634 m (15,200 ft) is the country's highest mountain. The southern Alps lie in the canton of Ticino. The eastern Alps contain the Parc Naziunal Svizzer, Switzerland's national park.

KEY

☐	Western Alps
☐	Eastern Alps
☐	Southern Alps
☐	Swiss upland
☐	Jura mountains

Western Alps

Southern Alps

Direction of tectonic thrust

Adriatic Plate

Mantle

ALPINE LANDSCAPE

Shaped by the action of ice, the landscape of the Alps was created during a succession of ice ages that occurred 600,000 to 10,000 years ago. During periods of glaciation, the ice sheet was up to 2,000 m (6,500 ft) thick. Typical of the glacial landscape are sharp ridges, steep gullies, flat-bottomed valleys carved out by advancing glaciers, glacial lakes and hanging valleys with waterfalls creating streams.

The Parc Naziunal Svizzer is situated in the Rhaetian Alps, which form part of the Eastern Alpine Group. Its pristine Alpine landscape, covering 180 sq km (70 sq miles) in Graubünden, ranges from evergreen forest to desolate rocky areas and permanent snow at high altitudes.

Swiss Architecture

Tympanum of Basel's Romanesque Münster

SERENE ROMANESQUE abbeys, lofty Gothic cathedrals, lavishly decorated Baroque churches and town houses with painted façades all form part of Switzerland's architectural heritage. For most of its history, however, Swiss architecture reflected various European influences – German in the north and east, French in the west, and Italian in the south – without developing a distinctive style until the mid-20th century. Swiss vernacular architecture, however, has always been distinctive. It is epitomized by the Alpine chalet, of which there are several local variants.

Painted façade *of a fine 16th-century town house in Stein-am-Rhein, Schaffhausen.*

ROMANESQUE (10TH–12TH CENTURIES)

The Grossmünster *in Zürich, begun in the 11th century, was stripped of its interior decor during the Reformation.*

As elsewhere in western Europe, the flowering of the Romanesque style in Switzerland was due largely to the diffusion of religious orders, which spearheaded a renewal in religious architecture. Romanesque buildings are characterized by massive walls, rounded arches, groin vaulting, and a restrained use of decorative carving. Among the finest examples of the style in Switzerland are the Benedictine monastery at St Gallen, the Münster zu Allerheiligen in Schaffhausen, and its culmination, Basel's remarkable Münster.

The Romanesque crypt of Basel's 13th-century Münster

GOTHIC (13TH–15TH CENTURIES)

Characterized by pointed arches, ribbed vaulting and flying buttresses, the Gothic style emphasizes vertical perspectives, with stained-glass windows admitting light to lofty interiors and decoration on towers and portals. Fine examples of Swiss Gothic architecture include the Cathédrale St-Pierre in Geneva and Cathédrale de Nôtre-Dame in Lausanne, both of French inspiration, and the Münster in Bern, in the German Gothic style. Important Gothic secular buildings include the Château de Vufflens and Château de Chillon, and Bellinzona's three castles, Montebello, Sasso Corbaro and Castelgrande.

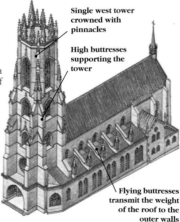

Single west tower crowned with pinnacles

High buttresses supporting the tower

Flying buttresses transmit the weight of the roof to the outer walls

The Cathédrale St-Nicolas *in Fribourg, built in the 14th and 15th centuries, exemplifies the High Gothic style.*

The Château de Chillon, *built by the Dukes of Savoy on an islet near Montreux, is one of the finest extant examples of Gothic fortified architecture in Switzerland.*

RENAISSANCE (15TH–16TH CENTURIES)

Coinciding with the Reformation, the Renaissance reached Switzerland in the late 15th to early 16th centuries. The style is most clearly seen in secular buildings, such as town halls, mansions with arcaded courtyards and fine town houses, like those in Bern. While the Gothic style tended to persist in the country's German-speaking regions, Renaissance influence was strongest in central and southern Switzerland.

The Rathaus in Luzern, completed in 1606, is built in the style of a Renaissance Florentine palazzo but its mansard roof reflects Swiss traditions.

The Collegio Pontificio di Papio in Ascona, built around 1584, has a fine Renaissance arcaded courtyard with a double tier of beautifully proportioned arches.

BAROQUE (17TH–18TH CENTURIES)

The end of the Thirty Years' War in 1648 was marked by a renewal in building activity in Switzerland. In the country's Catholic regions many new churches were built, and older ones remodelled, in the Baroque style. Characterized by extensive ornamentation, painted ceilings, scrollwork and gilding, the Baroque in Switzerland came under foreign influences and has north Italian and south German variants. The finest examples of Baroque architecture in Switzerland are the Klosterkirche in Einsiedeln, completed in 1745, and St Gallen Cathedral, completed in 1768.

The Klosterkirche at Einsiedeln has an ornate gilt and polychrome ceiling typical of the Baroque style.

St Gallen Cathedral, a fine example of Swiss Baroque architecture

THE SWISS CHALET

Characteristic of Switzerland and other adjacent Alpine areas, the chalet was originally a shepherd's house. Although there are many regional variations, the chalet is typically built of timber, generally on a square plan, and is covered with a low-pitched roof made of wood, slate or stone. The roof usually projects both at the eaves and at the gables, and the gable end is sometimes filled with a triangular area of sloping roof. Many chalets also have balconies, which may be fronted with decoratively carved railings.

Doors of wooden houses are of panel construction, and are usually covered with decorations and reinforced with ornamental metalwork.

Half-timbered chalet at the Freilichtmuseum Ballenberg

Rural house typical of the Bern region of the Mittelland during the Baroque period. The roof is designed to enable it to withstand heavy coverings of snow.

Tunnels and Railways

T HE BUILDING OF SWITZERLAND's renowned
railways, tunnels and viaducts began
in the mid-19th century, driven by the
needs of a precociously industrialized
economy and made possible by the techno-
logical advances of the age. As track was
laid along seemingly inaccessible mountain
routes, tunnels were driven beneath
mountains and viaducts built to span deep
valleys. By the end of the 19th century,
narrow- and full-gauge rail networks,
including rack-and-pinion track on the
steepest inclines, covered the country.
While part of the rail network caters for
visitors, it is used mainly by modern
express, intercity and high-speed trains.

*The Brienzer
Rothornbahn*
*is the oldest rack
railway still in use.
Steam-driven
trains climb to an
altitude of 2,350 m
(7,700 ft), enabling
passengers to enjoy
breathtaking views.*

An intercity train *of
Swiss Federal Railways
crosses the River Sarine
on the Grandfey
viaduct, in the
Fribourg region.*

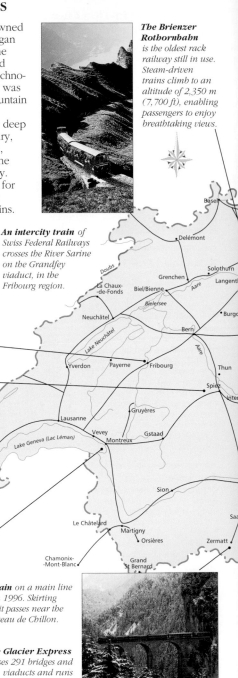

The funicular train *from
Mülenen takes visitors up the
Niesen, whose peak rises to
2,362 m (7,752 ft). From the
summit there is a magnificent
view of the Thunersee, Spiez
and the Jungfrau range.*

An intercity train *on a main line
that opened in 1996. Skirting
Lake Geneva, it passes near the
beautiful Château de Chillon.*

The Glacier Express
*crosses 291 bridges and
viaducts and runs
through 91 tunnels
on its scenic route between
Zermatt and St Moritz.*

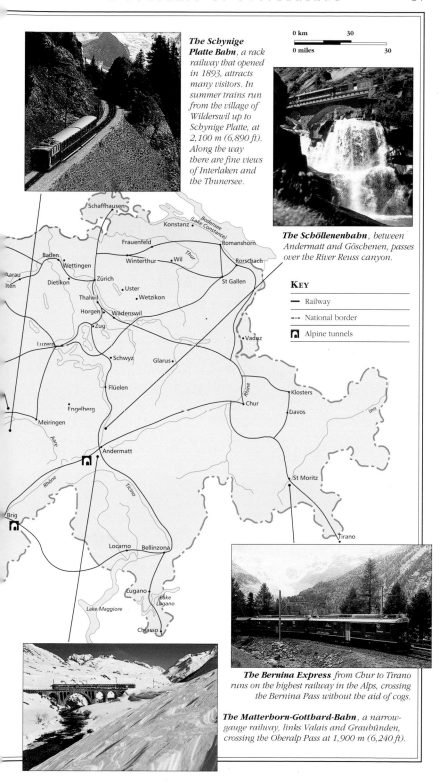

The Schynige Platte Bahn, *a rack railway that opened in 1893, attracts many visitors. In summer trains run from the village of Wilderswil up to Schynige Platte, at 2,100 m (6,890 ft). Along the way there are fine views of Interlaken and the Thunersee.*

0 km · 30
0 miles · 30

The Schöllenenbahn, *between Andermatt and Göschenen, passes over the River Reuss canyon.*

KEY

— Railway

-·- National border

🔲 Alpine tunnels

The Bernina Express *from Chur to Tirano runs on the highest railway in the Alps, crossing the Bernina Pass without the aid of cogs.*

The Matterhorn-Gotthard-Bahn, *a narrow-gauge railway, links Valais and Graubünden, crossing the Oberalp Pass at 1,900 m (6,240 ft).*

Sport in Switzerland

WITH ITS EXTENSIVE MOUNTAINOUS terrain, falls of thick, powdery snow and long winter season, Switzerland is a world leader in winter sports. It was here, in the late 19th century, that winter sports were born and where, in the early 20th century, the first European competitions took place. From downhill skiing and ski-jumping to snowboarding and bobsleigh, winter sports are an important part of Swiss life. The country hosts many prestigious world-class events, and the Swiss themselves figure prominently in international competititions, including the Winter Olympics.

The Lauberhorn Race is held near Wengen, in the Bernese Oberland. This demanding 4-km (3-mile) race, with a downhill run and a slalom, is regarded as the benchmark of Alpine skiing.

Swiss downhill skiers, including Pirmin Zurbriggen, Michael von Grünigen, Vreni Schneider, Michaele Figini, Maria Walliser and Sonja Nef, were among the world's best.

Former skiing champion Heidi Zeller-Baehler in an international event

CROSS-COUNTRY SKIING

AS ITS NAME implies, Nordic, or cross-country, skiing originated in Scandinavia. It was brought to Switzerland in the 19th century and was popularized mainly by British tourists.

Switzerland now hosts one of the world's greatest cross-country skiing competitions. This is the Engadine Ski-marathon, held in early March in the upper Engadine Valley, in Graubünden. While the men's race is run over a distance of 42 km (26 miles), from Maloja to S-chanf, the women's race is run over 17 km (10 miles), from Samedan to S-chanf.

Davos, also in Graubünden, hosts the Davos Nordic, an international cross-country championship, in mid-December, and a Cross-Country Skiing Week, in late November, an event open to competitors of all standards from beginner to professional.

The international championship organized by the Fédération Internationale du Ski takes place in the Flüela valley, above Davos.

DOWNHILL SKIING

THE MOST EXHILARATING of all alpine sports and a rigorous test of strength, balance and nerve, downhill skiing developed from cross-country skiing. It became a competitive sport in 1911.

Two of Switzerland's greatest downhill skiing events are the Inferno, first held in 1928, and the Lauberhorn Race, first held in 1930. Both take place in mid-January. The Inferno is a 15-km (9-mile) race from the top of the Schilthorn down to the village of Lauterbrunnen.

SKI JUMPING

THIS SPORT IS as exhilarating for participants as it is thrilling for spectators, yet in Switzerland it is less popular than downhill skiing.

The country hosts several international ski-jumping competitions. They take place on the slopes around Engelberg, a relatively small resort south of Luzern, and near St Moritz, one of the great centres of winter sports in Switzerland. St Moritz hosts the Continental Cup, an international ski-jumping competition, which is held on 26 December each year.

As in downhill skiing, some of the world's finest ski-jumpers are Swiss. Prominent among them is the Olympic gold-medallist Simon Ammann.

Ski-jumper in one of many competitions held in Switzerland

ICE-SKATING AND ICE HOCKEY

PLAYED NOT ONLY in winter, on Switzerland's many frozen lakes, but also at other times of the year on artificial ice rinks, ice-skating and ice hockey are popular with amateurs. Professional skaters and ice-hockey teams also have a large following. Both ice-skating, which has a century-old tradition in Switzerland, and ice hockey were introduced to the country by the British and both are now established in the main-stream of Switzerland's competitive winter sports.

Major international ice-hockey competitions are held in Switzerland. One of the longest-established is the Spengler Cup, first held in 1923. It takes place in Davos, one of Switzerland's main winter sports centres, in late December.

Snowboarder Jonas Emery in a half-pipe

SNOWBOARDING

THIS ENERGETIC sport is extremely popular in Switzerland and although it is relatively new, it has developed dramatically as courses have become more challenging. Snowboarding became an official Olympic event in 1998.

Tournaments takes place throughout Switzerland all through the winter sports season. The country's main international snowboarding competition is the Xtreme Snowboard Contest, which is held in March on the slopes of Bec des Rosses, near Verbier. The winter sports resort of Davos, with its numerous downhill runs, is renowned as a mecca for snowboarders. In 2003, the world championship snowboarding finals organized by the Fédération Internationale du Ski were held in Arosa.

LUGE AND BOBSLEIGH

THE INTERNATIONAL capital of luge and bobsleigh racing is undoubtedly St Moritz, where these sports were invented. Both developed from competitive toboggan-ing, which was pioneered by the British in the early 19th century. The luge is a racing toboggan on which the rider lies feet forward, whereas the bobsleigh is a racing sledge with seating.

The most celebrated luge race, in which competitors can reach speeds of up to 150 km per hour (95 mph), is the Cresta Run, the origins of which go back to 1884.

The world's oldest bob-sleigh race is the Olympia Bob Run, first held in 1890. The course, which runs from near the lake at St Moritz down to Celerina, is built of natural ice, and stretches for 1,722 m (over 1 mile). It is the longest of its kind in the world. European and international championships are held here.

CURLING

FOR THOSE WHO have not heard of this sport, curling is a game played on ice by two opposing teams, who propel a smooth, heavy stone towards a target. It originated in Scotland and was intro-duced to Switzerland in the 19th century. A Curling Club was founded in St Moritz in 1880, and a year later the town hosted Europe's first curling competition. The game now enjoys phenomenal popularity in Switzerland, and Swiss curling teams have won medals at the Winter Olympics.

Among the many curling tournaments held in Switzer-land are the Jackson Cup, which has been hosted by St Moritz for the past 100 years, and the international Coppa Romana, held in Silvaplana in January. It is Europe's largest open-air curling tournament.

Trotting race on a frozen lake in St Moritz

OTHER SPORTS

AMONG THE MORE recently developed winter sports are trotting races and the White Turf horse races that are run on the frozen lake at St Moritz.

Switzerland has also won renown in other sporting spheres. Roger Federer and Martina Hingis, for example, are both well established as world-class tennis players. Somewhat unexpectedly for a landlocked country, Switzerland also won the America's Cup, with the yacht *Alinghi*, in 2003. In the realm of football, Switzerland is due to host the European Nations Cup in 2008.

A bobsleigh team at the start of a race

SWITZERLAND THROUGH THE YEAR

THE SWISS enjoy a great variety of festivals. These range from colourful spectacles in which entire towns, cities and villages take part, to sophisticated art, music and film festivals, some of which are internationally famous. Among these are the Lucerne Festival of classical music and Bern's International Jazz Festival (May).

While the country unites to celebrate its origins on National Day (1 August), a large proportion of popular festivals,

Alphorn, seen at folk festivals

such as Bern's onion fair in November, have a more local, though no less historic, significance. Many folk festivals, particularly those ushering in the arrival of spring, have pagan roots, and in mountain villages cows are honoured in ceremonies that mark the spring and autumn transhumance.

Between November and March, the country also hosts many winter sports events, including several world championships.

Chalandamarz, a children's spring festival in the Engadine on 1 March

SPRING

THE EARLY SPRING is a time of transition. As the winter sports season nears its end, cold dark days begin to brighten and the first of the spring festivals, at which winter is ritually despatched, take place. Open-air voting sessions resume, cows are ceremonially taken up to their summer pastures, and in the Valais the first cow fights of the year are held.

MARCH

Chalandamarz *(1 March)*, villages all over the Engadine. Children's spring festival, with costumed parades.
Engadine Ski Marathon *(2nd Sunday in March)*. Major cross-country skiing marathon run from Maloja to S-chanf by about 12,000 participants *(see p28)*.

International Motor Show *(first half of March)*, Geneva. Prestigious annual event.
O'Neill Xtreme *(mid-March)*. Snowboarding championships, sponsored by Swatch, held on Bec des Rosses, Verbier.
Snow and Symphony *(late March–early April)*, St Moritz. World-famous orchestras and soloists present a series of 15 concerts of classical music and jazz.
Oesterfestspiele *(around Easter)*. Luzern. Festival of Easter music.

APRIL

Sechseläuten *(3rd Monday in April)*, Zürich. Spring festival with parade of medieval guilds and the ritual burning of Böögg (Old Man Winter).
Basel World, Basel. Watch and jewellery fair.
Primavera Concertistica *(mid-April–June)*, Lugano. Classical music concerts.

Fête de la Tulipe *(mid-April–mid-May)*, Morges. Colourful tulip festival.
Fête du Soleil *(late April)*, Lausanne. Carnival with bands and markets.
Combat des Reines *(mid-April)*, Valais. Traditional cow fighting. Similar events continue throughout the summer.
Landsgemeinde *(last Sunday in April)*, Appenzell. Open-air cantonal voting session.

MAY

Landsgemeinde *(1st Sunday in May)*, Appenzell. An open-air cantonal voting session conducted by a show of hands.
International Jazz Festival *(early May)*, Bern. Major five-day festival of blues, jazz and gospel music.
Landsgemeinde *(early May)*, Glarus. Open-air cantonal voting session.
Combat des Reines *(early May)*, Aproz, near Sion, Valais. Cantonal cow-fighting championships.

Traditional cow fights, held in the villages of Valais in summer

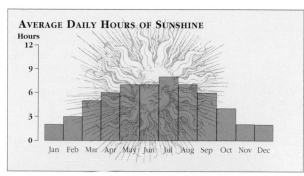

AVERAGE DAILY HOURS OF SUNSHINE

Hours

Jan Feb Mar Apr May Jun Jul Aug Sep Oct Nov Dec

Sunshine Chart
July is the sunniest month, but May, June and August also feature sunny weather. The cloudiest months are in winter, from November to January.

Dancers in traditional costume at a summer folk festival in Appenzell

SUMMER

IN MOUNTAIN VILLAGES summer is celebrated with a host of folk festivals, with much eating, drinking and merriment. Elsewhere, the first of many open-air events, including music festivals and summer sporting events, takes place. At the height of summer, Swiss National Day (1 August) is celebrated in every town and village of the country to commemorate the founding of the Confederation.

JUNE

Alpaufzug *(early June)*, Valais. Cows, adorned with flowers, are herded to high Alpine meadows, while celebrations are held in villages.
Corpus Christi, the Catholic cantons. Processions in local costume.

Participant in the Fêtes des Vignerons, Vevey

Art Basel *(mid-June)*, Basel. Major international contemporary art fair.
William Tell *(late June–mid-September)*, Interlaken. Open-air performances of Schiller's play about the Swiss hero.

JULY

Sittertobel: Rock and Pop Music Open-Air Festival *(early July)*, St Gallen.
Montreux Jazz Festival *(first two weeks in July)*, Montreux. Festival of jazz blues, rock, reggae and soul music. Free concerts on the promenade.
Allianz Swiss Open *(first two weeks in July)*, Gstaad. International men's tennis tournament.
International Rowing Regattas, Luzern. Races held on the Rotsee.
Avenches Opera Festival. World-class opera productions staged in the 8,000-seat Roman amphitheatre.

AUGUST

National Day *(1 August)*, throughout Switzerland. Celebrations, with fireworks, music, street illuminations and lantern processions, marking the birth of the Swiss Confederation in 1291.
Fêtes de Genève *(early August)*, Geneva. Ten days of classical, rave and folk music, as well as plays, firework displays and competitions.
International Film Festival *(early August)*, Locarno. One of the top international film events, with open-air screenings on Piazza Grande.
Street Parade *(either of the first two weekends in August)*, Zürich. Huge open-air gathering of techno-music fans.
Inferno Triathlon *(mid-August)*, Bernese Alps. Run over about 150 km (95 miles) from Thun to the Schilthorn.
Lucerne Festival *(mid-August–mid-September)*, Luzern. The famous festival of classical music, with international orchestras, conductors and soloists.
Älplerchilbi *(2nd half of August)*. Folk festival with alphorns and yodelling.

Celebrations on National Day in Oberhofen, on the Thunersee

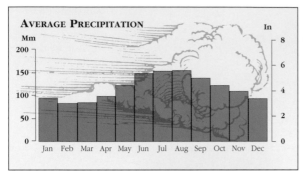

AVERAGE PRECIPITATION

Mm / In

Jan Feb Mar Apr May Jun Jul Aug Sep Oct Nov Dec

Precipitation
The heaviest rainfall in Switzerland occurs during the summer months. Winter brings heavy snowfalls, especially at high altitudes. However, the annual precipitation in some regions, such as Valais, is lower than the national average.

Autumn

WHEN THE TREES on the Alpine hillsides start to take on autumnal colours and the vines are heavy with ripe grapes, it is time to give thanks for a successful harvest. Colourful agricultural fairs are held across the country; chestnut and wine festivals take place everywhere and the cows are returned to their valley pastures, where they will spend the winter.

September

Jungfrau Marathon *(early September)*, Jungfrau. 3,000 runners compete along a route from Interlaken to Kleine Scheidegg.
La Bénichon *(early September)*, Fribourg. Festival of thanksgiving.
Knabenschiessen *(2nd weekend in September)*, Zürich. Shooting contest for young boys and girls.
Grape Harvest Festival *(late September)*, Neuchâtel. The largest of its kind in Switzerland. Others are held throughout the country.
Fête de la Désalpe *(last Saturday in September)*, Charmey. Celebrations as cows are brought down from their summer grazing in the high Alpine meadows.

October

Combats des Reines *(early October)*, Martigny. Cow fighting in the Roman amphitheatre, the ultimate winner being proclaimed Reine des Reines (Queen of the Herd).

Festivities marking the return of cows from their Alpine pastures

Autumn Fair *(early October)*, Basel. Switzerland's largest and oldest-established food fair and funfair.
La Bénichon *(3rd Sunday in October)*, Châtel-St-Denis. Harvest thanksgiving, with procession in traditional dress and banquet.

November

Räben-Chilbi *(2nd Saturday in November)*, Richterswil. Young people carrying lanterns made of turnips join in a procession.
Bach Festival *(two weeks in early November)*, Lausanne.
Gansabhauet *(mid-November)*, Sursee. Celebration of an ancient custom in which the central character is a goose.
Zibelemärit *(4th Monday in November)*, Bern. Onion fair, with confetti battle and other festive activities marking the beginning of winter.
Expovina, Zürich. Fair, with wine-tastings, at which wines imported from all over the world are put on display on ships moored along Bürkliplatz.
Jazz Festival, Zürich. Major international event taking place at several venues throughout the city.

September Grape Harvest, Neuchâtel

AVERAGE TEMPERATURES

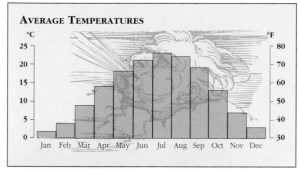

Temperatures
Temperatures are highest in June, July and August, though they rarely exceed 30° C (86° F). The coldest month is December, when temperatures often drop below freezing.

Ice sculptures at the World Snow Festival in Grindelwald

WINTER

ADVENT, CHRISTMAS and the Feast of St Nicholas are the main focus of fairs and festivals in December. New Year is exuberantly celebrated throughout the country. In some parts of Switzerland it is marked twice, first in accordance with the current Gregorian calendar, and again according to the older Julian calendar. This is also the season of a variety of winter sports events, from ice hockey and curling to horse-racing on ice. Between New Year and mid-March, countless carnival balls, folk festivals with masquerades and fancy dress keep spirits up through the cold winter months. They culminate in Fasnacht, a three-day festival held in many parts of Switzerland, which precedes Lent.

Carnival participant, in devil's costume

DECEMBER

St Nicholas Day *(on or around 6 December)*, all over Switzerland. Parades and fairs celebrating the arrival of Santa Claus.
Fête de l'Escalade *(1st Saturday in December)*, Geneva. Festival commemorating the Duke of Savoy's failed attempt to capture Geneva in 1602.
Spengler Cup *(late December)*, Davos. World ice-hockey tournament.
New Year's Eve, villages of Appenzell. Masked characters with cow-bells usher in the new year.

JANUARY

Vogel Gryff *(mid- to late January)*, Basel. Three-day folk festival with a ritual involving a lion, a griffin and Wild Man of the Woods.
Coppa Romana *(mid-January)*, Silvaplana. Europe's largest open-air curling contest.

World Snow Festival *(mid-January)*, Grindelwald. Fantastic ice-sculpture contest, held on a natural skating rink.
Hot-Air Balloon Week *(late January)*, Château d'Oex. Week-long spectacle as the skies fill with colourful hot-air balloons.
Cartier Polo World Cup on Snow *(late January)*, St Moritz. Polo played on the frozen lake at St Moritz.

FEBRUARY

Roitschäggättä *(week before Ash Wednesday)*, Lötschental. Nocturnal parades by men wearing grotesque masks.
White Turf *(1st half of February)*, St Moritz. International horse races held on the frozen lake.
Fasnacht *(late February to early March)*, Basel. Major spring carnival lasting three days and three nights, with thousands of costumed figures playing drums and piccolos. Also celebrated around the same time in Luzern, Bern and other towns.

PUBLIC HOLIDAYS

New Year's Day (1 Jan)
Good Friday (Karfreitag, Vendredi Saint)
Easter Monday (Ostermontag, Lundi de Paques)
Ascension Day (Himmelfahrt, Ascension)
Whit Monday (Pfingstmontag, Lundi de Pentecôte)
National Day (1 Aug)
Christmas Holiday (25 & 26 Dec)

THE HISTORY OF SWITZERLAND

T HE HISTORY OF SWITZERLAND *began in 1291, when three small cantons formed an alliance against their foreign overlords, the Habsburgs. As other cantons joined, the alliance expanded, but there followed centuries of instability, with bitter conflict between cantons and religious groups. It was not until 1848 that a central government was established and that modern Switzerland was born.*

HELVETI AND RHAETIANS

From about 500 BC, the lands that now comprise Switzerland were settled by two peoples, the Rhaetians, an Etruscan people who settled in a small area in the east, and the Helveti, a powerful Celtic tribe, who settled in the west. The Helveti established several small townships here, including La Tène, near Neuchâtel.

Bust of Marcus Aurelius from Avenches

FROM ROMAN TO FRANKISH RULE

By 58 BC Helvetia and Rhaetia, as they were known, were incorporated in the Roman Empire, the Helveti becoming allies of the Romans against warlike tribes to the north. Under Roman rule Aventicum (Avenches), capital of the Helveti, became a Roman province. Other towns with villas were built, agriculture flourished and new roads were laid out. In AD 260, Helvetia and Rhaetia were once again attacked by Germanic tribes. While the eastern region was taken by the Alemani, driving the Rhaetians into the hinterland, the western region was seized by Burgundians. In 401 the Romans abandoned their Alpine province.

By the 6th century, the Swiss territories of the Alemani and Burgundians had been taken by the Franks. These lands were later incorporated into Charlemagne's Holy Roman Empire, and in 843 they were divided between his grandsons.

ALLIANCE OF THE CANTONS

In 1033, Burgundy was reunited within the Holy Roman Empire. However, as imperial power declined, feudal dynasties came to prominence. The most powerful was that of the Habsburgs. In 1291, the free peasants of the Forest Cantons of Schwyz, Uri and Unterwalden formed an alliance against Habsburg power, their delegates meeting on Rütli Meadow to swear their mutual allegiance. This was the nucleus of what later became the Swiss Confederation. In the 14th century they were joined by the cantons of Luzern, Zürich, Glarus, Zug and Bern. In their attempts to break the Confederation, the Habsburgs suffered crushing defeats in a succession of battles with the Confederates, who eventually won their independence in 1499.

TIMELINE

5th century BC The Helveti and Rhaetians begin to settle in the Alps	**AD 69** Uprising of the Helveti against the Romans	**6th century** Franks conquer Aleman and Burgundian territories	**1033** Burgundy incorporated in the Holy Roman Empire
	260 First incursions by the Alemani		**1291** The three Forest Cantons form an alliance

200 BC	0	500	1000	1500

c. 500 BC The Helveti establish the settlement of La Tène	**401** The Romans abandon their Alpine province	**5th century** Settlement by the Alemani, Burgundians and Lombards	**1499** Switzerland gains independence

Reliquary in the shape of a foot

◁ **Representatives of the three Forest Cantons swearing the oath of allegiance on Rütli Meadow in 1291**

The Struggle for Independence

I N 1291, ON THE DEATH of Emperor Rudolf I, representatives of the cantons of Schwyz, Uri and Unterwalden decided to form an alliance against the power and tyranny of the Habsburgs. The oath of mutual allegiance that they swore at Rütli Meadow in August that year laid the foundations of the Swiss Confederation. The wars that the Confederates fought against the Habsburgs and the Burgundians in the 14th and 15th centuries demonstrated the superiority of agile peasant troops over heavily armed knights. The Swiss also became renowned for their valour as soldiers and were sought after as mercenaries throughout Europe.

Officer of the Swiss Guard
The reputation of the Swiss as courageous soldiers prompted Pope Julius II to form the Swiss Guard in 1506, to act as his bodyguards and to protect the Vatican.

Battle of Dornach (1499)
Confederate soldiers launched a surprise attack on troops commanded by Heinrich von Fürstenberg, who was killed in the battle.

Mercenary troops sent by Charles VII of France to aid the Habsburg cause march on Basel.

Battle of Morgarten (1315)
The army of Prince Leopold Habsburg suffered a crushing defeat when it fought against peasant Confederate forces at the Battle of Morgarten.

Shield of Schwyz
Originally plain red, as here, the shield of Schwyz was later charged with a white cross. A red cross on a white ground became the Confederation's emblem.

Confederate soldiers at the foot of a tower rally behind a banner with the emblem of Basel.

Crossbow
The crossbow was the basic weapon in the Swiss army's arsenal.

Defensive walls around Basel

Confederate defenders in a fortified camp around the church.

St Jakob's Church

William Tell's Arrow
According to legend, William Tell was sentenced to death by the Austrian bailiff Hermann Gessler for refusing to acknowledge Habsburg power but won a reprieve by shooting an apple off his son's head with his crossbow. William Tell later killed Gessler.

BATTLE OF ST JAKOB

In 1444, at the request of the Habsburg king Friedrich III, Charles VII of France sent a 40,000-strong army of mercenaries to Switzerland. In their fortified camp at St Jakob, on the River Birs, near Basel, defenders of the Confederation put up a heroic defence but were slaughtered.

Battle of Laupen (1339)
After the siege of Bern, the armies of Bern and Luzern give thanks to God for their defeat of the Duke of Burgundy and his ally, the canton of Fribourg.

Defeat of the Swiss at the Battle of Marignano (1515)

Reformation in Switzerland were the humanist Ulrich Zwingli (1484–1531), who was active in Zürich, and Jean Calvin (1509–64), who led the movement in Geneva. While the urban cantons embraced the Reformation, the poorer and more conservative cantons of central Switzerland remained faithful to Catholicism. Despite this rift, the cantons remained loyal to the Confederation throughout the wars of religion that swept through Europe in the 17th century.

THE PEAK OF TERRITORIAL POWER

Emboldened by independence, yet surrounded by territories held by the Habsburgs and other powers, the Swiss Confederation attempted to secure and expand its territory to the north, east and south. In 1512, Confederate troops conquered Lombardy, occupying Locarno and Lugano. However, their stand against combined French and Venetian forces at Marignano in 1515 ended in defeat, after which Switzerland abandoned its policy of expansion and moved towards military neutrality. The Confederation itself, however, continued to grow, Fribourg and Solothurn joining in 1481, Basel and Schaffhausen in 1501 and Appenzell in 1513. The cantons now numbered 13.

THE REFORMATION

The great religious and political movement to reform the Roman Catholic Church originated in Germany in the early 16th century and quickly spread throughout western Europe. At the vanguard of the

Bed made in Bern in the 16th century

PROSPERITY AND INDUSTRY

The Swiss Confederation's independence from the Austrian Empire was formally recognized by the Peace of Westphalia, which ended the Thirty Years' War (1618–48). Switzerland did not take part in the conflict, and this contributed to a boost in the country's economy.

During the war Switzerland had in fact played a key role in trade throughout Europe, and the arrival of refugees, particularly Huguenots, revitalized Switzerland's textile

Burning of religious paintings, in response to Zwingli's preaching against the worship of images

TIMELINE

1515 Battle of Marignano. The Confederation declares neutrality

1559 Jean Calvin founds the Calvin Academy in Geneva

1680s–1690s. The brothers Jakob and Johann Bernoulli, at Basel University, lay the foundations of the theory of probability and integral calculus

| 1500 | 1550 | 1600 | 1650 | 170 |

1525 Zwingli's reforms accepted by the church authorities in Zürich

1684 Peace of Westphalia guarantees Switzerland's neutrality

Louis XIV and representatives of the Swiss Confederation

William Tell victorious over the dragon of the French Revolution, a symbol of Swiss resistance

the short-lived and unpopular Helvetic Republic. The Swiss Confederation, as it was now known, was restored in 1803, although it remained under French control until the fall of Napoleon in 1815.

THE SWISS CONFEDERATION

Six further cantons – St Gallen, Graubünden, Aargau, Thurgau, Ticino and Vaud – joined the Confederation in 1803, and Valais, Neuchâtel and Geneva in 1815. Internal religious hostilities continued, however, and in 1845 seven Catholic cantons formed a military alliance known as the Sonderbund. Condemned as unconstitutional by the Protestant cantons, this led to civil war, and the defeat of the Catholic faction by Protestant forces.

A new constitution was drawn up in 1848, transforming what had until then been a loose confederation of cantons into a union ruled by a Federal Assembly in Bern, which was chosen as the Swiss capital. National unity was, however, tested again in 1857, when Prussia threatened to take the canton of Neuchâtel. The 100,000-strong Swiss army sent to the Rhine border repelled Prussian ambitions.

industry. Industrial expansion continued in the 18th century, when the weaving of silk, linen and cotton became mechanized, while clockmaking, introduced to Switzerland by French and Italian refugees in the 16th century, became one of the country's most important industries.

THE HELVETIC REPUBLIC

The principles of the French Revolution were supported by Switzerland's French-speaking regions, but this was a threat to the stability of the Confederation. In 1798, having conquered northern Italy, and wishing to control routes between Italy and France, Napoleon invaded Switzerland. Under Napoleon the 13 cantons of the Confederation were abolished and replaced with

The Swiss army bound for the Rhine to defend Neuchâtel in 1857

Economic Growth

AS EARLY AS THE 17th century, Switzerland already had active textile and clockmaking industries, the foundations of which were laid by Huguenot refugees from France. By the second half of the 18th century, aided by its neutrality in international politics, the growing affluence of the middle classes and long periods of domestic peace, Switzerland was becoming one of the most industrially advanced countries in Europe. Swiss economic growth accelerated in the 19th century, when the textile industry was mechanized and exports increased. This was also a boom period for precision engineering and the chemicals industry. Swiss foods, including Philippe Suchard's chocolate, Henri Nestlé's powdered milk and Julius Maggi's stock cubes became international brands.

Excited crowds gather around the Egyptian-style statue personifying industry.

Allegory of Justice

A locomotive, symbol of modern technical achievement.

Women workers operating belt-driven machinery.

An entrepreneur presenting his products to interested merchants.

The Swiss Pavilion at the Great Exhibition of 1851
The 270 exhibits in the Swiss Pavilion included textiles and lace, clocks and watches, and pharmaceuticals. There was also a model of Strasbourg Cathedral made by Jules Leemann, a sculptor from Bern.

Invention of the Telegraph
The first electric telegraph was built by the physicist George Lesage in Geneva in 1774.

Development of the Railway Network
Zürich's imposing Hauptbahnhof, or central station, was built in 1867.

Clock- and Watchmaking
The Swiss clock is a symbol of accuracy and reliability.

Allegory of Industry

ST GOTTHARD PASS

The gateway over the Alps between central and southern Switzerland, the St Gotthard Pass lies at 2,108 m (6,919 ft) above sea level. On one of the main transport routes between Germany and Italy, it is also one of Europe's crucial arteries. With international funding of 102 billion Swiss francs, work on building a tunnel and a railway line beneath the pass began in 1872. The project was completed in 1880.

Poster for St Moritz
From the 19th century, the popularity of Swiss resorts and tourist regions began to grow rapidly.

Driving a mail waggon
over the pass was arduous, sometimes dangerous and, because of heavy snow, possible only in summer.

Road Through the Alps
In the 19th century Switzerland's dramatic Alpine scenery began to attract numerous visitors.

Italian workers *who were employed to drill the tunnel staged a strike in 1875. Intervention by the army eventually brought a return to work.*

A group of clients, including a German visitor wearing a coat with a fur collar, and an American donning a wide-brimmed hat

APEX OF INDUSTRIAL DEVELOPMENT

This monumental fresco in the Musée d'Art et d'Histoire in Neuchâtel *(see p131)* portrays the achievements of Swiss industry in the 19th century. Through allegory the painting depicts the environment in which Swiss industry consolidated its position in the international market.

Swiss Chocolate
Among Swiss chocolate manufacturers whose brands became known worldwide in the 19th century was Philippe Suchard (1797–1884).

First assembly of the League of Nations, Geneva, in 1920

WORLD WAR I

At the outbreak of World War I, maintaining its neutrality was one of Switzerland's principal concerns. Relations between French- and German-speaking Swiss deteriorated, as both linguistic groups supported opposing sides in the war. However, appeals for national unity averted the danger of open conflict.

By 1915, some 100,000 Swiss troops had been mobilized to guard the country's frontiers. As the war went on, Switzerland embarked on a wide-ranging aid programme for some 68,000 prisoners of war and refugees. Political asylum-seekers who had come to Switzerland included many heads of state and political figures, including the Bolshevik leader Lenin and the Russian revolutionaries Trotsky and Zinoviev.

The revolutionary socialist ideas that they brought fomented unrest among Swiss workers, which culminated in the General Strike of 1918. The strike was quickly broken by the army but, as a result of their action, the workers won proportional representation, improved welfare and a 48-hour working week.

THE INTER-WAR YEARS

In 1920 Switzerland voted to join the newly formed League of Nations and, in tribute to the country's neutrality, Geneva was chosen as the organization's headquarters.

While the 1920s had been a period of prosperity, Switzerland, like the rest of Europe, fell prey to the Depression of the early 1930s. Also at this time, Switzerland's pacific stance and democracy were threatened by Nazi and Fascist sympathisers among its population.

By the late 1930s, as war seemed imminent, Switzerland's economy accelerated, fuelled partly by the booming arms industry in which the country was involved and by the fact that Swiss banks now played an important role in international finance.

General Henri Guisan, Commander-in-Chief of the armed forces, at the outbreak of war in 1939

TIMELINE

1901 Henri Dunant, founder of the International Red Cross, receives the first Nobel Peace Prize to be awarded

1918 General Strike and introduction of the 48-hour week

1934 Carl G. Jung, founder of modern psychology, becomes head of the Department of Psychology at Zürich University

1900	1910	1920	1930	1940	1950

1914–18 Switzerland maintains neutrality during World War I

1920 Switzerland joins the League of Nations

1922 The Simplon Tunnel opens

1939–45 Switzerland maintains neutrality during World War II

Drilling the Simplon Tunnel

Swiss artists and scientists were also coming to prominence. Among them were the artists Paul Klee (1879–1940) and Alberto Giacometti (1901–66), the architect Le Corbusier (1887–1965) and the psychologist Carl G. Jung (1875–1961).

Demonstration in 1963 by women demanding the right to vote in national elections

WORLD WAR II

In 1940, with Nazi Germany to the north and east, France under German occupation to the west and Fascist Italy to the south, Switzerland was surrounded. Invasion seemed inevitable, collaboration with Germany was suspected and the advantages of submitting to Germany were even contemplated. General Henri Guisan, Commander-in-Chief of the Swiss army, responded by assembling his officers on Rütli Meadow, where the Confederation had been established in 1291. Here he reaffirmed Switzerland's neutrality and demanded that all officers renew their vows of allegiance to the Confederation.

Although Switzerland was not directly drawn into World War II, it played a part in the conflict. The country acted as a secret meeting place between leaders of the Allied and Axis powers and set up anonymous bank accounts for German Jews. Swiss banks also provided currency for the purchase of military equipment and exchanged gold pillaged by the Germans for currency needed by the Third Reich.

Diego by Alberto Giacometti

POSTWAR YEARS TO THE PRESENT

Unlike all other European countries, Switzerland remained untouched by the upheaval of war and detached from the new world order that emerged in the postwar years. It was not until 1971 that women won the right to vote and the country continues to reject membership of the European Union, although popular opinion is divided on this issue. Switzerland did, however, vote to join the United Nations in 2002. In line with increasing globalization, Switzerland has softened its isolationist stance, and its relations with the EU remain at the top of the political agenda.

In 1998, the country was rocked by the "Nazi Gold" scandal, when it was discovered that Swiss banks were holding gold looted by the Nazis and the assets of Jews who had perished in the Holocaust. Under strong international pressure, Switzerland agreed to pay $1.2 billion in compensation to families of Holocaust victims, but the episode made a severe impression on the national psyche.

OUI
À L'EEE, CAR LES FEMMES, REGARDENT L'AVENIR EN FACE.
FEMMES SUISSES EN FAVEUR DE L'EEE

Poster for Swiss membership of the European Union

Carl G. Jung (1875–1961)

1971 Women obtain federal voting rights

1992 Switzerland rejects membership of the EU

2002 Switzerland votes to join the United Nations

1960	1970	1980	1990	2000	2010

1960 Professor Auguste Piccard's son Jacques reaches a record depth of 10,911 m (35,800 ft) in the Pacific Ocean in a bathysphere designed by his father

1998 The "Nazi Gold" scandal emerges

Celebratory salute on the 700th anniversary of the Swiss Confederation in 1991

SWITZERLAND REGION BY REGION

Switzerland at a Glance

FROM THE SNOW-BOUND Alps and verdant Jura mountains to the more densely populated plateau of the Mittelland that lies between them, Switzerland offers a wealth of different impressions. It has no coastline but the shimmering waters of its large, clean lakes amply make up for this. Picturesque mountain villages and atmospheric medieval towns of its remoter areas contrast with the cosmopolitan cities of Bern, Zürich, Lausanne, Luzern and Basel. For many, the Alps, which offer unrivalled skiing and other winter sports, as well as a pristine natural environment, are the country's greatest attraction. South of the Alps, the canton of Ticino is a different world, with a lively Italian culture and a warm Mediterranean-style climate.

Bern, the capital of Switzerland and the seat of its federal government, is a historic city with a medieval layout and many fine historic buildings. Its emblem is the bear.

0 km   25

0 miles   2

Lausanne, on the north side of Lake Geneva, is a vibrant cultural centre. The cathedral, in the medieval city centre, is one of Switzerland's most important Gothic buildings.

WESTERN SWITZERLAND
Pages 108–133

BERN
Pages 48–65

MITTELLAND, BERNESE OBERLAND AND VALAIS
Pages 66–91

GENEVA
Pages 92–107

Geneva enjoys a magnificent setting on the largest lake in western Europe. A city with a cosmopolitan culture, it is the headquarters of several international organizations.

The Matterhorn is the most distinctive and dramatic peak in the Swiss Alps. The resort of Zermatt lies in a valley at the foot of the mountain.

◁ **Ponte dei Salti, a 17th-century bridge near Lavertezzo, in Ticino**

Schaffhausen, the capital of Switzerland's northernmost canton, has an atmospheric medieval town centre. The Munot, a Renaissance fortress in the east of the city, towers over the Rhine.

Zürich, on the River Limmat, is Switzerland's largest city, and the centre of Swiss banking and trade in gold. The central landmark of the Old Town is the imposing twin-towered Grossmünster.

ORTHERN ITZERLAND *iges 134–157*

ZÜRICH *Pages 158–175*

Val Bregaglia is one of Graubünden's many scenic Alpine valleys. Surrounded by granite peaks and containing a variety of rock formations, it is regarded as a rock-climber's paradise.

CENTRAL SWITZERLAND AND TICINO *Pages 206–239*

EASTERN SWITZERLAND AND GRAUBÜNDEN *Pages 176–205*

The Hofkirche is one of Luzern's many fine buildings. This charming city, set on Lake Luzern and surrounded by mountains, is the cultural capital of central Switzerland.

Bellinzona, the capital of Ticino, owes its importance to its strategic position. It is the starting point of roads leading to the St Gotthard and San Bernardino passes.

BERN

WITH A PICTURESQUE SETTING *on the River Aare and fine buildings lining the cobbled streets of its medieval centre, Bern is one of the most beautiful of Switzerland's historic towns. Although it is the Swiss capital, it retains the atmosphere of a provincial town. Bern is also a university city, the seat of the Federal Assembly and the headquarters of several international organizations.*

Bern lies on a narrow, elevated spit of land set in a sharp, steep-banked bend of the River Aare. It was founded by Berthold V, Duke of Zähringen, in 1191, and its coat of arms features a bear. According to legend, the duke decided to name the new settlement after the first animal that he killed in the next hunt: this was a bear (Bär), and the duke duly named the town Bärn. After the demise of the Zähringen dynasty, Bern became a free town. Growing in power and prosperity, it joined the Swiss Confederation in 1353.

After a fire destroyed its timber buildings in 1405, the town was rebuilt in stone. It is from this period that the appearance of Bern's beautiful Old Town largely dates.

In 1528 the Bernese declared themselves in favour of the Reformation, and supported the Protestant cause. By the 16th century, Bern, led by a prosperous nobility, was a powerful city-state that, in the 17th and 18th centuries, further expanded its territory through the annexation of surrounding lands. Invaded by Napoleonic forces in 1798, Bern lost some of its territories but remained important enough to be chosen as the federal capital in 1848.

In the 20th century and into the 21st, Bern has continued to expand. Today, with a mostly German-speaking population, it is Switzerland's political and educational hub, and the base of major industries. Its historic Old Town is a UNESCO World Heritage Site.

he Rathaus, Bern's town hall, dating from the 15th century and with later alterations

Bundeshaus, the Federal Assembly building, from the Monbijoubrücke across the River Aare

...ern at a Glance

With many of its streets restricted to pedestrians and public transport, Bern's compact Old Town (Altstadt) is both easy and pleasant to explore on foot. Set on a narrow rocky ridge, the Old Town stretches, in the east, from the Nydeggbrücke, in the east, to the Käfigturm, a tower that was originally a city gate, in the west. The main artery through the Old Town is Marktgasse, lined with old houses that have been converted into shops. The museums in the Kirchenfeld district, on the opposite bank of the Aare, are easily reachable on foot via the Kirchenfeldbrücke.

SEE ALSO

- **Where to Stay** p244
- **Where to Eat** pp268–9

Statue of Samson subduing a lion, dating from 1545, on the Samsonbrünnen, a fountain in Kramgasse

KEY

▨	Street-by-Street map pp52–3
🚉	Railway station
🚌	Coach station
🅿	Parking
ℹ	Tourist information
➕	Hospital
🚓	Police station
✝	Church

Display in the Museum für Kommunikation

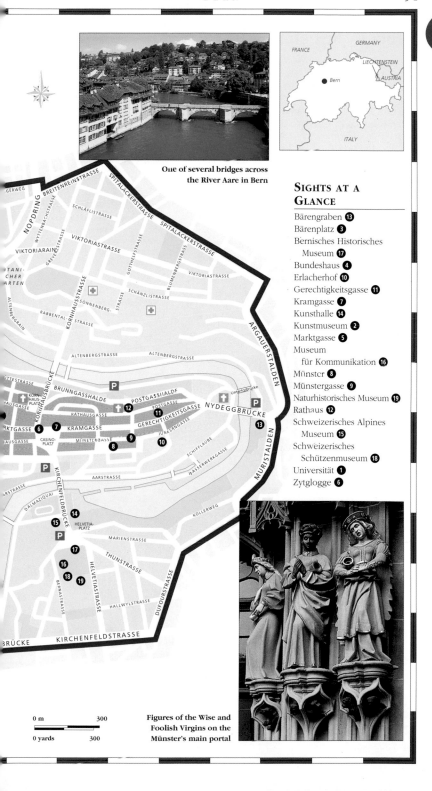

One of several bridges across
the River Aare in Bern

SIGHTS AT A GLANCE

Bärengraben ⑬
Bärenplatz ❸
Bernisches Historisches
  Museum ⑰
Bundeshaus ❹
Erlacherhof ⑩
Gerechtigkeitsgasse ⑪
Kramgasse ❼
Kunsthalle ⑭
Kunstmuseum ❷
Marktgasse ❺
Museum
  für Kommunikation ⑯
Münster ❽
Münstergasse ❾
Naturhistorisches Museum ⑲
Rathaus ⑫
Schweizerisches Alpines
  Museum ⑮
Schweizerisches
  Schützenmuseum ⑱
Universität ❶
Zytglogge ❻

Figures of the Wise and
Foolish Virgins on the
Münster's main portal

Street-by-Street: The Old Town

WITH LONG COBBLED STREETS lined with red-roofed houses and picturesque arcades, Bern's Old Town (Altstadt) is the best-preserved historic town centre in Switzerland. The layout of its streets, which are punctuated by colourfully painted fountains, has remained largely unchanged since the early 15th century. This was also the period when the Münster and the Rathaus, two of its great landmarks, were built. While the western district of the Old Town is filled with shops and busy street markets, the older eastern district has a more restful atmosphere.

The Kornhaus, or Granary, was built in the 18th century over large vaulted wine cellars. While the cellars have been converted into a restaurant, the Kornhaus now serves as a cultural centre.

Marktgasse
The main axis through the western part of the Old Town begins at the Käfigturm (Cage Tower). This tower was the city's western gate in the 13th and 14th centuries ❺

Französische Kirche is the oldest church in Bern.

SPEICHERGASSE

WAISENHAUSPLATZ

ZEUGHAUSGASSE

NEUENGASSE

MARKTGASS

Bärenplatz
This square overlies the spot where a moat once ran, along Bern's west side ❸

BÄREN-
PLATZ

Heiliggestkirche is Switzerland's finest Protestant church.

SPITALGASSE

BUNDES-
PLATZ

SCHAUPLATZGASSE

0 m	100
0 yards	100

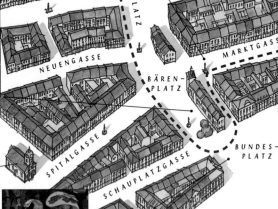

STAR SIGHTS

★ **Münster**

★ **Zytglogge**

Bundesplatz owes its name to the Bundeshaus, the Federal Assembly building, which is decorated with paintings depicting important episodes in Swiss history.

Rathaus
The town hall is fronted by a double staircase and a Gothic loggia that leads through to the main entrance ⓬

Gerechtigkeitsgasse
This is the eastern section of the main axis through the Old Town. The house at No. 68 is the Weavers' Guild, the façade featuring a gilt griffin. Another striking landmark is a fountain with a statue of Justice ⓫

LOCATOR MAP
See pp50–51.

★ Münster
The most striking feature of Bern's Gothic cathedral is the magnificent main portal, surrounded by painted figures ⑧

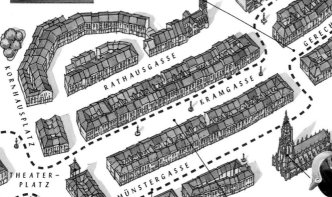

Münstergasse
On Tuesday and Saturday mornings the arcades along this street are filled with a bustling street market ⑨

Kramgasse
The main axis through the Old Town is continued by Kramgasse. This street begins at the Zytglogge, the clock tower marking the western limit of the oldest part of the Old Town ⑦

★ Zytglogge
From 1191 to 1250 the clock tower was the city's western gate, and it was later used as a prison. Its elaborate chimes begin at four minutes before the hour ⑥

KEY

- - - Suggested route

Universität ❶

Hochschulstrasse 4.

ALTHOUGH THE University of Bern was founded in 1834, the city's academic traditions go back to the 16th century. In 1528 a theological school was established, and it occupied a former Franciscan monastery that stood on the site of the Casino on what is now Casinoplatz.

In 1805 the school became an academy, which in turn was elevated to the status of university, its premises still being the former monastery.

As the university grew, with increasing numbers of students and the addition of new faculties, larger premises were required. These were built in 1899–1903, on the embankment of Grosse Schanze (the Great Rampart) that formed part of Bern's 17th-century defence system. This is now the main university building and is a monumental structure in an eclectic mixture of the Neo-Renaissance and Neo-Baroque styles.

Kunstmuseum ❷

See pp56–7.

Bärenplatz ❸

THIS ELONGATED esplanade has the appearance of a wide street rather than a square, particularly because it is seamlessly continued by another square, Waisenhausplatz, on its north side. Only a fountain marks the division between the two.

Bärenplatz (Bear Square) is named after the bear pit once located here, while Waisenhausplatz (Orphanage Square) owes its name to the former orphanage, in a fine Baroque building that is now the police headquarters.

Both squares were laid out on the course of the moat that was dug on the western side of the town in 1256. On the east sides of both squares stand the Dutch Tower and the **Käfigturm** (Cage Tower).

The Bundeshaus from a bridge on the River Aare

The Käfigturm has a steeply pitched roof with a slender lantern tower topped by a spire. Once part of the later wall that was built further to the west as Bern expanded, the Käfigturm was the town gate from 1250 until 1350. From 1643 to 1897 the tower was used as a prison and since 1999 it has served as a centre of political discourse, being the venue for political seminars, meetings with politicians and exhibitions.

On its southern side Bärenplatz adjoins Bundesplatz, an esplanade dominated by the Bundeshaus. Bundesplatz is also lined with cafés, and a fruit and flower market is held here on Tuesday and Saturday mornings.

🚻 **Käfigturm** 📞 031 322 70 07. ◯ 8am–6pm Mon–Fri, 10am–4pm Sat.

Bundeshaus ❹

Bundesplatz 3. 📞 031 322 85 22. ☑ 9am, 10am, 11am, 2pm, 3pm, 4pm Mon–Fri, when parliament is not in session. Meet at the east entrance, 30 mins in advance. Passports must be shown. ☑ www.parliament.ch

THE IMPOSING seat of the Federal Assembly stands on a cliff overlooking the Aare valley. Although it faces north onto Bundesplatz, its most attractive aspect is from the south – from Monbijoubrücke, a bridge on the Aare.

The Bundeshaus (parliament building) was designed by W. H. Auer in a bold Neo-Renaissance style, and completed in 1902. The central part of the building contains a spacious domed hall. The hall is decorated with paintings illustrating

FERDINAND HODLER (1853–1918)

One of the most outstanding Swiss painters of his time, Ferdinand Hodler was born in Bern but spent most of his life in Geneva. He initially produced exquisitely realistic landscapes and portraits but later became a leading exponent of Symbolism. Often allegorical, his Symbolist paintings have a haunting beauty and typically feature groups of stylized, symmetrically arranged figures. Hodler was also well known for his monumental wall paintings. His late work, which has a more spontaneous style, anticipated the development of Expressionism.

Self-portrait by Hodler

important events in Swiss history, the dome has stained-glass panels featuring the emblems of Switzerland's regions and cantons, and stained-glass windows with allegories of justice, education, public works and defence. The main assembly hall, in the south wing, is decorated with paintings depicting delegates of the cantons of Uri, Schwyz and Unterwalden swearing the oath of alliance on Rütli Meadow *(see p35)*.

When parliament is in session (indicated by a flag flying from the Bundeshaus), visitors may listen to debates from the public gallery.

The Bundeshaus is flanked by two other government buildings. That to the east was designed by Auer and built in 1892, that to the west was designed by F. Studer and built in 1857.

The Bundesterrasse, a wide promenade behind the Bundeshaus, offers a panoramic view of the Alps. A funicular near the western side of the Bundeshaus takes visitors down to the bottom of the Aare valley.

The Käfigturm, the former gate at the western end of Marktgasse

Marktgasse **❺**

L AID OUT IN THE 13th century, as the town expanded westwards, Marktgasse runs east to west from the Zytglogge, the original town gate, to the Käfigturm, the later gate.

Marktgasse is now the centre of Bern's shopping district,

and the arcades lining it are filled with shops, restaurants and cafés. Marktgasse also has two Renaissance fountains: the **Anna-Seiler-Brunnen**, commemorating the woman who founded Bern's first hospital, in 1354, and the **Schützernbrunnen** (Marksman Fountain).

At its eastern end Marktgasse forms a right angle with Kornhausplatz, which follows the line of the earliest town walls. On this square is the macabre **Kindlifresserbrunnen** (Ogre Fountain), with an ogre eating an infant.

Off the northwestern side of Kornhausgasse stands the **Französische Kirche** (French Church). Built in the 12th century as part of a monastery, it is the oldest church in Bern. It was taken over by French Protestants, most of them Huguenot refugees, in the 17th century.

Zytglogge **❻**

Marktgasse. 🖼 *May–Jun: 11:30am daily; Jul–Aug: 11:30am & 4:30pm daily; Sep–Oct: 11:30am daily.* 🖼

T HIS CLOCK tower is Bern's central landmark. It was the town's west gate from 1191 to 1250, when it was superseded by the Käfigturm. Rebuilt after the fire of 1405, the Zytglogge was then used to imprison prostitutes.

Its astronomical clock was made by Caspar Brunner in 1527–30. The clock contains mechanical figures, including bears and a crowing cock, that begin their procession on the clock's east face at four minutes before the clock strikes the hour.

The guided tour allows visitors to observe the clock's mechanism at close quarters, see the rooms in the tower and admire the view from the observation platform.

Café in an arcade on Kramgasse

Kramgasse **❼**

W ITH Gerechtigkeitsgasse, its eastern extension, Kramgasse marks the main axis of Bern's early medieval town plan, which was laid out in the late 12th century. Both sides of Kramgasse are lined with fine historic buildings and guild houses fronted by long arcades.

Also on Kramgasse are three fountains: the **Zähringer-brunnen** (1535), with a bear in armour holding the standard of Berthold von Zähringer, Bern's founder; the **Samson-brunnen** (1545), with a figure of Samson subduing a lion; and the un-adorned **Kramgass-brunnen** (1779).

At Kramgasse 49 is the **Einsteinhaus**, where the great German physicist and mathematician Albert Einstein lived from 1903 to 1905 and where he began to develop the theory of relativity while working at the patent office. Einstein's small apartment is now a museum. It contains a writing desk and other objects dating from his brief residence in Bern.

🏛 **Einsteinhaus**, Kramgasse 49. 📞 031 312 00 91. 🕐 *Mar–Oct: 10am–5pm Tue–Fri, 10am–4pm Sat.*

Kunstmuseum ❷

BERN'S MUSEUM OF FINE ARTS houses a collection of paintings of international importance. Spanning the 14th to the 20th centuries, it includes Early Renaissance paintings, 16th- and 17th-century Old Master paintings, and 19th- and 20th-century French paintings, including works by Delacroix, Manet and Monet, and Cubist paintings by Cézanne, Braque and Picasso. Swiss artists, among them Ferdinand Hodler and Albert Anker, are well represented. The collection of 2,000 works by Paul Klee, currently shown in rotation, is moving to the new Zentrum Paul Klee in Schöngrün, eastern Bern, in 2005.

Ice on the River
This winter landscape of broken ice carried downstream by a wide river was painted in 1882 by the French Impressionist Claude Monet.

Main entrance

★ **The Chosen One**
Consisting of an alignment of stylized figures, this painting by Ferdinand Hodler, dating from 1893–4, is typical of the artist's mature style. He called this method of painting Parallelism.

GALLERY GUIDE
The collection of Old Master paintings is displayed in the basement. The 19th-century paintings are exhibited on the ground floor. The 20th-century collection occupies the first floor and the wing, a modern extension.

★ **The Temptation of St Anthony by Demons**
This painting by the 16th-century Bernese artist Niklaus Manuel Deutsch is one of a pair. Its pendant depicts the temptation of St Anthony by women.

Moulin de la Galette, Montmartre
This well-known Parisian café is one of many atmospheric Montmartre street scenes painted by Maurice Utrillo (1883–1955).

VISITORS' CHECKLIST

Hodlerstrasse 8–12.
☎ 031 328 09 44.
⏰ 10am–9pm Tue, 10am–5pm
Wed–Sun. 🅿 ◨ ⬚
🌐 www.kunstmuseumbern.ch

First floor

★ Ad Parnassum
Paul Klee produced this painting at a time when he was fascinated with Pointillism, painting with small dots of pigment.

Blue Horse
This painting by Franz Marc reflects the artist's fondness for the colour blue and his love of horses, to which he ascribed great spirituality.

Ground floor

Drunken Doze
The museum's large collection of paintings by Picasso includes works from his early Blue Period, including this portrait.

Basement

KEY

- ☐ Old Master Paintings
- ☐ 19th-century Paintings
- ☐ Modern Paintings
- ☐ Temporary Exhibitions

STAR EXHIBITS

★ **Ad Parnassum**

★ **The Chosen One**

★ **The Temptation of St Anthony**

Münster ⑧

A SPLENDID EXAMPLE of the German-influenced Late Gothic style, Bern's Münster is the most recent of Switzerland's great Gothic cathedrals. The architect was Matthäus Ensinger of Strasbourg, who designed it as a three-aisle basilica with fan vaulting, side chapels and a tower. Work on the cathedral began in 1421 and continued into the 16th century. It was not, however, until 1893, when the spire was added, that the building was finally completed. Exactly 100 m (328 ft) high, the Münster is the tallest church in Switzerland. The tower is still inhabited by tower-keepers.

Nave
Flanked by square pillars, the lofty nave culminates in the stained-glass windows of the choir. On the keystones are busts of Christ, Mary and other biblical figures.

The rib vaulting, by Daniel Heintz, dates from the 1570s.

Pulpit
Like the Münster's other furnishings, the finely carved pulpit (1470) was badly damaged during the Reformation. The figures are later replacements.

★ **Tympanum**
A striking depiction of the Last Judgment fills the tympanum in the 15th-century central portal. While the damned occupy the left half of the tympanum, the saved are on the right.

Main entrance

★ **Stained Glass**
*The choir is lit by stained-
glass windows (1441–50). The
central panel depicts Christ's
Passion and Crucifixion.*

Flying buttresses
transmit the weight of
the roof outwards and
downwards to the outer walls.

STAR FEATURES

★ **Stained Glass**

★ **Tympanum**

Münstergasse ⑨

RUNNING parallel to
Kramgasse, Münstergasse
links Theaterplatz with
Münsterplatz, which is lined
with arcaded buildings.
On Tuesday and
Saturday mornings,
this square is filled
with a busy meat and
cheese market, and
on the first Saturday
of each month a
handicraft market
is held here.

At the junction of
Münstergasse and
Theaterplatz stands
the **Stadt- und
Universitäts-
bibliothek**, the City
and University
Library. This 18th-
century building stages
exhibitions of books and
manuscripts on the history of
Bern and on literary subjects.

At the point where Münstergasse joins Münsterplatz stands
the **Mosesbrunnen** (1791),
a fountain with the figure of
Moses holding the Ten
Commandments. He points to
the second of them, which
forbids idolatry, a stricture
that was one of the main
tenets of the Reformation.

**Figure of Moses on
the Mosesbrunnen**

Colourful flags along Münstergasse

On the south side of the
Münster is the Münster-
plattform, a terrace with trees
and Baroque pavilions from
which there are beautiful
views over the Aare.

🏛 **Stadt- und Universitäts-
bibliothek.** Münstergasse 61.
📞 *031 320 32 11.* **Exhibitions**
8am–9pm Mon–Fri, 8am–noon Sat.

Erlacherhof ⑩

Junkerngasse 47. Closed to visitors.

EAST OF Münsterplatz,
Münstergasse is continued
by Junkerngasse, a street
once inhabited by Bern's
wealthiest citizens.

At no. 47 is the **Erlacherhof**,
a Baroque mansion built by
Hieronymus von Erlach,
mayor of Bern,
and completed
in 1752. It is
designed in the
French style, with
wings set at a right
angle to the main
building, enclosing
a grand courtyard.
To the rear is a
formal garden, also
in the French style.

The Erlacherhof is now
the official residence of the
mayor of Bern and the seat
of the city's government.

Gerechtigkeits-
gasse ⑪

SOME OF THE oldest and
most beautiful arcaded
buildings in Bern line this
street. Many of them were
built as guild houses, and
their façades are heavily
decorated with motifs
reflecting the relevant trade.

Gerechtigkeitsgasse, or
Street of Justice, also has a
fountain, the **Gerechtigkeits-
brunnen**, which features a
figure personifying Justice.

In the side alley at no. 31
is the Berner Puppentheater
(see p63), a puppet theatre
that stages shows for children
and also produces puppet
plays for adult audiences.

At its eastern extremity,
Gerechtigkeitsgasse leads to
Nydegggasse. This is where a
castle stood, probably about
100 years before Berthold V
chose the location as a secure
spot on which to establish a
new town *(see p49)*. In the
late 15th century the castle
was replaced by a small church,
the **Nydeggkirche**, and in the
19th century a stone bridge,
the **Nydeggbrücke**, was built
over the deep gorge of the
Aare, connecting the Old Town
with Bern's eastern district.

Brown bears in the Bärengraben, the bear pits east of the Old Town

Rathaus ⓬

Rathausplatz. 🎧 *031 633 75 50.*
📧 *by prior arrangement.*

THE SEAT OF THE canton and city of Bern's legislative assemblies since it was built in 1406–16, the Rathaus is an attractive building with an elegant Gothic façade *(see illustration on p49).*

Since the 15th century the Rathaus has undergone major restoration, and the ground floor was completely rebuilt in 1939–42. However, it still retains its authentic Gothic character, making it typical of Bernese architecture. The building is fronted by a double staircase with balustrades decorated with tracery. Beneath the balustrades are pair of stone reliefs featuring human figures. On the loggia at the top of the staircase are a clock and statues set on canopied consoles.

Near the Rathaus stands the **Kirche St Peter- und St Paul**, a Catholic church in the Neo-Gothic style, completed in 1858.

One of the pair of stone reliefs on the façade of the Rathaus

Bärengraben ⓭

Bärengraben. 🕐 *Summer: 8am–5:30pm; winter 9am–4pm.*

BROWN BEARS, indelibly associated with Bern since the town was founded in 1191 *(see p49),* have been kept in pits *(Bärengraben)* on the far side of the Nydeggbrücke, across the river from the Old Town's eastern extremity, since the early 16th century.

Despite constant protests from animal-rights activists, who demand that this attraction be closed, or that the number of bears here be at least reduced, the Bärengraben continue to be very popular with visitors.

Next to the bear pits, in a former tram depot, is one of the town's two tourist offices, where there is also a restaurant serving local cuisine and beer brewed on the premises. The tourist office also presents the **Bern Show**, a visual history of Bern told through a model of the city, slides and spoken commentary.

The steep path from the Bärengraben leads up to the **Rosengarten**. Laid out on a hillside, this rose garden contains over 200 varieties of roses as well as other species of flowers. The Rosengarten also offers a scenic view of the Old Town, across the Aare.

📺 **Bern Show.** Am Bärengraben. Grosse Muristalden. 🎧 *031 328 12 12.* 🕐 *Mar–May: 10am–4pm daily; Jun–Sep: 9am–6pm daily; Oct: 10am–4pm daily; Nov–Feb: 11am–4pm Fri–Sun. Show (in English) every 20 mins.*

Kunsthalle ⓮

Helvetiaplatz 1. 🎧 *031 350 00 40.*
🕐 *2–5 pm Mon, 10am–7pm Tue, 10am–5pm Wed–Sun.* 📧

KIRCHENFELDBRÜCKE leads from Casinoplatz, in the Old Town, over the Aare to Helvetiaplatz, on the south bank of the river, where many of Bern's museums are located.

The Kunsthalle, a building in the Modernist style, was founded in 1918 and has retained its prominence as a showcase for modern art. It has no permanent collection but stages a continuous programme of exhibitions. Past events include one-man shows of the work of such artists as Paul Klee, Alberto Giacometti and Henry Moore. Details of upcoming shows here are available from the Kunsthalle itself and from Bern's tourist offices.

Landscape by Alexandre Calame, Schweizerisches Alpines Museum

Schweizerisches Alpines Museum ⓯

Helvetiaplatz 4. 🎧 *031 351 04 34.*
🕐 *2–5pm Mon, 10am–5pm Tue–Sun.* 📧

THROUGH VIDEOS, photographs, dioramas, models, and paintings inspired by the Alps' magnificent scenery, the Swiss Alpine Museum describes the geology, topography, climate and natural history of the Alps, and documents all aspects of human activity in the mountains.

The displays include a graphic explanation of how

glaciers are formed, and a scale model of the Bernese Oberland. Separate sections are devoted to various aspects of Alpine life, including transport, industry, tourism and winter sports. The daily life and culture of Alpine people are also described, as are modern concerns for environmental protection.

One exhibit in the section devoted to the history of mountaineering is *The Climb and the Fall*, a diorama by Ferdinand Hodler illustrating the conquest of the Matterhorn *(see p54)*.

Mural, Bernisches Historisches Museum

Museum für Kommunikation ⓰

Helvetiastrasse 16. **(** *031 357 55 55.* ☐ *10am–5pm Tue–Sun.* 🖼 🛆

THE HISTORY OF the human endeavour to communicate over long distances is compellingly presented at the Museum of Communication. The displays span the gamut from bonfires to satellites, and multimedia presentations usher the visitor into the complex world of modern telephone exchanges and state-of-the-art mail-sorting systems.

The museum also holds one of the world's largest collections of postage stamps. Numbering over half a million, they include such rarities as an 1840 Penny Black. A programme of temporary exhibitions complements the museum's permanent displays.

Bernisches Historisches Museum ⓱

Helvetiaplatz 5. **(** *031 350 77 11.* ☐ *10am–5pm Tue, 10am–8pm Wed, 10am–5pm Thu–Sun.* 🖼 🛆

LAID OUT ON seven floors of a Neo-Gothic building reminiscent of a medieval fortified castle, the artefacts displayed at Bern's Museum of History are highly diverse. Among the most interesting exhibits here are some of the original sandstone figures from the west front of the Münster *(see pp58–9)* and a spine-chilling depiction of the Dance of Death, a copy of a 16th-century monastic wall painting.

The pride of the museum, however, is its collection of twelve Burgundian tapestries, the oldest of which date from the 15th century. Among the most notable is the Millefleurs-tapisserie (Thousand Flowers Tapestry), which once belonged to Charles the Bold, Duke of Burgundy.

Other sections are devoted to archaeology, with displays of Stone Age, Ancient Egyptian, Roman and Celtic artefacts. Exhibits of coins and medals and of items of armour can be seen, as well as a spectacular collection of Islamic artefacts. A scale model of Bern as it was in 1800 is also on show.

Schweizerisches Schützenmuseum ⓲

Bernastrasse 5. **(** *031 351 01 27.* ☐ *2–5pm Tue–Sat, 10am–noon & 2–5pm Sun.* 🖼

THE ORIGINS of the Swiss Rifle Museum go back to 1885, when the participants in a shooting festival decided to create a rifle section within the Bernisches Historisches Museum. The pieces now form a museum collection in their own right.

Consisting of a vast array of guns, the collection illustrates the history of firearms from the early 19th century. Also on display are cups, medals and other trophies awarded at shooting festivals.

Naturhistorisches Museum ⓳

Bernastrasse 15. **(** *031 350 71 11.* ☐ *2–5pm Mon, 9am–5pm Tue, 9am–6pm Wed, 9am–5pm Thu–Fri, 10am–5pm Sat–Sun.* 🖼

WITH ROOTS going back to the early 19th century, Bern's Museum of Natural History is one of the oldest museums in Switzerland.

It is best known for its numerous dioramas in which stuffed animals are shown in re-creations of their natural habitats. There are sections devoted to the reptiles, birds and mammals of Africa, Asia and the Arctic, but the most impressive displays are those focusing on the wildlife of the Alps. Also on view is the stuffed body of Barry, a St Bernard famous for his feats of mountain rescue in the 19th century *(see p84)*. The museum also has a large collection of Alpine minerals and fossils.

A manually-operated telephone exchange, Museum für Kommunikation

ENTERTAINMENT IN BERN

BERN'S VIBRANT cultural scene offers entertainment of every kind, from ballet to jazz and in styles ranging from the classic to the avant-garde. The city's many cultural centres host a varied programme of art and photography exhibitions as well as other cultural events. Classic plays presented at the Stadttheater are complemented by fringe productions staged in many

small independent theatres. While the prestigious Bern Symphony Orchestra makes the city a focus of the classical music repertoire, Bern also has a long-standing tradition of hosting major jazz and rock festivals. Like those of many other capital cities, the streets and squares of Bern are enlivened by street musicians. The city is also well endowed with nightclubs and dance venues.

Street musician in Bern

INFORMATION/TICKETS

THE BEST SOURCE of information on entertainment and cultural events in Bern is the city's tourist office (**Bern Tourismus**). *Bern Aktuell*, a free guide available at the tourist office, gives listings of mainstream events in German, French and English. The Thursday edition of *Berner Zeitung*, the daily newspaper, includes *Agenda*, a supplement with listings in German.

THEATER VIS-A-VIS
Tel: 031 / 311 72 55
Gerechtigkeitsgasse 44

Signboard for a theatre on Gerechtigkeitsgasse

Tickets for major events can be purchased at the tourist office and from agencies, including **BZ-BilletZentrale**, **Ticket Corner** and **Konzert-kasse Casino**.

THEATRE AND CINEMA

THE FOCAL POINT of theatrical entertainment in Bern is the **Stadttheater**, where classic and contemporary

productions (in German or in French) are staged. Plays from the mainstream repertoire are also staged at the **Kornhaus** arts centre. Two other major theatrical venues in Bern are the **DAS Theater ander Effingerstrasse**, which specializes in modern drama, and the **Theater am Käfigturm**, which is often used by visiting drama companies.

Bern also has an unusually large number of fringe theatres, many of them tucked away in the cellars of houses along the streets of the Old Town. Information about fringe performances is available from the Stadttheater's box office.

Bern's 25 cinemas screen a regular programme of international mainstream films in their original language. Art-house films are shown at the Kunstmuseum (*see p57*).

Poster advertising a concert by the Bern Symphony Orchestra

FESTIVALS

BERN HOSTS no fewer than four annual jazz festivals. The jazz weekend in the Dampfzentrale takes place in January, followed two weeks later by the Be-Jazz Winterfestival. The city's largest and best-known annual musical event is the week-long **Internationales Jazzfestival Bern**, which takes place from late May to early June, with concerts staged at many venues throughout the town.

A dance festival – Berner Tanztage – and the church music festival are held in June.

The **Gurtenfestival** is over the penultimate weekend in July. This large-scale rock-music event is staged in Gurtenpark, over the Aare to the south of the Old Town. Altstadtsommer is a series of summer concerts organized in the Old Town.

The Stadttheater, on Kornhausplatz

The Kultur Casino Bern, on Herrengasse

CULTURAL CENTRES

BERN'S MAIN cultural centre is the **Kornhaus**, a former granary. This large building is the venue for a wide range of events, including exhibitions of architecture, design and photography, and seminars, concerts and theatrical productions.

Another of the town's major cultural centres is the **Kulturhallen Dampfzentrale**, installed in a disused boiler house. The spacious auditorium here is used as a dance, film and jazz theatre, and the centre also has a restaurant, pub and bar.

The **Reitschule** (also known as the Reithalle) was established in the 1980s when protesters took over a former riding school. Fashionably alternative and politically controversial, the Reitschule is run as a cooperative and stages film shows and concerts. There is also a nightclub and a café bar.

MUSIC AND CLUBS

MOST CONCERTS given by the renowned Bern Symphony Orchestra take place in the **Kultur Casino Bern**. The orchestra also plays at other venues, including the Kornhaus, and in churches.

Bern boasts several music clubs, some devoted to a variety of musical styles. They include the famous **Marian's Jazzroom**, where traditional jazz is played. Other clubs specialize in rock, funk and other types of popular music. Peculiar to Bern are music clubs occupying disused factories, a fact that is often reflected in their names. Very popular are the concerts organized in Musig-Bistrot, **Gaskessel** and **Wasserwerk**, which concentrates on techno music and which have a bar, disco and live music on certain nights.

Gaskessel is also a popular nightclub. Others include **Guayas**, on Parkterrasse, with Latino-funk and salsa, and Babalu, on Gurtengasse, which specializes in techno and house music.

GAMBLING

BERN'S MAIN CASINO is the Jackpot Spielcasino above the Allegro hotel at Kornhausstrasse 3. As well as slot machines and gambling tables, it has a restaurant and bars.

CHILDREN

BERN OFFERS several indoor and outdoor entertainments for the young. The **Berner Puppentheater** puts on puppet shows that will amuse children even if they do not speak German.

With its European animals, **Dählhölzli Tierpark Zoo** offers a close-up experience of many kinds of wildlife.

Historic surveying equipment, Schweizerisches Alpines Museum

DIRECTORY

INFORMATION/ TICKETS

Bern Tourismus
Bahnhofplatz and
Laupenstrasse 20.
📞 031 328 12 28.
🌐 www.berne.ch

BZ-BilletZentrale
Zeughausgasse 14.
📞 031 327 11 88.

Ticket Corner
📞 0848 800 800.

**Konzertkasse
Casino**
Herrengasse 25.
📞 031 311 42 42.

THEATRES

Stadttheater
Kornhausplatz 20.
📞 031 329 51 51.

**Theaterkasse im
Kornhaus**
Kornhausplatz 18.
📞 031 329 51 51.

**DAS Theater an der
Effingerstrasse**
Effingerstrasse 14.
📞 031 382 72 72.

Theater am Käfigturm
Spitalgasse 4.
📞 031 311 61 00.

FESTIVALS

Gurtenfestival AG
📞 031 386 10 00.
🌐 www.gurtenfestival.ch

**Internationales
Jazzfestival Bern**
📞 031 309 61 71.
🌐 www.jazzfestival.ch.

CULTURAL CENTRES

Kornhaus
Kornhausplatz 18.
🌐 www.kornhaus.org

**Kulturhallen
Dampfzentrale**
Marzilistrasse 47.
📞 031 311 63 37.

Reitschule
Bollwerk.
📞 031 306 69 69.

MUSIC & CLUBS

Kultur Casino Bern
Herrengasse 25.
📞 031 311 42 42.

Marian's Jazzroom
Engestrasse 54.
📞 031 309 61 11.

Gaskessel
Sandrainstrasse 25.
📞 031 372 49 00.

Wasserwerk
Wasserwerkgasse 5.
📞 031 312 12 31.

Guayas
Parkterrasse 16.
📞 031 306 69 69.

CHILDREN

Puppentheater
Gerechtigkeitsgasse 31.
📞 031 311 95 85.

**Dählhölzli
Tierpark Zoo**
Tierparkwege. 🚌 18.
📞 031 357 15 15.

SHOPPING IN BERN

BERN'S SHOPPING district lies along Gerechtigkeitsgasse Kramgasse, Marktgasse and Spitalgasse, streets that form a continuous east–west axis through the centre of the Old Town. Shops also line Postgasse, which runs parallel to Gerechtigkeits-gasse on its northern side.

Beneath arcades with vaulted roofs that cover the pavement below are shops selling an almost endless variety of goods. On offer here is a range of souvenirs,

Chocolate bear from Bern

including bears in all imaginable guises, as well as Swiss-made shoes, high-quality clothes and leather goods, fine jewellery and watches, Swiss army knives and musical boxes, handwoven textiles and woodcarvings, and, of course, the famous Swiss chocolate. On the squares at the Old Town's western extremity are several open-air markets, with colourful flower and produce stalls, and two large department stores on Spitalgasse.

Display of handcrafted goods at Heimatwerk, on Kramgasse

MARKETS AND FAIRS

TWICE A WEEK several of the squares in Bern's Old Town are filled with lively open-air markets. On Tuesday and Saturday mornings from April to October a large fruit, vegetable and flower market is held on Bärenplatz and the adjoining Bundesplatz, and there is also a meat and dairy produce market on Münster-gasse. A general market takes place on Waisenhausplatz all day Tuesday and Saturday, and on the first Saturday of the month from April to October there is a handicrafts market on Münsterplatz. A flea market is held on Mühleplatz, in the Matte district, on the third Saturday of the month from May to October.

Bern's annual fairs are major attractions. The magnificent Geranienmarkt, or Geranium Fair, takes place on Bundes-

platz in mid-May. On the fourth Monday of November a party atmosphere breaks out as Zibelemärit, the onion fair, gets under way *(see p32)*. A **Christmas market**, with gifts and handicrafts, is held on Waisenhausplatz and Münsterplatz daily through December.

ART AND ANTIQUES

THE BEST art galleries and antique shops in Bern are located on Kramgasse, Postgasse and Gerechtigkeitsgasse. Some art galleries, including the **Altstadt Galerie**, on Kramgasse, also hold exhibi-tions of contemporary art. Antique dolls and toys, meanwhile, are the speciality of **Puppenklinik**, on Gerechtigkeitsgasse.

Traditional Swiss cut-out

CRAFTS AND SOUVENIRS

THE SWISS TAKE PRIDE in their traditional handicrafts, particularly those associated with Alpine culture and folklore. Handicrafts from all Switzerland, including wood carvings, ceramics, music boxes, jewellery and hand-woven textiles, linen and embroidery are available at **Heimatwerk**, on Kramgasse.

A wide selection of pocket knives, particularly the multi-functional Swiss Army knives, is available at **Klötzli**, on Rathausgasse.

Kunsthandwerk Anderegg, on Kramgasse, specializes in beautifully handmade toys from Switzer-land and other countries.

Fruit and vegetable stall in the market, Bärenplatz

Window display at Bucherer, a jeweller's on Marktgasse

WATCHES AND JEWELLERY

FINE JEWELLERY and the clocks and watches that have brought Swiss craftsmanship international renown have many retail outlets in Bern. Two of the city's best clock, watch and jewellery shops are **Bucherer**, on Marktgasse, and **Gubelin**, on Bahnhofplatz.

MUSIC AND BOOKS

HAVING CLOSE associations with music, Bern has several excellent music stores. While **Musik Müller**, in Zeughausgasse, concentrates uniquely on musical instruments, **Musikhaus Krompholz**, on Spitalgasse, also stocks a good range of CDs, as well as sheet music,

musical scores and all kinds of books on music.

Bern also has the largest and reputedly the best bookshop in Switzerland. This is **Stauffacher**, on Neuengasse. You will find a good range of books in English here.

SHOES AND LEATHER GOODS

LEATHER shoes and accessories made by the internationally known Swiss shoe manufacturer **Bally** are available from a large branch of its outlets on Spitalgasse. Another major outlet for high-quality leather goods is

Doll in traditional Swiss costume

Hummel Lederwaren, on Marktgasse and at the train station. Stock here includes luggage, briefcases, purses and wallets, and a range of accessories, made in Switzerland and elsewhere in Europe.

CHOCOLATE

LIKE EVERY OTHER Swiss city, Bern has several shops offering tempting arrays of Swiss chocolates and other confectionery. Just two of them are **Eichenberger**, on Bahnhofplatz, which is famous for its hazelnut *Lebkuchen* (spicy honey biscuits), and **Tschirren**, on Kramgasse, which has been making and selling its own chocolates for over 80 years.

DEPARTMENT STORES

BERN'S TWO main department stores are **Loeb** and **Globus**, both located on Spitalgasse, on the western side of the Old Town. Their many departments stock an enormous variety of goods, and they are also known for their clothes, including designer labels, for both men and women.

DIRECTORY

MARKETS

Bundesplatz/Bärenplatz.
(Fruit, vegetables, flowers).
🔲 *8am–noon Tue & Sat.*

Münstergasse.
(Meat and dairy).
🔲 *8am–noon Tue & Sat.*

Waisenhausplatz *(General).*
🔲 *8am–6pm Tue & Sat.*

Mühleplatz *(Handicrafts and collectables).*
🔲 *May–Oct: 3rd Sat of the month.*

ART & ANTIQUES

Altstadt Galerie
Kramgasse 60.
📞 *031 311 25 26.*

Puppenklinik
Gerechtigkeitsgasse 36.
📞 *031 312 07 71.*

CRAFTS & SOUVENIRS

Heimatwerk
Kramgasse 61.
📞 *031 331 30 00.*

Klötzli
Rathausgasse 84.
📞 *031 311 00 80.*

Kunsthandwerk Anderegg
Kramgasse 48.
📞 *031 331 02 01.*

WATCHES & JEWELLERY

Bucherer
Marktgasse 38.
📞 *031 328 90 90.*

Gubelin
Bahnhofplatz 11.
📞 *031 311 54 33.*

MUSIC & BOOKS

Musikhaus Krompholz
Spitalgasse 28,
📞 *031 311 53 11.*

Musik Müller
Zeughausgasse 22,
📞 *031 311 41 34.*

Stauffacher
Neuengasse 25.
📞 *031 311 24 11.*

SHOES & LEATHER GOODS

Bally
Spitalgasse 9.
📞 *031 311 54 81.*

Hummel Lederwaren
Marktgasse 18.
📞 *031 311 20 66.*
Bahnhofshop
📞 *031 311 20 39.*

CHOCOLATE

Eichenberger
Bahnhofplatz 5.
📞 *031 311 33 25.*

Tschirren
Kramgasse 73.
📞 *031 311 17 17.*

DEPARTMENT STORES

Loeb
Spitalgasse 47–51.
📞 *031 320 71 11.*

Globus
Spitalgasse 17–21.
📞 *031 320 40 40.*

MITTELLAND, BERNESE OBERLAND AND VALAIS

THESE THREE REGIONS *occupy the western central section of Switzerland. The Mittelland, or Swiss Heartland, is a fertile area of rolling hills. While the Bernese Oberland, a massif in the heart of Switzerland, contains some of the country's most spectacular peaks, the Valais, in the south, has Switzerland's highest mountains, including the Matterhorn and the Eiger, and its best ski resorts.*

The Mittelland, the heart of the Swiss farming industry, is made up mostly of the small canton of Solothurn and the northern part of the large canton of Bern. Unlike Bern and Basel, Solothurn remained Catholic after the Reformation. By contrast, the predominantly German-speaking people of the canton of Bern embraced the Reformation and have been Protestant since the 16th century.

The southern part of the canton of Bern makes up the Bernese Oberland, a mountainous area that rises to the south of two lakes, the Thunersee and the Brienzersee. These lakes are bordered by the towns of Thun, Interlaken and Brienz. A land of natural wonders, the Bernese Oberland has some dramatically high peaks, with excellent skiing pistes, but also many gentler valleys that are ideal countryside for hiking.

The Valais, a Catholic and French-speaking canton, occupies the Rhône valley and the Pennine Alps. It is divided into two regions: Lower Valais, a French-speaking and Catholic region to the west, and Upper Valais, which is German-speaking and Protestant, to the east. The lower-lying parts of the Valais are industrial. By contrast, its more mountainous regions, with the large international resorts of Verbier, Crans-Montana, Zermatt and Saas Fee, support a thriving year-round tourist industry.

Wooden chalets in Blatten, a village in the Lötschental, Upper Valais

◁ The majestic Matterhorn, above Zermatt, in the canton of Valais

Exploring the Mittelland, Bernese Oberland and Valais

EACH OF THESE REGIONS is exceptionally scenic. While the area contains some of Switzerland's most historic towns, including Bern, Solothurn and Sion, it also has many natural wonders. The Thunersee and the Brienzersee, two beautiful lakes, lie at the foot of the Bernese Oberland, a paradise for skiers and hikers. The region also includes the Eiger, Monch and Jungfrau. To the south, in the Valais, lie the sunny Rhône valley and the rugged Pennine Alps, which culminate in the Matterhorn.

GETTING AROUND

As Bern has only a small airport, with relatively infrequent flights, it is best reached by train, which carries cars and travels through the Lötschberg Tunnel. The A1 motorway runs from Zürich, via Olten and Solothurn, to Bern. Bern also has motorway links with Thun and Biel/Bienne. Two routes lead south to the Rhône valley. While the A6 follows the Aare valley, the A11 skirts the mountains, running west. The motorway linking Martigny with Sion and Sierre runs along the Rhône valley. Interlaken is the hub of a network of Alpine train and cable-car lines, with destinations that include the Jungfraujoch, the Schilthorn and Schynige Platte.

Hillsides covered with vineyards in the Rhône valley

SEE ALSO

- **Where to Stay** pp244–9.

- **Where to Eat** pp269–273.

KEY

- ▬ Motorway
- ▬ Main road
- ▬ Scenic route
- = Other roads
- = River
- ☆ Viewpoint

View of Zermatt and the Matterhorn

Scenic alley in Sion

Sights at a Glance

Basel

Aarau

OLTEN ①

5

A1 E25

Luzern

LANGENTHAL

MMENTAL

Luzern

mme

0 km   20

0 miles   20

FREILICHTMUSEUM
BALLENBERG ← Luzern

BRIENZ ⑩   ⑪

⑫ MEIRINGEN

⑨ BRIENZER SEE   11

⑧ INTERLAKEN   ⑯ GRINDELWALD   6

WENGEN   ⑰   Andermatt

MÜRREN   ⑱

ANDERSTEG   ⑬ JUNGFRAUJOCH
ALETSCH
GLACIER   ㊳

⑥   ㊱ BRIG
SIMPLON PASS

㊲   Stresa

SAAS FEE
㉟

RMATT   ㉞ MONTE ROSA

ATTERHORN

Olten ❶

Road map D2. 🏘 *19,000.* 🚉 🚌
ℹ️ *Klosterplatz 21; 062 212 30 88.*

THE SMALL TOWN of Olten has a picturesque location on the banks of the River Aare. Pedestrian access to the old part of the town is provided by the Alte Brücke, a covered bridge dating from 1802.

The Old Town is dominated by the tall Gothic belfry of a church that was demolished in the 19th century. There are many fine historic houses, particularly on Hauptgasse and along the Old Town's riverbank. Also of interest are the 17th-century monastery church and the Neo-Classical Stadtkirche, dating from 1806–12 and decorated with paintings by Martin Disteli. Many works by this artist, together with 19th- and 20th-century paintings and sculpture, are exhibited in the **Kunstmuseum**.

🏛 Kunstmuseum
Kirchgasse 8. 📞 *062 212 86 76.* ⏰ *Tue–Fri 2–5pm, Sat–Sun 11am–5pm.* ♿

Houses along the banks of the Aare in Olten

Weissenstein ❷

Road map C2. ℹ️ *Solothurn, Hauptgasse 69; 032 626 46 00.*

SOME OF THE MOST spectacular views of the Mittelland can be enjoyed from the summit of the Weissenstein, a ridge of the Jura that rises like a rampart 1,284 m (4,214 ft) high. It is situated 40 km (25 miles) southwest of Olten and 10 km (6 miles) north of Solothurn. It is accessible by

road or rail to Oberdorf, from where you can either hike to the summit or take a chair lift (closed on Mondays).

On the ridge is the Weissenstein Hotel, which has a restaurant. The hotel is a good base for hiking, rock-climbing and paragliding in summer, and for sledging in winter. Other attractions include a botanical garden with plants and flowers of the Jura, a small regional museum, the Nidleloch, a limestone cave, and the Planetenweg, or Planet Trail, a walk with a schematic layout of the Solar System.

Solothurn ❸

See pp72–3.

Biel/Bienne ❹

Road map C3. 🏘 *55,000.* 🚉 🚌
🚢 ℹ️ *In the train station; 032 329 84 84.* 🎭 *Bieler Lauftage (Jun), Bieler Seefest (Jul–Aug), Zibelemärit (Oct).*

BIEL, KNOWN AS Bienne in French, is the second-largest town in the canton of Bern. It was founded in the 13th century, and from then until the 19th century it was ruled by the prince-bishops of Basel. Biel/Bienne's principal industry is watchmaking, its factories producing such leading brands as Omega and Rolex. It is Switzerland's only officially bilingual town: two-fifths of its inhabitants speak German, and the rest French.

The town is set on the shores of the Bielersee (or Lac de Bienne) at the point where the River Schüss (or Suze) flows into it. The Old Town, which has narrow cobbled streets and decorative fountains, is set on a hill. Its nucleus is a square known as the **Ring**, which is surrounded by fine arcaded houses. One of them is the house of the guild of foresters. This beautiful building has a 16th-century circular corner turret topped by an onion dome. Also on the square is the 15th-century church of

St Benedict, with impressive late Gothic stained-glass windows.

At the intersection of Burggasse and Rathausgasse, west of the Ring, stands the Rathaus, the Gothic town hall, which dates from the 1530s. It is fronted by a Fountain of Justice. The late 16th-century Zeughaus, or arsenal, nearby is now used as a theatre.

Biel/Bienne has several museums and galleries. The **Museum Neuhaus** contains re-creations of 19th-century patrician interiors, as well as paintings and exhibits relating to the town's history and industries, and a section devoted to cameras and the cinema. The dynamic **Kunsthaus Centre d'Art** stages a programme of changing exhibitions of contemporary art and photography, and shows relating to the cinema.

Foresters' guildhouse, Biel/Bienne

🏛 Museum Neuhaus
Schüsspromenade/Prde de la Suze 26. 📞 *032 328 70 30.* ⏰ *Tue, Thu–Sun 11am–5pm, Wed 11am–7pm.* ♿
🏛 Kunsthaus Centre d'Art
Seevorstadt/Faubourg du Lac 71–75. 📞 *032 322 55 86.* ⏰ *2pm–6pm Wed–Fri, 11am–6pm Sat–Sun.* ♿

ENVIRONS: **Twann**, a medieval town, **La Neuveville**, which has cobbled streets, **Erlach**, which has a castle, and **St Petersinsel** can all be visited by boat from Biel/Bienne. There are also boat trips on the lake, which enable visitors to enjoy views of vineyards on the surrounding hillsides. A riverboat service runs between Biel/Bienne and Solothurn.

Schloss Burgdorf, the castle of the Zähringers, in the Emmental

The Emmental ❺

Road map C3. 🚉 🚌 🚶 *Langnau, Schlossstrasse 3; 034 402 42 52.* ⓦ *www.emmental.ch*

THE EMMENTAL, the long, wide valley of the River Emme, has an outstandingly beautiful landscape of green meadows, which provide grazing for cows. The valley, which has excellent cycling and hiking routes, is also dotted with traditional wooden chalets with high roofs, eaves almost reaching to the ground and windows with decorative carvings.

The local culture of the Emmental is traditional and conservative, with a farming economy. This is also where the famous Emmental cheese is made, most of it by hand. At the **Schaukäserei** (show dairy) in Affoltern visitors can see every stage in the process of producing this holey, nutty-tasting cheese. It is also on sale in the dairy's shop and on the menu in its restaurant. Many inns along the valley also serve this highly prized local speciality.

Burgdorf is a small town in the north of the Emmental. The old part of the town, on top of a hill, has arcaded houses, a Gothic church and a castle, founded by the Zähringers in the 7th century. **Trubschachen**, a village further up the valley, has pottery workshops where the colourful local ware is made and offered for sale.

The Emmental also has the longest arched wooden bridge in Europe. Built in 1839, the Holzbrücke spans the Emme just downstream of the villages of **Hasle-Rüegsau**.

🏛 **Schaukäserei**
Affoltern. 📞 *034 435 16 11.*

Thun ❻

Road map C3. 🚶 *41,000.* 🚉 🚌
ⓘ *Bahnhofstrasse; 033 251 00 00.*
ⓦ *www.thuntourismus.ch*

THE HISTORIC MARKET town of Thun is set on the River Aare, at the northern end of the Thunersee. The origins of Thun go back to 1191, when Berthold V, Duke of Zähringen, built a castle on a hill above the river here.

Thun's Old Town spreads out beneath the castle, on the right bank of the river. Obere Hauptgasse, the main street running parallel to the river, is split into two levels. The walkway is built on the roofs of the arcaded buildings lining the street, so that pedestrians step downstairs to enter the shops below. Stepped alleys off Obere Hauptgasse lead up to the castle, **Schloss Thun**, from which there are impressive views of the town and the Bernese Oberland. Inside the castle's massive turreted keep, which looms

Detail of a fountain in Thun

over Thun, is a museum documenting the town's history. Other rooms in the castle contain collections of clocks, dolls and household objects, weapons and uniforms, glass and ceramics, coins and toys. The huge Knights' Hall, with an imposing fireplace, is used as a concert hall. Also on the hill is the Stadtkirche, the town's church. A short walk east of the castle and down to the river leads to the **Kunstmuseum**, which contains a collection of Swiss and international modern art.

On the left bank of the river is Schadau Park. Near the lake here stand a Neo-Gothic folly and a cylindrical pavilion, whose interior walls are painted with the **Wocher Panorama**. This visual record of daily life in Thun was painted by Marquard Wocher in 1814, and is the oldest such panorama in the world.

⚓ **Schloss Thun**
Schlossberg 1. 📞 *033 223 20 01.* 🕐 *Feb–Mar: 1–4pm daily; Apr–Oct: 10am–5pm daily; Nov–Jan: 1–4pm Sun.* 🌀

🏛 **Kunstmuseum**
Hofstettenstrasse 14. 📞 *033 225 84 20.* 🕐 *10am–5pm Tue, 10am–9pm Wed, 10am–5pm Thu–Sun.* 🌀

🏛 **Wocher Panorama**
Seestrasse 45, Schadaupark. 📞 *033 223 24 62.* 🕐 *May–Oct: 10am–5pm Tue–Sun; Jul–Aug: 10am–6pm daily.* 🌀

Schloss Thun, from the left bank of the River Aare

Solothurn ❸

THIS BEAUTIFUL BAROQUE city, known in French as Soleure and in Italian as Soletta, is the capital of the canton of Solothurn. It was founded by Celts and later became the second-largest Roman town north of the Alps after Trier. Having remained Catholic through the Reformation, Solothurn was chosen as the residence of French ambassadors to the Swiss Confederation. It was during this period, from 1530 to 1792, that the city's finest buildings were constructed. Today Solothurn is a vibrant city, with watchmaking and precision-engineering industries.

Clock on the Zytglogge

Exploring Solothurn

The historic nucleus of Solothurn, on the River Aare, occupies a small area on the north bank, a short walk from the railway station on the opposite side. The Kreuzackerbrücke, which spans the river, linking the old and new towns, leads to Klosterplatz. From here, Solothurn's main historic sights, including vestiges of fortifications on the northeastern side of the town, are within easy reach.

From Solothurn boat trips depart for Biel/Bienne, and follow a particularly beautiful stretch of the Aare.

Baroque pulpit in St Ursen Kathedrale

🛡 St Ursen Kathedrale

Hauptgasse. **☎** 032 626 46 47. **Treasury** ⬜ *by prior arrangement.*
Built from 1763 to 1773, Solothurn's monumental Neo-Classical cathedral takes the form of a three-aisle basilica with a transept and a dome over the crossing. A bell tower rises next to the presbytery at the eastern end.

Set on a hill, the cathedral is reached by steps flanked by ornamental fountains. The two-tier façade, which shows the influence of the Italian Baroque, is faced by Corinthian columns divided by a frieze. The frieze contains figures, among which are those of the city's patron saints, Ursus and Victor, who were martyred by the Romans in Solothurn.

The cathedral's interior features elaborate stucco-work. The treasury, in the crypt, contains an interesting collection of liturgical vestments dating from the 10th century.

🏛 Altes Zeughaus

Zeughausplatz 1. **☎** 032 623 35 28. ⬜ *May–Oct: 10am–noon & 2–5pm Tue–Sun; Nov–Apr: 2–5pm Tue–Fri, 10am–noon & 2–5pm Sat–Sun.* 🖼
The former arsenal is a large four-storey Baroque building dating from 1609–14. Above the upper storey is a crane that was used to lift heavy armoury from ground level to the upper floors.

The arsenal now serves as a museum of militaria. It contains a large collection of swords, suits of armour and cannons, and a tank used in World War II. Of particular interest is the collection of arms and uniforms used by Swiss mercenaries who served

as bodyguards to French kings. Many of these mercenaries came from Solothurn.

🏛 Riedholzschanze

Solothurn was fortified several times in the course of its history. The oldest walls surrounded a Roman camp, and their remains can be seen on Friedhofplatz and at Löwengasse. A later ring of walls, with gates and towers, was built in the Middle Ages. In the early 16th century the city's defences were modernized with the addition of two gates, Bieltor and Baseltor, and three towers, Buristurm, Krummturm and Riedholz-turm, all of which still stand. In 1667 work on new fortifications, with bastions, began. Although these were later levelled out to make way for streets and parks, Riedholz-schanze, a bastion at the northeastern corner of the old town, survives.

🏛 Kunstmuseum

Werkhofstrasse 30. **☎** 032 622 23 07. ⬜ *10am–noon & 2–5pm Tue–Fri, 10am–5pm Sat–Sun.* 🖼
This small art gallery contains some very fine works. Among its Old Master paintings are the exquisite *Madonna of Solothurn* (1522) by Hans Holbein the Younger, and *The Madonna in the Strawberries* (1425) by an anonymous artist. Most of the exhibition space is devoted to Swiss and French painting of the 19th and 20th centuries. There are landscapes by Caspar Wolf, Alexandre Calame and Giovanni Giacometti, and a dramatic depiction of William Tell

Part of the façade of the Altes Zeughaus, once the city's arsenal

The imposing entrance of the Rathaus

emerging from the clouds by Ferdinand Hodler *(see p54)*, and many paintings by Van Gogh, Degas, Cézanne, Matisse, and Picasso. A section is devoted to comtemporary Swiss artists, including Deiter Roth, Markus Raëtz and Meret Oppenheim.

⊞ Rathaus
Rathausplatz.

Solothurn's town hall, on the east side of Rathausplatz, is in an ornate Mannerist style. The building's complex appearance is the result of work on the building having occurred in successive stages over many years.

The Gothic building that was begun in 1476 was not completed until 1711, when the town hall acquired its narrow three-part façade, with a central tower and onion domes crowning the lateral sections. The interior has a spiral staircase known as the Schnecke (Snail), which curves upwards, leading to the grand hall.

🔒 Jesuitenkirche
Hauptgasse.

Dating from 1680 89, Solothurn's Jesuit church is a magnificent example of High Baroque architecture. While the exterior is sparsely decorated, the interior glistens

The Baroque nave and high altar of the Jesuitenkirche

with frescoes and is encrusted with stuccowork by masters from Ticino.

On the high altar, which dates from the early 18th century, is a huge altarpiece by Franz Carl Stauder depicting the Assumption of the Virgin. Stones, some with Roman inscriptions, are also displayed in the church.

⊞ Zytglogge
Marktplatz.

Its lower part dating from the 12th century and its upper from the 15th, the clock tower is Solothurn's oldest surviving building. The astronomical clock was made in 1545. It contains mechanical figures, including a knight, a figure of Death and the King of Jesters, which form a procession on the hour.

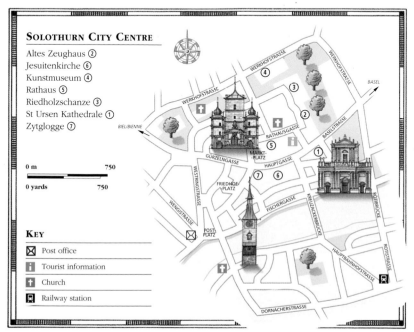

SOLOTHURN CITY CENTRE

Altes Zeughaus ②
Jesuitenkirche ⑥
Kunstmuseum ④
Rathaus ⑤
Riedholzschanze ③
St Ursen Kathedrale ①
Zytglogge ⑦

0 m   750
0 yards   750

KEY

⊠ Post office

🛈 Tourist information

✝ Church

🚆 Railway station

Thunersee **❼**

A BEAUTIFUL LAKE in a spectacular mountain setting, the Thunersee forms a slender arc between Thun and Interlaken in the valley of the River Aare. Some 18 km (11 miles) long and almost 4 km (3 miles) wide, the lake offers many kinds of water sports, including sailing, windsurfing, water-skiing and diving. The surrounding areas are ideal for hiking and cycling. A ferry service links the towns, villages and other places of interest on the lakeshore, and vintage steamships take visitors on tours of the lake.

Niesen ⑥
A funicular from Mülenen takes visitors to the summit of the Niesen, which rises to 2,362 m (7,750 ft) and offers a fine view of the Thunersee and its surroundings.

Hilterfingen ①
As well as a sailing school, Hilterfingen has a mid-19th-century castle, Schloss Hüneg. It is in the Neo-Renaissance style, with Art Nouveau interiors.

Bern

Gstadd

Wimmis

Simme

Thunersee

Merligen

Krattigen

Leissigen   A8

Kandersteg

0 km   3

0 miles   3

Spiez ⑤
The medieval castle in Spiez is set on a spur jutting into the lake. Near the castle is a Romanesque church with a fine Baroque interior.

Aeschi ④
In summer this beautiful resort is a particularly convenient starting-point for hikers. In winter it is an excellent base for cross-country skiers.

TIPS FOR VISITORS

Tour length: about 50 km (30 miles).
Stopping-off places: There are restaurants in every village around the lake.
Boat tours of the lake: BLS Schiffsbetrieb, Lachenweg 19, Thun.
☎ 033 334 52 11.

The Hôtel du Lac at Interlaken and the jetty on the Brienzersee

Oberhofen ②
The lakeside castle here dates from the 12th century. It is now an outpost of the Bernisches Historisches Museum *(see p61)*.

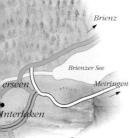

Beatenberg ③
Set high above the lakeshore, this resort overlooks the Bernese Alps. It offers facilities for skiers.

KEY

▬	Motorway
▬	Suggested route
▬	Scenic route
=	Other roads
=	River, lake
- -	Funicular
☆	Viewpoint

Interlaken ❽

Road map D4. 🏃 *13,500.* 🚌 🚊
ℹ *Höheweg 37; 033 826 53 00.*
🆆 *www.interlakentourism.ch*
🎪 *Musikfestwochen (Aug).*

INTERLAKEN LIES ON a narrow strip of land between the Thunersee and the Brienzersee. In prehistory the isthmus between the lakes, known as the Bödeli, was inhabited by Celts. The present town owes its name to the monastery that was founded here in the 12th century. It was named Inter Lacus, meaning "between lakes" in Latin.

Today Interlaken is a popular resort that makes an excellent base for mountaineers and hikers in summer and for skiers in winter. Interlaken is also a rail junction on the route by rack railway up to the Jungfrau region *(see p79)*, to Wengen *(see p83)* and beyond. A funicular also takes visitors up to the summit of the Heimwehfluh (669 m/2,195 ft).

Interlaken's newest attraction is the **Mystery Park**, a theme park that introduces visitors to the great unsolved mysteries of the world. It consists of several pavilions, in which elaborate displays focus on the meaning of mysterious ancient monuments, such as the pyramids of Egypt, question how the ancient Maya devised their complex calendar, and investigate the origins of religion in ancient cultures. A further section is devoted to outer space and the search for extraterrestrial intelligence.

Rugen Forest, on the south side of Interlaken, is the bucolic setting for open-air productions of Schiller's play *Wilhelm Tell*. On the opposite side of the Aare is Unterseen. The **Touristikmuseum** here documents the evolution of tourism in the Jungfrau region since the 19th century.

ENVIRONS: Alpine fauna can be seen at the zoo at **Harder**, accessible by cable car from Interlaken **Schynige Platte**, which can be reached by rack-railway from Wilderswil, south of Interlaken, is a 2,000-m (6,564-ft) high plateau offering magnificent views of the two lakes and their mountain setting. There is also a botanical garden here, with alpine plants and flowers.

🏛 **Mystery Park**
Obere Bönigstrasse 100, Interlaken.
☎ *0848 50 60 70.* ☐ *10–6pm daily*
⬤ *25 Dec & 1 Jan.* 🅿
🎭 **Wilhelm Tell**
Performances: late Jun–mid-Sep: Sat–Sun. Tickets from Tell-Büro, Höeweg 37; 033 822 37 22, and tourist offices in the region.
🏛 **Touristikmuseum**
Obere Gasse 26, Unterseen.
☎ *033 822 98 39.* ☐ *May–Oct: 2–5pm Tue–Sun.* 🅿

Flower clock in front of the Kursaal in Interlaken

The small town of Brienz, at the eastern tip of the Brienzersee, with the Brienzer Rothorn in the background

Brienzersee ⑨

Road map D4. 🚗 🚌 🛈
Brienz; 033 952 80 80. **Boat trips
on the lake** 📞 *033 822 17 36.*
Grandhotel Giessbach 📞 *033 952
25 25.* 🕐 *Apr–Oct.*

L YING EAST OF Interlaken
and the Thunersee *(see
pp74–5)*, the clear waters of
the Brienzersee stretch out in
a setting of forested slopes
and waterfalls, with majestic
mountains rising in the background. Some 14 km (9 miles)
long and almost 3 km (2 miles)
wide at its broadest point, the
Brienzersee is slightly smaller
than the Thunersee and much
less developed, with fewer
sports centres lining its shores
and less boating activity. As
such, it is much more
appealing to anglers.
    From Interlaken, places of
interest around the shore can
be visited by bicycle or by
taking a boat trip on the lake.
On the north side of the lake
are the ruins of **Goldswil**
castle and the village of
Ringgenberg, where there
is a small Baroque church.
The small town of **Brienz** lies
at the eastern tip of the lake.
On the south side is Axalp,
where there are excellent
restaurants and the
magnificent **Giessbachfälle**,
waterfalls that can be viewed
from the terrace of the Grand
Hotel Giessbach, reachable
by a funicular.

Brienz ⑩

Road map D3. 🏛 *3,000.* 🚗
🚌 🛈 *Hauptstrasse 143; 033 952
80 80.* 🆆 *www.alpenregion.ch*

L OCATED AT THE eastern end
of the Brienzersee, Brienz
is the main town on the lakeshore. It is a good base not
only for mountain hikers but
also for anglers and watersports enthusiasts. Axalp,
nearby, has a small ski and
snowboarding centre.
    Being the centre of Swiss
woodcarving, Brienz is full of
shops selling all kinds
of wooden objects. The
workshops of its renowned
woodcarving school, the
Schule für Holzbildhauerei,
are open to visitors during
term-time. Students can be

Alley in Brienz, lined with
traditional houses

seen at work, and there is
also an exhibition of their
finished pieces.
    Another speciality of
Brienz is violin-making. The
Geigenbauschule, where
future violin-makers learn their
craft, also welcomes visitors.
The school's workshops are
open to visitors, and there
is an exhibition of instruments.

ENVIRONS: The summit of the
Brienzer Rothorn, which
rises to 2,350 m (7,710 ft)
about 5 km (3 miles) north
of Brienz, can be reached
by steam-driven rack railway.
It is one of the few still in
use, though the carriages are
sometimes pulled by a diesel
locomotive. The 7-km (4-mile)
route up the mountain passes
through tunnels. The short
walk from the summit station
is rewarded by breathtaking
views of the Brienzersee and
the Bernese Alps.

🏛 **Schule für Holzbild-
hauerei**
Schleegasse 1 📞 *033 952 17 51.*
Exhibition 🕐 *8–11:30am & 2 ·5pm
Mon–Thu, 8–11:30am & 2–4:15pm Fri.*
🏛 **Geigenbauschule**
Oberdorfstrasse 94. 📞 *033 951 18 61.*
🕐 *By prior arrangement.*

Freilichtmuseum
Ballenberg ⑪

See pp80–81.

◁ Schloss Oberhofen, the 13th-century castle on the northern shore of the Thunersee

Meiringen ⓬

Road map D4. 🎿 4,500. 🚆 🚌
🛈 *Bahnhofstrasse 22; 033 972 50 50.*

THIS SMALL TOWN lies in the heart of the Hasli valley, the Upper Aare valley east of the Brienzersee. It is a skiing and snowboarding resort in winter, and a base for hiking and mountain biking in summer.

Meiringen lies near the **Reichenbachfälle**, the waterfalls chosen by the writer Arthur Conan Doyle as the scene of Sherlock Holmes' "death" after a struggle with Professor Moriarty. The **Sherlock Holmes Museum**, in the basement of a church, features a representation of Holmes' drawing room at 221B Baker Street, London. A statue of the fictional detective graces Conan Doyle Place.

Also of interest in Meiringen is the small church at the top of the town. It was built in 1684 over the crypt of an early Romanesque church. The town has two regional museums, one of which is open only in summer.

🏛 **Sherlock Holmes Museum**
Bahnhofstrasse 26. 📞 *033 971 42 21.*
🔲 *May–Sep: 1:30–6pm Tue–Sun; Oct–Apr: 4:30–6:30pm Wed & Sun.*
♿

ENVIRONS: From Meiringen a funicular takes visitors to the top of the **Reichenbach-fälle**. From here there is a stupendous view of the cascading waters. Equally impressive is the **Aareschlucht**, a deep gorge cut by the Aare between Meiringen and Innertkirchen. Viewing platforms allow visitors to penetrate into the depths of the cleft.

🏞 **Reichenbachfälle**
📞 *033 972 9010. Funicular every 15 mins: mid-May–mid-Oct: 8–11:45am & 1:15–5:45pm daily.*
🏞 **Aareschlucht**
📞 *033 971 40 48.* 🔲 *Apr–Oct: 9am–5pm; Jul–Aug: 8am–6pm, 9–11pm Wed & Fri, with artificial illumination.*

The Eiger, Mönch and Jungfrau, the highest peaks in the Jungfrau massif

Statue of Sherlock Holmes in Meiringen

Jungfraujoch ⓭

Road map D4. 🛈 *Interlaken; 033 826 53 00.* 🅦 *www.jungfrau.ch*

SOUTH OF INTERLAKEN lies the Bernese Oberland's most impressive mountain scenery, centred on a giant triple-peaked ridge: the Eiger (3,970 m/ 13,025 ft), the Mönch (4,099 m/ 13,448 ft) and the Jungfrau (4,158 m/13,642 ft). A network of rail and cable-car routes from Interlaken (*see p75*) makes it easy to travel around this area.

The best-known rail excursion, heavily promoted in Interlaken and around Switzerland, is to the Jungfraujoch. This icy saddle, which lies just below the summit of the Jungfrau, has been dubbed the "Top of Europe", and at 3,454 m (11,333ft) above sea level, the train station here is the highest in Europe.

As there are two different routes up to the Jungfraujoch, this excursion can easily be done as a circular journey. Trains head from Interlaken to Lauterbrunnen, where you change to the rack railway that climbs up through Wengen (*see p82*) and on further up to the dramatic station at Kleine Scheidegg, which nestles directly beneath the famous North Face of the Eiger. Different trains head from Interlaken to Grindelwald (*see p82*), where you again change to the rack railway, which from the other direction climbs up to Kleine Scheidegg. From Kleine Scheidegg, a separate line heads up to the Jungfraujoch itself.

The engineering on the lower sections of the rail route, around Wengen, is impressive enough but the topmost line, above Kleine Scheidegg, is extraordinary. It runs through steep tunnels blasted out of the heart of the Eiger. At the top, which can sometimes be quite crowded, there are cafeteria-style restaurants, a post office (where mail is stamped with a unique "Top of Europe" postmark), a set of ice sculptures, and other attractions. It is, however, far more rewarding to focus on the spectacular views, eastward out to the Black Forest, in Germany, westward to the Vosges, in France, and south into Italy.

There are also opportunities for walking, although they are limited. Some trails head out across the snows. You should, however, be aware that at this altitude the air is thin, and you may feel dizzy walking up steps or exerting yourself in any way. If this happens, the best cure is to rest, then head down again.

The Eiger, a major landmark in the Bernese Alps

Freilichtmuseum Ballenberg ⑪

F ROM SIMPLE ALPINE CHALETS to entire farmsteads, about 100 historic rural buildings fill this huge open-air museum. The buildings, some of wood, others of stone or brick, come from several regions of Switzerland. Carefully dismantled, they were transported and reconstructed here, most being saved from demolition. In this 66-hectare (160-acre) wooded park, the buildings are grouped according to their area of origin, and each group is linked by paths. The museum grounds also have gardens and fields with crops and farm animals. All the buildings are authentically furnished.

★ Richterswil House
Built in 1780 at Richterswil, near Zürich, this two-family house is an example of the half-timbered buildings typical of northeastern Switzerland, particularly the Zürich area. The house was once inhabited by a vineyard-owner.

Villnachern Family House
Built of limestone in the mid-17th century, this was probably the home of a wealthy family.

House from La Chaux-de-Fonds, Neuchâtel (18th century).

House from Burgdorf, Bern (1872)

Winery from Schaffhausen (17th century)

Pigsty from Brugg, Aargau (19th century).

Barn from Faulensee, Bern (1702)

Three attached from Cugnasco (1843–5?)

Fire-station from Mühledorf, Bern (1834)

Farmhouse with dovecote from Lancy, Geneva (1762)

Tentlingen House (1790)

House from Malvagli Ticino (1515–64)

Therwil House
Built in stone, with a wooden outbuilding, this house is typical of the architecture of the Jura. It dates from 1675.

★ Ostermundigen House
This large house was built in 1797. Although it is made of wood, the façade was painted grey to resemble stone. In the work areas of the house, the rooms are set up as exhibition galleries.

WORKSHOPS

Some of the houses at the museum have workshops where craftsmen using authentic tools and original machinery demonstrate some of the crafts and trades of Switzerland's regions. Among these crafts are weaving, spinning, pottery, wickerwork, lace-making and cheese-making. The museum also stages fairs and festivals in which folk traditions are revived

VISITORS' CHECKLIST

Road map D4. 🚃 🚌 Brienzwiler.
Freilichtmuseum Ballenberg,
3 km (2 miles) east of Brienz.
📞 033 952 10 30. 🌐 www.
ballenberg.ch. **Interiors** ◯
mid-Apr–Oct: 10am–5pm daily.
Ticket office & park ◯ mid-
Apr–Oct: 9am–6pm daily. 🎫

0 m   200
0 yards   200

Törbel Mill House

This mill house from Valais was built in the 19th century. Since the late Middle Ages, the power of mountain streams has been used to grind grain.

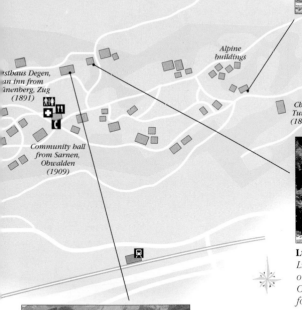

Alpine buildings

stbaus Degen, an inn from inenberg, Zug (1891)

Chapel from Turtig, Valais (18th century)

Community hall from Sarnen, Obwalden (1909)

Lütschental Cheese Store
Like other houses and outbuildings of the Bernese Oberland, this storehouse for cheese has a ridge roof with protruding eaves and gable ends.

Brülisau House
This wooden house, typical of the architecture of eastern Switzerland, was built in 1754.

STAR SIGHTS

★ **Ostermundigen House**

★ **Richterswil House**

The parish church in Kandersteg

Kandersteg ⑭

Road map C4. 🏔 *800.* 🚉
ℹ️ *Hauptstrasse; 033 675 80 80.*
🖳 www.kandersteg.ch

THE QUIET village of
Kandersteg stretches out
along the valley of the River
Kander, west of the Jungfrau
massif. Kandersteg is located
at the north entrance to the
Lötschberg Tunnel, through
which trains run for 15 km
(9 miles) under the Lötschberg
to emerge at Goppenstein, in
eastern Valais.

Apart from its attractive
16th-century parish church,
Kandersteg's main interest to
visitors is as a resort. In winter,
the gentle slopes around the
village make ideal skiing pistes
for beginners. In summer the
village is a popular base for
hiking and mountaineering or
simply for exploring the
stunningly beautiful lakes and
mountains in the vicinity.

The **Oeschinensee**, a small
lake surrounded by towering
cliffs, lies above Kandersteg
and can be reached by taking
a chairlift from the eastern
edge of the village. Fit hikers
can enjoy a walk back down
to Kandersteg. The **Blausee**,
a small boating lake
surrounded by a pine forest,
is a ten-minute drive north
of Kandersteg.

The Blümlisalphorn (3,664 m/
12,025 ft) and Hockenhorn
(3,297 m/10,820 ft), two peaks
within reach of Kandersteg,
offer mountaineers a more
demanding challenge.

Adelboden ⑮

Road map C4. 🚉 🏔 *3,650.*
ℹ️ *Dorfstrasse 23; 033 673
80 80.* 🖳 www.adelboden.ch

LOCATED AT THE head of
Engstligental, a wide
valley, Adelboden is an
attractive village with chalets,
pleasant streets and well-kept
gardens. The small parish
church here was built in 1433
and is of interest for its
frescoes and stained-glass
windows by Augusto
Giacometti. The village also
has an interesting museum
documenting local history
and daily life in the
Engstligental.

Adelboden is, however,
primarily a resort. With more
than 50 ski lifts and some
170 km (105 miles) of pistes,
it is one of the most popular
ski centres in Switzerland.
Adelboden also
offers facilities for
extreme sports
and ice-rinks for
skating and curling.
In summer it is a
base for mountain
biking and hiking.
The **Engstligen-
fälle**, spectacular
waterfalls tumbling
from Engstligenalp,
4 km (3 miles)
above Adelboden,
are accessible by
cable car. There are
several hiking trails, which
lead up to higher altitudes,
including Ammertenspitz
(2,613 m/ 8,573 ft) and also
down past the falls, that can
be started from here.

**Epitaph in Adelboden's
parish church**

Grindelwald ⑯

Road map D4. ℹ️ *Sportzentrum;
033 854 12 12.*
🖳 www.grindelwald.ch

THE ROAD AND railway line
into the mountains diverge
just south of Interlaken. One
branch continues into the
Lauterbrunnen valley, with
the villages of Lauterbrunnen,
Wengen and Mürren, and the
other heads east along the
Lütschen valley to Grindelwald.

Nestled beneath the giant
Wetterhorn, Mettenberg and
Eiger, this lively resort village
has long been one of the
most popular destinations in
the Alps. In winter it offers
good skiing, and in summer
excellent hiking. A one-hour
walk east of the village leads
to the trailhead for a scenic
stroll through woodland to
the awe-inspiring Oberer
Gletscher, a glacier
inching its way
down the
Wetterhorn.
Some of the
region's best hiking
trails lie in the area
around **First**, which
is served by its own
gondola. A classic
half-day route from
First gives a superb
ridge-top walk along
to the glittering
Bachalpsee tarn and
on to the summit
of the **Faulhorn** (2,681 m/
8,795 ft), where refreshment
can be found at a restaurant
and an inn. From here the
views of the sunrise and
sunset are breathtaking.

Snow-covered chalets at the resort of Wengen

Schloss Wimis, the 16th-century castle in the Nieder Simmental

Wengen ⑰

Road map C4. 👤 *1,050.*
ℹ️ *033 855 14 14.*
🆆 *www.wengen-murren.ch*

THE ROAD AND rail line from Interlaken terminate in Lauterbrunnen, an idyllic village on the floor of the stunning Lauterbrunnen valley, the world's deepest U-shaped valley. This is classic Swiss Alpine scenery, with the sheer cliffs, waterfalls, green meadows where cows graze, and snowy peaks.

Mountain trains climb from Lauterbrunnen towards the Jungfraujoch *(see p79)*, stopping midway at Wengen, a village of chalets and large hotels tucked on a shelf of southwest-facing pasture. Like its neighbours Grindelwald and Mürren, Wengen (which is impossible to reach by car) has been a magnet for summer and winter visitors for a century or more.

The skiing and snowboarding here are outstanding, and in summer the countryside around Wengen offers superb hiking. Trails lead down to the flowery meadows around Wengwald, and up to Männlichen (which can also be reached by cable car). From here visitors can enjoy spectacular views down over Grindelwald on one side and the Lauterbrunnen valley on the other.

Murren ⑱

Road map C4. 👤 *320* ℹ️ *033 855 14 14.* 🆆 *www.wengen-murren.ch*

FROM Lauterbrunnen there are two ways of reaching the small car-free village of Mürren, on the opposite side of the valley from Wengen. Both routes are spectacular. A funicular rises to Grütschalp, from where a train takes a scenic route along the cliff-edge to reach Mürren. Alternatively, buses head along the valley-floor road from Lauterbrunnen (past a magnificent set of waterfalls at Trümmelbach) to Stechelberg, from where a cable car climbs to Mürren, perched 800m (2,625 ft) above the valley floor. The views, down the valley and up to a dazzling panorama of snowy crags, are astounding. The cable car heads further up, to the ice-bound summit of the Schilthorn (2,970 m/9,747 ft), where there is a famous revolving restaurant.

The Simmental ⑲

Road map C4. 🚃 🚌
ℹ️ *Zweisimmen, Thunstrasse 8; 033 722 11 33.* 🆆 *www.simmental.ch*

THE SIMMENTAL, the long valley of the River Simme, is divided into two sections. Nieder Simmental, the lower section, runs from Spiez, where the Simme enters the Thunersee, westwards to Boltigen. Here the valley veers southwards, becoming Obere Simmental, the upper section. This part stretches up to the resort and spa town of **Lenk**, near the source of the Simme.

Several villages lie along the Simmental. **Erlenbach** is the starting point for white-water rafting down the Simme. **Zweisimmen**, at the confluence of the Kleine Simme and Grosse Simme, is the trailhead of roads that run along the valley floor up towards Lenk and Gstaad. From Lenk ski lifts take hikers and skiers up to Metschberg, Betelberg and Mülkerblatten.

The Saane River near Gstaad, excellent for white-water rafting

Gstaad ⑳

Road map C4. 👤 *2,500.* 🚃 🚌
ℹ️ *Promenade; 033 748 81 81.*
🎭 *Swiss Open Tennis Tournament (Jul), Menuhin Festival (Jul–Sep), Country Night Gstaad (Sep).* 🆆 *www.gstaad.ch*

FOR ONE OF Switzerland's smartest resorts, Gstaad is a surprisingly small village, its size out of proportion to its international fame and prestige. Lying at the junction of four valleys, Gstaad has about 250 pistes and numerous ski lifts on the slopes of Wispile, Eggli and Wasserngrat.

In summer Gstaad attracts numerous visitors who come here to enjoy rock climbing, hiking, cycling, tennis and extreme sports, such as rafting on the turbulent waters of the Saane.

By avoiding high-rise developments and remaining faithful to traditional Swiss-style architecture, Gstaad has maintained its romantic character. Its main street, the Promenade, is lined with shops, cafés, restaurants and art galleries. Craftsmen can be seen at work on woodcarvings and decorative paper cut-outs.

Luxuriously furnished interior of a chalet in Gstaad

Martigny ㉑

Road map B5. 🏔 *13,000.* 🚉 🚌
ℹ️ *Place Centrale; 027 721 22 20.*
🆆 www.martignytourism.ch

LOCATED AT THE confluence of the Drance and the Rhône, at the point where the latter curves northward, Martigny (Octodorus) was established by the Romans in about 15 BC. Excavations have revealed a complex of Roman buildings, including a temple dedicated to Minerva, baths and an amphitheatre.

The town is dominated by the **Tour de la Bâtiaz**, a 13th-century fortress set on a promontory. Other buildings of interest in Martigny's old district are the 16th-century **Maison Supersaxo** and the **Chapelle Notre-Dame-de-Compassion**, built in the 1620s.

Martigny's main attraction is the **Fondation Pierre Gianadda**, a museum built on the ruins of a Gallo-Roman temple. It consists of several collections. While the main gallery stages important temporary exhibitions, the Musée Archéologique Gallo-Romain contains statues, coins, pottery and bronzes uncovered during excavations. The Musée de l'Auto, in the basement, has about 50 vintage cars, including Swiss-made models. A small number of paintings, by Van Gogh, Cézanne, Toulouse-Lautrec and other important artists, are shown in the more intimate Salle Franck. Modern sculpture fills the Parc des Sculptures, an open area around the museum.

Roman head of a bull in Martigny

🏛 **Fondation Pierre Gianadda**
59 Rue du Forum. 📞 *027 722 39 78.*
⏰ *Jun–Oct: 9am–7pm daily; Nov–May: 10am–6pm daily.*

ENVIRONS: The small town of **St-Maurice**, 15 km (9 miles) north of Martigny, has an Augustinian abbey founded in 515. The church is part of the oldest surviving abbey north of the Alps. Northwest of

The mountain refuge at the Col du Grand-St-Bernard

Martigny lies the extensive Franco-Swiss skiing area known as the **Portes du Soleil**, which can be reached via the town of Monthey. The area comprises 12 resorts and has about 650 km (400 miles) of pistes.

St Bernard Pass ㉒

Road Map B5. 🚌 ℹ️ *Bourg St-Pierre; 027 787 12 06.*
🆆 www.st-bernard.ch

SITUATED ON the border with Italy at an altitude of 2,469m (8,103 ft), the St Bernard Pass, or Col du Grand-St-Bernard, is the oldest of all Alpine pass routes. An isolated nexus between western Europe and Italy, it has been used since at least 800 BC. Julius Caesar came over the pass in the 1st century BC, followed by

Charlemagne in 800, on the return from his coronation in Milan, and Napoleon in 1800.

The pass is named after Bernard of Menthon, Bishop of Aosta, who built a hospice for travellers here in 1049. In recognition of his missionary work, St Bernard was beatified after his death, in the 1080s, and was later made patron saint of the Alps.

The hospice on the pass has been inhabited by monks ever since and is still open to travellers all year round. The present building, which dates from the 18th century, incorporates a 17th-century church, in which a casket containing the remains of St Bernard is displayed. The treasury has a collection of liturgical vessels. There is also a **museum** with exhibits documenting the history of the pass since pre-Roman times and **kennels** where a small number of St Bernard dogs are kept.

ST BERNARD DOGS

Named after the hospice at the St Bernard Pass where they were kept by monks, these sturdy dogs, with a body weight of up to 100 kg (220 lb), are synonymous with mountain rescue. Athough the monks probably began to breed them in the Middle Ages, training them to sniff out travellers lost in snow or swallowed by avalanches, the earliest mention of St Bernards dates from the late 17th to early 18th centuries. Although the monks at the hospice still keep them, mountain rescue work is now done mostly with helicopters.

St Bernard with a handler

Because of its elevation and heavy snowfalls in winter, the pass itself can be used only between mid-June and October. However, since 1964, the St Bernard Tunnel, running 6km (4 miles) under the pass, has provided a year-round route between Switzerland and Italy.

Verbier ㉓

Road map C5. 🏔 2,000. 🚌
ℹ Place Centrale; 027 775 38 88.
Ⓦ www.verbier.ch 🎿 Xtreme Verbier (Mar); Verbier Festival & Academy (late Jul).

FEW SWISS RESORTS match Verbier in terms of its beautiful location and the range of winter and summer activities that it offers, which attract 1 million visitors each year. At an altitude of 1,400 m (4,595 ft), the resort lies on a wide plateau that opens to the south onto views of Mont Blanc and Grand Combin. Just below Verbier lies a picturesque valley, the Val de Bagnes.

The slopes of the surrounding mountains, which include Pierre Avoi, Mont Fort and Mont-Gelé, are a paradise for skiers and snowboarders. Verbier has 100 chair lifts and over 300 km (185 miles) of pistes, including glacier runs that stay open throughout the summer.

Summer sports here include golf, tennis, angling, horse riding and mountain biking. The town is also a good starting point for hikes along the Val de Bagnes, at the head of which is a dam, the Barrage de Mauvoisin, and for climbing the mountains in the vicinity, including Pierre Avoi (2,472 m/8,113 ft), which offers a breathtaking view of Mont Blanc.

Verbier also hosts Xtreme Verbier, in which the world's best and most fearless snowboarders descend the slopes of the Bec des Rosses at breakneck speed. In summer the town hosts the serene Verbier Festival and Academy, an international festival of classical music and poetry.

The Romanesque church at St Pierre-de-Clages

St Pierre-de-Clages ㉔

Road map B5. 🏔 600. 🚌 🚉
🎭 Fête du Livre (late August).

THE TINY VILLAGE of St Pierre-de-Clages is set on the southern, vineyard-covered slopes of the Rhône valley. Apart from an annual literary festival, the village's main attraction is its beautiful Romanesque church. Dating from the late 11th to the early 12th century, it originally formed part of a Benedictine priory. The rib-vaulted interior is almost entirely devoid of decoration, and this pleasing austerity is accentuated by the bare stonework of the walls and columns. The stained glass dates from 1948.

Sion ㉕

See pp86–7.

Barrage de la Grande Dixence ㉖

Road map C5. 🚌 late Jun–mid-Oct.

ONE OF THE largest dams in the world and the greatest feat of modern engineering in Switzerland, the Barrage de la Grande Dixence is a hydroelectric dam 284 m (932 ft) high across the River Dixence, at the head of the Val d'Hérémence.

The Lac des Dix, an elongated stretch of water filling the valley above the dam, is surrounded by mountains. Rising to the west is Rosablanche (3,336 m/10,949 ft); to the east Les Aiguilles Rouges (3,646 m/11,966 ft), and to the south Mont Blanc de Cheilon (3,870m/12,701ft) and Pigne d'Arolla (3,796m/12,458 ft). A cable car ferries visitors from the foot of the dam, where there is a restaurant, up to the level of the lake. From here you can take a boat to the Cabane des Dix, a mountain refuge, walk around the lake or go on a hike – for example, to the small resort of Arolla, which lies in the next valley.

Val d'Hérémence joins Val d'Hérens (see p88) at the level of Hérémence. This small town is a good base for skiing on the eastern slopes of Mont Rouge and for hiking in the mountains.

Interior of the Romanesque church at St Pierre-de-Clages

Sion ㉕

THE CAPITAL OF THE canton of Valais, Sion (Sitten in German) is a pleasant town with a rich heritage. It lies on a plain on the north bank of the Rhône, at the foot of two hills, each of which is crowned by a medieval castle. A Roman settlement named Sedunum was established here in the 1st century. The two castles that tower above the town are vestiges of its powerful bishopric, which ruled over Valais for centuries. In the Middle Ages Sion was also an important producer of wine and fruit, for which the fertile Rhône Valley is still renowned. Sion's excellent wines are also highly prized.

Sion, seen from Valère, one of two hills overlooking the town

Exploring Sion

Sion's old town, with quiet cobbled streets and fine houses, is easily explored on foot. Access to the castles is via Rue des Châteaux, which leads to a car park on an area of level ground between the two hills. From here steep paths lead left to Tourbillon and right to Valère. Both hills offer panoramic views of the town and of the vineyard-covered hillsides all around.

♣ Château de Tourbillon

(027 606 47 45. ◯ Mid-Mar–mid-Nov: 10am–6pm Tue–Sun. **Chapel** 11am, 3pm, 4pm.
Standing on the higher of the two hills, this great medieval fortress is surrounded by crenellated walls set with tall square towers. The castle was built in the late 13th century as the fortified residence of Bishop Boniface de Challant. It was besieged and rebuilt on several occasions and in 1788 it was destroyed by fire. Although the castle itself is now in ruins, much of the ramparts remain. The small chapel, with ribbed vaulting and carved capitals, contains medieval wall paintings.

♣ Château de Valère

Church (027 606 47 10.
◯ Jun–Sep: 10am–6pm Tue–Sat, 2–6pm Sun; Oct–May: 10am–5pm Tue–Sat, 2–5pm Sun.

🏛 Musée Cantonal d'Histoire

(027 606 47 15. ◯ Jun–Sep: 11am–6pm Tue–Sat; Oct–May: 11am–5pm Tue–Sat.
Built in the 12th to 13th centuries, with a square tower, curtain wall and rampart walk, the Château de Valère is in fact a fortified church, Notre-Dame-de-Valère. It stands on the site of an 11th-century fortress and a Roman building.

Romanesque capitals and Gothic frescoes grace the interior. Other notable features are the 17th-century stalls and a remarkable organ. Built in 1390, it is the oldest playable organ in the world.

Next to the church stands a 12th-century building that was originally the canon's residence. It now houses the Musée Cantonal d'Histoire, in which exhibitions on local history are shown. The grand hall has wall paintings and a finely carved fireplace.

🏛 Musée Cantonal des Beaux-Arts

19 Place de la Majorie. **(** 027 606 46 90. ◯ Jun–Sep: 1–6pm Tue–Sun; Oct–May: 1–5pm Tue–Sun.
This art gallery occupies two 15th-century houses that were once the residence of episcopal officers. Ranging from the 17th century to the present, the collection concentrates mainly on paintings by Valais artists, including some folk art.

🏛 Musée Cantonal d'Archéologie

12 Rue des Châteaux. **(** 027 606 47 00. ◯ Jun–Sep: 1–6pm Tue–Sun; Oct–May: 1–5pm Tue–Sun.
Offering a glimpse of the wealth of archaeological finds made in Valais, this small museum contains Neolithic pieces, including carved steles, and a large array of Roman artefacts. Greek and Etruscan pieces complete the displays.

Notre-Dame-de-Valère, the fortified church on a hill overlooking Sion

Rue du Grand-Pont, with the white-fronted Hôtel de Ville

⊞ Hôtel de Ville

12 Rue du Grand-Pont.
◯ 8am–noon & 2–6pm Mon–Fri.
With its clocktower crowned by a cupola and lantern, Sion's 17th-century town hall stands out among other fine buildings on Rue du Grand-Pont.

The town hall, which dates from 1657–65, has finely carved wooden doors at the entrance. Stones with Roman inscriptions are embedded in the walls of the hall within. Among them is a stone with a Christian inscription dating from 377, the earliest of its kind in Switzerland.

The council chamber on the upper floor of the town hall has rich furnishings and decorative woodwork.

⊞ Maison Supersaxo

Rue de Conthey. ◯ 8:30am–noon & 2–6pm Mon–Fri.
This ornate late Gothic mansion was built in about 1505 for Georges Supersaxo, the local governor. A wooden spiral staircase leads up to the grand hall, which has a wooden ceiling lavishly painted in the late Gothic style. The centrepiece of the ceiling is a painted medallion by Jacobinus de Malacridis depicting the Nativity. Busts of the Prophets and the Magi fill alcoves lining the walls.

Nativity medallion in Maison Supersaxo

⛪ Cathédrale Notre-Dame du Glarier

◯ 1–5pm Tue–Sun.
Although the main part of the cathedral dates from the 15th century, it contains earlier elements, including a 12th-century Romanesque belfry crowned by an octagonal steeple. Interesting features of the interior

include tombs of the bishops of Sion, early Baroque stalls and a wooden triptych depicting the Tree of Jesse.

The Église St-Théodule, the late Gothic church just to the south of the cathedral, dates from 1514–16. The 19th-century building opposite the cathedral is the Bishop's Palace.

⊞ Tour des Sorciers

Avenue de la Gare. ☎ 027 606 47 30. ◯ Jun–Sep: 1–6pm Tue–Sun; Oct–May: 1–5pm Tue–Sun. 🚫
The Witches' Tower, so named because of its conical roof, is the only remaining part of Sion's medieval fortifications. It once defended the town's northwestern aspect and is now used as a space for temporary exhibitions.

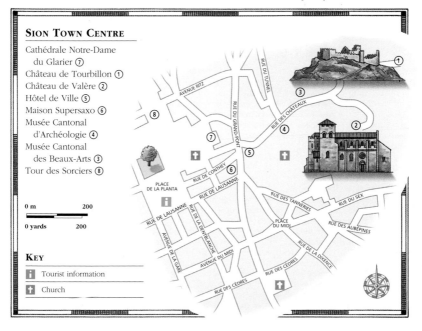

SION TOWN CENTRE

0 m   200

0 yards   200

KEY

| ℹ️ | Tourist information |
| 🕇 | Church |

The Pyramides d'Euseigne, striking rock formations in the Val d'Hérens

Val d'Hérens ㉗

Road map C5. 🚌 ℹ️ *Sion, 6 Rue du Pré-Fleuri; 027 327 35 70.*
🆆 *www.matterhornstate.ch*

STRETCHING SOUTHEAST from Sion, the Val d'Hérens (Eringertal in German) reaches into the Pennine Alps. This tranquil valley has enchanting scenery and villages with wooden chalets. Women wearing traditional dress can be seen working in the fields.

A striking geological feature of the Val d'Hérens is a group of rock formations known as the **Pyramides d'Euseigne**. These jagged outcrops of rock, which are visible from the valley road, jut out of the hillside like fangs. They were formed during the Ice Age by the erosive action of wind, rain and ice. Each point is capped by a rock, which protected the softer rock beneath from erosion, so producing these formations.

The village of Evolène, 15 km (9 miles) south of the village of Euseigne, is a good base for hiking. At the head of the valley is the hamlet of Les Haudères, where there is a Geology and Glacier Centre, with an interesting museum. Beyond Les Haudères the Val d'Hérens extends into the Val d'Arolla. The road ends at the small resort of Arolla.

Crans-Montana ㉘

Road map C4. 🏔️ *4,500.* 🚌
ℹ️ *027 485 08 00.* 🆆 *www. crans-montana.ch* 🏌️ *European Masters Golf Tournament (Sep).*

THE FASHIONABLE SKI resort of Crans-Montana lies on a plateau north of the Rhône valley, with a clear view of the Valais Alps to the south. In the late 19th century, as the fashion for mountain holidays grew, Crans and Montana expanded but they have remained two separate villages.

Crans-Montana can be reached by road from Sion. From Sierre it is accessible either by a road that winds up through vineyards and pasture, or by funicular. This well-equipped resort has a network of cable cars and ski lifts, and over 160 km (100 miles) of pistes that are suitable for beginners and intermediate skiers.

Window with flowers, a typical sight in Valais

Summer activities include golf, paragliding and hot-air ballooning. There is also year-round cross-country skiing on the Plaine Morte Glacier above Crans-Montana. A plateau lying at an altitude of 2,267 m (7,437 ft), Plaine Morte offers stunning views of the Valais Alps, with Mont Blanc to the southwest. From here mountain trails lead to Bella Lui and Bisse du Roh.

Sierre ㉙

Road map C4. 🏔️ *11,000.* 🚊 🚌
ℹ️ *Place de la Gare; 027 455 85 35.*
🆆 *www.sierre.ch*

LOCATED IN THE Rhône valley, Sierre (Siders in German) lies on the border between French- and German-speaking Valais. Enjoying an exceptionally sunny climate, it is surrounded by vineyards, and contains several historic buildings, including a 16th-century castle, the **Château des Vidomnes**. The Baroque town hall contains a small museum of pewter objects.

The local winemaking tradition is documented by the **Musée Valaisan de la Vigne et du Vin**, a wine museum whose collections are displayed in two places. One part occupies a wing of the 16th-century Château de Villa in Sierre, and the other the 16th-century Zumofenhaus in Salgesch (Salquenen in French), a village east of Sierre. The two locations are linked by a Sentier Viticole, or wine route, running for 6 km (4 miles) through villages and their vineyards, with wine-tasting stops along the way.

🏛️ **Musée Valaisan de la Vigne et du Vin**
Château de Villa, 4 Rue Ste-Catherine.
📞 *027 456 35 25.* ⏰ *Mar: 2–5pm Fri–Sun; Apr–Oct: 2–5pm Tue–Fri; Nov–Dec: 2–5pm Fri–Sun.* 🅿️

The 16th-century Château des Vidomnes in Sierre

Characteristic wooden houses in Grimentz, Val d'Anniviers

Val d'Anniviers ③⓪

Road map C4. 🚌 🛈 *0848 84 80 27.* Ⓦ www.sierre-anniviers.ch

Surrounded by the high peaks of the Pennine Alps and washed by the River La Navisence, the verdant Val d'Anniviers begins opposite Sierre and runs southwards up to Zinal. The valley is dotted with villages, which offer visitors winter skiing and summer hiking and cycling.

From Soussillon you can make a trip to the picturesque village of **Chandolin**, which has wooden chalets and spectacular views. From Vissoie it is worth going to **Saint-Luc**, a village situated high up in the mountains, with a breathtaking view of the Val d'Anniviers. From Saint-Luc you can proceed further up, to the top of Bella Tola (3,025m/9,928 ft).

Grimentz is a fascinating village, full of traditional tall wooden chalets built on the underlying bedrock. From here hiking trails lead up to the Moiry dam, and the **Glacier de Moiry**. The highest-lying village in the valley is **Zinal**. This resort, with several villages, is a ski centre in winter and a good base for hiking in summer. From Zinal it is possible to hire a guide for the climb to the summit of the Zinal-Rothorn (4,221m/13,853 ft), the Pyramide des Besso, Oberes Gabelhorn and Pointe de Zinal. There are many easier peaks for less ambitious climbers, and several highly scenic rambling routes.

Leukerbad ③①

Road map C4. 🏔 *1,600.* 🚌 🛈 *Rathausstrasse 8; 027 472 71 71.* Ⓦ www.leukerbad.ch

Lying at the head of the Dala valley, at an altitude of 1,400 m (4,595 ft), Leukerbad (Loèche-les-Bains in French) is one of the highest and largest spa resorts in Europe. The therapeutic properties of its hot springs, which are rich in calcium, sulphur and gypsum, have been appreciated since Roman times.

Leukerbad has several public spa complexes, with indoor and outdoor pools and many other facilities, including various treatments and rehabilitation programmes.

Leukerbad also has skiing pistes. Above the resort, and accessible by cable car, lies the Gemmi Pass, on the hiking trail to Kandersteg (*see p82*) and the Bernese Oberland.

Zermatt ③②

Road map C5. 🏔 *4,200.* 🚌 🛈 *Bahnhofplatz 5; 027 966 81 00.* Ⓦ www.zermatt.ch

Nestling at the foot of the Matterhorn (*see p90*) and surrounded by mountains over 4,000 m (13,000 ft), Zermatt is one of Switzerland's largest and best-known resorts. As it is closed to motorized traffic, Zermatt must be reached by train from Brig, Visp or Täsch.

Switzerland's ski capital in winter, Zermatt is a centre of hiking and mountaineering in summer. Skiing on glaciers in the vicinity is also possible all through the summer.

The **Alpines Museum** in Zermatt documents the history of mountaineering in the region, with a display devoted to Edward Whymper, who led the first ascent of the Matterhorn in 1865. The small Anglican church here was built in the 19th century for English climbers scaling the neighbouring peaks. The town square, surrounded by historic houses, features a fountain with a statue of a marmot.

From Zermatt a cable car runs to the summit of the Kleines Matterhorn (3,883m/12,744 ft), and a rack railway climbs to the Gornergrat (3,089m/10,138 ft) from where there are breathtaking views of the Matterhorn and the Gornergletscher.

Marmot on a fountain in Zermatt

Municipal baths in Leukerbad

The Matterhorn, for expert climbers only

Matterhorn ❸

Road map C6. ℹ️ *Zermatt, Bahnhofplatz; 027 966 81 00.* 🌐 www.zermatt.ch

ALTHOUGH THE Matterhorn is not the highest mountain in Switzerland, it is certainly the most awesome. It virtually straddles the Swiss-Italian border, and with its distinct pyramidal peak, which reaches 4,478m (14,692 ft), it has become one of Switzerland's national symbols. Shrouded in legend, it has claimed several lives and remains inaccessible to all but the most expert climbers. The best views of it are from the centre of Zermatt *(see p89).*

The Matterhorn (Cervino in Italian) was first conquered on 14 July 1865 by a team led by Edward Whymper. The expedition ended in tragedy when three of the English mountaineers and a Swiss guide were killed during the descent. Their tombs lie in Zermatt along with those of others who lost their lives on the mountain.

The Matterhorn is still a challenge for climbers. Each year several thousand expeditions reach the summit. The most difficult ascent route is on the east face, which was not conquered until 1932.

Monte Rosa ❸4

Road map C5.

RIGHT ON THE international border, Monte Rosa is divided into Swiss and Italian territory. Although it is not as famous as the Matterhorn, Monte Rosa has the highest peak in Switzerland and the second-highest in the Alps after Mont Blanc. This is the Dufourspitze, which culminates at 4,634m (15,209 ft).

Because of its shape, Monte Rosa does not present as much of a challenge to climbers as the Matterhorn. Situated on its Italian side, near the summit at 4,556m (14,953 ft), is the Capanna Regina Margherita, the highest mountain shelter in Europe, built in 1893. The Monte Rosa massif is encircled by the Gornergletscher, a vast glacier; stretching lower down are the slopes of Stockhorn and Gornergrat, with long pistes and many ski lifts.

Saas Fee ❸5

Road map D5. 👥 *1,700.* 🚌 📞 *027 958 18 58.* 🌐 www. saas-fee.ch 🎪 *Alpaufzug (Jun), Älplerfest (mid-Aug).*

A VILLAGE WITH a history going back to the 13th century, Saas Fee, in the Pennine Alps, has evolved into a resort since the early 19th century. It is the main town in the Saas Valley, through which flows the River Saaser Vispa. Saas Fee has a magnificent setting at the foot of the Dom (4,545 m/14,916 ft) and is surrounded by several other tall peaks.

The resort is closed to motorized traffic. It has many traditional wooden chalets, which are built on high stone foundation walls. Although Saas Fee's commercial orientation has tended to obliterate its traditional rural culture, several local traditions are enacted for the benefit of visitors. These include processions marking Corpus Christi, cow fights and yodelling contests, folk festivals celebrating Swiss National Day, and the Alpaufzug festival in late spring, which marks the time when cows are taken up to their summer pastures. The Saaser Museum, which is devoted to regional folk traditions and culture, includes the reconstruction of a typical local house, and a large collection of crafts and costumes.

Saas Fee also has many modern hotels and guest houses, ski lifts, a piste, cross-country ski trails, a large indoor skating rink, and a promenade full of shops, restaurants and bars. Summer skiing is also possible on the Feegletscher (Fairy Glacier) in the Mischabel massif.

In summer visitors have a choice of countless trails, from easy to demanding, leading to the surrounding peaks or to other sites, such as the Mattmarksee, an artificial lake. A cable car also runs up to Felskinn. From here the Alpine Metro runs to Mittelallalin, where there is a revolving restaurant.

Monument to a guide in Saas Fee

Brig ❸6

Road map D4. 👥 *10,000.* 🚉 ℹ️ *Bahnhofplatz 1; 027 921 60 30.* 🌐 www.brig.ch

BRIG IS A major town in the Upper Valais. It lies at the crossroads of the main Alpine routes leading over the Simplon, Furka, Grimsel and Nufenen passes and through the Lötschberg Tunnel. Located on the Rhône, the town takes its name from the bridges that span the river at this spot, where a Roman settlement once stood. During the 17th century, the trade

The towers of the Stockalper Palace in Brig

route to Italy, leading over the Simplon Pass, was controlled by the Stockalper family of merchants. Kaspar Jodok Stockalper von Thurm gave Brig its finest monument, a Renaissance-Baroque palace built in 1658–78. The building is set with three tall square towers crowned by cupolas known as Caspar, Melchior and Balthasar. The palace has an attractive arcaded courtyard and a chapel dedicated to the Three Kings, with an exquisite silver altarpiece made by Samuel Hornung of Augsburg. The palace houses various offices and a history museum.

Brig also has other historic buildings, town houses and churches, including the pilgrimage church in Glis, built in 1642–59.

Simplon Pass ㊲

Road map D5. ℹ 027 979 12 21. 🌐 www.simplon.ch

L YING AT AN altitude of 2,005m (6,580 ft), the Simplon Pass is one of the most important routes between Switzerland and Italy, and between western and southern Europe. It also marks the border between the Pennine and Lepontine Alps. The route, once used by the Romans, has played an important role in trade since the Middle Ages.

The strategic importance of the pass was recognized by Napoleon, on whose orders a new road was built here in 1800–08. It is about 64 km (40 miles) long and runs from Brig, over the pass and through the village of Simplon, to the Italian town of Domodossola.

Aletsch Glacier ㊳

Road map D4 ℹ *Riederalp; 027 928 60 50.* 🌐 www.riederalp.ch

T HE LONGEST GLACIER in the Alps, the Aletsch Glacier (or Grosser Aletschgletscher) stretches for about 25 km (15 miles) from the Jungfrau *(see p79)* to a plateau above the Rhône valley. At its widest point the glacier is 2 km (1 mile) across.

Together with the Jungfrau and Bietschhorn mountain ranges, the Aletsch Glacier has been declared a UNESCO Natural Heritage Site.

The best starting point for a hike to the Aletsch Glacier is the small mountain resort of **Riederalp**, just above the Rhône valley. It is closed to motor traffic but can be reached by cable car from Mörel.

The tourist information centre in Riederalp contains a small alpine museum with a traditional cheese dairy. Within walking distance is the secluded Villa Cassel at **Riederfurka**. The Pro Natura Zentrum Aletsch here is a scientific centre that provides information on alpine glaciers and the environmental protection of this region.

Hikers beside the Aletsch Glacier

GENEVA

WITH ITS BEAUTIFUL LAKESIDE *setting, Geneva is a serene whose modest size belies its wealth and its importance on th... world stage. French-speaking yet Calvinistic, it is a dynamic centre of business with an outward-looking, cosmopolitan character tempered by a certain reserve. It is also the European headquarters of the United Nations and the birthplace of the International Red Cross.*

A city with a population of just 180,000, Geneva is the capital of the canton of the same name. Sharing 95 per cent of its border with France, the canton is joined to the rest of Switzerland only by a narrow strip of land on its north side.

Loosely bound to the Holy Roman Empire from the 9th century, Geneva was later controlled by Savoy, from which it won independence in 1536. In 1602, when the Savoyards attempted to retake the city, they were repulsed. This event is commemorated to this day by a festival known as L'Escalade (Scaling the Walls).

By the 16th century, the city of Geneva was established as a prosperous centre of trade. When Jean Calvin began to preach here, Geneva also became a stronghold of the Reformation. Known as the Protestant Rome, it attracted Protestant refugees from all over Europe, who further increased the city's wealth and boosted its cosmopolitan character. Briefly an independent republic, Geneva was annexed by France from 1798 to 1813. In 1815, the city and its canton joined the Swiss Confederation.

The seat of over 200 international organizations, Geneva is today the capital of international diplomacy. It is also the home of the European Laboratory for Particle Physics (CERN), one of the world's most advanced scientific laboratories.

International flags on the approach to the Palais des Nations, in Geneva's International Area

...solée du Duc de Brunswick, in the style of Scaglieri's tomb in Verona, on Geneva's South Bank

...oring Geneva

AT THE WESTERN extremity of Lake Geneva
...at the point where the Rhône flows away
...wards France, Geneva is divided by water.
On the South Bank (Rive Gauche) is the
16th-century Old Town (Vieille Ville), once
surrounded by walls. Plainpalais, southwest
of the Old Town, is the university district,
while further south is Carouge, a
picturesque suburb with a population
of artists. The North Bank (Rive
Droite), dominated by grand quayside hotels, is Geneva's main
commercial area. Further north
lies the Cité Internationale,
base of international
organizations. Both river-
banks have pleasant
green areas. From
La Rade, the harbour,
rises the Jet d'Eau,
Geneva's famous fountain.

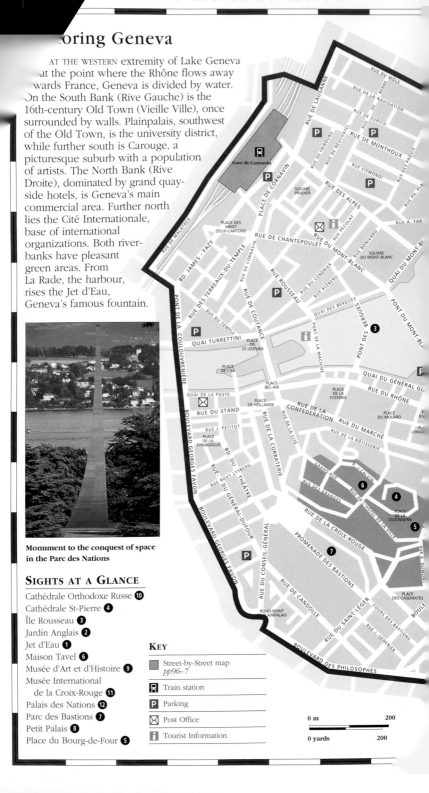

**Monument to the conquest of space
in the Parc des Nations**

SIGHTS AT A GLANCE

KEY

Street-by-Street map
pp96–7

Train station

Parking

Post Office

Tourist Information

0 m   200

0 yards   200

SEE ALSO

- *Where to Stay* pp249–50.
- *Where to Eat* pp273–4.

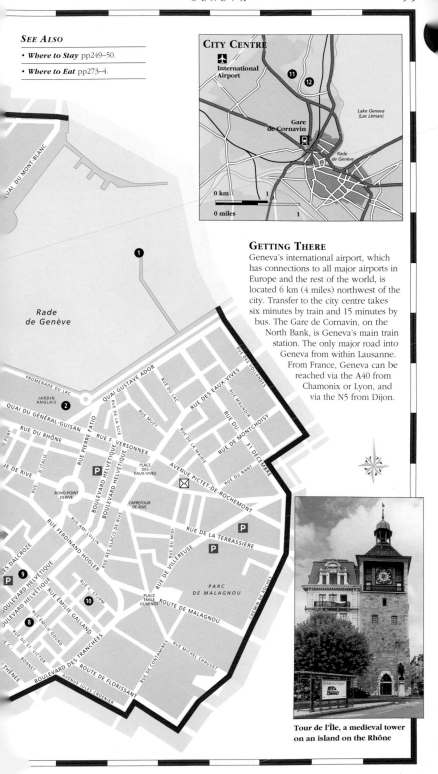

CITY CENTRE

✈ **International Airport**

⑪ ⑫

Lake Geneva (Lac Léman)

Gare de Cornavin

Rade de Genève

0 km ⸻ 1

0 miles ⸻ 1

GETTING THERE

Geneva's international airport, which has connections to all major airports in Europe and the rest of the world, is located 6 km (4 miles) northwest of the city. Transfer to the city centre takes six minutes by train and 15 minutes by bus. The Gare de Cornavin, on the North Bank, is Geneva's main train station. The only major road into Geneva from within Lausanne. From France, Geneva can be reached via the A40 from Chamonix or Lyon, and via the N5 from Dijon.

QUAI DU MONT-BLANC

Rade de Genève

PROMENADE DU LAC

JARDIN ANGLAIS ②

QUAI DU GÉNÉRAL-GUISAN

QUAI GUSTAVE ADOR

RUE DU LAC

RUE DES EAUX-VIVES

RUE DES VOLLANDES

RUE MALNOA

S PORT

RUE DU RHÔNE

RUE MUZY

RUE DE LA SCIE

RUE DE LA MAIRIE

RUE DU 31 DÉCEMBRE

RUE DE MONTCHOISY

RUE D'ITALIE

JE DE RIVE

RUE PIERRE FATIO

RUE F. VERSONNEX

BOULEVARD HELVÉTIQUE

PLACE DES EAUX-VIVES

AVENUE PICTET-DE-ROCHEMONT

RUE DU NANT

ROND-POINT DERIVE

BOULEVARD HELVÉTIQUE

CARREFOUR DE RIVE

RUE AMI-LULIN

RUE FERDINAND HODLER

RUE DES GLACIS-DE-RIVE

RUE DE LA TERRASSIÈRE

ÈS DALCROZE

⑨

BOULEVARD HELVÉTIQUE

RUE C. STURM

RUE DE VILLEREUSE

RUE DU MIDI

⑩

PLACE EMILE GUVENOT

ROUTE DE MALAGNOU

PARC DE MALAGNOU

CHEMIN DE ROCHES

BOULEVARD HELVÉTIQUE

RUE ÉMILIE GALLAND

⑧

RUE ÉMILIE GOURD

RUE DU ST-VICTOR

RUE DES TRANCHÉES

RUE MICHEL CHAUVET

RUE DE CONTAMINES

THÉNÉE

BONNET

E C.

BOULEVARD DES TRANCHÉES ROUTE DE FLORISSANT

AVENUE JULES CROSNIER

Tour de l'Île, a medieval tower on an island on the Rhône

Street-by-Street: Old Town

SET ON ELEVATED GROUND on the south bank of the
Rhône, the Old Town (Vieille Ville) clusters around
the cathedral and Place du Bourg-de-Four. This
atmospheric district, whose main thoroughfare is the
pedestrianized Grand' Rue, has narrow cobbled streets
lined with historic limestone houses. While the southern limit of the Old Town is marked by the Promenade
des Bastions, laid out along the course of the old city
walls, its northern side slopes down to the quay,
which is lined with wide boulevards
and the attractive Jardin Anglais.

★ Cathédrale St-Pierre
*Geneva's cathedral, completed
in the 13th century, stands on
the site of several earlier
buildings, including a bishop's
palace, whose mosaic
floor survives* ④

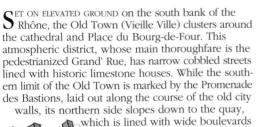

Maison Rousseau
*The birthplace of the 18th-
century writer and philosopher
Jean-Jacques Rousseau is at
40 Grand' Rue.*

Hôtel de Ville,
where the first
Geneva Convention
was signed, in 1864.

★ Maison Tavel
*The oldest house in Geneva,
this elegant residence was built
in 1334. It is now a museum
documenting daily life in
Geneva through the ages* ⑥

LOCATOR MAP

★ **Place du Bourg-de-Four**
This central square was used as a market place in the Middle Ages. It is still lined with old inns, as well as modern cafés and restaurants ❺

0 m 50
0 yards 50

KEY

--- Suggested route

STAR SIGHTS

★ **Cathédrale St-Pierre**

★ **Maison Tavel**

★ **Place du Bourg-de-Four**

Jet d'Eau, emblem of Geneva and Europe's tallest fountain

Jet d'Eau ❶

Off Quai Gustave-Ador.

STANDING IN isolation on a jetty on the south bank of Lake Geneva, the Jet d'Eau is a powerful fountain that sends a plume of water shooting 140 m (460 ft) into the air, at a rate of 500 litres (113 gallons) per second and a speed of 200 km per hour (125 mph). It came into existence almost by accident.

In the late 19th century a purely functional fountain was set up to relieve excess water pressure while a reservoir system was being installed. Such was the fountain's popularity that the authorities decided to construct a permanent fountain, which became more spectacular as increasingly powerful pumps were installed. Visible from afar and floodlit after dark, the Jet d'Eau is the pride of Geneva and has been adopted as the city's emblem.

Floral clock at the entrance to the Jardin Anglais

Jardin Anglais ❷

Quai du Général-Guisan.

LAID OUT ON the lakeside at the foot of the Old Town, the Jardin Anglais (English Garden) offers a view of the harbour, and of the buildings along the quay on the north bank. The entrance to the garden is marked by a large floral clock, the **Horloge Fleurie**. Created in 1955 as a tribute to Switzerland's clock-making tradition, it consists of eight intersecting wheels with 6,500 flowering plants. The **Monument National** nearby commemorates Geneva's accession to the Swiss Confederation in 1814.

Protruding from the lake at a point just north of the Jardin Anglais are two stones brought down by glaciers during the Ice Age. They are known as the **Pierres du Niton** (Neptune's Stones), and the larger of the two was once used as the reference point from which altitude was measured in Switzerland.

Île Rousseau ❸

Pont des Bergues.

A WALKWAY jutting out at a right angle from the centre of the Pont des Bergues leads to a medieval bastion in the Rhône. Now known as the Île Rousseau, it is named after Jean-Jacques Rousseau (1712–78), the writer and philosopher of the Enlightenment who was one of Geneva's most distinguished citizens.

Statue of Jean-Jacques Rousseau

Rousseau, the son of a clockmaker, left Geneva at the age of 16. Although he praised the city in his writings, his views elicited the disapproval of the authorities and his books were burned. However, in 1834, 56 years after his death, a statue was installed on the bastion that now bears his name.

Cathédrale St-Pierre ❹

BUILT OVER A SPAN of some 70 years from 1160 to 1230, with later additions, Geneva's vast cathedral is in a mixture of styles. Basically Gothic, it incorporates earlier Romanesque elements and has an incongruous Neo-Classical portal, which was added in the 18th century. In 1536 it became a Protestant church, losing most of its lavish Catholic decoration. Only the stalls and the stained glass in the chancel escaped the purge. The result, however, is a plain interior of awesome austerity. The cathedral stands on the site of a Roman temple and a complex of later buildings, part of the remains of which can be seen at the archaeological site nearby.

Calvin's Chair
Calling for a radical reform of the Church, Jean Calvin preached many sermons in the cathedral, reputedly seated in this chair.

The Nave
The groin-vaulted nave combines Romanesque and early Gothic elements. The arches are surmounted by a triforium.

Chapelle des Macchabées
This side chapel in the flamboyant Gothic style was added in the early 15th century. With later frescoes and stained glass, it is a contrast to the austere nave.

STAR FEATURES

★ **Capitals**

★ **Stalls**

Main entrance

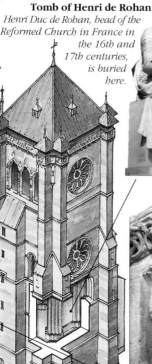

Stained glass of St Andrew
The stained-glass windows in the presbytery are copies of the original 15th-century windows. These are on display in Geneva's Musée d'Art et d'Histoire.

Tomb of Henri de Rohan
Henri Duc de Rohan, head of the Reformed Church in France in the 16th and 17th centuries, is buried here.

★ **Capitals**
Masterpieces of Romanesque and Gothic stonework, these capitals are among the few decorative features to have survived the Reformation.

★ **Stalls**
The stalls, with intricately carved back panels and canopy, originally stood near the choir.

Place du Bourg-de-Four, filled with café tables

Place du Bourg-de-Four **⑤**

PROBABLY OVERLYING Geneva's Roman forum, the Place du Bourg-de-Four was the city's market place in the Middle Ages. Today, graced by an 18th-century fountain and lined with 16th-century houses, art galleries and antique shops, and with busy cafés and restaurants, the square is still the hub of Geneva's Old Town.

The imposing **Palais de Justice** on the southeastern side of the square was built in 1707–12 and has been used as the city's law courts since 1860. Nearby, on Rue de l'Hôtel-de-Ville on the southwestern side of the square, stands the **Hôtel de Ville**, with a Renaissance façade. Built in the 15th century with additions in the 16th, 17th and 18th centuries, it was originally the city hall and now serves as the seat of the cantonal authorities. The ramp in the courtyard allowed cannons to be pulled up into the building and enabled dignitaries to ride their horses to the upper floors. The Tour Baudet, a tower dating from 1455 and the oldest part of the city hall, once housed the cantonal archives. On the ground floor of the Hôtel de Ville is the Alabama Room, where the Geneva Convention was signed in 1864 and where the International Red Cross was recognized as a humanitarian organization. It was also here that the League of Nations assembled for the first time, in 1920.

Opposite the Hôtel de Ville stands the **Ancien Arsenal**, a granary that became a weapons store in the 18th century.

Musée d'Art et d'Histoire ❾

THE HUGE COLLECTION of paintings, sculpture and artefacts on display at Geneva's museum of art and history covers a timespan ranging from prehistory to the mid-20th century. While the large archaeological section contains pieces from Mesopotamia, Egypt, Greece, Rome and other ancient cultures, the displays of applied arts feature pottery, furniture, stained glass and other fine objects, as well as reconstructions of period interiors. The painting and sculpture galleries contain works ranging from the Impressionist to the Surrealist periods and beyond. Swiss artists, including those of the Geneva school, are well represented.

★ **Miraculous Draught of Fishes**
This painting is part of the altarpiece that Konrad Witz made for the Cathédrale St-Pierre (see pp98–9) in 1444. In the background is a view of Geneva.

★ **Palace Drawing Room**
The drawing room of the Palais Cartigny in Geneva is reconstructed here. Dating from about 1805, it was designed and furnished in the Neo-Classical style.

Ground floor

Main entrance

★ **Greek Rhyton**
This beautiful drinking vessel, with a handle in the shape of a horseman, dates from the 4th century and comes from Asia Minor.

Greek Vase
Decorated by the Master of Bari, this beautiful vase from Taranto dates from c. 350 BC. It is a fine example of Greek red-figure vase-painting.

Lower ground fl[oor]

First floor

VISITORS' CHECKLIST

2 Rue Charles-Galland. 022
418 26 00. 10am–5pm
Tue–Sun. w mah.ville-ge.ch
@ mah@ville-ge.ch

Le Quai des Pâquis à Genève
The French painter Camille Corot was a regular visitor to Geneva. He completed this view of the lake in 1863.

Ferme à Monfoucault
Rural scenes such as this one, painted in 1874, were frequently chosen as subjects by the French Impressionist painter Camille Pissarro (1830–1903).

Mezzanine

GALLERY GUIDE
While the lower ground floor contains the museum's collection of antiquities, the ground floor is devoted to prehistory and the applied arts. On the mezzanine are the reconstructions of palatial rooms. The first floor contains the museum's galleries of painting and sculpture.

KEY
- Antiquities
- Applied arts
- Prehistory
- Reconstructed palace rooms
- Painting and sculpture gallery
- Temporary exhibitions

Costume for *Nightingale*
This elegant dress is one of the costumes that Henri Matisse (1869–1954) designed for a production of the ballet The Nightingale, *directed by Sergei Diaghilev and staged at the Paris Opéra in 1920.*

Hodler's Furniture
Side chairs, armchairs, a table and a bookcase comprise the set of oak furniture that Josef Hoffman, of the Vienna Workshops, designed for the 19th-century Swiss painter Ferdinand Hodler (see p54).

STAR EXHIBITS

★ **Greek Rhyton**

★ **Miraculous Draught of Fishes**

★ **Palace Drawing Room**

SHOPPING IN GENEVA

GENEVA HAS BEEN described as a shopper's paradise. Catering for a wealthy clientele, the city's smartest shops glitter with trays of diamond-studded watches and opulent jewellery, and attract attention with seductive displays of clothes by international designers. A leading centre of the art market, the city also has many art galleries and antique shops.

Box of Swiss praline chocolates

Away from the city's smartest streets, however, are shops that offer more affordable goods, from watches at more modest prices to high-quality craft items and a variety of handmade souvenirs. Swiss specialities such as chocolate, cheese and the locally produced wines are also available. Beyond the city centre are colourful street markets selling everything from books to collectables.

Colourful display of painted cow bells in a souvenir shop in Geneva

OPENING HOURS

MOST SHOPS in Geneva are open from 8am to 6.30pm Monday to Friday, and from 8am to 4pm or 5pm on Saturday. Late opening for shops in the city centre is until 8pm on Thursdays. The only shops open on Sunday are those selling souvenirs, and supermarkets and general stores at petrol stations, at the airport and the train station.

DEPARTMENT STORES

THE **Migros**, Coop, **Globus** and **Manor** supermarket chains and department stores all have large branches in Geneva. **Bon Génie** specializes in designer clothing and high-class cosmetics. One of the city's largest shopping centres is Balexert. Another new shopping centre is La Praille, near the stadium.

MARKETS

GENEVA'S largest outdoor markets are held at **Plaine de Plainpalais**, southwest of the Old Town. A fruit and vegetable market takes place here on Tuesday and Friday mornings, and there are interesting flea markets all day Wednesday and Saturday, where you may be able to discover some real finds, such as old watches, furniture ranging from antique to modern, ornaments and clothes from all over the world. Lively markets are also held on Wednesday and Saturday mornings in Place du Marché, near Carouge, and in Boulevard Helvétique, in the city centre. A crafts and local produce market is held every Thursday in **Place de la Fusterie**.

WATCHES AND JEWELLERY

WITH BRANCHES ON Place du Molard, Rue du Mont-Blanc and Rue de la Fontaine, the **Gübelin** chain of shops offers a choice of clocks and watches by leading Swiss makers, and a range of jewellery and pens. **Bucherer** and **Cartier**, both on Rue du Rhône, one of Geneva's smartest streets, are two other upmarket watch and jewellery shops.

SOUVENIRS

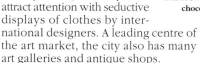

Swiss watch

GENEVA abounds in shops selling high-quality goods associated with Switzerland, from pen-knives and cuckoo clocks to fine linen, leather goods and a wealth of high-quality craft items, as well as a more affordable range of watches and jewellery. **Swiss Corner, Little Switzerland, Ours de Berne** are three of the best.

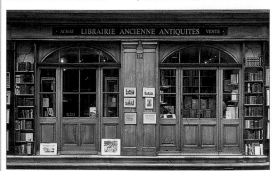

Bookstore and antique shop at 20 Grand' Rue, in the Old Town

Logo of Rolex, a leading Swiss watchmaker

ART AND ANTIQUES

THE GREATEST concentration of antique shops and art galleries in Geneva is along Grand' Rue, in the Old Town. While many galleries along this street are filled with expensive Old Master paintings, others specialize in more affordable types of art, such as modern paintings and graphics, and a variety of attractive prints.

The Carouge district, to the south of the Old Town, has many small specialist studios and craft shops where craftsmen can be seen at work.

BOOKS

A GOOD RANGE of books in English is stocked by **ELM English Books**, on Avenue Pictet-de-Rochemont. Another store that is worth a visit is **Bookworm**, on Rue Sismondi, which sells secondhand books on a wide range of subjects. Librairie du Voyageur, on Rue de Rive, specializes in travel books.

CONFECTIONERY

THE LOCAL chocolate manufacturer is Favarger. Its brand products may be bought in factory outlets, as well as in Mercury chain stores and the food halls of department stores. Several traditional manufacturers have their own factory outlets in various parts of the city. There are also many chocolate shops in Geneva's Old Town. Two of the best are the **Chocolaterie du Rhône** and the **Chocolaterie Stettler**, which sells such specialities as *pavés de Genève* (Genevese chocolate squares).

Chocolate rabbit

CHEESE AND WINE

A GREAT VARIETY of Swiss cheeses *(see pp264–5)* can be purchased in many specialist shops all over the city. Among them are **La Fromagerie,** on Rue de Cornavin, and **Philippe Muller,** on the Boulevard Helvétique.

The area around Geneva is a prime wine-growing region *(see pp266–7)*. Bottled wine of an excellent quality can be bought directly from winegrowers in several villages around the city. Many outlets allow customers to sample the wines before they buy.

Colourful flower stall in a street in Geneva

DIRECTORY			
DEPARTMENT STORES	**MARKETS**	**Cartier** 35 Rue du Rhône. ☎ 022 819 54 054.	**Bookworm** 5 Rue Sismondi. ☎ 022 731 87 65.
Migros Plainpalais-Centre 64 Rue de Carouge. ☎ 022 807 09 60.	Plaine de Plainpalais. *(fruit, vegetables, souvenirs)* Tue & Fri, 8am–1pm. Plaine de Plainpalais. *(flea market)* Wed & Sat 8am–5pm.	**SOUVENIRS** **Swiss Corner** Rue des Alpes. ☎ 022 731 06 84.	**CONFECTIONERY** **Chocolaterie du Rhône** 3 Rue de la Confédération. ☎ 022 311 56 14.
Globus Grand Passage 48 Rue du Rhône. ☎ 022 319 50 50.	Place de la Fusterie. *(handicrafts)* Thu 8am–7pm. Place de la Fusterie. *(books)* Fri 8am–6:45pm.	**Little Switzerland** 28 Rue du Cendrier. ☎ 022 731 23 69.	**Chocolaterie Stettler** 5 Rue du Mont-Blanc. ☎ 022 732 17 44.
Manor 6 Rue Cornavin. ☎ 022 909 46 98.	**WATCHES AND JEWELLERY**	**Ours de Berne** Place du Port. ☎ 022 310 12 57.	**CHEESE**
Bon Génie 34 Rue du Marché. ☎ 022 818 11 11.	**Gübelin** 1 Place du Molard. ☎ 022 310 86 55.	**BOOKS** **Elm English Books** 16 Avenue Pictet-de- Rochemont. ☎ 022 737 20 20.	**La Fromagerie** 1 Rue de Cornavin. ☎ 022 731 35 05.
	Bucherer 45 Rue du Rhône. ☎ 022 319 62 66.		**Philippe Muller** 29 Boulevard Helvétique. ☎ 022 735 21 40.

WESTERN SWITZERLAND

A PREDOMINANTLY FRENCH-SPEAKING REGION, *western Switzerland consists of three distinct geographical areas: the mountainous terrain of the Swiss Jura in the north, the western extremity of the Mittelland plateau in the east, and the Alpine region in the southeast. Western Switzerland's geographical hub is Lake Geneva (Lac Léman), on whose banks lie Geneva, Lausanne, Vevey and Montreux.*

Western Switzerland is a region of lakes and rolling hills, great cities and atmospheric medieval towns, and small villages with beautiful ancient churches. It consists of the cantons of Geneva, Vaud, Jura, Fribourg and Neuchâtel. While the area is bordered by France on its western side, the canton of Geneva is surrounded on three sides by French territory. Western Switzerland forms part of the region known as Suisse Romande, or Romandie, and it has a strong French-Swiss cultural identity.

While Geneva's high profile in global events and its role as a centre of world banking give it an international character, Lausanne, with its great cathedral and its university, is a centre of culture and intellectual life. Fribourg, straddling the River Sarine, is a bilingual town, French being spoken on the west side of the river and German on the east. The purest French in Suisse Romande is supposed to be spoken in Neuchâtel.

It was in western Switzerland, particularly in the Jura, that the country's world-famous watchmaking industry was born and where it continues to flourish today. The region is also renowned for its fine wines, most especially from the vineyards that border Lake Geneva. Western Switzerland also has one of the country's most memorable sights, the beautiful Château de Chillon, set serenely beside the sparkling blue waters of Lake Geneva.

The city of Fribourg, dominated by the Gothic tower of the 13th-century Cathédrale St-Nicolas

◁ medieval Château de Chillon, set on an islet on the eastern shore of Lake Geneva

Exploring Western Switzerland

A REGION WITH A DIVERSE landscape, western Switzerland has many atmospheric towns and internationally famous cities. The Jura mountains in the west have much to offer hikers and cross-country skiers, and the southeastern part of the region has many ski resorts. With Lake Geneva as its focal point, the centre of the region is a land of great lakes, with vineyards covering sunny hillsides. The cities of Geneva, Lausanne, Fribourg and Neuchâtel are bustling centres of industry and culture with a wealth of museums and historic buildings. By contrast, the sophisticated towns of Vevey and Montreux, situated on the shores of Lake Geneva, offer relaxation in an unequalled setting.

Escaliers du Marché, leading off Place de la Palud, in Lausanne

GETTING THERE

The main gateways to western Switzerland are Geneva's and Basel's international airports. From Geneva, the A1 motorway gives access to the whole region. Western Switzerland is also served by a rail network. Trains depart both from Geneva's airport and from the city itself. While the main rail route runs from Geneva north to Neuchâtel and Biel/Bienne, fast trains also run along the shores of Lake Geneva to Fribourg and beyond, both northwards to Bern, and southwards via Montreux to Valais. Most of the rail route is extremely scenic.

Rooftops in Murten/Morat, from the town walls

Pontarlier

Pontarlier

STE-CROIX
19

GRANDSON

YVERDON-LES-BAINS

VALLORBE
17

16

ROMAINMÔTIER

Lac
de Joux

A1 E23

5

LAUSANNE
1

MORGES

LAKE 2
GENEVA
(LAC LÉMAN)

Lons-le-Saunier

A1 E25 E62

1

NYON

St-Claude

Chamonix-
Mont-Blanc

GENEVA (GENÈVE)

Rhône

Lyon   Annecy

KEY

▬ Motorway

▬ Main road

▬ Scenic route

= Other roads

= River

☆ View point

0 km   20

0 miles   20

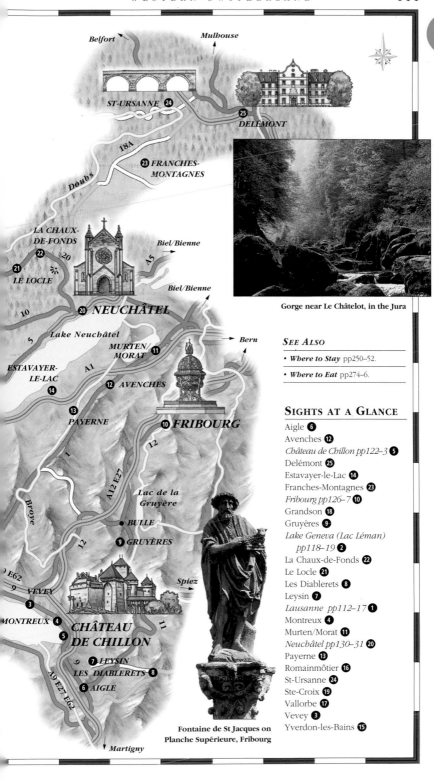

Belfort

Mulhouse

ST-URSANNE 24

25
DELÉMONT

18A

Doubs

23 FRANCHES-
MONTAGNES

LA CHAUX-
DE-FONDS
22   Biel/Bienne

20

45

21
LE LOCLE

Biel/Bienne

10

20 NEUCHÂTEL

Lake Neuchâtel

MURTEN/
MORAT 11   Bern

5

ESTAVAYER-
LE-LAC
14   A1

12 AVENCHES

13
PAYERNE

10 FRIBOURG

12

A12 E27

Lac de la
Gruyère

BULLE

Broye

12

9 GRUYÈRES

E62

9
VEVEY

3

MONTREUX 4

5   CHÂTEAU
DE CHILLON

Spiez

11

9 7 LEYSIN
LES DIABLERETS 8

6 AIGLE

Martigny

Gorge near Le Châtelot, in the Jura

Fontaine de St Jacques on
Planche Supérieure, Fribourg

See Also

- *Where to Stay* pp250–52.
- *Where to Eat* pp274–6.

Sights at a Glance

Lausanne

With an outstandingly beautiful setting on the north shore of Lake Geneva, Lausanne is one of Switzerland's finest cities. It was founded in the 4th century as a Roman lakeshore settlement but for greater safety its inhabitants later moved to higher ground on the hills above the lake. This area is now Lausanne's Old Town (Vieille Ville). It became a bishopric in the late 6th century, and its university was founded in 1540. Lausanne is a centre of the cultural and economic life of French-speaking Switzerland. It is also the seat of the Federal Supreme Court and the location of the International Olympic Committee's headquarters.

Detail of the 18th-century Église St-Laurent

Exploring Lausanne

A city of steep gradients, Lausanne is set on three hills that rise in tiers from the lakeshore. The hub of the city is Place St-François. To the north is the city's shopping district, centred on Rue du Bourg. Further north lies the Old Town (Vieille Ville), dominated by Lausanne's great cathedral *(see pp114–15)*. The district of Bel Air, to the west, overlooks a valley where the Flon stream once flowed. The Grand-Pont, a bridge across the valley, offers fine views of Bel-Air and of the Old Town, which rises behind it.

🏛 Bel-Air Métropole

1 Place Bel-Air. **[** *021 311 11 22.*
Set on a steep slope, at the foot of the Old Town, the Bel-Air Métropole was the first high-rise structure to be built in Switzerland. Standing 50 m (165 ft) high, the Bel-Air Métropole contains offices,

residential apartments and the Théâtre Métropole. Completed in 1931, the building gives Lausanne's townscape a touch of metropolitan verve, while the theatre has become one of its cultural hubs.

🔒 Église St-Laurent

Rue St-Laurent.
Less than a hundred paces from Bel-Air, amid the well-preserved houses of the Old Town, stands the Protestant Église St-Laurent. It was built in 1716–19, on the ruins of a 10th-century church. Its façade, designed by Rodolphe de Crousaz in the second half of the 18th century, is one of the few examples of Neo-Classical architecture in Lausanne.

🏛 Place de la Palud

The south side of this market square is dominated by Lausanne's town hall, a two-storey arcaded building fronted by the arms of the city. Built in the Renaissance style, it dates from the 15th century. It was here, on 10 April 1915, that the administrative headquarters and central archives of the International Olympic Committee were officially established.

Place de la Palud is a popular meeting area. A street market takes place here on Wednesdays and Saturdays,

and once a month the square is filled with a crafts fair.

At the centre of the square is the 16th–18th century Fontaine de la Justice, with an allegorical figure of Justice. The covered wooden stairs beyond the fountain are known as the Escaliers du Marché. They lead up to Rue Viret, from where further steps lead up to the cathedral.

The bare Gothic interior of the Église St-François

🏛 Place St-François

At the centre of this square stands the Église St-François, built in the 13th and 14th centuries as the church of the Franciscan monastery. The monastery was dissolved during the Reformation and the church stripped of its decoration. Although the façade was restored in the 1990s, the interior is disappointingly bland.

The streets leading off Place St-François are among the city's smartest. Rue du Bourg, which is lined with old houses, contains the city's most upmarket art galleries, jewellers' shops and boutiques, as well as bars and jazz clubs.

Figure on the Fountain of Justice

🏛 Musée Historique

4 Place de la Cathédrale.
[*021 315 41 01.*
⏰ *11am–6pm Tue–Thu, 11am–5pm Fri–Sun.*
Lausanne's museum of history fills the restored rooms of the former bishop's palace, which dates from

1373–83. The museum's collections constitute a detailed account of the city's history from prehistory to the present day. A particularly interesting exhibit is the model of Lausanne as it was 1638.

🔒 Lausanne Cathedral

See pp114–15.

🏛 Palais de Rumine

6 Place de la Riponne.
Musée Cantonal des Beaux-Arts 📞 021 316 34 45. ⏰ 11am–6pm Tue–Wed, 11am–8pm Thu, 11am–5pm Fri–Sun.📷
Musée d'Archéologie et d'Histoire 📞 021 316 34 30. ⏰ 11am–6pm Tue–Thu, 11am–5pm Fri–Sun. 📷

The imposing Neo-Renaissance Palais de Rumine, built in 1896–1906, housed Lausanne's university until the latter moved to new premises on the outskirts of the city. The building now contains the university library and five museums.

The Musée Cantonal des Beaux-Arts, on the ground floor, displays a fine collection of Swiss paintings of the 18th to the 20th centuries. Of

Wall decoration, Palais de Rumine

particular interest here are 19th-century landscapes of the Vaud countryside and works by François Bocion and Giovanni Giacometti, father of the more famous Alberto Giacometti.

The museum of archaeology and history, on the sixth floor, is devoted to finds made during local excavations. The exhibits range from the Bronze Age to the medieval period, and one of the finest is the gold bust of Marcus Aurelius *(see illustration on p35)*, discovered at Avenches in 1939.

The other three museums are devoted to geology, palaeontology and zoology.

⚜ Château St-Maire

Place du Château. ⬤ *Closed to visitors.*
This massive brick and sandstone edifice was built in 1397–1427 as the palace of the bishops of Lausanne, who ruled the city. When they were overthrown, the chateau became the residence of new overlords, the bailiffs of Bern. The fight for the

VISITORS' CHECKLIST

Road map G3. 🏃 250,000.
🚉 🚌 ⛴
ℹ 9 Place de la Gare (in the train station); 021 613 73 73. 4 Place de la Navigation (next to Ouchy metro station).
🌐 www.lausanne-tourisme.ch

independence of Lausanne and canton of Vaud was led by Jean Davel, who was beheaded in 1723 on the orders of the Bernese authorites. A monument to his memory stands in front of the chateau. The building is now the seat of the cantonal authorities of Vaud.

Château St-Maire, fronted by a statue of Jean Davel

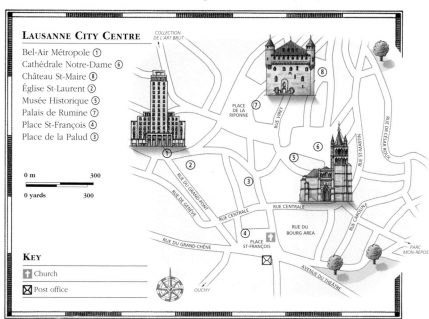

0 m   300

0 yards   300

KEY

🏛 Church

✉ Post office

COLLECTION DE L'ART BRUT
PLACE DE LA RIPONNE
RUE VIRET
RUE ST-MARTIN
RUE DE CÉSAR ROUX
RUE DU GRAND-PONT
RUE DE GENÈVE
RUE CENTRALE
RUE CENTRALE
RUE CAROLINE
RUE DU BOURG AREA
RUE DU GRAND-CHÊNE
PLACE ST-FRANÇOIS
AVENUE DU THÉÂTRE
PARC MON-REPOS
OUCHY

Cathédrale Notre-Dame

BEGUN IN THE MID-12TH CENTURY and completed in the 13th, the Cathédrale Notre-Dame in Lausanne is the finest Gothic building in Switzerland. It is built on the site of a Roman camp and overlies the foundations of Carolingian and Romanesque basilicas. With a central nave flanked by aisles, a transept over which rises a tower, an apse and an ambulatory, the cathedral's design and decoration show the influence of the French Gothic style. Consecrated by Pope Gregory X in 1275, Notre-Dame has been a Protestant cathedral since the Reformation. The top of the southwest tower commands a spectacular view of the city and Lake Geneva.

Nave
Alternating thick and slender columns line the nave. The thick columns support the central vaulting.

Stalls
Decorated with expressive figures of saints, the stalls in the Chapelle St-Maurice are masterpieces of late Gothic woodcarving.

North tower, containing the Chapelle St-Maurice

★ Chapelle St-Maurice
Located in the northwest tower, the chapel is filled with exquisitely carved late Gothic stalls dating from the early 16th century.

Montfalcon Portal
The entrance at the west end, known as the Montfalcon Portal, is decorated with replicas of Gothic carvings dating from 1515–36.

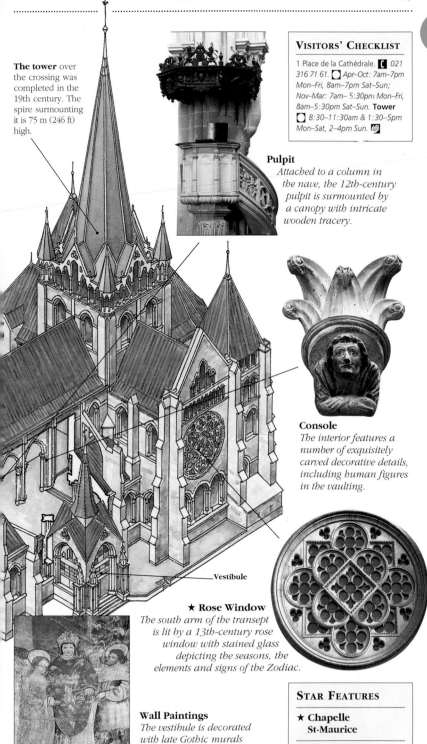

The tower over the crossing was completed in the 19th century. The spire surmounting it is 75 m (246 ft) high.

VISITORS' CHECKLIST

1 Place de la Cathédrale. 021 316 71 61. Apr–Oct: 7am–7pm Mon–Fri, 8am–7pm Sat–Sun; Nov–Mar: 7am– 5:30pm Mon–Fri, 8am–5:30pm Sat–Sun. **Tower** 8:30–11:30am & 1:30–5pm Mon–Sat, 2–4pm Sun.

Pulpit
Attached to a column in the nave, the 12th-century pulpit is surmounted by a canopy with intricate wooden tracery.

Console
The interior features a number of exquisitely carved decorative details, including human figures in the vaulting.

Vestibule

★ **Rose Window**
The south arm of the transept is lit by a 13th-century rose window with stained glass depicting the seasons, the elements and signs of the Zodiac.

Wall Paintings
The vestibule is decorated with late Gothic murals dating from the early 16th century.

STAR FEATURES

★ **Chapelle St-Maurice**

★ **Rose Window**

Beyond the city centre

West of Place St-François is the offbeat district of Flon, which is filled with art galleries and upmarket shops. North of the Old Town stretches the extensive Parc de l'Hermitage. To the south of the city centre lies the old fishing village of Ouchy, now a popular lakeside resort and the location of the Musée Olympique.

🏛 Collection de l'Art Brut

Château de Beaulieu, 11 Avenue des Bergières. 📞 021 315 25 70.
🚌 2 from Place St-François.
🕐 11am–6pm Tue–Sun. 📷
🌐 www.artbrut.ch

Art Brut is the name that the French painter Jean Dubuffet (1901–85) gave to art created by people living on the fringe of society, including criminals, psychotics, patients at psychiatric hospitals or other institutions, and spiritualist mediums, who had no artistic training. The ideas for art came from their own imaginations, free from established cultural influences and the history of a fine arts tradition. The originality, freshness and often indecency of Art Brut inspired Dubuffet in his search for creative expression, and in 1945 he began to amass a private collection. In 1971 he presented it to the city of Lausanne, and the Collection de l'Art Brut opened in 1976.

Only about 1,000 pieces from the present holding of about 30,000 are on display at any one time. The exhibits are laid out on four floors in converted stables at the 18th-century Château de Beaulieu, northwest of the city centre.

Ranging from paintings, drawings and painted fabrics to wood carvings, sculptures and even an illustrated novel, these extraordinary works of art have a striking force and spontaneity. Alongside each exhibit is a short biography of the artist, giving the visitor some insight into the mental attitude and personal circumstances in which these works were created.

🏛 Fondation de l'Hermitage

2 Route du Signal. 📞 021 312 50 13. 🚌 3 from the main train station or 🚌 16 from Place St-François.
🕐 10am–6pm Tue–Wed, 10am–9pm Thu, 10am–6pm Fri–Sun. 📷
🌐 www.fondationhermitage.ch

The imposing Neo-Gothic villa set in magnificent parkland north of Lausanne was built in 1842–50 by Charles-Juste Bugnion, a wealthy banker, and donated to the city by his descendants. Now known as the Fondation de l'Hermitage, it is a gallery with a permanent collection of nearly 800 French paintings. Of particular note are the Impressionist and Post-Impressionist paintings, as well as the works of 20th-century Vaudois artists. The Fondation also stages two or three large-scale temporary exhibitions every year of the work of world-class artists.

The Parc de l'Hermitage, the extensive grounds in which the villa is set, is landscaped with exotic trees.

At its northern extremity is the Signal de Sauvabelin, a hill which rises to a height of 647 m (2,120 ft) and offers views of Lausanne and Lake Geneva, with the Alps in the background. Beyond the hill are woods and the Lac de Sauvabelin, where there is a reserve for ibexes and other alpine animals.

🏛 Parc Mon-Repos

Avenue Mon-Repos.

This landscaped park, laid out in the 19th century to the southeast of the city centre, is the most elegant of all Lausanne's gardens. It contains a Neo-Gothic tower, a Neo-Classical temple, a conservatory and a rockery with a cave and a waterfall. At the centre of the park stands an 18th-century villa, which at the time that it was built was surrounded by vineyards. The 18th-century French writer Voltaire lived in the villa during his stay in Lausanne.

Statue in Parc Mon-Repos

The villa also has associations with the Olympic Games. The Olympic spirit was resurrected by the French aristocrat Baron Pierre de Coubertin (1863–1937), who believed that sport plays an essential role in the development of citizens and nations. De Coubertin set up the International Olympic Committee (IOC) in Paris in 1894, with himself as president, and two years later the first modern Olympic Games were held in Athens. During World War I De Coubertin moved the IOC's head office to Switzerland. From 1922 until his death, the villa at Mon Repos was his residence and until the 1970s it was also the headquarters of the IOC, and the location of the first Olympics museum to be set up.

At the north end of Parc Mon-Repos stands the building of the Federal Tribunal, Switzerland's supreme court.

Le Cinema (c.1950) by Collectif d'enfants at the Collection de l'Art Brut

Hôtel du Château d'Ouchy, one of many lakeside hotels in Ouchy, on the outskirts of Lausanne

Ouchy

On Lake Geneva, 2 km (1 mile) south of central Lausanne, accessible by metro (M2 line).

Once a fishing village, Ouchy, on the outskirts of Lausanne, is now a popular lakeside resort. It has a beautiful setting on Lake Geneva, with views of the surrounding mountains, and a tree-lined promenade along the lakeshore. Cruises on the lake depart from here.

All that remains of the 12th-century castle that once defended the harbour is a tower, which now forms part of the Neo-Gothic Château d'Ouchy, built in the 1890s. The chateau is now a hotel and restaurant *(see p276)*.

Several late 19th- to early 20th-century hotels line the lakeshore. They include the Beau-Rivage Palace, a fine example of Art Nouveau architecture, and the Hôtel d'Angleterre, the house where Lord Byron stayed when he came to Lausanne and where he wrote *The Prisoner of Chillon (see pp122–3)*.

🏛 Musée Olympique

1 Quai d'Ouchy. 📞 *021 621 65 11.*
W *www.olympic.org* ⬤ *May–Sep: 9am–6pm daily; Oct–Apr: 9am–6pm Tue–Sun.*
The Olympics Museum illustrates the history of the Olympic movement, from the athletes of Ancient Greece to the modern Olympic Games.

It is Lausanne's main attraction, drawing over 200,000 visitors a year. Multimedia presentations, archive film footage, interactive equipment, photographs and postage stamps show the development of individual sport disciplines and the achievements of Olympic champions, many of whom have donated their medals to the museum.

The museum is set in parkland planted with Mediterranean trees and shrubs. The upper floor has a restaurant with a large terrace offering fine views of Lake Geneva and the surrounding mountains.

Figures of cyclists in the Parc Olympique

🏛 Musée Romain

24 Chemin du-Bois-de-Vaux. 📞 *021 625 10 84* W *www.lausanne.ch/mrv* ⬤ *11am–6pm Tue–Wed, 11am–8pm Thu, 11am–6pm Fri–Sun.*
About ten minutes' walk west of Ouchy are the remains of Lousonna and Vidy, two Roman towns that flourished from 15 BC to the 4th century AD. The ruins have been excavated, and the finds that were uncovered are on display in the Musée Romain nearby.

The objects are laid out in the reconstruction of a Roman house. They include glassware and pottery, combs, toga pins and jewellery, and coins and votive figures, as well as some fine examples of classic Roman mosaics.

Entrance to the Olympics Museum in the Parc Olympique

Lake Geneva (Lac Léman) ❷

LYING IN AN ARC bordered by the Jura mountains to the west, the French Alps to the south, and the Mittelland to the northeast, Lake Geneva, known as Lac Léman in French, is the largest lake in the Alps. While most of the southern shore is French territory, the greater part of the lake lies within Switzerland. Its shores are dotted with towns and villages, many of which are the departure points of boat trips on the lake. An important stop on the Grand Tour of Europe in the 19th century, Lake Geneva attracted and inspired many Romantic writers. With the mountains reflected in its still blue waters, it is one of Switzerland's most spellbinding sights.

★ **Vufflens-le-Château**
Built in the 15th century in the North Italian style, the castle here is one of Switzerland's most magnificent Gothic fortresses. It has a turreted keep, a central courtyard and living quarters within its towers.

Rolle
A village at the heart of the La Côte wine-producing area, Rolle has a moated castle built by the Duke of Savoy in the 13th century. The castle is built to a triangular plan, with a tower at each corner.

Geneva
This is the largest city on the lakeshore. The headquarters of several international organizations, Geneva has a prominent place on the world stage.

LONS-LE-SAUNIER

Vufflens-le-Château

Rolle

A1 E25 E62

1

LONS-LE-SAUNIER

Divonne-les-Bains

Nyon

Thon-les-Ba

N5 E21

Gex

Coppet

Douvaine

N5

Ferney-Voltaire

Meyrin

Vernier

Geneva

Annemasse

N 206

A40 E25

CHAMONIX-MONT-BLANC

LYON

A40 E25

ANNECY

STAR SIGHTS

★ **Vevey**

★ **Vufflens-le-Château**

KEY

▬	Motorway
▭	Major road
▭	Minor road
▭	River
☆	Viewpoint

Cully
One of many scenic villages on around Lake Geneva, Cully is a centre of the local wine trade. The sun-drenched hillsides above it are covered with vineyards.

VISITORS' CHECKLIST

Road map A4, B4. 🚆 🚌 ⛴
ℹ *Lausanne, 60 Avenue d'Ouchy; 021 613 26 26.*
🌐 www.region-du-leman.ch
Boat Trips: *Compagnie Générale de Navigation; 848 811 848*

St-Saphorin
This romantic winemaking village has steep cobbled streets and a 7th-century church that was remodelled in the 16th century, in the flamboyant Gothic style.

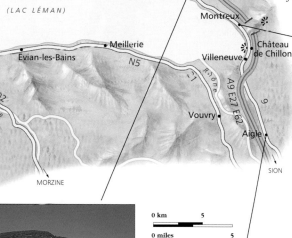

Montreux
Stretching along the lakeshore, Montreux is a cosmopolitan resort. Renowned for its music festivals, it is also an important cultural centre.

★ Vevey
This stately and traditional resort offers a choice of cultural events. It is renowned for the Fête des Vignerons, a grape-harvest festival held here every 25 years.

Aigle
At the intersection of the Ormonts and Rhône valleys, Aigle is the capital of the Chablais winemaking region. Its 12th-century castle, which contains the Musée de la Vigne et du Vin, is surrounded by vineyards.

The lakeside resort of Vevey, with mountains in the background

Vevey ❸

Road map B4. 16,000.
Montreux, 5 Rue du Théâtre; 021 962 84 84.
www.montreux-vevey.com
Street Artists Festival (Aug)

WITH MONTREUX, Vevey is one of the two best-known holiday resorts of the Swiss Riviera, the stretch of land bordering the north-western shores of Lake Geneva between Lausanne and Villeneuve. The region began to develop as a centre of tourism in the 19th century. Known for its sophisticated ambience, Vevey soon attracted an international clientele, which included the Austrian painter and playwright Oskar Kokoschka, the writer Ernest Hemingway and the comedian Charlie Chaplin, who spent the last 25 years of his life in Vevey and who was buried here in 1977.

Known in Roman times as Viviscus, Vevey was once Lake Geneva's main port. It continued to flourish through the Middle Ages and by the 19th century was the first industrial town in the canton of Vaud. It was here, in 1867, that Henri Nestlé established the powdered milk factory that revolutionized baby foods. Now the world's largest food manufacturer, the Nestlé company still has its international headquarters in Vevey.

The most attractive part of Vevey is its Grande Place (also known as Place du Marché). On Tuesdays and Saturdays this huge square is filled with a market, and in summer regional growers offer wine tastings. A folk arts market is also held here on Saturday mornings in July and August. La Grenette (1808), a handsome building on the north side of the square, was once the town's granary.

The narrow alleys of Vevey's historic quarter continue to the east of Grande Place. On Quai Perdonnet stands a statue of Charlot, the French name by which Charlie Chaplin is known here. Nearby is the **Musée de l'Alimentation**, a museum devoted to the history of food products. To the east of the train station is the **Musée Jenisch**. Besides a large collection of paintings and sculpture by 19th- and 20th-century Swiss artists, this gallery is the home of the Fondation Oskar Kokoschka, which contains 800 Expressionist paintings by this Austrian artist. The Musée Jenisch also houses an outstanding collection of prints, which includes not only the largest assemblage of lithographs of Rembrandt in Europe but also works by such major artists as Albrecht Dürer and Jean-Baptiste Corot.

Musée de l'Alimentation
1 Rue du Léman. *021 924 41 11.*
10am–6pm Tue–Sun.

Musée Jenisch
2 Avenue de la Gare. *021 921 29 50.* *11am–5:30pm Tue–Sun.*

Statue of Freddie Mercury in Montreux

Montreux ❹

Road map B4. *20,000.*
5 Rue du Théâtre; 021 962 84 84.
www.montreux-vevey.com
Narcissus Festival (spring); Montreux Jazz Festival (Jul).

OFTEN DESCRIBED as the jewel of the Swiss Riviera, Montreux is an upmarket resort that is renowned for its annual jazz festival. The town began to develop as an international tourist resort in about 1815, and its golden age lasted until the outbreak of World War I in 1914. In the 19th century the charm of the area captivated artists, writers and musicians, including Lord Byron and Mary Shelley, Leo Tolstoy and Hans Christian Andersen.

Montreux has many Belle Époque hotels. The most famous of them is the Montreux Palace on Grand'Rue, west of the town centre. Opposite this hotel is the Centre des Congrès, a modern conference centre. It contains the Auditorium Stravinsky, a concert hall built in 1990 and dedicated to Igor Stravinsky (1882–1971), who composed *The Rite of Spring* in Montreux.

The metal-framed market hall in Place du Marché was built in 1890 with funds donated by Henri Nestlé, founder of the powdered milk company. At the end of the square, on the lakeshore, is a statue of Freddie Mercury, vocalist in the band Queen. Montreux was his second home and it was here that he died, in 1991.

East of the statue, on the lakeshore promenade, is a casino rebuilt after a fire that has entered into rock legend. On 4 December 1971, during a concert given by Frank Zappa and the Mothers of Invention, a rocket-flare was fired into the ceiling and the building was suddenly engulfed by flames. As clouds of smoke soared above the waters of

Château d'Aigle, once a bailiff's castle and now the home of a museum of wine and winemaking

the lake, Ian Gillan, of the band Deep Purple, who was watching from his hotel room, was inspired by the sight to write *Smoke on the Water*.

Château de Chillon **5**

See pp122–3.

Aigle **6**

Road map B4. 6,500.
5 Rue Colomb; 024 466 30 00.
W www.aigle.ch

AIGLE IS THE capital of the Chablais, a wine-growing region that lies southeast of Lake Geneva and produces

Wooden chalets along a street in the ski resort of Leysin

some of Switzerland's finest wines *(see p266– 7)*. Set among vineyards covering the foothills of the Alpes Vaudoises, the town is dominated by a turreted castle, the Château d'Aigle. Built in the 12th century by the Savoyards, it was severely damaged in the 15th century but was later rebuilt to serve as the residence of the region's Bernese bailiffs.

The castle now houses the **Musée de la Vigne et du Vin**, whose exhibits illustrate the age-old methods of vine-cultivation and wine-making. The 16th-century Maison de la Dîme opposite the castle contains the **Musée International de l'Étiquette**, which documents the history of wine labels over 200 years.

Musée de la Vigne et du Vin and **Musée International de l'Étiquette**
024 466 21 30. Apr–Jun: 10am–12:30pm & 2–6pm Tue–Sun; Jul–Aug: 10am–6pm daily; Sep–Oct: 10am–12:30pm, 2–6pm Tue–Sun.

Leysin **7**

Road map B4. 2,700.
Place Large; 024 494 22 44.
W www.leysin.ch

THE SMALL VILLAGE of Leysin, now a popular winter and summer resort, occupies a sun-drenched mountain

terrace with views across to the Dents du Midi and down onto the Rhône valley. Lying at an altitude of 1,260 m (4,135 ft), Leysin enjoys an unusually dry and sunny climate. Once a centre for the treatment of tuberculosis, the village later evolved into a ski resort. Cable cars carry visitors up to the Tour de Mayen (2,326 m/7,634 ft) and to Berneuse (2,037 m/6,685 ft), where there is a revolving restaurant that enables diners to admire a panoramic view of the Alps.

Les Diablerets **8**

Road map B4. 1,300.
Rue de la Gare; 024 492 33 58.
W www.diablerets.ch

SET AMONG ALPINE meadows in the Ormonts valley, the small ski resort of Les Diablerets lies at an altitude of 1,150 m (3,775 ft) in the Alpes Vaudoises. Above it rise the peaks of Les Diablerets, 3,210 m (10,535 ft) high and among which lies the glacier of the same name.

With six cable cars, 18 lifts and 120 km (75 miles) of ski runs, the resort offers year-round skiing. The Glacier de Tsanfleuron, a southern extension of the Glacier des Diablerets, makes an ideal piste for downhill skiing in summer.

Château de Chillon ❺

THIS ENCHANTING MEDIEVAL CASTLE, set on a rocky spur on the eastern shore of Lake Geneva, is one of Switzerland's most evocative sights. Built for the Dukes of Savoy, its origins probably go back to the 11th century but its present appearance dates from the 13th century. In 1536, the castle was captured by the Bernese, and from then until 1798 it was the seat of the region's Bernese bailiffs. The centre of court life, the castle was also used as a prison. Its most famous captive was François de Bonivard, imprisoned there from 1530 to 1536 for political incitement.

Heraldic Hall
This ceremonial hall is decorated with the coats of arms of the Bernese bailiffs.

Defences
Surrounded by thick walls, the castle is also defended by three semicircular turrets.

A guest room, the Camera Paramenti, and another bedchamber are located here.

Aula Nova
The former banqueting hall contains a museum, with furniture, pewter vessels, armour and weapons.

Grand Burgrave Hall
This great hall has a wooden ceiling resting on columns that support arches. The walls are richly decorated with paintings.

The covered bridge leading to the gatehouse was originally a drawbridge

★ **Grand Ducal Hall**
This large room, also known as the Aula Magna, has chequered walls and its original 15th-century wooden ceiling, which is supported by black marble columns.

VISITORS' CHECKLIST

Road map B4. 🚉 🚌 📞 *021 966 89 10.* ⬜ *Mar: 9:30am–5pm daily; Apr–Sep: 9am–6pm daily; Oct: 9:30am–5pm; Nov–Feb: 10am–4pm daily.* 📷

Bergfrieg, the tower that was the castle's final defence, is one of its oldest elements.

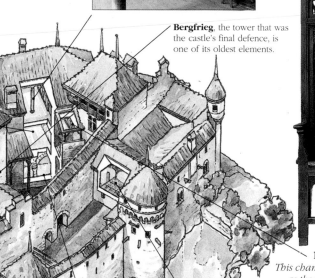

Ducal Chamber
This chamber, also known as the Camera Domini, has a wooden beamed ceiling and contains Gothic furniture.

Chapel
The castle's chapel, dedicated to St George, is in the early Gothic style, with a rib-vaulted ceiling. The walls and ceiling are covered with frescoes.

★ **Bonivard's Prison**
The castle's vaulted underground chambers were once used as a prison. François de Bonivard, who spent six years in captivity here, was immortalized by Lord Byron in The Prisoner of Chillon, a poem that he wrote in Ouchy in 1816.

STAR FEATURES

★ **Bonivard's Prison**

★ **Grand Ducal Hall**

Gruyères **9**

Road map B4. **1,200.** **To Pringy.** **026 921 10 30.** **W** www.gruyeres.ch

VISIBLE FROM AFAR against the backdrop of Alpine scenery, the well-preserved medieval village of Gruyères is a popular destination for visitors, and is often crowded during the summer. As its only street is restricted to pedestrians, vehicles must be left in the parking areas below.

The village has houses dating from the 15th to the 17th centuries and is crowned by a castle, the **Château de Gruyères**. Built in the 11th century, the castle was continuously inhabited by the counts of Gruyères until the mid-16th century, when the bankrupted 19th count fled and his lands were divided between the lords of Bern and Fribourg.

In 1848, the castle was acquired by the Bovys, a wealthy Genevese family who carried out extensive and much-needed restoration. In 1939 the castle passed into the ownership of the cantonal authorities of Fribourg. It now contains a museum. Displayed in rooms with frescoes and grand fireplaces, the exhibits include 16th-century Flemish tapestries and booty taken after the Battle of Murten (1476). Delicate landscapes by the French Impressionist painter Jean-Baptiste Corot (1796–1875), who stayed at the castle, are also on view.

At **La Maison du Gruyère**, a working dairy in Pringy, at the foot of the village, visitors can watch the famous local cheese being made. The dairy also has a restaurant and a shop selling local produce.

⚜ Château de Gruyères
C 026 921 21 02. **O** Apr–Oct: 9am–6pm daily; Nov–Mar: 10am–4:30pm daily.
⚜ La Maison du Gruyère
Pringy. **C** 026 921 84 00.
O Apr–Sep: 9am–7pm daily; Oct–Mar: 9am–6pm daily.
W www.lamaisondugruyere.ch

Fribourg **10**

See pp126–7.

Murten/Morat **11**

Road map B3. **5,000.**
i Französische Kirchgasse 6; 026 670 51 12. **W** www. murtentourismus.ch

THE RESORT TOWN of Murten (Morat in French) lies on the eastern shore of the Murtensee (Lac de Morat). It has strong historical associations. It was at Murten, on 22 June 1476, that the forces of the Swiss Confederation crushed the army of Charles the Bold, Duke of Burgundy, killing 12,000 of his soldiers, while losing only 410 of their own. According to legend, a messenger ran 17 km (10 miles) from Murten to Fribourg with news of the victory, dropping dead with exhaustion on his arrival. His sacrifice is commemorated by an annual run between Murten and Fribourg that takes place on the first Sunday in October.

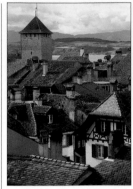

View from Murten's fortified walls

The town was founded by the Zähringer dynasty in the 12th century, and is still encircled by walls dating from the 12th to the 15th centuries. Hauptgasse, the main street through the old town, is lined with 16th-century arcaded houses with overhanging eaves. The rampart walk, reached from several points along Deutsche Kirchgasse, offers views of the Murtensee, the castle and the old town's brown-tiled houses. At the western end of the town is a 13th-century castle, with a courtyard that provides a fine view over the lake. At the eastern end stands Berntor (or Porte de Berne), a Baroque gatehouse with a clock dating from 1712. The **Musée Historique**, in a disused mill on the lakeshore, contains prehistoric finds from local excavations and items relating to the Burgundian Wars.

🏛 Musée Historique
C 026 670 31 00. **O** Apr–Nov: 11am–5pm Tue–Sun.

Avenches **12**

Road map B3. **2,000.**
i 3 Place de l'Église; 026 676 99 22.
W www.avenches.ch
◈ Opera Festival (Jul); Rock Oz'Arènes (Aug); Musical Parade (military bands; Sep).

ORIGINALLY THE capital of the Helveti, the Celtic tribe that once ruled western Switzerland, Avenches was conquered by the Romans in the 1st century BC. Named

The Château de Gruyères, seat of the counts of Gruyères for 500 years

Aventicum, it became the capital of the Roman province of Helvetia. At its peak in the 2nd century AD, Aventicum was larger than the present town of Avenches. Encircled by 6 km (4 miles) of walls set with watchtowers, it supported a population of 20,000. By 260, however, much it had been razed by the Alemani, a Germanic tribe, and by 450 it had lost its importance.

Vestiges of the Roman city can still be seen to the east of the medieval town centre. The most complete of these remains is the amphitheatre, with seating for 6,000. Other features include the Tornallaz, a tower that is the only surviving part of the old city walls, the forum, the baths and a 12-m (40-ft) Corinthian column known as the Tour du Cigognier.

The **Musée Romain**, in a medieval square tower within the amphitheatre, contains an impressive display of Roman artefacts discovered during excavations at Aventicum. The exhibits range from items of daily life, such as pottery, tools and coins, to bronze and marble statues of Roman deities, mosaics and wall paintings, and a replica of a gold bust of Marcus Aurelius *(see illustration on p35)*.

🏛 **Musée Romain**
📞 026 675 17 27.
🕐 *Apr–Sep: 10am–noon & 1–5pm Tue–Sun; Oct–Mar: 2–5pm Tue–Sun.*
♿

The Roman amphitheatre in Avenches

Nave of the Romanesque abbey church in Payerne

Payerne ⓭

Road map B3. 🏘 *7,000.* 🚌 ℹ
10 Place du Marché; 026 660 61 61.

T HE SMALL market town of Payerne, in the canton of Vaud, is distinguished by its remarkable church, one of the most beautiful Romanesque buildings in Switzerland.

The **Église Abbatiale** was built in the 11th century as the abbey church of a Benedictine monastery, of which little remains. Stripped of its decoration during the Reformation, the church's interior is bare, but this only

Knocker on the abbey church in Payerne

serves to accentuate its impressive grandeur and the contrasting colours of its soaring limestone and sand-stone columns. The portico features 12th-century frescoes and one of the chapels in the apse has 15th-century Gothic paintings.

🔒 **Église Abbatiale**
📞 *026 662 67 04.* 🕐 *May–Oct: 10am–noon & 2–6pm Tue–Sat,. 10:30am–noon & 2–6pm Sun; Nov–Apr: 10am–noon & 2–5pm Tue–Sat, 10:20am–noon & 2–5pm Sun.*

Estavayer-le-Lac ⓮

Road map B3. 🏘 *4,000.* 🚌
ℹ *Place du Midi; 026 663 12 37.*
🌐 *www.estavayer-le-lac.ch*

S URROUNDED ON three sides by the canton of Vaud, this small town on the southern shore of Lake Neuchâtel lies within an enclave of the canton of Fribourg. A popular yachting centre, Estavayer-le-Lac is also a pleasant medieval town with arcarded streets.

Its focal point is the Château de Cheneaux, a fine Gothic castle that is now the seat of local government.

The **Musée Communal**, housed in a 15th-century mansion, contains an eclectic assemblage of exhibits, including kitchen implements. It also boasts an unusual curiosity, namely a collection of 108 stuffed frogs arranged in poses that parody the social life of the mid-19th century. The scenes were created by François Perrier, an eccentric resident of Estavayer who served in the Vatican's Swiss Guard and who produced this bizarre display in the 1860s.

🏛 **Musée Communal**
Rue du Musée. 📞 *026 663 24 48.*
🕐 *Mar–June: 10am–noon & 2–5pm Tue–Sun; Jul–Aug: 10am–noon & 2–5pm daily; Sep–Oct: 10am–noon & 2–5pm Tue–Sun; Nov–Feb: 2–5pm Sat–Sun.* ♿

Street-by-Street: Fribourg ⑩

WITH STEEP COBBLED streets, immaculately preserved Gothic houses and numerous fountains, Fribourg (Freiburg in German) is one of Switzerland's most attractive towns. Set on a rocky peninsula within a bend of the River Sarine (Saane in German), it was founded in 1157 by Berthold IV of Zähringen, and joined the Swiss Confederation in 1481. Despite the Reformation, Fribourg remained Catholic, and a Catholic university was founded here in 1889.

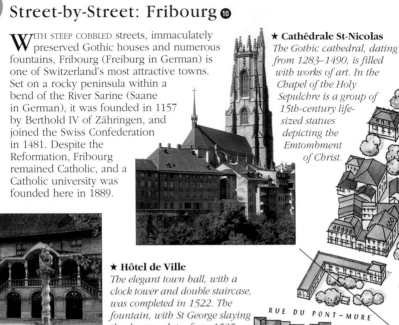

★ **Cathédrale St-Nicolas**
The Gothic cathedral, dating from 1283–1490, is filled with works of art. In the Chapel of the Holy Sepulchre is a group of 15th-century life-sized statues depicting the Emtombment of Christ.

★ **Hôtel de Ville**
The elegant town hall, with a clock tower and double staircase, was completed in 1522. The fountain, with St George slaying the dragon, dates from 1525.

RUE DU PONT–MURE

RUE DES EPOUSES

Tilleul de Morat is the remains of a linden tree planted in memory of the man who brought news of victory over Charles the Bold at Murten (Morat).

GRAND–RUE

Maison de Ville
The Baroque town house next to the Hôtel de Ville was designed by Hans Fasel and built in 1730–31.

KEY

– – – Suggested route

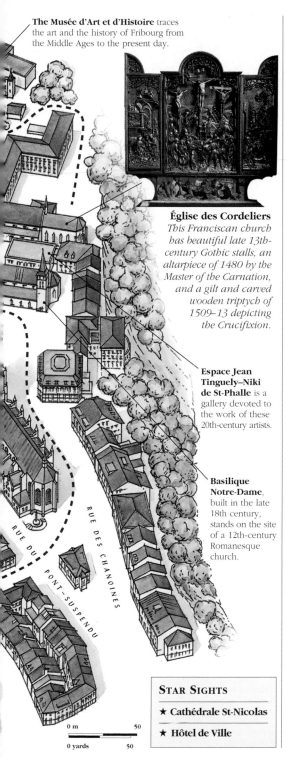

The **Musée d'Art et d'Histoire** traces the art and the history of Fribourg from the Middle Ages to the present day.

Église des Cordeliers
This Franciscan church has beautiful late 13th-century Gothic stalls, an altarpiece of 1480 by the Master of the Carnation, and a gilt and carved wooden triptych of 1509–13 depicting the Crucifixion.

Espace Jean Tinguely–Niki de St-Phalle is a gallery devoted to the work of these 20th-century artists.

Basilique Notre-Dame, built in the late 18th century, stands on the site of a 12th-century Romanesque church.

RUE DU PONT-SUSPENDU

RUE DES CHANOINES

0 m   50
0 yards   50

STAR SIGHTS

★ **Cathédrale St-Nicolas**

★ **Hôtel de Ville**

VISITORS' CHECKLIST

Road map B3. 🛉 *40,000.*
ℹ *1 Avenue de la Gare;
026 350 11 11.*
ⓦ *www.fribourgtourism.ch*
🎭 *Carnival (late Feb); Festival des Musiques Sacrées (Jul).*

Exploring Fribourg

While Fribourg's major historic sights are clustered around the cathedral, there is much else of interest in this ancient district of the town.

On Rue de Morat, north of the cathedral, is the **Éspace Jean Tinguely–Niki de St-Phalle**. This vast gallery contains kinetic sculptures by Jean Tinguely, who was born in Fribourg, and installations by his wife, Niki de St-Phalle. South of the cathedral, streets lead down to Place du Petit St-Jean, on the peninsula. **Rue d'Or**, just north of the square, is lined with Gothic houses. The peninsula is connected to the south bank of the river by the **Pont de Berne**. This wooden bridge leads to Place des Forgerons, where there is a Renaissance fountain and vestiges of fortifications.

Around Planche Supérieure, a square to the east of the peninsula, are the Église St-Jean and a museum of archaeology. From here, the Pont de St-Jean leads across the river to Neuveville, a low-lying area above which stands the town hall.

Pont de Berne, a wooden bridge across the Sarine in Fribourg

🏛 Musée Suisse de la Marionette

2 Derrière-les-Jardins. 📞 *026 322 85 13.* 🕐 *10am–noon Mon–Fri, 2–6pm Sat–Sun.* 🈲
This unusual museum has an interesting collection of puppets and other theatrical dolls, both antique and modern. An exhibition of theatrical masks rounds off the display.

The 13th-century Château d'Yverdon, focal point of Yverdon-les-Bains

Yverdon-les-Bains ⓯

Road map B3. 🏔 *22,000.* 🚉 🚌
🛈 *1 Avenue de la Gare; 024 423
61 01.* 🅆 *www.yverdon-les-bains.ch*

Sɪᴛᴜᴀᴛᴇᴅ ᴀᴛ ᴛʜᴇ southwestern
extremity of Lake Neuchâtel,
Yverdon-les-Bains is Vaud's
second town after Lausanne.
The Celtic settlement that was
originally established here
later became a Gallo-Roman
camp, Eburodunum, and the
Romans built thermal baths
here so as to use the hot
sulphurous springs. Yverdon's
town centre overlies the Roman
settlement. The focal point is
the **Château d'Yverdon**, a
massive castle built by Peter II
of Savoy in the 13th century.

Part of the castle now
houses a museum of local
history, with a collection of
Gallo-Roman finds and other
exhibits. A section of the
museum is devoted to the life
and work of Johann Heinrich
Pestalozzi (1746–1827), the
Swiss educational reformer
who set up a school for
deprived children in the
castle in 1805. Influenced by
the writings of Jean-Jacques
Rousseau, his revolutionary
teaching methods were based
on a flexible school
curriculum suited to the
character of each child.

Place Pestalozzi, opposite
the castle, is dominated by
the Hôtel de Ville, the town
hall built in 1768–73 on the
site of a former market hall.
The collegiate church on the
west side of the square dates
from 1757. The arched pedi-
ment of its Baroque façade
features an allegory of Faith.

Of particular interest to fans
of science fiction is the
Maison d'Ailleurs (House
of Elsewhere). This museum
concentrates on imaginary
worlds, from those described
by Homer, Thomas More and
Jules Verne to 20th-century
science fiction. The numerous
exhibits here include toys, such
as Star Trek and Star Wars
figures, ray-guns, a mock-up
of a spaceship and a library
of science-fiction literature.

Yverdon's thermal baths lie
on Avenue des Bains, about
1 km (half a mile) southeast of
the town centre. The **Centre
Thermal** is one of Switzerland's largest and most modern
spa centres. With indoor and
outdoor pools, saunas and
physiotherapy, the centre is
used by some 1,300 people
every day. Rich in minerals,
the water here is particularly
effective in curing respiratory
ailments and rheumatism.

🏰 **Château d'Yverdon**
◻ *Jun–Sep:10am–noon & 2–5pm
Tue–Sun; Oct–May: 2–5pm Tue–Sun.*
🗝
🏛 **Maison d'Ailleurs**
14 Place Pestalozzi. 🄲 *024 425
64 38.* ◻ *2–6pm Wed–Sun.* 🗝
💧 **Centre Thermal**
Avenue des Bains.
🄲 *024 423 02 32.* ◻ *8am–10pm
Mon–Fri; 9am–8pm Sat–Sun & public
holidays*

Envɪʀᴏɴs: Beyond Clendy,
the northern suburb of
Yverdon-les-Bains, is a
Neolithic stone circle. It
stands near the shore of Lake
Neuchâtel and is one of
several similar ancient
monuments around the lake.

Romainmôtier ⓰

Road map A4. 🏔 *400.* 🚉 🚌
🛈 *024 453 14 65.*
🅆 www.romainmotier.ch

Tʜᴇ sᴍᴀʟʟ ᴠɪʟʟᴀɢᴇ of
Romainmôtier, set in
beautiful wooded hills,
is worth a detour for its
remarkable abbey church.
One of Switzerland's most
beautiful Romanesque
religious buildings, the **Église
Abbatiale de Romainmôtier**
was built between the late
10th and early 11th centuries
by monks from the Abbaye
de Cluny, in France. The
interior contains fine 13th-
and 14th-century frescoes
and a medieval statue of
the Virgin. Although the
15th-century monastery
was dissolved in 1536, in the
wake of the Reformation,
the abbey church and part
of the cloister have survived.

⛪ **Église Abbatiale de
Romainmôtier**
🄲 *024 453 14 65.* ◻ *7am–8pm
daily.*

**The nave of the Romanesque
Église Abbatiale de Romainmôtier**

Vallorbe ⓱

Road map A3. 🏔 *3,000.* 🚉 🚌
🛈 *11 Rue des Grandes-Forges; 021
843 25 83.*

Tʜɪs sᴍᴀʟʟ ɪɴᴅᴜsᴛʀɪᴀʟ town
lies near the Franco-Swiss
border. From the Middle Ages
up to recent times, the town
was an iron-smelting centre.
It was also at Vallorbe that
the tunnel beneath the Jura

World War II tank at the Fort de Pré-Giroud, near Vallorbe

was built, thus creating the Paris–Istanbul rail route.

This is reflected in the **Musée du Fer et du Chemin de Fer** (Iron and Railway Museum), which traces the history of the Swiss iron industry, with a section that is devoted to the Swiss railways.

About 3km (2 miles) southwest of Vallorbe are the **Grottes de Vallorbe**. These are caves with stalactites and stalagmites. The caves form a tunnel over the River Orbe, which surges through a gorge. A short distance west of Vallorbe is the **Fort de Pré-Giroud**, which was built as a surveillance post on the eve of World War II to observe the French border. Disguised as a chalet, it is a large underground bunker with space for over 100 people.

🏛 Musée du Fer et du Chemin de Fer
11 Rue des Grandes-Forges. 📞 021 843 25 83. ⏰ Apr–Oct: 9:30am–noon & 1:30–6pm daily; Nov–Mar: 9:30am–noon & 1:30–6pm Mon–Fri. ▣
♣ Grottes de Vallorbe
⏰ Apr–May: 9:30am–4:30pm daily; Jun–Aug: 9:30am–5:30pm ▣ ▣.

Grandson ⑱

Road map B3. 🏚 2,000. 🚊 🚌
ℹ Château de Grandson; 024 445 29 26.

DOMINATED BY ITS great medieval castle, the town of Grandson is associated with a momentous event in the history of the Swiss Confederation. This was the defeat of Charles the Bold, Duke of Burgundy, at the Battle of Grandson on 2 March 1476.

In February 1476, the duke's army laid siege to Grandson and its castle, eventually securing the surrender of the garrison, who were put to death. However, after raising an army of 18,000, the Confederates marched on Grandson to wreak revenge on the duke and his army. Fleeing in panic, the Burgundians abandoned their arms, horses and tents, as well as the ducal treasury. The booty is now displayed in the Historisches Museum in Bern *(see p61)*.

Built between the 11th and 14th centuries, the **Château de Grandson** rises proudly from the shore of Lake Neuchâtel. It contains a model of the battlefield and a diorama illustrating the town's history from the Middle Ages to the present day. In the basement is an automobile museum with exhibits including a white Rolls Royce that belonged to Greta Garbo and Winston Churchill's Austin Cambridge car.

Capital in the Église St-Jean-Baptiste in Grandson

♣ Château de Grandson
Place du Château. 📞 024 445 29 26. ⏰ Apr–Oct: 8:30am–6pm daily; Nov–Mar: 8:30–11am & 2–5pm Mon–Fri, 8:30am–5pm Sun. ▣

Ste-Croix ⑲

Road map B3. 🏚 4,500. 🚊 🚌
ℹ 6 Rue Neuve; 024 454 27 02.

APPROPRIATELY KNOWN as the Balcony of the Jura, the town of Ste-Croix lies at an altitude of 1,092 m (3,584 ft) and commands a wide view of the Alps, the Swiss Upland and the Jura mountains.

Since the early 19th century Ste-Croix has been the world capital of musical-box manufacture. Two local museums are devoted to this art. In the course of a guided tour of the **Musée du CIMA** (Centre International de la Méchanique d'Art) the guide sets in motion a mesmerizing assortment of musical boxes with performing acrobats, drummers and accordionists, and other figures.

🏛 Musée du CIMA
2 Rue de l'Industrie. 📞 024 454 44 77. ⏰ 1:30–6pm Tue–Sun. ▣ ▣

ENVIRONS: The **Musée Baud**, in the village of L'Auberson, 6 km (4 miles) west of Ste-Croix, has similar exhibits. The collection was created by members of the Baud family of musical-box makers.

🏛 Musée Baud
23 Grand-Rue, L'Auberson. 📞 024 454 24 84. ⏰ Jul–mid-Sep: 2–5pm daily; mid-Sep–June: 2–4pm Sat, 10am–noon & 2–6pm Sun. ▣ ▣

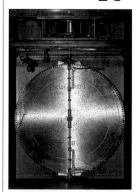

One of the musical boxes in the Musée du CIMA in Sainte-Croix

Neuchâtel

LYING ON THE WESTERN SHORE of Lake Neuchâtel, no more than about 20 km (12 miles) from the French border, Neuchâtel is a graceful town with a strikingly Gallic atmosphere. It is also notable for its pale yellow limestone buildings, which famously led the writer Alexandre Dumas to describe the town as looking as if it were carved out of butter. Neuchâtel, a university town, owes its wealth to its watchmaking and precision-engineering industries, which go back to the 18th century. The region is also renowned for its fine wines, which are celebrated each September at the Fête des Vendanges wine festival.

Église Collégiale, fronted by a statue of Guillaume Farel unveiled in 1876

Exploring Neuchâtel

Neuchâtel's graceful Old Town (Ville Ancienne) is filled with houses built of soft, yellow sandstone, and its streets have numerous fountains. While Place des Halles, the old market square, has many busy cafés, the town's smartest district lies on the lakeshore northeast of the harbour. The rampart walk around the castle walls gives you a panoramic view of the town.

♣ Château de Neuchâtel

Rue de la Collégiale.
C 032 889 60 00,
📷 Apr–Sep: 10am,
11am, noon, 2pm,
3pm, 4pm Mon–Fri,
10am, 11am, 2pm,
3pm, 4pm Sat, 2pm,
3pm, 4pm Sun. 📷

Coat of arms in the Château de Neuchâtel

For over 1,000 years, the castle of the lords of Neuchâtel has been the seat of authority. Today it houses the law courts and the cantonal government. While the west wing dates from the 12th century, the rest of the castle was built in the 15th and 17th centuries. The interior has been altered many times. Of particular interest, however, is the castle's Salle des États, the state room decorated with the coats of arms of the families who married into Neuchâtel's ruling dynasty.

♠ Église Collégiale

The early Gothic collegiate church, in a combination of Romanesque and Burgundian Gothic styles, was consecrated in 1276.

The Reformation was introduced to Neuchâtel by Guillaume Farel (1489–1565), who led the religious movement in western Switzerland, and in 1530 the church became a centre of Protestant worship.

It houses a Gothic tomb known as Le Cénotaphe. This memorial, dating from 1372, consists of life-sized figures of the counts of Neuchâtel arranged in pious poses. It is an outstanding example of medieval sculpture. The other elements of the tomb were added in the 15th century, some being taken from other churches.

During the Reformation the church's other furnishings and decoration, narrowly escaped destruction at the hands of iconoclastic zealots. The commemorative plaque in the choir proclaims that the cult of images was abolished here in 1530. In accordance with the strictures of the Reformation, Farel's tomb has no monument of any kind. Neuchâtel's great reformer is, however, commemorated by a plaque in the south aisle, and by a 19th-century statue in front of the church.

🏛 Maison des Halles

Place des Halles.
The elegant turreted Renaissance market hall dates from the 16th century. Here grain was sold on the ground floor, and cloth on the upper floor. The richly ornamented eastern wall bears the coat of arms of the Orléans-Longueville family.

The influence of French culture brought to Neuchâtel by this dynasty can be seen in the Louis XIII and Louis XIV style of many of the houses in Place des Halles and in the streets around this central square.

Place des Halles, with the turreted Maison des Halles in the background

☗ Hôtel de Ville

Rue de l'Hôtel de Ville.

The large Neo-Classical town hall stands in the eastern part of the Old Town, near the harbour. Completed in 1790, it was designed by Pierre Adrien Paris, court architect to Louis XVI.

⚏ Musée d'Art et d'Histoire

Quai Léopold-Robert. [032 717 79 25. ◯ 10am–6pm Tue–Sun. ◐

Neuchâtel's unusual and fascinating art and history museum is divided into three main sections. Devoted to art, the upper floor is crammed with paintings by 19th- and 20th-century Swiss artists, including Ferdinand Hodler and Albert Anker. There is also a collection of French Impressionist paintings.

The ground floor and the mezzanine are devoted to the history of the canton of Neuchâtel and to local decorative arts. The star attractions here are three automata that demonstrate the ingenuity and sophistication of 18th-century Swiss watchmakers.

The figures were made by Pierre Jaquet-Droz, a watchmaker of La Chaux-de-Fonds, and his son Henri-Louis between 1768 and 1774. Le Dessinateur (The Draughtsman) produces six different drawings, including a profile of Louis XV and a picture of a butterfly. La Musicienne (The Musician) is a young woman playing an organ. Her bosom heaves as she breathes, and she bends forward, sits up and plays several melodies, striking the keyboard with her fingers. The most sophisticated auto-maton is L'Écrivain (The Writer), who composes a text consisting of 40 letters, dipping his quill pen in an inkpot as he writes.

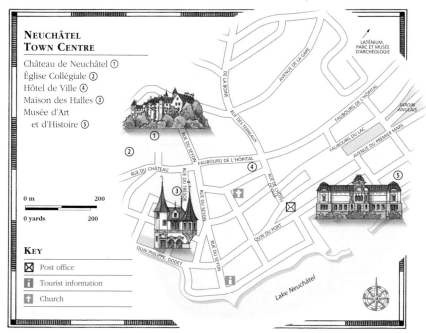

La Musicienne, in the Musée d'Art et d'Histoire

The automata are on permanent display but visitors can see each of them performing when they are put into action on the first Sunday of each month.

VISITORS' CHECKLIST

Road map B3. ⚏ *33,000.*
⚏ ⚏ ⓘ *Hôtel des Postes;*
032 889 68 90.
[W] *www.neuchateltourisme.ch*
⚏ *Fête des Vendanges*
(Grape Harvest Festival; last weekend in Sep).

⚏ Laténium, Parc et Musée d'Archéologie de Neuchâtel

Espace Paul Vouga, Hauterive, 3 km (2 miles) northeast of the town centre.

⚏ *1.* [*032 889 69 17.*
◯ *10am–5pm Tue–Sun.* ◐
[W] *www.latenium.ch*

Covering 3 hectares (7 acres), the Laténium is a large and modern museum complex that opened in 2001.

Its primary purpose is to illustrate the history of human activity and settlement in the region of Lake Neuchâtel from the end of the Ice Age to the Middle Ages. Among many fine displays, the centrepiece is the section devoted to the lakeside settlement of La Tène, which was founded by Celts in the 5th century BC. Stunning examples of Celtic metalwork and other fine objects paint a vivid picture of their lives.

NEUCHÂTEL TOWN CENTRE

Château de Neuchâtel ①
Église Collégiale ②
Hôtel de Ville ④
Maison des Halles ③
Musée d'Art
    et d'Histoire ⑤

0 m   200
0 yards   200

KEY

☒ Post office

ⓘ Tourist information

✚ Church

LATÉNIUM, PARC ET MUSÉE D'ARCHEOLOGIE

Lake Neuchâtel

Château des Monts, home of the Musée d'Horlogerie in Le Locle

Le Locle ㉑

Road map B3. 🚉 🚌 ℹ️ *31 Rue Daniel Jeanrichard; 032 931 43 30.* 🌐 www.lelocle.ch

ALTHOUGH IT HAS nothing of outstanding interest to visitors, the town of Le Locle has the distinction of being the birthplace of Swiss watchmaking. In 1705 the young watchmaker Daniel Jeanrichard arrived from Neuchâtel to settle in Le Locle, where he set up a workshop. The apprentices that he trained then established workshops of their own in La Chaux-de-Fonds, so launching the Swiss watchmaking industry.

The **Musée d'Horlogerie**, which is in a stately 18th-century mansion with beautiful interiors, presents a large collection of timepieces from around the world, as well as several elaborate automata.

ENVIRONS: About 2km (1 mile) west of Le Locle are the **Moulins Souterrains du Col-des-Roches**. In use from the 16th to the 19th centuries, these underground mills were built to harness the waters of the River Biel, whose energy was used to work machinery. Having fallen into disuse, they have now been restored and their wells and galleries are open to visitors.

🏛 Moulins Souterrains du Col-des-Roches
📞 *032 931 89 89.* 🗓 *May–Oct: 10:15am, 11:30am, 2:45pm, 4:15pm; Nov–Apr: 2:15pm & 3:45pm Tue–Thu, 2:15pm, 3:15pm, 4:15pm Sat–Sun.* 🖼

La Chaux-de-Fonds ㉒

Road map B3. 🏔 *37,800.* 🚉 🚌 ℹ️ *1 Rue Espacité; 032 919 68 95.*

IF LE LOCLE IS the birthplace of the Swiss watchmaking industry, La Chaux-de-Fonds may be regarded as its cradle. The largest town in the canton of Neuchâtel, La Chaux-de-Fonds lies in the Jura at an altitude of 1,000 m (3,280 ft). Introduced to the town in the early 18th century, watchmaking was initially a cottage industry. In time it was industrialized and La Chaux-de-Fonds became the leading centre of Swiss watchmaking. The industry reached its peak in the late 18th and 19th centuries.

After it was destroyed by a fire in 1794, the town was rebuilt to a grid pattern, with long, wide avenues. It is now dotted with several modernist buildings.

La Chaux-de-Fonds' illustrious past is celebrated in the magnificent **Musée International d'Horlogerie**. The museum's collection of some 3,000 pieces from around the world illustrates the history of timekeeping from its beginnings in antiquity to state-of-the-art instruments able to record time lapses of infinitesimal fractions of a second. In purely visual terms, many of the finest pieces on display were made in La Chaud-de-Fonds during the town's apogee. Musical,

Carillon at the Musée International d'Horlogerie, La Chaux-de-Fonds

---

A WORLD-FAMOUS INDUSTRY

The earliest watchmaking workshops in Switzerland were established in the 17th century by Huguenot refugees who had settled in Geneva. Soon after, many other workshops were set up in the Jura, most notably at La Chaux-de-Fonds. In the 19th century, innovations in precision mechanics introduced by Abraham-Louis Breguet enabled watchmaking to be industrialized, and the canton of Neuchâtel then became its leading centre. In 1967, the Centre Horloger Neuchâtelois produced the first quartz watch. This nearly led to the collapse of the Swiss watchmaking industry. Now able to mass-produce cheap watches, other countries quickly gained the largest market share. However, thanks to the inexpensive and fashionable Swatch and an image update, Switzerland regained supremacy, and now produces 95 million watches a year.

Giant pocket watch as a shop sign

astrononomical, atomic and quartz clocks are also on display. The museum has audiovisual facilities, a library and a restoration workshop for antique clocks and watches. At the entrance is a tubular steel carillon that sounds every 15 minutes.

La Chaux-de-Fonds is also the birthplace of the modernist architect Charles-Édouard Jeanneret, known as Le Corbusier (1887–1965). Before he moved to Paris in 1917, Le Corbusier built several houses here, and an itinerary taking in buildings that he designed and places associated with him is available from the town's tourist office. Only one, however, is open to visitors. This is the Villa Schwob, better known as the **Villa Turque** (Turkish Villa) because of its Islamic-style features. Built in 1916 for Anatole Schwob, a wealthy industrialist, the villa launched Le Corbusier's career.

Musée International d'Horlogerie
29 Rue des Musées. *032 967 68 61.* www.mih.ch *10am–5pm Tue–Sun.*

Villa Turque
167 Rue du Doubs. *032 912 31 47.* *1st & 3rd Sunday of the month & by appointment.*

Franches-Montagnes ㉓

Road map B2.
Saignelégier, 6 Place du 23 Juin; 032 952 19 52. *Marché-Concours (2nd weekend in Aug).*

The part of the Jura mountains that lies within the canton of Jura itself are known as the Franches-Montagnes. The area received its name in the 14th century, when the prince-bishop of Basel, who owned the territory that now constitutes the canton of Jura, granted its inhabitants a *franchise*, or exemption from taxation, so as to encourage migration to this sparsely populated region.

The Franches-Montagnes lie at an altitude of 1,000–1,100 m (3,300–3,600 ft) in the southwest of the canton of Jura. With forests, pastures and picturesque low houses, this outstandingly beautiful plateau has extensive hiking trails, and cycling and cross-country skiing routes. It is also famous for horse-breeding.

The region's principal town is **Saignelégier**. Every year, in the second week in August, it hosts the Marché Concours National des Chevaux, a horse fair and horse show that draws sellers, competitors and spectators from Switzerland and eastern France.

Portal of the church at St-Ursanne

St-Ursanne ㉔

Road map C2. *1,100.* *Place Roger-Schaffter; 032 461 37 16.* www.jura.ch/st-ursanne

A charming medieval walled town with fortified gates, St-Ursanne is set in a deep canyon washed by the River Doubs. The town grew up around the hermitage that Ursicinus, a disciple of St Columba, established here in the early 7th century.

The focal point of the town is its beautiful Romanesque and Gothic **church**. It has a fine Romanesque portal, with statues of the Virgin and St Ursicinus. There is an old stone bridge across the River Doubs, on the south side of St-Ursanne, which provides a good view of the town and its setting. The bridge features a statue of St John Nepomuk, who is the little-known patron saint of bridges.

Delémont ㉕

Road map C2. *11,500.* *9 Place de la Gare; 032 422 97 78.*

The capital of the canton of Jura, Delémont is a quiet town with a well-preserved medieval centre. From 1212 until 1792 it served as the summer residence of the prince-bishops of Basel.

Historic buildings in the old town, which has cobbled streets and fountains topped by statues, include the Château de Delémont, the prince-bishops' 18th-century mansion, the Hôtel de Ville, built in 1745 in the Baroque style, and the 18th-century Église St-Marcel, in a Rococo and Neo-Classical style. The **Musée Jurassien d'Art et d'Histoire** contains artefacts relating to local history from prehistoric times to the 18th century.

Musée Jurassien d'Art et d'Histoire
52 Rue du 23-Juin. *032 422 80 77.* *2–5pm Tue–Sun.*

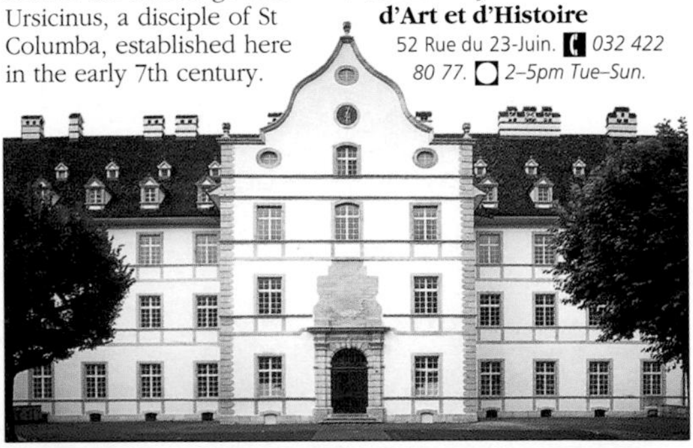

Façade of the prince-bishops' palace in Delémont

NORTHERN SWITZERLAND

B ORDERED BY THE RHINE *to the north and the Jura to the southwest, northern Switzerland is a largely Protestant, German-speaking region with a strongly industrial economy. It consists of the half-cantons of Basel-Stadt and Basel-Landschaft in the west, Aargau in the centre, and part of the canton of Zürich in the east.*

Being the most industrialized and densely populated region of Switzerland, this northern, relatively flat area is less scenic than other parts of the country. With Zürich, Switzerland's richest and most populous city, and Basel, its most industrial, northern Switzerland is noticeably less oriented towards tourism than other areas further south. However, as well as several fine historic towns, the region has an exceptionally large number of world-class museums and art galleries. It is here, in Switzerland's industrial heartland, that privately acquired wealth has been translated into some of the world's most exquisite art collections.

The Rhine marks part of Switzerland's northern border and also connects this landlocked country to the sea. Set on the Rhine, Basel is Switzerland's only port, with a direct shipping link to Rotterdam and out the North Sea.

Besides being a large industrial port, Basel is a major centre of the pharmaceuticals and chemicals industries. With the oldest university in Switzerland and the Kunstmuseum, an art gallery of international standing, Basel is also one of the country's cultural capitals.

Winterthur, another of Switzerland's major industrial centres, also has a wealth of art galleries and museums. The beautiful city of Zürich, in the east of the region, is Switzerland's financial capital and burgeoning centre of popular culture.

Baden's Old Town, on the west bank of the River Limmat

◁ **The clock on the façade of Basel's brightly painted Rathaus**

Exploring Northern Switzerland

FLANKED BY BASEL in the west and Winterthur and Zürich in the east, this region is bordered by the Rhine to the north, while to the south lies the Mittelland. Just outside the great city and port of Basel lie the extensive remains of the Roman town of Augusta Raurica. Other focal points here include the spa resort of Baden, and the attractive towns of Zofingen and Aarau, capital of Aargau. While small towns and villages dot the landscape of vineyards in the east of the region, the industrial town of Winterthur has several exceptional art galleries. The lakeside city of Zürich is the Swiss capital of finance as well as a vibrant centre of culture.

A side altar in the monastery church at Wettingen

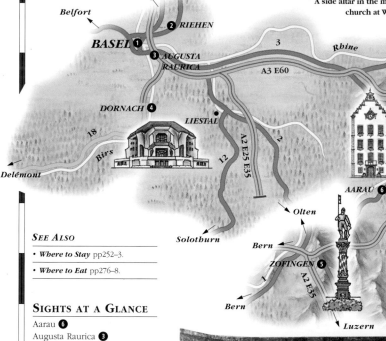

SEE ALSO

• *Where to Stay* pp252–3.

• *Where to Eat* pp276–8.

Paintings in the Reformierte Kirche in Eglisau

GETTING THERE

With international airports and rail links to the country's major towns, Basel and Zürich are the two main hubs of northern Switzerland's transport network. Motorway links from Zürich include the A1 north to Winterthur and west to Baden, and the A51 to Eglisau. From Baden, the A3 runs west as far as Basel, which is also connected to Bern and western Switzerland via the A2. The more scenic A7 follows the Rhine as far as Kaiserstuhl then turns south to Winterthur.

The Benedictine monastery in Muri

Houses in Basel's
northern district,
Kleinbasel

KEY

- Motorway
- Main road
- Scenic road
- River

Basel ❶

THE ORIGINS OF THE CITY of Basel (Bâle in French) lie in a Roman settlement, Basilia, that was established in 44 BC. Under Frankish control from the 7th century, it became part of the German empire in the early 11th century. Located at a point where the Rhine becomes navigable, it is Switzerland's only port. Basel is a major centre of commerce and industry, specializing in pharmaceuticals. The city also hosts Art Basel, the world's largest contemporary art fair, and is famous for its festivals, the largest of which are Vogel Gryff and Fasnacht, an exhuberant masked carnival.

Exploring Basel

Straddling the Rhine, Basel is divided into two districts. Grossbasel (Greater Basel), on the south bank, is the oldest part of the city. On the north bank lies Kleinbasel (Lesser Basel), a largely residential area, and the Messe, the city's great conference centre.

The Spalentor seen from Spalenvorstadt

🕎 Spalentor

This monumental Gothic gate stands on the west side of the Old Town (Altstadt), at the entrance to Spalenvorstadt, a narrow alley lined with picturesque shuttered houses. Built in 1370, the Spalentor formed part of the defensive walls that once encircled Basel. The tower consists of a pair of crenellated turrets framing a square central section, which has a pointed roof laid with glazed tiles. The gate, which has wooden doors and a portcullis, is embellished with sculptures and on its west side it bears the arms of the city.

🏛 Jüdisches Museum der Schweiz

Kornhausgasse 8. 📞 061 261 95 14. ⏰ 2–5pm Mon & Wed, 11am–5pm Sun.

Through a variety of artefacts dating back to the 13th century, including liturgical objects and items used at religious feasts, the museum illustrates Jewish religion and customs, and the history and daily life of Jewish people. It is the only Jewish museum in Switzerland.

Basel's Jewish community of 2,000 is the second-largest in the country after Geneva's. It was in Basel that the first Zionist Congress took place, in 1897.

🎓 University

Petersplatz 1.

Founded in 1460, Basel's university is the oldest in Switzerland. Among the illustrious figures with whom it is associated are the humanist Erasmus of Rotterdam (1466–1536), the physician Paracelsus (1493–1541), the mathematician Jakob Bernoulli (1654–1705), and the philosophers Friedrich Nietzsche (1844–1900) and Karl Jaspers (1883–1969).

The present university building is the Kollegienhaus, a great Modernist edifice on the east side of Petersplatz. It was completed in 1946. The entrance to the building is embellished with mosaics depicting the university's founders and the main hall has stained-glass windows.

Additional university buildings are located in Petersgraben and in other parts of the city. The university's botanical garden lies east of Petersplatz, beyond which is the university library.

Bust of the Basel poet J. P. Hebel (1760–1826)

🏛 Puppenhausmuseum

Steinenvorstadt 1. 📞 061 225 95 95. ⏰ 11am–5pm Tue–Wed, 11am–8pm Thu, 11am–5pm Fri–Sun.

With more than 6,000 items laid out on four floors, the Doll's House Museum in Basel is the largest of its kind in Europe. Most of the exhibits date from the late 19th to the early 20th centuries, although there are also some contemporary pieces. All the doll's houses and miniature shops on display are meticulously decorated and furnished. The collection also includes mechanical toys, teddy bears and other stuffed toys by leading makers.

Shuttered houses along Spalenvorstadt in the Old Town

⚜ Pharmaziehistorisches Museum Basel

Totengäslein 3. 📞 061 264 91 11. 🕐 10am–6pm Tue–Fri, 10am–5pm Sat.

Appropriately for a world centre of the pharmaceuticals industry, Basel has a museum devoted to the history of medicinal chemistry. Its collection ranges from instruments and medicines used by apothecaries through the ages to a display of traditional remedies from tribal Africa. There are also reconstructions of a pharmacy and a laboratory.

Microscope, Pharmazie-historisches Museum

♨ Marktplatz

Every weekday morning Marktplatz is filled with the stalls of a fruit, flower and vegetable market, and on public holidays it becomes the hub of Basel's great seasonal festivals. The square is lined with fine buildings, particularly those dating from late 19th to early 20th centuries. In the square stands a fountain with statues of the Virgin and saints.

Just north of Marktplatz is Mittlere Rhein-brücke. Near the bridge is a curious figure of a bearded man, the Lällekeenig (Tongue King), which has become the symbol of Basel. It is a static replica of an amusing 19th-century mechanical figure that rolled its eyes and stuck out its tongue at the inhabitants of Kleinbasel, on the north bank. The original figure is in the Historisches Museum.

♨ Rathaus

Marktplatz 9.

The main feature of Marktplatz is the eyecatching Rathaus, the Gothic town hall whose bright red façade is decorated with allegorical figures. The central arcaded section of the building dates from 1504–21. The present façade (see *illustration on p134*) has been restored so as to re-create its appearance as it was in about 1600. The tower and annexe date from the 19th century. The inner courtyard, with a Mannerist stairway, is painted with 16th-century (though heavily restored) frescoes.

Figure of Justice, a painting on the façade of the Rathaus

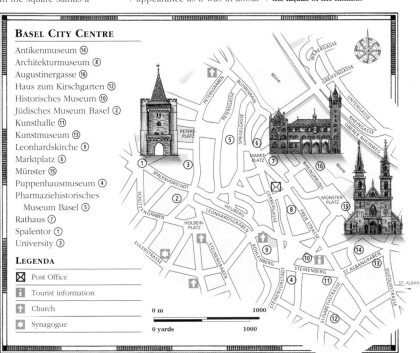

BASEL CITY CENTRE

LEGENDA

⊠ Post Office

ℹ Tourist information

✠ Church

✡ Synagogue

0 m 1000
0 yards 1000

Street-by-Street: Old Town

THE NUCLEUS OF BASEL'S medieval Old Town, or Altstadt, lines the escarpment of the south bank of the Rhine. The hub of the Old Town is Barfüsserplatz, a buzzing square lined with cafés and crossed by trams, and its major landmarks are the Münster, Basel's great Romanesque-Gothic cathedral, and the unmistakable Rathaus, the brightly painted town hall on Marktplatz. With smart shopping streets, several churches, steep alleyways and leafy courtyards, this is Basel's busiest district. However, as many streets in the Old Town are closed to motor traffic, it is a pleasant area to explore on foot.

Mittlere Rheinbrück
a stone bridge spanni the Rhine, links Grossbas on the south ban to Kleinbasel, a district on t north ban

Martinskirche
Dating from the 14h century, this is the oldest parish church in Basel.

Marktplatz has for centuries served as a market place. It is also the hub of the city's festivals.

★ Rathaus
The town hall has a brightly and elaborately painted façade and a clock surmounted by figures.

Barfüsserplatz
This square, named after the Discalced, or barefooted, Franciscans, is surrounded by buildings dating mostly from the 19th and 20th centuries.

STAR SIGHTS

★ Historisches Museum

★ Münster

★ Rathaus

KEY

- - - Suggested route

Museum der Kulturen
Basel's ethnographic museum contains an extensive collection, including some oustanding examples of Pre-Columbian sculpture.

```
0 m                    75
0 yards                75
```

Münsterplatz
The cathedral square overlies the site of a Roman camp.

Augustinergasse, a street lined with picturesque houses and mansions, runs along the excarpment on the south bank of the Rhine.

★ Münster
Basel's magnificent medieval cathedral dominates the city from an elevated terrace above the Rhine.

AUGUSTINERGASSE

MÜNSTER–PLATZ

FREIE STRASSE

RITTERGASSE

STREITGASSE

MÜNSTERGASSE

★ Historisches Museum
Housed in a former Franciscan church, the museum illustrates the history of Basel, with particular emphasis on life in the city during the Middle Ages.

Exploring Basel

WITH OVER 30 museums and art galleries, ranging from the cutting-edge Kunsthalle to the venerable Kunstmuseum, Basel is one of Switzerland's most cultured cities. East of the Old Town lies St-Alban-Vorstadt, a quiet district of medieval streets where it is pleasant to stroll. Opposite the Old Town, on the north bank of the Rhine, lies Kleinbasel, a prosperous suburb. At Basel's port (Hafen), downstream from the Old Town, an obelisk marks the point at which the Swiss, German and French borders meet.

The Tinguely Fountain, outside the Kunsthalle

🔒 Leonhardskirche
Kohlenberg. ◯ 9am–5pm Tue–Sat.
The Gothic church of St Leonard overlooks the city from its hilltop location. It stands on the site of an 11th-century church, whose Romanesque crypt survives. Following the earthquake that destroyed much of Basel in 1356, the church was rebuilt in the Gothic style. The interior features 15th- and 16th-century Gothic paintings and an exquisite rood screen of 1455. The musical instruments on display in a wing of the adjoining monastery are part of the collection of the Historisches Museum.

Emblem of Basel in the Leonhardskirche

🏛 Historisches Museum
Barfüsserplatz. 🔲 061 205 86 00.
◯ 10am–5pm Mon & Wed. 📷
Occupying the Barfüsserkirche, a former Franciscan church, this fascinating museum traces the history of Basel from Celtic times. Exhibits include wooden chests, pottery and silver-mounted vessels, Gothic, Renaissance and Baroque liturgical vessels and other items from the cathedral treasury, as well as tapestries, altarpieces and weapons. A section is devoted to Basel's trade guilds.

🏛 Kunsthalle
Steinenberg 7. 🔲 061 206 99 00. ◯ 11am–5pm Tue, 11am–8:30pm Wed, 11am–5pm Thu–Sun. 📷
Thanks to the Kunsthalle, Basel's position at the forefront of trends in modern art is well established. One of the city's most prominent cultural institutions, the Kunsthalle hosts a continuous programme of exhibitions of the work of leading contemporary artists.
The Kunsthalle is located opposite the Stadttheater, another institution at Basel's cultural hub. On the square between the two buildings stands a fountain that incorporates several of Jean Tinguely's kinetic sculptures, with moving elements.

🏛 Architekturmuseum
Steinenberg 7. 🔲 061 261 14 13.
◯ as Kunsthalle. 📷
The Kunsthalle also houses Basel's museum of architecture. Concentrating on architecture of the early 20th century onwards, the museum hosts temporary exhibitions of the work of Swiss architects, and of international architecture as well as related subjects such as architectural photography and the links between art and architecture.

🏛 Haus zum Kirschgarten
Elisabethstrasse 27–29. 🔲 061 205 86 78. ◯ 10am–5pm Tue, 10am–8pm Wed, 10am–5pm Thu–Fri, 1–5pm Sat. 📷
This Rococo mansion was built in 1775–80 as the residence of J. R. Burckhardt, the owner of a silk mill. Furnished in period style, it has now been opened as a museum illustrating patrician life in the 18th and 19th centuries. On the first and second floors there are elegantly furnished drawing rooms, a dining room, a music room and a kitchen.
The topmost floor contains a display of dolls, rocking horses and other toys. The basement is filled with a fine collection of clocks and ceramics, including Italian faience, and of porcelain made at Meissen and other major European factories.

The wide nave of the Leonhardskirche

🏛 Kunstmuseum
See pp146–7.

🏛 Antikenmuseum
St-Alban-Graben 5. **[** *061 271 22 02.* ◯ *10am–5pm Tue–Sun.* 🖼 ⅃

Basel's museum of antiquities is devoted to the four great early civilizations of the Mediterranean basin, namely those of ancient Greece, Etruria, Rome and Egypt. The display of Greek pieces includes a fine collection of vases from the Archaic to the Classical periods, marble sculpture, bronze figurines, pottery, coins and jewellery. The collections of Etruscan pottery and of Roman and Egyptian art are equally impressive.

🛉 Münster
See pp146–7.

🏛 Augustinergasse
Museum der Kulturen and **Naturhistorisches Museum.** Augustinergasse 2. **[** *061 266 55 00.* ◯ *10am–5pm Tue–Sun.* 🖼 ⅃

Augustinergasse is a picturesque alley that runs north from Münsterplatz, along the escarpment on the south side of the Rhine. As well as a Renaissance fountain with a figure of a basilisk, the street contains several fine 14th- and 15th-century houses.

The Neo-Classical building at no. 2 houses the **Museum der Kulturen** and the **Naturhistorisches Museum**. The former, a museum of anthropology, presents a collection of items from various cultures around the world. Among the finest pieces here are wooden reliefs from Tikal, the ancient Mayan site in Guatemala. The Natural History Museum contains an extensive collection of minerals, and sections devoted to palaeontology and zoology.

🏛 St Alban
Basler Papiermühle. St Alban-Tal 37. **[** *061 272 96 52.* ◯ *2–5pm Tue–Sun.* 🖼 **Museum für Gegenwartskunst.** St Alban-Rheinweg 60. **[** *061 272 81 83.* ◯ *11am–5pm Tue–Sun.* 🖼 **Plug In.** St Alban-Rheinweg 64. **[** *061 283 60 50.* ◯ *4–10pm Wed, 4–8pm Thu–Sat.*

The district of St Alban takes its name from the church of a former Benedictine monastery

The St Alban-Tor, a 13th-century gate, in the district of St Alban

founded on the outskirts of Basel in the 11th century. It is an attractive district, with a mix of old and modern buildings. The canal that runs through St Alban was used to power the monastery's mills. One of these, the **Basler Papiermühle**, now houses a museum of paper, writing and printing. Visitors can watch paper being made by hand. The **Museum für Gegenwartskunst**, in a modern building a short distance from the mill, showcases art from the 1960s to the present day. **Plug In**, another museum nearby, is devoted to modern media.

Statue in Kleinbasel

Kleinbasel
The first permanent bridge over the Rhine at Basel was built in 1226. A small fortress was then established on the

north bank, and the settlement that grew up around it became part of the city in the late 14th century. For many centuries, Kleinbasel, as the district was known, was inhabited mainly by the poorer sector of the city's population.

🏛 Museum Jean Tinguely
Paul-Sacher Anlage 1. **[** *061 681 93 20.* ◯ *11am–7pm Tue–Sun.* 🖼 ⅃

This pale pink sandstone building, designed by the Swiss architect Mario Botta, stands in Solitude Park, on the banks of the Rhine. The museum is devoted to the work of Jean Tinguely, who is famous for his kinetic sculptures. Born in Fribourg in 1925, he was educated in Basel. He settled in New York in 1960, but in 1968 returned to Switzerland, where he stayed until his death in 1991.

The nucleus of the collection consists of works by Tinguely donated by his wife, the artist Niki de St-Phalle. These, with many later gifts, bequests and purchases, trace Tinguely's artistic development.

While the mezzanine contains engine-driven contraptions that visitors can set in motion, the upper floor contains various items associated with Tinguely. The central exhibit on the ground floor is a huge sculpture, *Grosse Méta Maxi-Maxi Utopia* (1987). The museum also stages exhibitions concentrating on individual aspects of Tinguely's work.

The Museum Jean Tinguely, fronted by one of the artist's sculptures

Münster

WITH DARK RED SANDSTONE walls and a patterned roof, Basel's monumental cathedral is a conspicuous and majestic presence. The church that originally stood on the site was built in the 8th century. The present cathedral was begun in the 12th century. Partly damaged by an earthquake in 1356, it was rebuilt in the Gothic style, although elements of the earlier building were incorporated into the structure. In the 16th century, as a result of the Reformation, the cathedral was stripped of almost all its furnishings and decoration. However, some fine Romanesque and Gothic sculpture, and 14th-century frescoes in the crypt, survive. All the stained glass dates from the 19th century.

★ Crypt Paintings
The ceiling of the crypt is covered with frescoes of scenes from the life of the Virgin and the childhood of Christ. One of the finest is this Nativity scene.

Stained-glass Window
The ambulatory is lit by 19th-century stained-glass windows with medallions depicting the Nativity, the Crucifixion and the Resurrection of Christ.

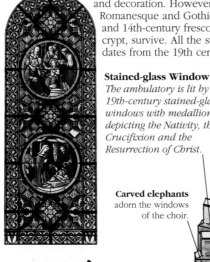

Carved elephants
adorn the windows of the choir.

Tomb of Queen Anna
Queen Anna of Habsburg, consort of Rudolf of Habsburg, died in 1281 and was entombed with her infant son, Karl. Their portraits appear on the lid of the sarcophagus.

★ Galluspforte
The magnificent Romanesque portal closing the north arm of the transept dates from about 1180. The carvings depict the judgment of St Gallus.

STAR FEATURES
★ Crypt Paintings
★ Galluspforte
★ Panel of the Apostles

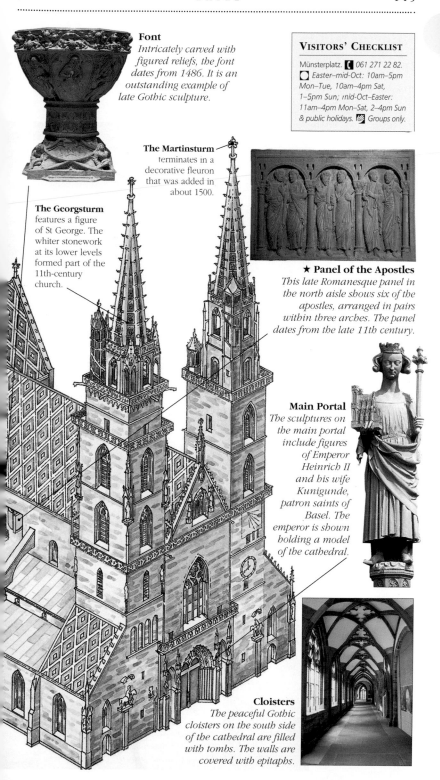

Font
Intricately carved with figured reliefs, the font dates from 1486. It is an outstanding example of late Gothic sculpture.

VISITORS' CHECKLIST

Münsterplatz. [phone] 061 271 22 82.
[symbol] Easter–mid-Oct: 10am–5pm
Mon–Tue, 10am–4pm Sat,
1–5pm Sun; mid-Oct–Easter:
11am–4pm Mon–Sat, 2–4pm Sun
& public holidays. [symbol] Groups only.

The Martinsturm
terminates in a decorative fleuron that was added in about 1500.

The Georgsturm
features a figure of St George. The whiter stonework at its lower levels formed part of the 11th-century church.

★ **Panel of the Apostles**
This late Romanesque panel in the north aisle shows six of the apostles, arranged in pairs within three arches. The panel dates from the late 11th century.

Main Portal
The sculptures on the main portal include figures of Emperor Heinrich II and his wife Kunigunde, patron saints of Basel. The emperor is shown holding a model of the cathedral.

Cloisters
The peaceful Gothic cloisters on the south side of the cathedral are filled with tombs. The walls are covered with epitaphs.

Kunstmuseum

T HE PRESTIGIOUS Kunstmuseum in Basel is one of the world's greatest art galleries, and the largest in Switzerland. Its collections fall into four main categories: 15th- and 16th-paintings and drawings, including an extensive collection of German art and the largest assemblage in the world of works by Hans Holbein the Younger; 17th-century Dutch and Flemish paintings; 19th-century Swiss, German and French paintings, with works by Delacroix, Manet, Monet and Pissarro; and 20th-century art, including works by Rousseau, Cézanne, Picasso, Dalí and Giacometti. The museum occupies a spacious building dating from the 1930s. Its courtyard is filled with sculptures, among which is Rodin's louring *Burghers of Calais.*

The Jungle
Henri Rousseau, known as Le Douanier, painted this picture in 1910, the year of his death. In the setting of a luminously painted and dreamlike forest, a man is attacked by a leopard.

GALLERY GUIDE
While the ground floor is reserved for temporary exhibitions, the galleries on the first floor are hung with works of the period 1400–1800 and 19th-century painting. The second floor is devoted to 20th-century art.

Senecio
This lyrical portrait of a boy by Paul Klee dates from 1922, and is one of several works by this artist in the gallery's collection.

Mermaids at Play
Arnold Böcklin, who was born in Basel, was one of the most important Swiss artists of the late 19th century. This work of Romantic fantasy is typical of his atmospheric yet rather sentimental style.

★ Ta Matete
The gestures of the figures in Ta Matete (The Fair), as well as the colours used in the composition, make this a powerful example of Paul Gauguin's Symbolist style. The work dates from 1892.

Main entrance

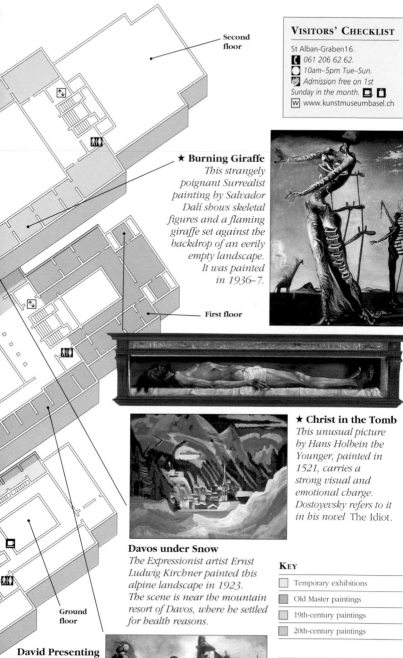

VISITORS' CHECKLIST

St Alban-Graben16.
061 206 62 62.
10am–5pm Tue–Sun.
Admission free on 1st
Sunday in the month.
www.kunstmuseumbasel.ch

Second floor

★ Burning Giraffe
This strangely poignant Surrealist painting by Salvador Dalí shows skeletal figures and a flaming giraffe set against the backdrop of an eerily empty landscape. It was painted in 1936–7.

First floor

★ Christ in the Tomb
This unusual picture by Hans Holbein the Younger, painted in 1521, carries a strong visual and emotional charge. Dostoyevsky refers to it in his novel The Idiot.

Davos under Snow
The Expressionist artist Ernst Ludwig Kirchner painted this alpine landscape in 1923. The scene is near the mountain resort of Davos, where he settled for health reasons.

KEY

☐	Temporary exhibitions
☐	Old Master paintings
☐	19th-century paintings
☐	20th-century paintings

Ground floor

David Presenting Saul with the Head of Goliath
Dating from1627, this small-scale painting of the well-known biblical story is one of Rembrandt's earlier works.

STAR EXHIBITS

★ Burning Giraffe

★ Christ in the Tomb

★ Ta Matete

Riehen ②

Road map C2. 👥 20,800. 🚉
Ⓦ www.riehen.ch

Now almost engulfed by the encroaching outskirts of Basel, the small town of Riehen is linked to the city by a tram line. This charming place, northeast of Basel's city centre, is filled with smart villas and old country houses and has much to interest visitors.

Wettsteinhaus, the residence of a 17th-century mayor, houses the **Spielzeugmuseum**. This superb toy museum contains exhibits ranging from dolls to board games. Also in the house are the **Dorfmuseum**, which documents daily life in Riehen in 1900, and the **Rebbaumuseum**, devoted to the local winemaking industry.

Riehen's largest museum is the exceptional **Fondation Beyeler**. It was set up by Hilda and Ernst Beyeler, art collectors who assembled some 200 pieces. These were put on public display in 1997, in a building designed by the Italian architect Renzo Piano. Most of the paintings in the collection date from the late 19th and 20th centuries. Among them are Impressionist paintings by Monet, works by Cézanne, Van Gogh, Picasso and Matisse, and canvases by Miró, Mondrian, Bacon, Rothko, Warhol and other major artists of the 20th century. A selection of artefacts from other parts of the world, including Africa and Oceania, complements the paintings. The foundation also stages temporary exhibitions of modern art.

🏛 **Spielzeugmuseum, Dorfmuseum & Rebbaumuseum**
Baselstrasse 34. 📞 061 641 28 29.
🕐 2–5pm Wed–Sat, 10am–5pm Sun. 📷
🏛 **Fondation Beyeler**
Baselstrasse 101. 📞 061 645 97 00.
🕐 10am–6pm Mon–Tue, 10am–8pm Wed, 10am–6pm Thu–Sun. 📷 ♿

The Goetheanum in Dornach, the world centre of anthroposophy

Augusta Raurica ③

Road map C2. 🚉 🚌 ⛴

The Roman town of Augusta Raurica lies 11 km (7 miles) southeast of Basel, at the confluence of the Ergolz and the Rhine. It was founded in 27 BC and at its height in about AD 200 it had a population of 20,000. By about AD 350, the town had been largely destroyed by the Alemani, a northern tribe.

Carefully excavated, Augusta Raurica is now a large and fascinating open-air museum. The site includes restored temples, amphitheatres, baths and sewers, as well as a forum and numerous houses.

Some of the many objects unearthed during excavations are displayed in the **Römermuseum**, in the adjacent village of Kaiseraugst. They include a hoard of silver discovered at the foot of the town's fortress. The reconstruction of a Roman house furnished with pieces found at the site illustrates daily life in the town. In the animal park, visitors can see some of the domestic animals that were kept in Roman times.

Tombstone of Dannicus in Augusta Raurica

🏛 **Römermuseum**
Giebancherstrasse 1, Kaiseraugst.
📞 061 816 22 22 🕐 Mar–Oct: 1–5pm Mon, 10am–5pm Tue–Sun; Nov–Feb: 1:30–5pm Mon, 10am–noon & 1:30–5pm Tue–Sun. 📷

Dornach ④

Road map C2. 👥 6,000. 🚉 🚌
ℹ Ⓦ www.dornach-tourismus.ch

The small town of Dornach, on the southern outskirts of Basel, is the location of the world centre of anthroposophy. Founded in about 1912 by the Austrian-born social philosopher Rudolf Steiner (1861–1925), anthroposophy holds that spiritual development, nourished by myth-making and other creative activities, is of prime importance to humanity. In the development of this philosophy, Steiner was strongly influenced by the writing of the German poet Goethe.

The **Goetheanum**, a huge concrete building overlooking Dornach, is the seat of the Universal Anthroposophical Society. Replacing the original building, which was destroyed by fire in 1922, the present Goetheanum was completed in 1928. According to the principles of anthroposophy, it has no right angles, and is regarded as being a prime example of Expressionist architecture. The interiors, completed in 1998, are decorated so as to depict anthroposophy's themes.

The centre of the building contains an auditorium with seating for 1,000 people. It is used for concerts and operas and for plays produced according to the movement's principles. The auditorium is also used for conferences on anthroposophy and for other gatherings. The Free University of Spiritual Science is also housed here.

⛩ Goetheanum
Rüttiweg 45. 📞 061 706 42 42. ○ 8:30am–6pm daily. 📷 2pm daily. ⌨

Zofingen ❺

Road map D2. 🏠 9,000. ℹ Marktgasse 10. 📞 062 745 00 05. Ⓦ www.zofingen.ch

ZOFINGEN, IN THE canton of Aargau, is a charming town whose history goes back to the 12th century. Its well-preserved old town is surrounded by a green belt laid out along the course of the former fortifications. Almost all the town's sights are clustered around three neighbouring squares, Alter Postplatz, Kirchplatz and Niklaus-Thut-Platz.

On one side of Alter Postplatz stands Alte Kanzlei, a notable Baroque building. In the centre of the square is an historic arcaded market hall that is still used as a market today. Kirchplatz (Church Square) takes its name from the Stadtkirche, a parish church built in the Romanesque style and enlarged in the 15th century, when it acquired Gothic elements, and again in the mid-17th century, when the west tower, in the Renaissance style, was added. Notable features of the church's interior are its Gothic stalls and stained-glass windows.

Fountain with the figure of a knight, in Niklaus-Thut-Platz, Zofingen

The centre of Niklaus-Thut-Platz is marked by a fountain with a statue of Arnold Winkelried, hero of the Battle of Sempach fought in 1386, when the Confederates routed the Austrians. Among the fine buildings surrounding the square are the Metzgern-Zunfthaus (butchers' guild house), dating from 1602, and the Baroque town hall, whose council chamber is furnished in the Neo-Classical style.

Aarau ❻

Road map D2. 🏠 15,500. ℹ Graben 42; 062 824 76 24. Ⓦ www.aarauinfo.ch

THE CAPITAL OF the canton of Aargau, Aarau has a scenic location on the River Aare. The old part of the town is built on terraces that rise steeply from the riverbank.

Aarau was granted the privileges of township in the 13th century. Part of Habsburg territory for many years, it passed to Bernese control in 1415. Briefly the capital of the Helvetic Republic (see p39), Aarau became the capital of Aargau in 1803. Its wealth is derived from the textiles industry.

The town's highest point is marked by Schlössli, an 11th-century castle that now houses a museum of history. Other notable buildings are the 16th-century town hall with a Romanesque tower and the Stadt-kirche, a Gothic church built in the 15th century. Some of the houses that line the narrow streets of Aarau's old districts have stepped gables and are decorated with floral motifs.

The town also has an art gallery, the **Aargauer Kunsthaus**, with a fine collection of modern paintings, and Naturama, a museum of natural history.

Decoration on a house in Aarau

🏛 Aargauer Kunsthaus
Aargauerplatz. 📞 062 835 23 30. ○ 10am–5pm Tue–Wed, 10am–8pm Thu, 10am–5pm Fri–Sun. ⌨

ENVIRONS: The small town of Lenzburg, about 10 km (6 miles) east of Aarau, has an interesting castle. A museum of local history fills some of its rooms.

The castle at Lenzburg, near Aarau

Muri ❼

Road map D2. 🏘 *6,000.*
ℹ *Marktstrasse; 056 664 70 11.*
Ⓦ *www.muri.ch*

THE SPLENDIDLY restored
Benedictine monastery in
Muri constitutes this town's
main attraction. **Kloster Muri**
was founded by Ita von
Lothringen and Count
Redebot von Habsburg in
1027 and was inhabited by a
community of monks until
1841. It then fell into
disrepair and was gutted by
fire in 1889. In 1960, after it
had been meticulously
restored, a small group of
Benedictine monks returned
to the monastery, where they
ran a hospice.

The oldest surviving parts
of the monastery's church
include its Romanesque
presbytery, crypt and
transept. Some Gothic
elements also survive. The
main body of the church,
however, is in the Baroque
style. Built to an octagonal
plan and crowned by a
dome, it dates from the
17th century. Most of the
church furnishings were
made in the late 17th and
18th centuries.

The peaceful cloisters
adjoining the church are the
burial place of the hearts of
Emperor Karl I and his wife
Zita. An exhibition of
paintings by the Swiss artist

**The twin-towered church of
Kloster Muri**

Caspar Wolf and items from
the monastery's treasury are
also on display here.

🛈 **Kloster Muri**
Church ⬜ until 8pm daily. **Museum**
⬜ May–Oct: 2–5pm daily. 🖼

Kloster Königsfelden ❽

Road map D2. 🚉 **Klosterkirche,
Windisch**. ℹ *056 441 88 33 .*
⬜ Apr–Oct: 9am–noon & 2–5pm
Tue–Sun; Nov–Mar: 10am–noon
& 2–4pm Tue–Sun. 🖼

THE FRANCISCAN abbey
of Königsfelden lies
between the quaint villages
of Brugg and Windisch. It
was founded in 1308 by
Elizabeth von Habsburg
to mark the spot where
her husband Albrecht
I was murdered
by Duke Johann
of Swabia. The
monastery was
later given to a
community of
Franciscan monks
and nuns of the Order
of St Clare. After
Elizabeth's death,
building work on
the abbey was
continued by her
daughter, Agnes
of Hungary.

During the
Reformation both of
these religious
communities were
dissolved and in
1804 the monastery
buildings were converted into
a psychiatric hospital. When
the hospital moved to new
premises later in the 19th
century, most of the
monastery buildings were
dismantled.

The church, however,
survives. Built in 1310–30,
it takes the form of a
monumental Gothic basilica
with a wooden ceiling. In the
aisles are wooden panels with
depictions of knights and
coats of arms. The eleven
large stained-glass windows
in the presbytery are some of
the finest in Switzerland.
Made between 1325 and 1330
and restored in the 1980s, the

**Baroque pulpit in the
church at Wettingen**

windows show scenes from
the lives of Christ, the Virgin,
the Apostles and the saints.

Baden ❾

See pp154–5.

Wettingen ❿

Road map D2. 🏘 *18,000.*
ℹ *Seminarstrasse 54; 056 426
22 11.* Ⓦ *www.wettingen.ch*

SET AMONG HILLS bordering
the scenic Limmat valley,
Wettingen is a small town
with a magnificent Cistercian
abbey, **Zisterzienserkloster**.
The monastery was dissolved
in 1841, and the complex
now serves as a school.
Its church and the
adjoining cloisters are
open to visitors.
The abbey
church was
founded in
1227 and was
remodelled several
times. Although the
Renaissance stalls
survive, the church's
interior is furnished
and decorated in
an extravagant
Baroque style,
with an ornate gilt
pulpit, altars and
statuary.
The Gothic cloisters,
whose arcades were glazed
in modern times,
now contain a
display of stained
glass ranging from
the 13th to the 17th centuries.

🛈 **Zisterzienserkloster**
☎ *056 437 24 10.* **Church**
⬜ Apr–Oct: 2–5pm daily. 🏞 🖼
Cloisters ⬜ Apr–Oct: 2–5pm
Sat–Sun.

Regensberg ⓫

Road map D2. 🏘 *500.*

THE ATTRACTIVE wine-growing
village of Regensberg lies
on a minor road off the highway running between Zürich
and Waldshut, via Dielsdorf.
Set on a hillside amid
vineyards, it is one of the

Half-timbered houses in the village of Regensberg

best-preserved medieval villages in Switzerland. Its main square and oldest streets are lined with half-timbered houses.

The history of Regensberg goes back to 1245. The oldest building in the town is the castle's circular crenellated keep, from the top of which there is a fine view of the vineyards and countryside around. The castle itself dates from the 16th and 17th centuries and now serves as a school for children with learning difficulties. Also of interest is the early 16th-century parish church, which overlies the foundations of a medieval building.

Kaiserstuhl ⓬

Road map D2.
W www.kaiserstuhl.ch

L YING ON A gently sloping hillside on the left bank of the Rhine, on the border with Germany, Kaiserstuhl is a beautiful small medieval town. Its historic centre, which is contained within an irregular triangle, is a listed conservation area.

The upper corner of the triangle is marked by Oberer Turm (Upper Tower), a medieval bastion that once formed part of the town's fortifications. Nearby stands the Baroque Landhaus, Zur Linde. Kaiserstuhl's historic centre also contains many beautiful old houses, most of them having shuttered windows and steeply pitched roofs. Also of interest is Mayenfisch, a Baroque mansion, and a former Augustinian monastery, whose 16th-century building now accommodates the offices of the local authorities. The parish church of St Catherine has a fine pulpit and notable stalls.

Oberer Turm, the medieval tower in Kaiserstuhl

From Kaiserstuhl, visitors can cross the bridge over the Rhine, arriving at Hohentengen, on the north bank, where there is a castle, Schloss Röteln.

ENVIRONS: The spa town of Zurzach lies about 12 km (7 miles) west of Kaiserstuhl. Of interest to visitors here is the town's historic centre, as well as museums and a castle, Schloss Zurzach, which contains a display of paintings by August Deusser. Zurzach also has two churches, the Obere Kirche, in the Gothic style, and the Verenamünster, with Romanesque and Gothic elements incorporated into later rebuilding in the Baroque style.

Eglisau ⓭

Road map E2. 🏠 *3,150*. 🚉
W www.eglisau.ch

L IKE KAISERSTUHL, Eglisau also lies on the left bank of the Rhine, on the German border. The town is surrounded by gentle hills covered in vineyards. Its origins go back to medieval times, when it was established at what was then a ford across the river, on an ancient route leading south to Zürich.

When a hydroelectric dam was built across the Rhine, the picturesque houses that once stood on the river bank were engulfed by water. Eglisau's historic covered bridge was also lost. The higher part of the old town, with its 18th-century domed church, now stands just above water level. This historic centre is filled with half-timbered houses with steeply pitched roofs. Some of the houses are decorated with colourful murals.

The belvedere behind the church offers a view of the river. Nearby, a high viaduct reminiscent of an ancient aqueduct carries a railway line past the town.

ENVIRONS: Some 10 km (6 miles) northeast of Eglisau is the small town of Rheinau. Its early 11th-century Benedictine monastery, with a fine Baroque church, is set on an island in the Rhine.

Polychrome wall painting on a house in Eglisau

Baden ⑨

ONE OF SWITZERLAND'S oldest health resorts, Baden (meaning "Baths") is a peaceful, stately town. The therapeutic properties of its hot sulphur springs, which the Romans knew as Aquae Helvetiae, have been exploited since ancient times. From the Middle Ages, Baden's location on the River Limmat contributed to its becoming an important centre of trade, and its beautiful Old Town (Altstadt) is the legacy of this historical status. Still a popular health resort with facilities for large numbers of visitors, Baden today is also a thriving industrial town, specializing in electro-mechanical engineering.

Exploring Baden

A good starting point for a stroll around Baden's Old Town is the Landvogteischloss, the castle on the east bank of the Limmat. From here, the rest of the Old Town, on the hillside to the west, is reached by crossing a wooden bridge. A short walk north along the river leads to the spa area.

🏛 Schweizer Kindermuseum

Ländliweg 7. █ 056 222 14 44. ◯ 2–5pm Wed–Sat, 10am–5pm Sun.
Housed in a mansion, this museum contains a collection of toys and everyday objects that illustrate various aspects of childhood, including children's mental development and education. Young visitors are encouraged to play with many of the exhibits.

Coat of arms on the Stadtturm

⛪ Ruine Stein

The ruins of a castle overlook the Old Town from the top of a hill, beneath which runs a road tunnel. Originating in the 10th century, the castle was rebuilt in the 13th century as an arsenal and fortress for Austrian forces, when Baden and the surrounding area were under Habsburg rule. The castle was destroyed in 1712, during conflicts between Protestant and Catholic cantons. Now surrounded by greenery, these ruins make a pleasant place for a stroll. The hilltop offers a splendid view over the River Limmat and the Old Town.

⛪ Stadtturm

This tall four-sided tower, built in the 15th century, originally guarded the entrance to the Old Town. It is set with four corner turrets and is crowned by a belfry. The tower also features a clock, and its façade is decorated with paintings.

🔒 Pfarrkirche Mariä Himmelfahrt

Kirchplatz. █ 056 222 57 15.
The Church of the Assumption, Baden's parish church, was built in the second half of the 15th century. Although it was remodelled on several occasions, acquiring Baroque features in the 17th century and Neo-Classical elements in the early 19th, it retains its original Gothic outline, and is crowned by a pointed cupola. The church treasury, with a collection of liturgical objects, is open to visitors.

The Stadthaus (town hall), north of the church, contains a beautifully restored council chamber, the Tagsatzungssaal, where Switzerland's parliament once sat. Dating from 1497, the chamber is lined with fine wood panelling and original stained-glass windows featuring the emblems of the Swiss cantons.

⛪ Holzbrücke

This picturesque wooden bridge spans the Limmat at a point just downstream from the Landvogteischloss. Built in 1810 to replace an earlier bridge, the Holzbrücke is an attractive single-span structure covered by a ridge roof *(see illustration on p135)*.

Landvogteischloss, the Gothic bailiff's castle

♜ Landvogteischloss

█ 056 222 75 74. ◯ 1–5pm Tue–Fri, 10am–5pm Sat–Sun. 🏛
The massive 15th-century Gothic castle on the east bank of the Limmat was built in the 15th century, and from 1415 to 1798 was the residence of Baden's bailiffs.

The Baroque interior of the Pfarrkirche Mariä Himmelfahrt

Rooftops of Baden's Old Town

The castle keep now houses a museum of local history. Its archaeological section includes Roman pottery, coins and other objects found in and around Baden. There are also displays of weapons, religious items, traditional costumes of the Aargau region, and a set of interiors furnished and decorated in the style of successive historical periods.

A modern wing, which extends along the riverbank, contains displays of objects relating to Baden's more recent history, focusing mainly on the town's industrial development from the 19th century onwards.

Spa area

Baden's spa centre, in a bend of the Limmat, consists of a large park with several treatment centres. The spa's 19 springs spout warm sulphur-rich waters that are especially effective in curing rheumatism and respiratory ailments.

Besides several hotels with their own thermal pools, the spa area has public pools, individual tubs, whirlpool baths, saunas, solariums, and facilities offering massage and other treatments.

Museum Langmatt

Römerstrasse 30. 056 222 58 42.
Apr–Oct: 2–5pm Tue–Fri, 11am–5pm Sat–Sun.

On Römerstrasse, a short walk westwards from the spa area, stands a charming villa that once belonged to the art connoisseur Sidney Brown (1865–1941). Designed by Karl Moser, the villa was built in 1900–01. A few years later it was extended by the addition of a wing which, like the house itself, contains an exquisite art collection.

The nucleus of the collection consists of French Impressionist paintings, with works by Corot, Monet, Pissarro, Renoir, Sisley, Degas and Cézanne. The collection also includes and 18th-century Venetian town scapes, and other examples of French art, including several works by Fragonard and Watteau and paintings by Van Gogh and Gauguin. Some of the rooms contain 17th- and 18th-century French furniture.

VISITORS' CHECKLIST

Road map D2. 15,000.
Bahnhofplatz 1; 056 210 91 91.
www.welcome.baden.ch

Fountain in the gardens around the Museum Langmatt

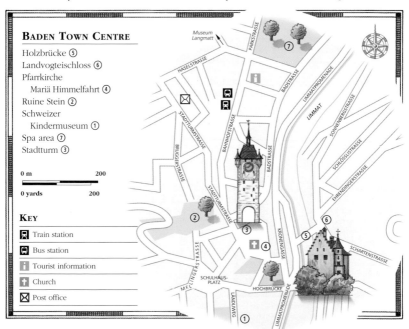

BADEN TOWN CENTRE

Holzbrücke ⑤
Landvogteischloss ⑥
Pfarrkirche
    Mariä Himmelfahrt ④
Ruine Stein ②
Schweizer
    Kindermuseum ①
Spa area ⑦
Stadtturm ③

0 m   200
0 yards   200

KEY

Train station
Bus station
Tourist information
Church
Post office

Winterthur ⑭

A THRIVING INDUSTRIAL centre now associated chiefly with textiles and mechanical engineering, Winterthur is the canton of Zürich's second-largest town after Zürich itself. Despite its industrial character, Winterthur is a pleasant town, with many leafy streets and open green spaces. It also has several outstanding art galleries, the most celebrated of which contain paintings donated by Oskar Reinhart (1885–1965), a native of Winterthur who became a wealthy industrialist and one of Europe's greatest art collectors.

Marktgasse, the main street in Winterthur's Old Town

Exploring Winterthur
Free of motorized traffic, Winterthur's old town centre is pleasant to explore on foot. A Museumbus circles the town every hour, stopping at each of Winterthur's principal museums and art galleries.

🛈 Stadtkirche
◻ *10am–4pm daily.*
This Gothic parish church, which was built on the site of an 8th-century shrine, dates from the mid-13th century and was extended several times until the 16th century. It takes the form of a vaulted basilica with a square apse flanked by Baroque towers. Decorative features of the interior include an organ screen, a font, which dates from 1656, wall paintings and fine 19th-century stained-glass windows.

Stained-glass window in the Stadtkirche

🏛 Kunsthalle Winterthur
Marktgasse 25. **☎** *052 267 51 32.*
◻ *2–5pm Tue–Fri, 10am–noon & 2–4pm Sat, 2–4pm Sun.*
The former Waaghaus (Weigh House) has been converted into a spacious exhibition hall, the Kunstalle Winterthur, which organizes temporary shows of modern art. Marktgasse, the Old Town's pedestrianized main artery and its principal shopping street, is lined with several other fine historic buildings. Among the oldest and most attractive is Zur Geduld (Patience House), which dates from 1717.

🏛 Rathaus
Marktgasse 20. **☎** *052 267 51 26.*
◻ *2–5pm Tue–Sat, 10am–noon & 2–5pm Sun.*
Winterthur's Neo-Classical town hall was built in 1782–4 on the site of a former Gothic structure. In 1878, the ground floor was converted into a shopping arcade. The upper floors, however, have remained intact.

The rooms here include a stucco-decorated Festsaal, and former residential quarters and offices that now contain two museums. On the first floor is the private collection of paintings amassed by Jakob Briner and consisting mainly of 17th-century Dutch Old Masters. On the floor above is a collection of miniatures donated by E.S. Kern.

Detail on the façade of the Rathaus

🏛 Museum Oskar Reinhart am Stadtgarten
Stadthausstrasse 6. **☎** *052 267 51 72.* ◻ *10am–8pm Tue, 10am–5pm Wed–Sun.*
Oskar Reinhart amassed one of the greatest private art collections of the 20th century. He donated part of his collection to the town in 1951, and the rest was bequeathed to Winterthur after his death.

The collection on display in the Stadtgarten includes works by such major artists as Holbein, Grünewald, Cranach, Poussin, El Greco, Chardin and Goya. It also includes works by German, Austrian and Swiss artists of the late 18th to the early 20th centuries. These range from German Romantic painting to portraits of children. The Swiss artists Albert Anker, Ferdinand Hodler and Giovanni Giacometti are well represented. The bulk of Oskar Reinhart's collection is, however, exhibited at Römerholz, his villa on the edge of the town.

🏛 Sammlung Oskar Reinhart am Römerholz
Haldenstrasse 95. **☎** *052 269 27 40.*
◻ *10am–5pm Tue–Sun.*
The villa where Oskar Reinhart lived from 1926 until his death contains about 200 works of art from his collection. Most of these are French Impressionist paintings, with stunning canvases by Manet, Degas, Renoir and Monet.

The main entrance to the Kunstmuseum

🏛 Kunstmuseum

Museumstrasse 52. 📞 *052 267 51 62* ⭕ *10am–8pm Tue, 10am–5pm Wed–Sun.* 🎨

An excellent collection of 19th-and 20th-century paintings by an international span of artists fills the rooms of the Kunstmuseum.

Exhibits include paintings by Monet and Van Gogh, and Cubist works, including paintings by Picasso, as well as Surrealist works. Important painters and sculptors, such as Rodin, Hodler, Miró, Brancusi, Mondrian, Kandinsky and Alberto Giacometti are also well represented.

The building also houses a natural history museum and a museum that is designed specifically for children.

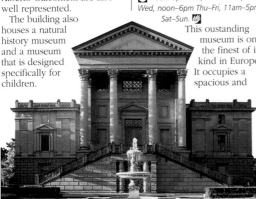

🎭 Stadthaus

Stadthausstrasse 4a.
The imposing Neo-Renaissance Stadthaus houses the town's main concert hall. Built in 1865–9, it was designed by Gottfried Semper, a professor of architecture at Zürich's Technical University. Semper also designed Dresden's opera house. The Stadthaus in Winterthur is considered to be one of Gottfried Semper's finest buildings.

🏛 Fotomuseum

Grüzenstrasse 44. 📞 *052 233 60 86* ⭕ *noon–6pm Tue, noon–7:30pm Wed, noon–6pm Thu–Fri, 11am–5pm Sat–Sun.* 🎨

This oustanding museum is one the finest of its kind in Europe. It occupies a spacious and

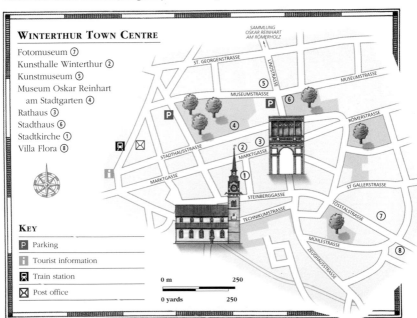

The Neo-Renaissance Stadthaus, designed by Gottfried Semper

well restored warehouse about ten minutes' walk from the town centre. On view here is a comprehensive range of photographs, from the early beginnings of photography to the most recent examples of the art, by an international span of photographers. The museum also stages a programme of world-class exhibitions.

🏛 Villa Flora

Tösstalstrasse 44. 📞 *052 212 99 66.* ⭕ *2–5pm Tue–Sat, 11am–3pm Sun.* 🎨

Post-Impressionist paintings collected by Hedy and Arthur Hahnloser-Bühler between 1907 and 1932 hang in the rooms of this mid-19th-century villa. Among them are fine examples of the work of the Nabis, including Bonnard and Vuillard, and of the Fauves, including Matisse and Rouault.

WINTERTHUR TOWN CENTRE

Fotomuseum ⑦
Kunsthalle Winterthur ②
Kunstmuseum ⑤
Museum Oskar Reinhart
    am Stadtgarten ④
Rathaus ③
Stadthaus ⑥
Stadtkirche ①
Villa Flora ⑧

KEY

🅿 Parking

ℹ Tourist information

🚉 Train station

⊠ Post office

0 m   250

0 yards   250

ZÜRICH

AN INTERNATIONAL CENTRE *of banking and industry, Zürich is Switzerland's capital of finance and its richest city. Zürich's exuberant popular culture and vibrant arts scene also make it one of the liveliest cities in Europe. With a lakeshore setting and elegant quays, Zürich is a beautiful city, and the cobbled streets and squares of its historic centre are lined with many fine buildings.*

Capital of the densely populated canton of the same name, the city of Zürich lies on the north shore of the Zürichsee at the point where the River Limmat flows north out of the lake. By the 1st century BC, a Celtic settlement, Turicum, had been established on the Lindenhof. This hill, now in the heart of the old city, was later the site of a Roman fortress. In the 9th century, a Carolingian palace was built on the Lindenhof, and a trading settlement developed at its base. Briefly under the control of the Zähringen dynasty, Zürich passed to the Holy Roman Empire in 1218 and joined the Swiss Confederation in 1351.

By the early Middle Ages, the silk, wool, linen and leather trade had already brought Zürich's merchants great wealth. However, having become too powerful, this merchant class was overthrown and replaced by guilds, who in turn held power until the late 18th century.

In the 16th century, mainly because of the activities of Ulrich Zwingli, who preached from the Grossmünster, the city's great cathedral, Zürich embraced the Reformation. Becoming rich and influential, the city then reached its apogee, only to fall into relative obscurity in the 17th and 18th centuries. In the 19th century, Zürich underwent rapid industrial growth and, thanks to Switzerland's stability and neutrality, emerged from the aftermath of both world wars as a major centre of finance. Zürich enjoys a prestigious position in international banking. It is the base of the world's largest gold market and its stock exchange is one of the most important in the world.

Zürich seen from the tower of the Grossmünster, with St Peters Kirche on the left

◁ **Monument on Bahnhofplatz to Alfred Escher, reviver of Zürich's economy in the 19th century**

Exploring Zürich

SPANNED BY ELEGANT low bridges, the Limmat bisects
the city as it flows north out of the Zürichsee. On
the west bank is the Old Town (Altstadt), Zürich's
medieval heart, dominated by the Fraumünster and
St Peters Kirche. While the Old Town is now the
city's commercial centre, Bahnhofstrasse, which
follows the western course of the former city
walls, is its smartest shopping street. On the east
bank, where the Grossmünster is the principal
landmark, lie the historic districts of Niederdorf
and, south of Marktgasse, Oberdorf. A pleasant
walk south along Utoquai leads to Zürichhorn Park, the city's largest green space.

**Relief depicting a Bacchic procession, at the
Johann Jacobs Museum in Zürichhorn Park**

SIGHTS AT A GLANCE

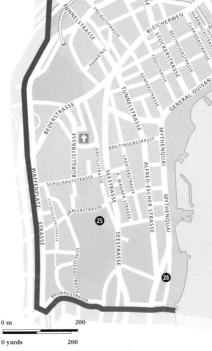

0 m   200

0 yards   200

The Münsterbrücke, spanning the Limmat in Zürich

GETTING THERE

Zürich's international airport lies 11 km (7 miles) north of the city centre, just ten minutes away by rail. Zürich also has many rail links with towns and cities all over Switzerland and Europe. Roads into Zürich include the A52 from the southeast, the A3 from the southwest and the N1 from the north and east.

The Hauptbahnhof, Zürich's main station

SEE ALSO

- **Where to Stay** pp253–5.
- **Where to Eat** pp278–80.

KEY

🛈	Tourist information
✝	Church
⊠	Post office
🚇	Train station

Schweizerisches Landesmuseum ❶

THE VAST COLLECTIONS of the Swiss National Museum illustrate the country's history and culture from prehistoric times to the present day. The museum has outposts at several locations around the country but its headquarters, and the largest repository of its collections, are in Zürich. Highlights here include artefacts from Switzerland's rich archaeological past, and a section devoted to the Middle Ages. Other displays illustrate the impact of the Reformation on Swiss culture. There are also reconstructions of period interiors, displays of costume, and models showing aspects of Swiss life, such as weaving, watchmaking and commerce.

Army Uniform
Uniforms like this one, of about 1720, were worn by Louis XIV's Swiss bodyguards. From the 15th century Swiss mercenaries served as royal bodyguards at many European courts.

Battle of Murten
In this panorama hundreds of toy soldiers re-enact the Battle of Murten of 1476, when Charles the Bold, Duke of Burgundy, laid siege to Murten but was routed by Bernese forces.

GALLERY GUIDE
Laid out in chronological order, the collections on the ground and first floors cover a timespan from the Neolithic period to modern times. On the second floor are a collection of costumes and a series of reconstructed rooms. The third floor contains a collection of toys and a display of costumes. The basement is devoted to farming life.

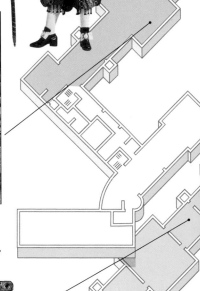

Ground floor

Main entrance

Processional Crucifix
A masterpiece of the enameller's art, this magnificent Romanesque crucifix was made in Limoges, France, in about 1200.

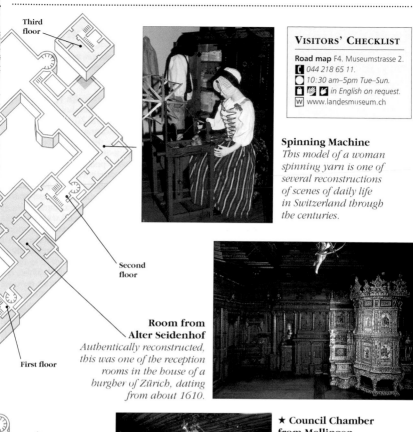

Third floor

Second floor

First floor

Basement

VISITORS' CHECKLIST

Road map F4. Museumstrasse 2.
044 218 65 11.
10:30 am–5pm Tue–Sun.
in English on request.
www.landesmuseum.ch

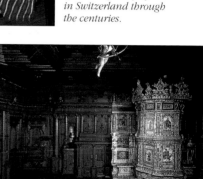

Spinning Machine
This model of a woman spinning yarn is one of several reconstructions of scenes of daily life in Switzerland through the centuries.

Room from Alter Seidenhof
Authentically reconstructed, this was one of the reception rooms in the house of a burgher of Zürich, dating from about 1610.

★ Council Chamber from Mellingen
Beautiful Gothic panelling and woodcarvings dating from 1467 decorate the council chamber of Mellingen's town hall, reconstructed here.

KEY

☐	Middle Ages
☐	Renaissance and Baroque
☐	Daily life, costumes and toys
☐	19th and 20th centuries
☐	Agricultural life
☐	Temporary exhibitions

★ Abbey Pharmacy
Dating from the second quarter of the 18th century, this well-preserved pharmacy from the Benedictine abbey in Muri is one of the museum's most remarkable exhibits.

STAR EXHIBITS

★ **Abbey Pharmacy**

★ **Council Chamber from Mellingen**

Universität ⑰

Rämistrasse 71. **Archäologische Sammlung** Rämistrasse 73.
☎ 044 634 28 11. ◯ 1–6pm Tue–Fri, 11am–5pm Sat–Sun.

Set on a hillside east of Niederdorf, Zürich's university buildings overlook the city. Athough the present complex dates from 1911–14, the university was founded in 1833. It is now the largest in Switzerland, and is a prominent centre of research and higher education.

The university's collection of archaeological artefacts (**Archäologische Sammlung**) is displayed in the adjoining building. It contains some fine Egyptian, Etruscan and Mesopotamian pieces.

Technische Hochschule ⑱

Rämistrasse 101. **Graphische Sammlung der ETH** ☎ 044 632 40 46. ◯ 10am–5pm Mon–Tue, 10am–7pm Wed, 10am–5pm Thu–Fri. **Thomas-Mann-Archiv** Schönberggasse 15. ☎ 044 632 40 45. ◯ 2–4pm Wed & Sat.

The federal institute of Technology, or ETH, was founded in 1835 and is now one of the most highly regarded technical colleges in Europe. It occupies a Neo-Renaissance building designed by Gottfried Semper, a prominent German architect who was also the institute's first professor of architecture.

While the building is of architectural interest in its own right, it is also worth a visit for its collection of drawings and graphic art (**Graphische Sammlung**) and for the temporary exhibitions that often fill its corridors. The ETH also owns the **Thomas-Mann-Archiv**, in a building nearby. The archive is the entire literary legacy of this great German writer, who died in Zürich in 1955.

The terrace of the ETH building commands a magnificent view of the city. Just to the north of the ETH is the

Le Corbusier Haus, near Zürichhorn Park

upper station of the Polybahn, a funicular that runs down to Central, a large square on the east side of the Bahnhofbrücke.

Kunsthaus ⑲

See pp170–71.

Opernhaus ⑳

Falkenstrasse 1. ☎ 044 268 64 00.

Zürich's neo-baroque opera house was designed by the Viennese architects Hermann Helmer and Ferdinand Fellner and completed in 1891 *(see illustration on p172)*. The elegant façade is fronted by two tiers of columns and a balcony framed by porticoes. Allegorical statues crown the roof. One of the city's most prestigious cultural venues, the Opernhaus stages a world-class programme of operas and ballets.

Statues on the façade of the Opernhaus

Zürichhorn Park ㉑

Chinagarten ◯ Mar–Oct: 11am–7pm daily. ⚑ **Atelier Hermann Haller** Höschgasse 6. ☎ 044 383 42 47. ◯ Jul–Sep: noon–6pm Wed–Sun. **Le Corbusier Haus** Höschgasse 8. ☎ 044 383 64 70. ◯ Jun–Sep: 2–5pm Sat–Sun. ⚑ **Johann Jacobs Museum** Seefeldquai 17. ☎ 044 388 61 51. ◯ 2–7pm Fri, 2–5pm Sat, 10am–5pm Sun.

This pleasant park to the south of the city centre stretches out beyond Utoquai, along the east shore of the Zürichsee and around the Zürichhorn, a promontory. The park contains sculptures by well-known modern artists. At the northern end stands a stone sculpture by Henry Moore, and at the southern end a large kinetic sculpture that Jean Tinguely created for Expo 64 in Lausanne. The piece is entitled *Heureka*, and from April to October at 11.15am and 5.15pm every day its mechanism is set in motion.

In the eastern part of the park high walls enclose the **Chinagarten**. This Chinese garden, laid out in 1994, was a gift from Kunming, the Chinese city that is twinned with Zürich. It is filled with plants and small ornaments typical of the Chinese art of creating a formal garden *(see illustration on p173)*.

The park is bordered by several interesting buildings. On Höschgasse is the **Atelier Hermann Haller**, the studio of this Swiss sculptor. Designed by Haller (1880–1950), it is a rare example of wooden Bauhaus architecture. The colourful pavilion next to it is **Le Corbusier Haus**. Designed by Le Corbusier, it is one of the last projects that this Swiss-born architect worked on before his death in 1965. The building contains a museum of graphic art.

The **Johann Jacobs Museum**, at the junction of Kausstrasse and Seefeldquai, documents the social history of coffee in Europe. Exhibits include paintings and drawings, and porcelain and silver vessels made for the enjoyment of this prized beverage.

Museum Bellerive ②

Höschgasse 3. 🕻 044 383 43 76. ◯ 10am–8pm Tue–Thu, 10am–5pm Fri, 11am–5pm Sat–Sun.

SPECIALIZING IN THE applied arts, as well as in design, decoration and crafts, the Museum Bellerive displays its permanent collection in the form of a continuous programme of temporary exhibitions. The museum's extensive holdings include furniture, tapestry, jewellery, stained glass and other pieces produced by the English Arts and Crafts Movement in the late 19th century, and Art Nouveau glass, jewellery and ceramics. The work of Swiss craftsmen and designers also figures prominently in the museum's collections.

Sammlung E.G. Bührle ②

Zollikerstrasse 172. 🕻 044 422 00 86. ◯ 2–5pm Tue, 5–8pm Wed, 2–5pm Fri & Sun.

Sculpture by Henry Moore in Zürichhorn Park

A SMALL BUT exquisite collection of Impressionist and Post-Impressionist paintings and other works of art is on public display in a mansion south of Zürichhorn Park. The collection was formed by the Swiss industrialist Emil G. Bührle between 1934 and 1956 and was opened to the public after his death in 1965. Besides paintings by Delacroix, Courbet and Corot, the collection includes little-known works by Monet, Degas, Van Gogh and Gauguin, as well as Dutch and Italian Baroque painting and fine Gothic woodcarving.

Zürichsee ②

Zürichsee Schifffahrtgesellschaft Mythenquai 333. 🕻 044 487 13 33.

THIS BEAUTIFUL glacial lake stretches in a 40-km (25-mile) arc from Zürich to the foot of the Glarner Alps. The many boat trips departing from Zürich range from short trips to cruises of half a day, taking in several lakeshore towns and villages. The main landing stage in Zürich is at Bürkliplatz. Being unpolluted, the lake's clear waters are also safe for swimming.

Museum Rietberg ②

Gablerstrasse 15. 🕻 044 206 31 31. **Villa Wesendonck** ◯ 10am–5pm Tue, 10am–8pm Wed, 10am–5pm Thu–Sun. **Park-Villa Rieter** ◯ 1–5pm Tue–Sat, 10am–5pm Sun.  single charge for both villas.

THE VAST ASSEMBLAGE of ethnographic pieces and Oriental artefacts that make up the collections of this museum are displayed in two villas set in parkland on the west side of the Zürichsee. **Villa Wesendonck**, a Neo-Renaissance mansion in which the composer Richard Wagner once stayed, houses the main collection. This consists of wooden, bronze and ceramic objects from Africa, India, China, Japan and other Southeast Asian countries. The neighbouring **Park-Villa Rieter** is devoted to Asian art. Two floors of the house are filled with changing selections of Indian, Chinese and Japanese prints and paintings.

Städtische Sukkulentensammlung ②

Mythenquai 88. 🕻 044 344 34 80. ◯ 9–11:30am & 1:30–4:30pm daily.

WITH MORE THAN 8,000 species of cacti, spurges, agaves, aloes and other succulents, this collection is one of the largest of its kind in Europe. Succulents from every arid region of the world, from giant agaves to the tiniest cacti, are presented here in a fascinating display.

The Zürichsee, with Bürkliplatz in the left foreground and the Grössmunster in the right background

Kunsthaus ⑲

SWITZERLAND'S GREATEST art gallery, the Kunsthaus contains important works of art ranging from medieval religious paintings and Dutch Old Masters to Impressionist and Post-Impressionist paintings. The gallery's holdings also exemplify the major art movements of the 20th century. Highlights of this superb collection include paintings by the 19th-century Swiss artists Ferdinand Hodler and Albert Anker, the largest assemblage of the work of Edvard Munch outside Scandinavia, paintings by Marc Chagall and paintings and sculpture by Alberto Giacometti. The Kunsthaus also stages large-scale temporary exhibitions.

Au-dessus de Paris
The poetic imagery of Marc Chagall's paintings was inspired by his Russian Jewish origins. Floating figures, like those in this 1968 painting, are a recurring theme in his work.

Second floor

The Entire City
A leading Dadaist and Surrealist painter, Max Ernst created many scenes with an eerie, dreamlike quality. This painting dates from 1935–6.

First floor

Falstaff in a Laundry Basket
Many paintings by the Swiss artist Henri Füssli were inspired by literature. This one, dating from 1792, illustrates a scene from Shakespeare's play The Merry Wives of Windsor.

Ground floor

War
In this dramatic painting dating from 1896, Arnold Böcklin depicted war as one of the terrifying Horsemen of the Apocalypse.

Main entrance

Bird in Space
This elegant sculpture, created by Constantin Brancusi in 1925, is an abstract synthesis of the movement and apparent weightlessness of a bird in flight. Ovoid shapes typify Brancusi's mature work.

VISITORS' CHECKLIST

Heimplatz 1. ☎ 044 253 84 84.
🕐 10am–9pm Tue–Thu,
10am–5pm Fri–Sun. 🎟
Admission free on Wed.
🔲 www.kunsthaus.ch

Guitar on a Pedestal Table
Like this painting of 1915, many works from Pablo Picasso's Cubist period feature a guitar.

★ Cabanes Blanches
Some of Vincent van Gogh's most powerful and richly expressive paintings are the views of the Provençal countryside that he painted in the final years of his tortured life.

★ The Holy Family
This tender painting by Peter Paul Rubens, dating from c. 1630, is one of the most important pieces in the museum's collection of Flemish Baroque works.

Large Can of Campbell's Soup
Andy Warhol's arrestingly realistic depictions of cans of Campbell's soup and other seemingly mundane objects made him the leading exponent of Pop Art during the 1960s. This painting dates from 1962.

GALLERY GUIDE
After renovation, which is due to be completed in 2005, the collections in the Kunsthaus will be rearranged.

STAR EXHIBITS

★ Cabanes Blanches

★ The Holy Family

ENTERTAINMENT IN ZÜRICH

THE MOST VIBRANT of all Swiss cities, Zürich enjoys an extremely active, innovative and multifaceted cultural life. While the Schauspielhaus offers some of the best productions in German theatre, Zürich has its own symphony and chamber orchestras, and prestigious programmes of opera, ballet and classical music take place in the Opernhaus and Tonhalle, the main concert hall. Zürich's club scene, which is concentrated in the district of Zürich West and the Industrie-Quartier, has also burgeoned, and its nightclubs are among the liveliest of any European city. With art-house cinemas, small theatres, cutting-edge art galleries and a population of artists and musicians, Zürich West has become the hub of a lively underground culture. Boisterous street festivals with parades and music are also part of Zürich's cultural life.

The Opernhaus, Zürich's main venue for ballet and opera

INFORMATION/TICKETS

MAINSTREAM CULTURAL events taking place in Zürich are listed in several publications. *Zürich News*, a fortnightly publication with information in English and German, is available free from the tourist office and from the reception desks of most hotels. *Züritipp*, in German, appears as a supplement to the Friday edition of *Tages Anzeiger*, the daily newspaper, and is also available from the tourist office. *City Guide Zürich*, published quarterly by **Zürich Tourism**, is obtainable from the tourist office and can also be picked up at various points in the city.

While tickets for the theatre and opera and for classical concerts can be bought from the tourist office, tickets for almost all events can be bought from **Ticket Corner** or from **Billetzentrale**. Tickets can, of course, be purchased directly at the box offices of individual venues.

THEATRE, OPERA AND CLASSICAL MUSIC

HAVING NO FEWER than a dozen theatres, Zürich is a leading centre of the dramatic arts. Almost all productions are in German. Zürich's main theatre is the **Schauspielhaus**, which is known for its innovative productions. This theatre has two stages: the Schauspielhaus Pfauen, used for mainstream plays, and the Keller, where experimental theatre is staged.

Other productions are staged in the main auditorium (Halle) of the **Schauspielhaus Schiffbau**, in a former shipyard building in the newly fashionable district of Zürich West. The Schiffbau also has a studio stage.

The **Opernhaus** is one of Europe's leading opera and ballet theatres. As tickets for its highly regarded productions sell out rapidly, booking well in advance is usually necessary. Returns are, however, sometimes available.

The Tonhalle Orchestra and Zürich Chamber Orchestra both perform regularly at the **Tonhalle**. This grand Baroque building, completed in 1895, is renowned for its excellent acoustics. Its inaugural concert, in 1895, was given in the presence of the composer Johannes Brahms.

Music festival in the courtyard of the Schweizerisches Landesmuseum

Tickets for concerts at the Tonhalle are rarely available unless you can book well in advance. This is, however, less likely to apply to organ recitals and concerts of choral and chamber music given in many of Zürich's churches.

Participants in the August Street Parade

The Chinagarten, venue for open-air film screenings in summer

and disco, house and techno music, and **Kaufleuten**, with house and garage music. While **Rohstofflager** employs internationally known DJs, **Labor Bar**, with retro decor, offers the full range of musical styles. **Labyrinth**, meanwhile, is a focal point of Zürich's gay scene, although it also attracts a heterosexual clientele.

CINEMAS

MOST FILMS SCREENED in Zürich's many cinemas are shown in their original language. The initials E/d/f in listings and on posters indicate that a film is shown in English with German and French subtitles.

Large multi-screen complexes such as the **Cinemax** and **Kino Corso** screen international blockbusters and the latest releases. **Kino Arthouse Alba** and **Xenix**, by contrast, specialize in non-commercial productions. **Riff-Raff**, in Zürich West, is a four-screen cinema complex with a bistro and bar.

Most cinemas offer cheaper tickets on Mondays.

NIGHTCLUBS

ZÜRICH'S NIGHTCLUBS range from upmarket venues in the city centre to the more relaxed and innovative establishments concentrated in Zürich West. Among the smartest clubs are **Adagio**, with a medieval-style decor and jazz and rock, **Indochine**, with a Southeast Asian theme

Gun in a courtyard of the Schweizerisches Landesmusem

LIVE MUSIC

THE TOP LIVE MUSIC venue in Zürich is **Rote Fabrik**, an arts complex near the lakeshore in the city's southwestern suburbs. As well as staging concerts by international bands, Rote Fabrik is also an arts complex with facilities for film and theatre, and it has a bar and restaurant

Moods, which shares the Schiffbau building with Schauspielhaus Schiffbau, is the city's foremost jazz venue, with international and local performers providing a continuous programme of all styles of jazz.

SHOPPING IN ZÜRICH

BAHNHOFSTRASSE, which runs north to south from Zürich's train station, is reputed to be one of the most expensive shopping streets in the world. It is lined with smart boutiques, the windows of which are filled with glittering displays of the best watches and jewellery, as well as furs, porcelain, leather goods and other luxury items. However, Zürich also has an abundance of shops

The multifunctional Swiss army knife

offering a great variety of high-quality items that are at more affordable prices. This city is one of the best places to buy souvenirs such as excellent handcrafted work, as well as delicacies including Swiss cheeses and chocolates. Along the narrow streets in the Old Town, on the west bank of the Limmat, and the cobbled alleys of Niederdorf, on the east bank, interesting antique and souvenir shops can be found.

A souvenir stall with a range of handcrafted items

OPENING HOURS

MOST SHOPS in central Zürich are open from 9am to 6pm Monday to Saturday, with late closing on Thursday and earlier closing on Saturday. While some shops close on Mondays, many of those on Bahnhofstrasse are open on Sundays.

WATCHES AND JEWELLERY

EXPENSIVE watches by prestigious makers such as Patek Philippe and Rolex and fine jewellery by such internationally renowned designers as Cartier can be found in the upmarket shops that line Bahnhofstrasse. **Gübelin** and **Bucherer** both have branches here, as does **Swatch Store**, which offers a good range of Swiss-made though less expensive timepieces.

HANDCRAFTED ITEMS AND SOUVENIRS

ONE OF THE best outlets for high-quality handmade Swiss craft items, such as decorative glass, jewellery and ceramics, as well as Swiss designer clothing, is **Schweizer Heimatwerk**, which has several branches in the city and another at Zürich airport. **Dolmetsch**, on Bahnhofstrasse, stocks a large selection of penknives, watches and other Swiss-made items. The Schipfe district, along the River Limmat, has

A souvenir shop, with Swiss specialities

many handicraft shops. Other specialist handicraft shops can be found in the Niederdorf district and along Langstrasse.

LEATHER GOODS

MOST OF Zürich's high-class leather-goods shops are on Bahnhofstrasse. Among them are **Varesino**, which offers shoes, belts, briefcases, handbags and wallets. Another excellent leather shop is **Lederladen**, on Schipfe, which has a fine stock of handmade items.

BOOKSHOPS

AN EXTENSIVE RANGE of books in English is stocked by the **English Bookshop**, part of the Orell Füssli chain, on Bahnhofstrasse. The **Travel Bookshop**, on Rindermarkt, also stocks travel books in English, as well as maps and alpine trekking and mountaineering guides.
The upper area of the Niederdorf district contains many antiquarian bookshops, several specializing in particular subjects and many carrying selections of books in English.

ANTIQUES

THE STREETS of Zürich's Old Town contain many interesting antique shops. **Art of Living**, on Siehlstrasse, has a fine selection of decorative pieces, such as glassware and mirrors. **Greenwich**, on Rämistrasse, stocks antique watches.

Jelmoli, one of Zürich's leading department stores, on Seidengasse

CHOCOLATE

SHOPS OFFERING Switzerland's famous brands of chocolate abound in Zürich. A particularly pleasant place to sample and buy Swiss chocolate is the branch of **Confiserie Sprüngli** on Paradeplatz, where the shop also has a famous café. Other high-quality *chocolatiers* can be found in Hauptbahnhof and at Zürich airport.

Café Schober, on Napfgasse, in the heart of Niederdorf, is a confectioner's with a café that is renowned for serving mugs of hot chocolate. Café Schober also sells cakes.

Signboard of an antique shop

WINE

BECAUSE THEY are rarely exported, Swiss wines are one of the country's best-kept secrets *(see pp266–7)*. Zürich has several good vintners, with fine wines from the cantons of Valais, Vaud, Geneva and Neuchâtel.

Two of Zürich's leading vintners are **Baur au Lac Wein**, on Börsenstrasse, and **Wein Halle Zürich**, in Zeltweg. The latter stocks over 1,500 different wines from all over the world, including a good selection of Swiss wines. Some vintners invite customers to sample certain of the wines before they buy.

DEPARTMENT STORES

ZÜRICH'S TWO major department stores are **Jelmoli**, on Seidengasse, just west of Bahnhofstrasse, and **Globus**, on Löwenplatz, also west of Bahnhofstrasse. Both stock the full range of items associated with large department stores, including designer clothes for both men and women.

Both Jelmoli and Globus also have food halls selling high-quality foods from around the world. On offer here are many Swiss delicacies and specialities, including the finest cheeses *(see pp264–5)* and luxury chocolates.

Wine shop on Münstergasse, in the Niederdorf district of Zürich

DIRECTORY

INFORMATION

[W] www.zuerich.com
Contains information in English on shopping in Zürich.

WATCHES AND JEWELLERY

Gübelin
Bahnhofstrasse 36.
[044 221 38 88.

Bucherer
Bahnhofstrasse 50.
[044 211 26 35.

Swatch Store
Bahnhofstrasse 94.
[044 221 28 66.

HANDCRAFTED ITEMS/SOUVENIRS

Schweizer Heimatwerk
Bahnhofstrasse 2.
[044 221 08 37.

Rennweg 14.
[044 221 35 73.

Dolmetsch
Bahnhofstrasse 92.
[044 211 20 60.

LEATHER GOODS

Varesino
Bahnhofstrasse 69.
[044 211 87 57.

Lederladen
Schipfe 29.
[044 221 19 54.

BOOKSHOPS

English Bookshop
Bahnhofstrasse 70.
[044 211 04 44.

Travel Bookshop
Rindermarkt 20.
[044 252 38 83.

ANTIQUES

Art of Living
Siehlstrasse 93.
[044 212 10 12.

Greenwich
Rämistrasse 2.
[044 262 10 38.

CHOCOLATE

Confiserie Sprüngli
Bahnhofstrasse 21.
[044 224 47 11.

Café Schober
Napfgasse 4.
[044 251 80 60.

WINE

Baur au Lac Wein
Börsenstrasse 27.
[044 220 50 55.

Wein Halle Zürich
Zeltweg 26.
[044 253 75 75.

DEPARTMENT STORES

Jelmoli
Seidengasse 1.
[044 220 44 11.

Globus
Löwenplatz.
[044 226 60 60.

EASTERN SWITZERLAND AND GRAUBÜNDEN

TRAVERSED BY THE RHINE, *which flows through the Bodensee, eastern Switzerland is a relatively low-lying region. As well as several large towns, it has extensive rural areas with the lush pastures that help produce its famous cheeses. The high alpine region of Graubünden, to the south, is a magnet for mountaineers and winter-sports enthusiasts.*

Eastern Switzerland consists of the cantons of Thurgau, Schaffhausen, St Gallen, Appenzell Ausserrhoden and Appenzell Innerrhoden, and Glarus. The region is bordered by Germany to the north and by Liechtenstein and Austria to the east. With a majority of German- and Italian-speakers, and a small minority who speak Romansh (a language related to Latin), eastern Switzerland is officially trilingual, and religion is divided between Protestant and Catholic. The prosperity of this less populated region is based on the service industries, fruit growing and dairy products.

East of Glarus lies the tiny principality of Liechtenstein, a vestige of the Holy Roman Empire. Although separate from Switzerland, it maintains open borders with it.

Graubünden, bordered by Austria and Italy, occupies the southeastern corner of the country. This mountainous region corresponds to the Roman province of Rhaetia Prima. While German predominates in and around urban centres in the north of the canton, Romansh survives among the rural population. With some of the country's best ski slopes and greatest resorts, Graubünden is a major centre for winter sports, and half of its population is involved in the tourist industry. South of the Rhaetian Alps are the sunny valleys of Graubünden's Italian-speaking region.

A mountain stream and pine forest in the Parc Naziunal Svizzer, southeastern Graubünden

◁ A narrow street in Guarda, a village in the Lower Engadine

Exploring Eastern Switzerland and Graubünden

Besides several thriving towns, such as Schaffhausen and St Gallen, and the attractive medieval village of Stein am Rhein, eastern Switzerland has vast expanses of unspoilt countryside, where ancient rural traditions and ways of life continue. Further south is the peaceful Engadine valley, where the façades of historic houses have sgraffito decoration. The resorts of St Moritz, Klosters and Davos, in Graubünden, attract visitors with superb skiing, snowboarding and tobogganing, as well as hiking and mountaineering. The Parc Naziunal Svizzer, in the far southeastern corner of Graubünden, is a pristine wilderness with a network of hiking trails.

Barrels at a wine-harvest festival in Graubünden

SIGHTS AT A GLANCE

0 km   20

0 miles   20

SEE ALSO

- **Where to Stay** pp255–7.
- **Where to Eat** pp280–82.

Bridge on the route from the Julier Pass to the Engadine

⑤ BODENSEE (LAKE CONSTANCE)

GETTING THERE

The easiest way to reach eastern Switzerland is by road or rail from Zürich. Intercity rail services operate from Zürich to Schaffhausen, and to St Gallen and Liechtenstein. Rail links also connect all major towns in eastern Switzerland and Graubünden. Motorway links from Zürich include the A7 to Frauenfeld and the A1 to St Gallen. From the Bodensee (Lake Constance) the A13 runs south along the Rhine valley, passing through Liechtenstein, Bad Ragaz and Chur, where it is joined by the A3 from Zürich. Continuing southward, the A13 runs beneath the San Bernardino Pass and on towards Italy.

Cows with traditional decoration, at pasture in Appenzell

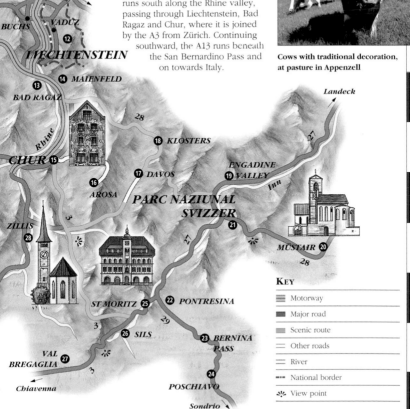

KEY

▬	Motorway
▬	Major road
▬	Scenic route
—	Other roads
═	River
- - -	National border
⁂	View point

Street-by-Street: Schaffhausen ❶

CAPITAL OF THE CANTON of the same name,
Schaffhausen is set on the north bank of the
Rhine, 4km (3 miles) above waterfalls known as
the Rheinfall. Lying at the point where boatmen
unloaded their cargoes, the town was an important
centre of trade from the early Middle Ages. The
cobbled streets of Schaffhausen's Old Town
(Altstadt) are lined with Gothic, Renaissance,
Baroque and Rococo buildings, some with
frescoed façades and others with graceful oriel
windows. The Munot, a circular keep
set on a hill to the east of
the town, was built in the
late 16th century, during
the unrest caused by the
Reformation. From the
keep there is a fine view of
the town and the river.

Fronwagplatz
*This square, once a site of medieval
markets, has two 16th-century
fountains, the Metzgerbrunnen
with a statue of a mercenary
and the Mohrenbrunnen,
with a statue of
a Moorish king.*

★ Rathaus
*The town hall,
completed in 1412
and decorated in
Renaissance style,
contains a beautiful
council chamber.*

Altes Zeughaus
The Old Armoury, in an imposing
Renaissance style, is fronted by
a doorway richly decorated with
relief carvings.

★ Haus zum Ritter
*The façade of the
Knight's House is
decorated with
intricate Renaissance
frescoes depicting
aspects of knightly
valour. They date
from 1568–70.*

Hallen für Neue Kunst is a gallery
with an international collection
of works of the 1960s and 1970s.

KEY

- - - - Suggested route

Kirche St Johann
This parish church was founded in the 11th century and completed in the early 16th. Some of its ancient wall paintings survive.

VISITORS' CHECKLIST

Road map E2. 🚶 *34,000.*
🚉 🚌 ℹ️ *Fronwagplatz 4;
052 632 40 20.*
W www.
schaffhausen-tourismus.ch

Schmiedstube
This ornate Baroque doorway, with depictions of the tools of the blacksmith's trade, fronts the Smiths' Guild House.

KIRCHHOF-
PLATZ

VORDERGASSE

Museum zu Allerheiligen,
in a former monastery, has prehistoric and medieval artefacts and a collection of Swiss paintings and sculpture.

MÜNSTER-
PLATZ

BAUMGARTEN-
STRASSE

★ Münster zu Allerheiligen
The beautiful Romanesque minster, originally part of a Benedictine abbey founded in the 11th century, was completed in the mid-12th century.

Schillerglocke
The Schiller Bell in the monastery cloisters was cast in 1486. Its sound inspired the German poet Friedrich Schiller to write Song of the Bell.

STAR SIGHTS

★ **Haus zum Ritter**

★ **Münster**

★ **Rathaus**

The medieval town of Stein am Rhein, with Kloster St Georgen in the foreground

Rheinfall ❷

Road map E2. **ℹ** *Neuhausen, Industriestrasse 39; 052 672 74 55.*

CREATING AN awe-inspiring spectacle of rainbow-tinted spray, the waters of the Rhine tumble off a cataract at at Neuhausen, 4km (3 miles) downriver from Schaffhausen. These waterfalls, known as the Rheinfall, are the largest in Europe. Although they are only 23 m (75 ft) high, they are remarkable for their width (about 150 m/492 ft) and their setting between tree-covered banks.

The best view of the falls is from **Schloss Laufen**, a turreted Renaissance castle overlooking the river from the south. From the castle, steps lead down to viewing platforms near the edge of the falls. Boat trips around the lake beneath the falls are also offered. A spectacular fireworks display is staged at the Rheinfall on National Day (1 August) each year.

Stein am Rhein ❸

Road map E2. *3,000.* 🚉 🚌 **ℹ** *Oberstadt 3; 052 742 20 90.* Ⓦ *www.steinamrhein.ch.*

WITH MANY medieval half-timbered buildings and 16th-century houses whose façades are painted with frescoes, Stein am Rhein is one of the most beautiful sights in Switzerland. Founded in Roman times, this small town began to prosper and expand in the late 11th century, when the German emperor Heinrich II founded

a Benedictine monastery here. The outline of the town walls can be made out, and two of the town gates, Obertor and Untertor, still stand. Rathaus-platz, the main square, is lined with houses painted with motifs reflecting their names, such as House of the Sun or House of the Red Ox, the town's oldest tavern *(see illustration on pp8–9)*. The 16th-century town hall, on one side of the square, contains the **Rathaussammlung**, a collection of paintings and objects that document the town's history.

Overlooking the Rhine stands Kloster St Georgen, a Benedictine monastery, and its 12th-century church. The well-preserved monastery rooms, decorated in the early 16th century, now house the **Klostermuseum St Georgen**, devoted to local history.

🏛 **Rathaussammlung**
Rathausplatz. **℡** *052 741 28 71.* ⏰ *10–11:30am & 2–5pm daily.* 🎫 📷

🏛 **Klostermuseum St Georgen**
Fischmarkt. **℡** *052 741 21 42.* ⏰ *Apr–Oct. 10am–5pm Tue–Sun.* 📷

Frauenfeld ❹

Road map E2. *19, 000.* 🚉 🚌 **ℹ** *Bahnhofplatz 75; 052 721 31 28.* Ⓦ *www.frauenfeld.ch*

LOCATED ON THE River Murg, west of Lake Constance, Frauenfeld is the capital of the canton of Thurgau. It is a picturesque town with many attractive burgher houses in its historic centre. They include the Baliere in Kreuzplatz, a half-timbered building that is now an art gallery, and the Luzemhaus, a Baroque building that houses a museum of natural history. The origins of Frauenfeld's castle go back to the 13th century. Its restored rooms house a museum of local history.

ENVIRONS: At **Ittingen**, about 4 km (3 miles) north of Frauenfeld, is the Kartause Ittingen, a Carthusian monastery founded in the 15th century. No longer inhabited by monks, the monastery is open to visitors. As well as a hotel, a restaurant and a farm shop, the monastery also has a museum illustrating monastic life and a gallery of 20th-century Swiss painting.

The riverside town of Frauenfeld, with a 13th-century castle keep

Bodensee (Lake Constance) ➎

BORDERED BY GERMANY and Austria, the Bodensee (Lake Constance) marks Switzerland's northeastern frontier. The lake, which is both fed and drained by the Rhine, is 65 km (40 miles) long and 15 km (9 miles) wide. Its western and southern shores, which belong to Switzerland, are lined with small resorts that have excellent fishing and watersports facilities. Boat trips depart from several points around the lakeshore.

Gottlieben ③
In 1415 the Czech reformer Jan Hus was held prisoner in the castle here.

Schloss Arenenberg ②
In 1817, this 16th-century castle became the property of Queen Hortense, mother of Napoleon III. Empress Eugenie, his wife, bequeathed it to Thurgau in 1906, and it is now open to visitors.

```
0 km          10
0 miles       10
```

Kreuzlingen ④
The Baroque Kirche St Ulrich is Kreuzlingen's finest building. This Swiss town is now a suburb of Konstanz (Constance), over the border in Germany.

Stuttgart
A98 E54
chaffhausen 33 31 E54 34 GERMANY
Radolfzell 33 Überlingen Ravensburg
Konstanz Meersburg 33 31 E54
13 Friedrichshafen Leutkirch
Winterthur Argen Kempten
Thur 14 Bodensee (Lake Constance) 31 E54 Lindau
13 Bregenz
AUSTRIA
Lustenau
Vaduz Feldkirch

Rorschach ⑤
This attractive lakeside resort has fine 16th- to 18th-century houses.

Steckborn ①
This small town has many fine historic houses. The 14th-century waterfront castle, or Turmhof, once belonged to the abbots of Reichenau. It now contains a museum of local history.

KEY

▬▬	Suggested route
▬▬	Motorway
▬▬	Scenic route
══	Other roads
▪-▪-	National border
☼	View point

TIPS FOR DRIVERS

Tour length: 50 km (30 miles).
Stopping-off points: The resorts around Lake Constance offer a wide choice of hotels and restaurants.
Additional attractions: There is a dolphinarium at Conny Land, near Lipperswil. ☐ summer: 9am–6pm daily. 🏊

St Gallen **6**

C APITAL OF THE CANTON of the same name, St Gallen is eastern Switzerland's largest town. Its origins go back to 612, when Gallus, an Irish monk, chose the spot for his hermitage. A Benedictine abbey was founded here in 747 and, with the establishment of a library in the 9th century, the abbey became a notable centre of learning and culture. By the Middle Ages, St Gallen was already an important producer of linen, exporting fine cloth all over Europe. In the 19th century, embroidery was St Gallen's major export, and the town is still renowned for this cottage industry.

Marktplatz, once St Gallen's market square

Exploring St Gallen
While the city's focal point is its magnificent cathedral (see pp186–7), its beautiful medieval centre contains many half-timbered houses and mansions with oriel windows. Most of St Gallen's museums are concentrated to the east of the Old Town (Altstadt).

🏛 Textilmuseum
Vadianstrasse 2. 071 222 17 44. 10am–noon & 2–5pm Tue–Fri, 10am–noon Sat.
Reflecting St Gallen's importance as a centre of the textiles industry, this museum is filled with a comprehensive array of pieces illustrating the art of weaving, as well as intricate embroidery and exquisite handmade lace. Local patterns and products, and the implements that were devised to produce them, are also shown.

Statue on a fountain in St Gallen

🏛 Stiftsbibliothek
Klosterhof 6d. 071 227 34 16. Apr–Nov: 10am–5pm Mon–Sat, 10am–4pm Sun; Dec–Mar: 10am–noon & 1:30–5pm Mon–Sat, 10am–noon & 1:30–4pm Sun.
Although most of the abbey was destroyed during the Reformation, its important library, the Stiftsbibliothek, was spared. The main room, designed by Peter Thumb in 1758–67, is a stunning Baroque masterpiece, with elaborate Rococo decoration. The wooden floor is intricately inlaid and the ceiling decorated with stuccowork by the Gigl brothers and with trompe-l'oeil paintings by Josef Wannenmacher.
The library contains more than 150,000 books and manuscripts, including an important collection of Irish manuscripts dating from the 8th to the 11th centuries, and rare works dating from the 8th century.

🔒 St-Laurenzenkirche
Marktgasse. 071 222 67 92. 9:30–11:30am & 2–4pm Mon–Sat.
This church was originally part of the abbey complex. During the 16th century it became the main centre of the Reformation in St Gallen. The building's present Neo-Gothic appearance is the result of remodelling carried out in the mid-19th century.

🏛 Marktplatz
Once the town's main market square, Marktplatz lies on the northern side of the Old Town. The square is surrounded by fine houses dating mainly from the 17th and 18th centuries. While most of them are built of brick and have intricately painted façades, others are half-timbered and decorated with relief carving. Many also have attractive oriel windows, a feature typical of St Gallen's architecture.
On Marktgasse, the street leading off the southern side of Marktplatz, is a watchmaker's shop with a small collection of musical boxes. These include some fascinating examples of Swiss ingenuity.

🏛 Bohl
This elongated esplanade, leading off the eastern side of Marktplatz, is dominated by the dazzlingly white façade of the Waaghaus, a weighhouse built in 1583. The building is now the seat of the city authorities, and is also used for concerts and exhibitions.

The late 16th-century Waaghaus, on Bohl

🏛 Natur- und Kunstmuseum

Museumstrasse 32. 📞 071 242 06 71. ⏱ 10am–noon & 2–5pm Tue–Fri, 10am–5pm Sat–Sun.

This late 19th-century museum building is divided into two parts. One is devoted to natural history, and contains displays relating to the region's plants and animals, as well as its minerals. The other is an art gallery, with works dating mainly from the 19th and 20th centuries.

🏛 Historisches Museum

Museumstrasse 50. 📞 071 242 06 42. ⏱ 10am–noon & 2–5pm Tue–Fri, 10am–5pm Sat–Sun.

The history of the town and region of St Gallen is the focus of the displays at this museum. Besides many archaeological pieces, there

The Natur- und Kunstmuseum

are documents, mementoes and reconstructed domestic rooms of various periods. Highlights include a scale reconstruction of St Gallen's abbey and a model of the city as it was in the 17th century. The museum also has an ethnographic collection, with Asian, African and South American artefacts.

🏛 Universität

Dufourstrasse 50. 📞 071 224 21 11.

The university of St Gallen is of interest to visitors for its modern architecture and its decoration. Created by innovative artists of the 20th century, the paintings and sculpture here are closely integrated with the buildings' physical structure.

The main building, which was completed in 1963, features a ceramic frieze by Joan Miró, wall paintings by Antoni Tàpies, a mosaic by Georges Braque and sculptures by Alberto Giacometti. A bronze sculpture by Jean Arp stands in the courtyard. A later building, completed

VISITORS' CHECKLIST

Road map F2. 👥 70,000. 🚌 🚉 ℹ *Bahnhofplatz 1a; 071 227 37 37.* 🎪 *Open Air St Gallen (popular music; last weekend in Jun).* Ⓦ *www.stgallen.ch*

in 1989, contains several works by the painters Gerhard Richter, Josef Felix Müller and Luciano Fabro.

🏛 Sammlung Hauser und Wirth

Grünbergstrasse 7. 📞 071 228 55 50. ⏱ mid-Jun–mid-Oct: 2–8pm Wed, 2–6pm Thu–Fri, 11am–6pm Sat–Sun; also 2–6pm Mon–Tue during Art Basel (mid-Jun). 🖼

The former locomotive depot next to St Gallen's main railway station has been converted into an exhibition space. It contains modern art that the collectors Ursula Hauser and Manuela and Ivan Wirth acquired from 1999 onwards. The collection includes paintings, photographs, sculpture, installations and video films created by an international range of avant-garde artists during the 1990s.

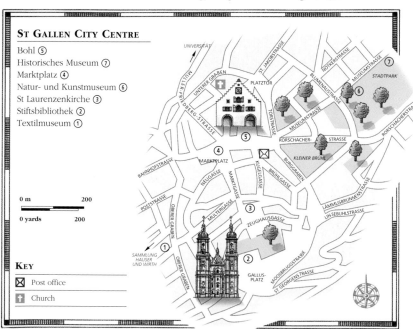

ST GALLEN CITY CENTRE

Bohl ⑤
Historisches Museum ⑦
Marktplatz ④
Natur- und Kunstmuseum ⑥
St Laurenzenkirche ③
Stiftsbibliothek ②
Textilmuseum ①

0 m   200
0 yards   200

KEY

⊠ Post office

✝ Church

St Gallen Cathedral

THE BENEDICTINE ABBEY in St Gallen was established in 747 and was at the height of its importance from the 9th to the 11th centuries. The Romanesque church and monastery, built during that period, have not survived, their only remains being the crypt containing the tombs of the abbots. The present Baroque cathedral and monastery were completed in 1766. The architects were Peter Thumb and Johann Michael Beer, and the interior decoration was executed by the foremost artists of the day. Such is the importance of the abbey, with its works of art and its library *(see p184)*, that it was made a World Heritage Site.

★ **Ceiling Frescoes**
The ceiling is decorated with dramatic frescoes by Josef Wannenmacher.

Main Altarpiece
The painting on the high altar, depicting the Assumption of the Virgin, is by Francesco Romanelli. Dating from 1645, it was later heavily retouched.

High altar

Thrones
Two thrones, made by Franz Joseph Anton Feuchtmayer and decorated by the Dirr brothers, stand among the choir stalls.

STAR FEATURES

★ **Ceiling Frescoes**

★ **Stalls**

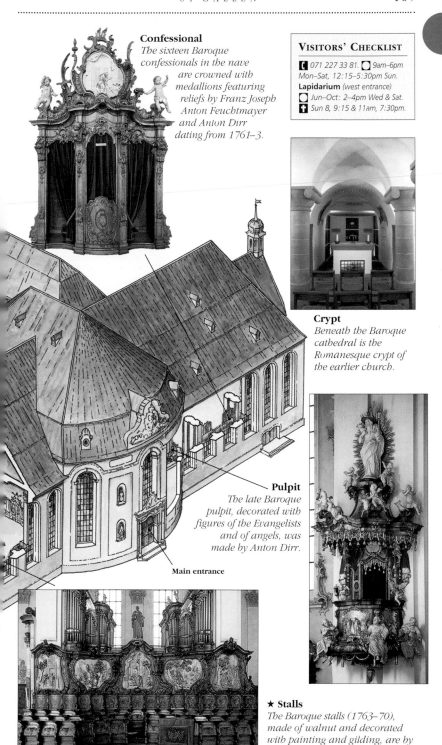

Confessional
The sixteen Baroque confessionals in the nave are crowned with medallions featuring reliefs by Franz Joseph Anton Feuchtmayer and Anton Dirr dating from 1761–3.

Crypt
Beneath the Baroque cathedral is the Romanesque crypt of the earlier church.

Pulpit
The late Baroque pulpit, decorated with figures of the Evangelists and of angels, was made by Anton Dirr.

Main entrance

★ Stalls
The Baroque stalls (1763–70), made of walnut and decorated with painting and gilding, are by Franz Joseph Anton Feuchtmayer and craftsmen from his studio.

Appenzell ❼

Road map F2. 🚗 🚌 ℹ️ Appenzell, *Hauptgasse 4; 071 788 96 41.* 🅆 www. appenzell.ch 🎏 *Landsgemeinde (last Sun in Apr, Appenzell).*

S URROUNDED ON ALL sides by the canton of St Gallen, the region known as Appenzell consists of two half-cantons, Appenzell Ausserrhoden in the north and west, and Appenzell Innerrhoden in the south. From the 10th to the 15th centuries, Appenzell formed part of the territory owned by the abbey at St Gallen *(see p184).* Having gained its independence, Appenzell joined the Swiss Confederation in 1513.

While Appenzell Ausser-rhoden, the larger of the two half-cantons, is Protestant and largely industrialized, Appenzell Innerrhoden is Catholic and markedly more bucolic, with a farming economy and a developed tourist industry. It is renowned for its cattle-breeding and its dairy products, most especially its cheeses. Along with its rural character, Appenzell Innerrhoden has strong folk traditions and a pristine natural environment.

Like many other towns in the region, **Appenzell**, capital of Innerrhoden, has a Landsgemeindeplatz, a square on which regular voting sessions are held *(see p30).* The well-preserved historic centre of this small town is

Interior of the Kirche St Mauritius in Appenzell

filled with colourfully painted wooden houses. Other buildings of interest here are the 16th-century town hall and the parish church, Kirche St Mauritius, built in the 16th century in the Baroque style and remodelled in the 19th century.

The history and culture of Appenzell is amply documented by the varied and extensive collections of the **Museum Appenzell**. These range from costumes and headdresses to embroidery and cowbells. The privately run **Museum im Blauen Haus** contains a similar, though much smaller, collection.

To the south of Appenzell lies the Alpstein massif, whose highest peak, the Säntis, rises to 2,504 m (8,218 ft). Popular with hikers and mountaineers, the Säntis can be reached by road or by cable car from Schwägalp. The summit commands an extensive panorama that takes in the Bodensee *(see p183)* and the Black Forest to the north, the Zürichsee to the southwest and the Glarner Alps to the south.

The picturesque village of **Urnäsch**, in Ausserrhoden and located northwest of the Säntis, also has a museum of local folk traditions. This is the **Museum für Appenzeller Brauchtum,**

House in Gais, with an ornate gable

whose collection includes reconstructed farmhouse interiors, as well as costumes and craft items. North of Urnäsch is **Herisau**, capital of Appenzell Ausserrhoden. The town has attractive wooden houses and a church with Rococo furnishings dating from 1520. A museum of local history occupies part of the town hall.

Stein, a quiet village east of Herisau, has an interesting folk museum and show dairy. While the displays at the **Appenzell Folklore Museum** illustrate the lives, culture and crafts of the local people, visitors to the **Appenzeller Showcase** can watch cheese being made by local methods.

The market town of **Gais**, at the centre of Appenzell, is of interest for its colourfully painted wooden houses, many of which have ornate gables. Gais is also an excellent base for exploring the region.

The small hilltop town of **Trogen**, north of Gais, is worth a visit for its Baroque church and traditional wooden houses.

🏛 **Museum Appenzell**
Appenzell, Hauptgasse 4.
📞 071 788 96 31.
🕐 Apr–Nov: 10am–noon & 2–5pm daily; Dec–Mar: 2–5pm Tue–Sun.
♿

Hauptgasse, the main street in Appenzell's historic district

🏛 **Museum in Blauem Haus**
Stein. 📞 071 787 12 84. 🕐 9am–6pm
Mon–Sat, 10am–5pm Sun.

🏛 **Museum für Appenzeller Brauchtum**
Urnäsch. 📞 071 364 14 87.
🕐 Apr–Oct: 1:30–5pm daily & by arrangement.

🏛 **Appenzeller Folklore Museum**
Stein. 📞 071 368 50 56.
🕐 10am–noon & 1:30–5pm
Mon–Sat, 10am–5pm Sun. 🗓

🏛 **Appenzeller Showcase**
Stein. 📞 071 368 50 70. 🕐
May–Oct: 9am–7pm daily; Nov–Apr: 9am–6pm daily. 📷 on request.

Toggenburg ❽

Road map E3. 🛈 Wildhaus, Hauptstrasse; 071 999 99 11.
🖥 www.toggenburg.org

WASHED BY THE River Thur, the Toggenburg is a long valley that lies on a north–south axis between Wil and Wattwil, then veers eastwards just above Alt St Johann, where it becomes Oberes Toggenburg. With the Alpstein massif to the north and Churfirsten to the south, Oberes Toggenburg then opens out onto the Rhine valley.

The Toggenburg has over 300 km (185 miles) of marked hiking trails and cycling routes, and its gentle slopes provide excellent skiing pistes. The valley is dotted with attractive small towns and villages. Among them are **Wil**, the main town, and **Lichtensteig**, which is of interest for its historic houses and museum of local history.

Wildhaus, a pleasant resort at the eastern extremity of

A 17th-century house in Lichtensteig, in the Toggenburg

Oberes Toggenburg, is the birthplace of Ulrich Zwingli, the leader of the Reformation in Switzerland. The farmhouse where he was born in 1484 is open to visitors. **Unterwasser** is worth a visit for its impressive waterfall, the Thurwasserfälle.

Rapperswil ❾

Road map E3. 👥 7,700. 🛈 Fischmarktplatz 1; 055 220 57 57.
🖥 www.rapperswil.ch

THIS SMALL TOWN, in the canton of St Gallen, is set on a promontory on the north side of the Zürichsee. Although the modern part of Rapperswil has nothing of great interest, the old district is a pleasant place to stroll.

Behind the lakeside promenade lie narrow streets lined with houses fronted by arcades, and small squares with cafés and restaurants

that serve fresh locally caught fish. From May to October the air here is filled with the delicate perfume of roses. Known as the City of Roses, Rapperswil has several walled rose gardens, including one within a Capuchin monastery and another that is specially designed for blind people.

Besides the 15th-century town hall and the parish church, Rapperswil's main feature is its Gothic castle, whose three forbidding towers rise above the town. From the castle there are views of Zürich to the north and of the Glarus Alps to the southwest.

Glarus ❿

Road map E3. 👥 5,500.
🛈 Bahnhof; 055 650 20 90.
🖥 www.stadt-glarus.ch
🎪 Landsgemeinde (1st Sun in May).

CAPITAL OF THE canton of Glarus, this small town is also the urban centre of Glarnerland, an isolated and mountainous region lying between the Walensee and the Klausen Pass. Largely rebuilt after it was destroyed by fire in 1861, Glarus is laid out on a grid pattern and as such is a classic example of 19th-century urban planning. Notable buildings here include the town hall, an art gallery with a collection of 19th- and 20th-century Swiss paintings, and the Neo-Romanesque parish church whose treasury contains a collection of liturgical vessels.

With beautiful lakes and valleys, the mountains around Glarus, particularly those of the Glärnisch massif, are popular with hikers. Many of the slopes have excellent skiing pistes.

ENVIRONS: South of Glarus, the main road continues to **Linthal**, from where a funicular ascends to **Braunwald**. This tranquil car-free resort is located on a plateau that offers superb hiking. Beyond Linthal the road leads through spectacular scenery over the **Klausen Pass** (1,948 m/6,393 ft) and down to Altdorf and Lake Lucerne (see p224).

Skiers on a cross-country trek in the Toggenburg

The Walensee, with the Churfirsten massif on its northern side, seen from the cable car to Tannenboden

Walensee ⓫

Road map F3. 🚆 🚌

THIS SLENDER LAKE marks the border between the cantons of St Gallen and Glarus. About 15 km (9 miles) long and just 2 km (1 mile) across at its widest point, it lies in a steep-sided valley, with the rugged Churfirsten massif on its northern side and the Glarner Alps to the southeast.

A railway line and the motorway linking Zürich and Chur run along the south side of the lake. Most of the towns and villages on the steep north shore are accessible only by boat or on foot. Cruises on the lake take in **Weesen**, a charming town on the western shore.

A short distance south is **Näfels**, which has a late Renaissance palace, the Freulerpalast. The building houses a museum of local history. The neighbouring town of **Mollis** contains well-preserved burgher houses and fine 18th-century mansions.

Walenstadt, on the lake's eastern shore, is a convenient base for exploring the surrounding mountains, taking in **Walenstadtberg**, about 8km (5 miles) northwest of Walenstadt, and **Berschis**, 6 km (4 miles) to the southeast, where there is a 12th-century chapel decorated with frescoes.

Liechtenstein ⓬

See pp192–3.

Bad Ragaz ⓭

Road map F3. 🚌 🚆 🚶 *4,580*
ℹ️ *Maienfelderstrasse 5; 081 302 10 61.* 🖥️ *www.badragaz-tourismus.ch*
🎭 *Maibär (spring festival, first week in May).*

BAD RAGAZ, set on the River Tamina, is one of Switzerland's foremost spa resorts. Its thermal springs are used to treat rheumatism and respiratory disorders, and also to promote general health. The resort has several

indoor and outdoor thermal pools. The best-known are Tamina-Therme, which are in the centre of the resort.

Bad Ragaz also has an early 18th-century parish church with Baroque wall paintings. The town hall contains a display of paintings and other graphic works of art of Bad Ragaz and its environs.

As well as skiing on the slopes of Pizol, Bad Ragaz offers golf, tennis and other sporting activities. It is also an excellent base for hiking in the surrounding hills.

ENVIRONS: About 5 km (3 miles) south of Bad Ragaz is **Bad Pfäfers**, a spa town with a beautiful Baroque church and a former Benedictine monastery that now houses a museum of local history.

Southwest of Bad Ragaz is the **Taminaschlucht**, a deep gorge carved out by the rushing waters of the Tamina. Also of interest is **Sargans**, with beautiful Neo-Classical buildings and a Gothic castle.

Maienfeld ⓮

Road map F3. 🚌 🚆 🚶 *2,390*
ℹ️ *Heididorf; 081 330 19 12.*
🖥️ *www.heididorf.ch*

THE VILLAGE OF Maienfeld, in the hills above Bad Ragaz, is the hub of the area that has been promoted as Heidiland. It was this region of the Swiss Alps that Johanna Spyri chose as the setting for *Heidi*, the story of an orphaned girl that has become a classic of children's literature.

Bad Ragaz, a spa resort and base for hiking trips

An easy walking trail leads from Maienfeld up to the hamlet of Oberrofels. Here visitors can see Heidi's House, a wooden chalet in which the fictional surroundings of Heidi's life with her grandfather are re-created.

Chur 15

See pp194–7.

Arosa 16

Road map F4. 🚌 🚉 🚗 *2,300.* ℹ️ *Poststrasse; 081 378 70 20* 🌐 *www.arosa.ch*

SET IN A BOWL in the narrow Schanfigg valley, Arosa is one of Switzerland's most beautiful resorts. Although it lies at an altitude of 1,800 m (5,900 ft), it enjoys a gentle climate, with many days of calm, sunny weather.

The town is divided into two areas. Ausserarosa is the main resort and Innerarosa the original village. The crafts and folk art on display in the **Schanfigg Heimatmuseum** here reflect mountain life in the days before the fashion for winter sports led to its transformation.

In winter the neighbouring slopes of Weisshorn, for experienced skiers, and of Hörnli and Prätschli, for intermediate skiers, provide superb downhill pistes. There are also extensive cross-country trails, a sleigh run and an ice rink. In summer visitors can enjoy over 200 km (125 miles) of hiking trails and mountain biking routes.

WInter sports on the slopes of the Schanfigg valley, near Arosa

Davos, with the peaks of Schatzalp and Parsenn in the background

There is also a golf course, and the resort's two lakes, the Obersee and Untersee, offer a variety of water sports.

🏛️ **Schanfigg Heimatmuseum**
Poststrasse, Innerarosa. 📞 *081 377 33 13.* ⏰ *Winter: 2:30–4:30 pm Tue & Fri; summer: 2:30–4:30 pm Mon, Wed & Fri.* ♿

Davos 17

Road map F3. 🚗 *10,900.* 🚉 🚌 ℹ️ *Promenade 67; 081 415 21 21.* 🌐 *www.davos.ch* 🎭 *International Festival of Classical Music (Jul–Aug); Spengler Cup Ice Hockey Tournament (Dec).*

BRASH AND FAST-PACED, Davos is one of the largest winter sports resorts in Switzerland and the Swiss capital of snowboarding. Originally a remote village, Davos developed into a health resort for tuberculosis sufferers in the 1860s, and was transformed into a winter sports resort in the 1930s.

Davos has close associations with the German writer Thomas Mann, who came here in 1911 and was inspired to write *The Magic Mountain*. Davos is also associated with the German Expressionist painter Ernst Ludwig Kirchner, who settled here in 1917. The largest collection of his work in the world, including many of the Alpine landscapes that he painted during his years in Davos, are displayed in the **Kirchner Museum**.

Poster in the Kirchner Museum, Davos

Although a 15th-century church and 16th-century town hall survive in its old district, Davos is geared primarily to its role as a leading winter sports resort. With those of its neighbour, Klosters, it has a total of 300 km (185 miles) of pistes and 75 km (50 miles) of snowboarding trails. These are particularly suitable for intermediate and experienced skiers and snowboarders. However, for beginners, there are several ski and snowboarding schools, and some less demanding slopes. Davos also has toboggan runs and a large natural ice rink, where ice hockey is played.

In summer visitors can enjoy golf and tennis, hiking along trails, rock climbing and trekking on horseback.

🏛️ **Kirchner Museum**
Promenade 82. 📞 *081 413 22 02.* ⏰ *10am–6pm Tue–Sun.* ♿

Klosters 18

Road map F3. 🚗 *3,800.* 🚉 🚌 ℹ️ *Alte Bahnhofstrasse 6; 081 410 20 20.* 🌐 *www.klosters.ch*

QUIETER AND SMALLER than Davos, its neighbour to the south, the discreetly chic ski resort of Klosters has an intimate atmosphere. Of the medieval monastery from which it takes its name, the only trace is Kirche St Jacob, which has stained-glass windows by Augusto Giacometti. The history of the village and its development into a resort are documented by displays in the **Nutli-Hüschi**, a 16th-century chalet.

Together with those of Davos, the resort has 300 km (185 miles) of downhill pistes and 50 km (30 miles) of cross-country skiing trails. These are suitable for a range of abilities, from beginner to experienced.

🏛️ **Nutli-Hüschi**
Montbielerstrasse. 📞 *081 410 20 20.* ⏰ *Dec–mid-Apr & Jul–mid-Oct: 3–5pm Wed & Fri.* ♿

Liechtenstein ⓬

L YING IN THE EASTERN Rhaetian Alps, Liechtenstein borders
Switzerland to the west and Austria to the east. It consists
of the estates of Schellenberg and Vaduz, which were
purchased by Johann von Liechtenstein in 1699 and 1712,
and it was established as a principality in 1719. This
German-speaking country, with a population of 34,000,
is a democratic monarchy, and it has close links to
Switzerland, with which it shares an open border. It is
one of the most highly industrialized countries in the
world. The capital, Vaduz, has the air of a pleasant
provincial town and is worth a visit for its impressive
art gallery, the Kunstmuseum Liechtenstein.

Triesenberg ③
This mountain village above the Rhine valley
was settled by immigrants from Valais in the
13th century. It is now a popular holiday resort.

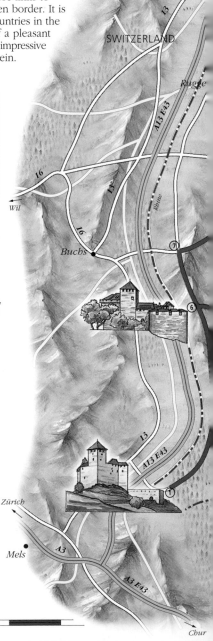

Triesen ②
The St Mamerten
Kapelle, a Gothic
chapel with a
Romanesque apse,
is one of Triesen's
historic buildings.

Balzers ①
Burg Gutenberg, a 13th-century castle, dominates
Balzers, Liechtenstein's southernmost town.
Although the castle is not open to visitors, its
courtyard is used as a venue for cultural events.

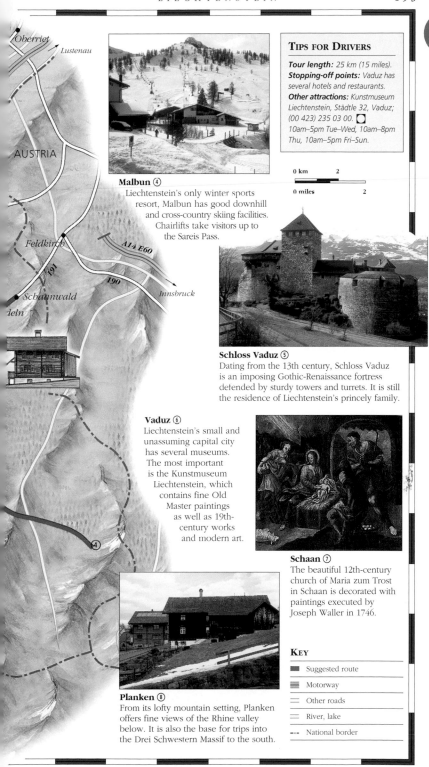

Oberriet
Lustenau

AUSTRIA

Feldkirch

191

A14 E60

190

Innsbruck

Schaanwald
deln

TIPS FOR DRIVERS

Tour length: 25 km (15 miles).
Stopping-off points: Vaduz has several hotels and restaurants.
Other attractions: Kunstmuseum Liechtenstein, Städtle 32, Vaduz; (00 423) 235 03 00. ☐ 10am–5pm Tue–Wed, 10am–8pm Thu, 10am–5pm Fri–Sun.

0 km   2

0 miles   2

Malbun ④
Liechtenstein's only winter sports resort, Malbun has good downhill and cross-country skiing facilities. Chairlifts take visitors up to the Sareis Pass.

Schloss Vaduz ⑤
Dating from the 13th century, Schloss Vaduz is an imposing Gothic-Renaissance fortress defended by sturdy towers and turrets. It is still the residence of Liechtenstein's princely family.

Vaduz ⑥
Liechtenstein's small and unassuming capital city has several museums. The most important is the Kunstmuseum Liechtenstein, which contains fine Old Master paintings as well as 19th-century works and modern art.

Schaan ⑦
The beautiful 12th-century church of Maria zum Trost in Schaan is decorated with paintings executed by Joseph Waller in 1746.

Planken ⑧
From its lofty mountain setting, Planken offers fine views of the Rhine valley below. It is also the base for trips into the Drei Schwestern Massif to the south.

KEY

▬	Suggested route
▤	Motorway
═	Other roads
=	River, lake
▪-▪	National border

Chur ⑮

Capital of the Bischöflicher Hof

L OCATED AT THE HEAD of the Rhine valley, Chur lies at the crossroads of ancient trade routes running between the Alpine passes to the south and the Bodensee to the north. The Romans founded a settlement here in the 1st century BC. Around AD 450 Chur became a bishopric and, under the rule of prince-bishops from the 12th to the 16th centuries, the town prospered. With the arrival of the Reformation, Chur passed to the secular rule of its merchant class, becoming the capital of the canton of Graubünden in 1803.

Exploring Chur

With the Obertor, a city gate, on its western side, the Old Town clusters around Kirche St Martin. The bishop's palace and the cathedral *(see pp196–7)* stand to the east. The narrow streets and squares of the Old Town are quiet and pleasant to explore.

The 8th-century crypt beneath the Kirche St Luzius

🔒 Kirche St Luzius

This massive church, which is dedicated to the missionary who is said to have brought Christianity to the region, crowns a vineyard-covered hill on the east side of the Old Town. The building overlies the crypt of an 8th-century structure, which can be visited. There is also a monastery attached to the church, which houses a seminary.

🔒 Chur Cathedral

See pp196–7.

🔒 Bischöflicher Hof

Hofplatz.
The complex of buildings set on the terrace that rises to the east of the Old Town make up the bishop's palace. Founded in the 6th century on the site of a Roman fort, the palace was extended on several occasions, and its thick walls reflect the ruling bishops' need for defence. The palace's present appearance is mainly the result of remodelling in the 18th and 19th centuries. Since it is still the residence of the bishops of Chur, it is not open to visitors.

🏛 Rätisches Museum

Haus Buol, Hofstrasse 1. [081 257 28 89. ◯ 10am–noon & 2–5pm Tue–Sun. 📷
The displays at this museum illustrate the history of Chur and its environs from prehistoric times to the 19th century.

Exhibits include archaeological finds from the time of the Rhaetians, who colonized the region in prehistory, and from Graubünden's Roman period. Medieval reliquaries and other precious pieces from the cathedral treasury are also displayed. Later exhibits include 17th-century furnishings and other objects. The culture and folk arts of Graubünden are also documented.

Stained-glass window by Augusto Giacometti in Kirche St Martin

🔒 Kirche St Martin

St Martinsplatz [081 252 22 92. ◯ 8:30–11:30am & 2–5pm Mon–Fri.
The late Gothic church of St Martin was completed in 1491, replacing an 8th-century church that was destroyed by fire. Among ` the most notable features of its interior are the carved stalls and the three stained-glass windows created by Augusto Giacometti in 1917–19.

🎪 Obere Gasse

Chur's smartest shopping street, Obere Gasse runs from St Martinsplatz to Obertor, the Gothic city gate on the banks of the Plessur. The historic houses along the street have been converted into boutiques, restaurants and

The Bischöflicher Hof, with the cathedral on the left

cafés. On Saturday mornings in summer, a market is held in Obere Gasse and Untere Gasse.

🚩 Rathaus

Poststrasse. ◯ *By prior arrangement;* *081 252 18 18.*
Built in 1465, the Gothic town hall stands on the site of an earlier building that was destroyed by fire. At ground level is an arcaded area that was once used as a marketplace. The upper floors of the town hall contain two finely decorated council chambers, one with a wooden ceiling and the other with Renaissance panelling. Both chambers have 17th-century tiled stoves.

The house at No. 57 Riechsgasse, nearby, is the birthplace of the Swiss painter Angelica Kauffmann. Born in 1741, she later moved to London, where she became a well-known portraitist and painter of mythological themes.

🚩 Regierungsplatz

Several historic buildings, now serving as the seat of the cantonal authorities, line this square on the north side of

The commemorative obelisk in the centre of Regierungsplatz

the Old Town. One of the finest is Graues Haus (Grey House), a stately three-storey residence dating from 1752.

VISITORS' CHECKLIST

Road map F3.
🏔 33,000.
🚉 🚌 ℹ️ *Grabenstrasse;* *081 252 18 18.*
W www.churtourismus.ch

The Vazerol-Denkmal, an obelisk in the centre of the square, commemorates the free association formed by the communes of Graubünden in the 14th century, when the local population began to organize itself against foreign domination.

Postplatz, at the northern end of Chur's Old Town

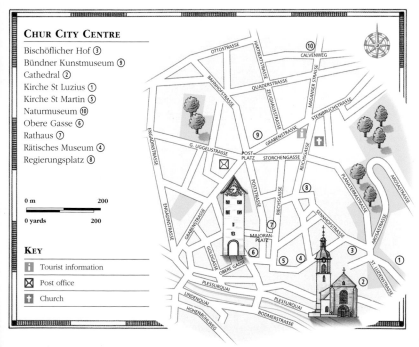

CHUR CITY CENTRE

Bischöflicher Hof ③
Bündner Kunstmuseum ⑨
Cathedral ②
Kirche St Luzius ①
Kirche St Martin ⑤
Naturmuseum ⑩
Obere Gasse ⑥
Rathaus ⑦
Rätisches Museum ④
Regierungsplatz ⑧

0 m   200
0 yards   200

KEY

ℹ️ Tourist information
✉️ Post office
✝️ Church

🏛 Bündner Kunstmuseum

Postplatz. 📞 081 257 28 68.
🕐 10am–noon & 2–5pm Tue–Wed,
10am–noon & 2–8pm Thu,
10am–noon & 2–5pm Fri–Sun. 💺

Chur's museum of fine arts
occupies a large Neo-
Renaissance villa dating
from 1874–5. It was built for
Jacques Ambrosius von Plant,
a merchant who traded in
Egypt. This accounts for the
Oriental character of the
building's interior decoration.

Most of the paintings and
sculptures that fill the rooms
of the villa are by artists who
were either born or worked
in Graubünden between the
18th and the 20th centuries.
They include Angelica
Kauffmann, Giovanni
Segantini, Ferdinand Hodler,
Giovanni and Alberto
Giacometti and Ernst Ludwig
Kirchner. The rooms at the
back of the villa are used for
temporary exhibitions.

🏛 Naturmuseum

Masanserstrasse 31. 📞 081 257
28 41. 🕐 10am–noon & 1:30–5pm
Tue–Sat, 10am–5pm Sun. 💺

This modern museum show-
cases the natural environment
of Graubünden. The well-
presented displays include
a large collection of minerals
from the region's mountains,
as well as plants and stuffed
animals.

ENVIRONS: A cable car
departing from the station
on Kasernenstrasse, about
five minutes' walk to the
south of Chur, carries visitors
up to the **Brambrüesch**, at
an altitude of 1,600 m (5,250
ft). This is one of the three
peaks of the Dreibündenstein
massif, which has many scenic
hiking trails. Its terrain also
makes it popular with
paragliders. From
Brambrüesch a chair lift goes
up to **Dreibündenstein**, at
2,180 m (7,155 ft). Hiking
trails from Dreibündenstein
lead to Pizokel and Calanda,
at 2,806 m (9,200 ft).

The spa town of **Bad
Passugg**, 5 km (3 miles)
southwest of Chur on the
road leading to Lenzerheide,
has iron-rich mineral springs.
Beyond Bad Passugg, the
road leads to the spa region
of Tschiertschen.

Chur Cathedral

BEGUN IN 1151 AND COMPLETED in the mid-
13th century, Chur's cathedral is in a
mixture of Romanesque and Gothic styles.
The earliest part of the basilica is its eastern
section. The nave, with Romanesque
columns and Gothic vaulting, and the
tower, topped by a lantern, are later
elements. The exterior was remodelled in
the early 19th century, after the building
was damaged by fire. The cathedral is
built to an irregular plan, the axis of
the sanctuary and that of the nave
being out of alignment. The
cathedral's finest feature is the
15th-century altar triptych,
which is under restoration.

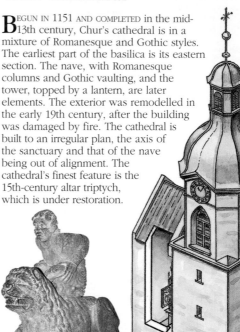

Crypt Figures
*The crypt is supported by
columns with capitals in
the form of animal figures.*

★ Capitals of the Nave
*The capitals of the columns
flanking the nave are
outstanding examples
of Swiss Romanesque
stone carving.*

★ Sanctuary
*The Gothic sanctuary is
decorated with delicate
tracery and figures of saints.*

Stalls
The intricate decoration on the 15th-century stalls are fine examples of late Gothic woodcarving.

VISITORS' CHECKLIST

Chur Cathedral (Kathedrale St Maria Himmelfahrt)
Hofplatz. 081 252 23 12.
8am–7pm daily. For the duration of its restoration, due to be completed in 2007, only part of the cathedral is open to visitors.

Pulpit
Figures of putti and relief carvings of biblical scenes adorn the Baroque pulpit.

Frescoes
Gothic frescoes cover the walls of the baptistry.

Stained-glass Window
The large stained-glass window in the west wall features medallions with scenes from the life of the Virgin.

Main entrance

Tomb of Ortileb von Brandis
The Gothic tomb of this 15th-century bishop of Chur was made in 1491.

STAR FEATURES

★ Capitals of the Nave

★ Sanctuary

Sgraffito decoration on the façade of a house in Guarda, Lower Engadine

Engadine Valley ⓳

Road map G4. ⓗ *Pontresina; 081 842 65 73.* Ⓦ www.engadin.ch

THE ENGADINE VALLEY begins at the foot of the Rhaetian Alps, near St Moritz, and extends northeastwards as far as the Austrian border. It is named after the River Inn (En in Romansch), which runs along the valley and on into Austria, where it joins the Danube.

This deep-cut valley lies between high cliffs. It is divided into an upper, south-western section and a lower, northeastern section. The Upper Engadine (Oberengadin in German, Engiadin' Ota in Romansh), lies between the Maloja Pass and Zernez. With glaciers and snowy peaks on either side, the valley floor of the Upper Engadine lies at an altitude averaging 1,800 m (5,900 ft) and is dotted with winter sports resorts, including Pontresina and St Moritz *(see p204)*.

The Lower Engadine (Unterengadin in German, Engiadina Bassa in Romansh) lies between Zernez and Martina. Remote, unspoilt and very picturesque, this region is dotted with attractive villages set on either side of the River Inn. Many of these villages have houses with painted façades or sgraffito decoration, in which the upper layer of plaster is cut away to create a design. Particularly fine sgraffito decoration can be seen in **Guarda**, a village overlooking the River Inn. The village of **Ardez** is also

notable for its painted houses, one of which is covered with a beautiful depiction of Adam and Eve in the Garden of Eden.

The principal town of the Lower Engadine is **Scuol** (Schuls in German), with a spa and a regional museum. On the opposite bank of the Inn lie the villages of **Vulpera**, which has picturesque houses and an 11th-century castle, and **Tarasp**, with a spa. Chaste Tarasp, a castle, perches on a rocky spur above the village. At **S-charl**, nearby, is a lead and silver mine that is open to visitors.

Most of the towns and villages in the Lower Engadine are good bases for exploring the Silvretta mountain range to the north and the Parc Naziunal Svizzer *(see pp202–3)* to the south.

Müstair ⓴

Road map G4. ⓗ *830* ⓘ *081 858 50 00.* Ⓦ www.muestair.ch

TUCKED AWAY at the bottom of Val Müstair (Münstertal in German), and almost on the border with Italy, lies a small town. This is Müstair (Münster in German), which takes its name from the Carolingian monastery here. Founded in about AD 780, reputedly by Charlemagne, and still inhabited by a community of Benedictine monks, the monastery is one of the most ancient buildings in Switzerland.

The monastery church, known in Romansh as the **Baselgia San Jon** and in German as Klosterkirche St Johann, is decorated with exceptionally well-preserved 12th- and 13th-century

House in Ardez, in the Engadine valley, with Adam and Eve decoration

Romanesque frescoes. Because of these, the church has been declared a UNESCO World Heritage Site. While the frescoes on the side walls depict scenes from the life of Christ, those in the presbytery show scenes from the life of St John. A depiction of the Last Judgment covers the west wall. Some of the frescoes have been moved to the Schweizerisches Landesmuseum in Zürich (see pp162–3). The church also contains a 12th-century statue of Charlemagne and an 11th-century relief of the Baptism of Christ. The small **museum** near the church contains Carolingian statuary and reliefs and Baroque figures.

Statue of Charlemagne in Müstair's church

🛈 Baselgia San Jon

Church ☐ Apr–Oct: 7am–8pm daily; Nov–Mar: 7:30am–6pm daily. **Museum** ☐ May–Oct: 9am–noon & 1:30–5pm Mon–Sat, 1:30–5pm Sun; Nov–Apr: 10am–noon & 1:30–4:30pm Mon–Sat, 1:30–4:30pm Sun. 🎫

Parc Naziunal Svizzer ㉑

See pp202–03.

Pontresina ㉒

Road map G4. 🏠 1,900. 🛈 Via Miastra; 081 838 83 00. ☒ www.pontresina.ch

THE RESORT OF Pontresina, in the Upper Engadine, lies at the foot of Val Bernina at an altitude of 1,800 m (5,900 ft). With several large hotels, it is a major resort and the base of Switzerland's leading school of mountaineering.

Among Pontresina's historic buildings is the Spaniola Turm, a Romanesque tower, and the chapel of Santa Maria. It contains Romanesque frescoes, some of which depict scenes from the life of Mary Magdalene. Exhibits in the **Museum Alpin** illustrate the history of the town and its surroundings.

Pontresina is a year-round resort. In winter the slopes of Diavolezza and Lagalb offer excellent downhill skiing. There are also many cross-country routes and snow-boarding pistes. In summer, Pontresina offers gentle walking along wooded paths in the vicinity as well as more demanding hiking and mountaineering up to the summits of Alp Ota and Munt della Bescha. The trail up Val Roseg leads to a glacier at the foot of Piz Roseg. Experienced climbers can tackle Piz Bernina, which at 4,049 m (13,289 ft) is the highest peak in the Rhaetian Alps.

🏛 Museum Alpin

Via Maistra. 🔂 081 842 72 73. ☐ Mid-Jun–mid-Oct & end Dec–mid-Apr: 4–6pm Mon–Sat .🎫

Bernina Pass ㉓

Road map G4.

AT AN ALTITUDE of 2,328 m (7,638 ft), the Bernina Pass (Passo del Bernina in Italian) is the highest point on the ancient route from St Moritz to Tirano, over the border in Italy. The pass marks the boundary between Romansh- and Italian-speaking Graubünden.

A road, the Berninastrasse, climbs up Val Bernina on the north side of the pass and descends Val di Poschiavo on its southern side. The pass is also served by ordinary trains

and by the Bernina Express (see p27). The breathtaking view from the pass takes in the peaks of the Rhaetian Alps to the north and Lago Bianco, an artificial lake, to the south.

Poschiavo ㉔

Road map G4. 🛈 Piazza Communale; 081 844 05 71. ☒ www.valposchiavo.ch

THE DESCENT down Val di Poschiavo, the valley on the south side of the Bernina Pass, reveals a very different aspect of Switzerland. Here the climate and vegetation, as well as the culture, are Mediterranean. Buildings show an Italian influence and cypress trees and palms grow in sheltered gardens.

Poschiavo (Puschlav in German) is the main town in the valley. At its heart is the Piazza Communale, a square lined with Italianate palazzi and two churches, a late 15th-century Catholic church and a 17th-century Protestant church. Other notable buildings include the Casa Torre, a Romanesque tower, and the Palazzo Albricci. The so-called Spaniolenviertel (Spanish quarter) has houses painted in a colourful Moorish style.

ENVIRONS: At Cavaglia, near Poschiavo, are remarkable geological features known as cauldrons. These are natural wells, up to 3 m (10 ft) in diameter, that were carved into the rock by the circular action of stones and water released by a melting glacier.

The Piazza Communale in Poschiavo, lined with Italianate palazzi

Parc Naziunal Svizzer ㉑

Established in 1914, the Parc Naziunal Svizzer was the first national park to be created in the Alps. This pristine nature reserve covers an area of 172 sq km (66 sq miles) and its topography ranges from sheltered valleys with forests of pine and larch to flower-covered meadows and rocky, snow-covered peaks. The park is populated by ibex, chamois and deer, eagles and vultures, and colonies of marmots. Many rare plants, including edelweiss and alpine poppy, grow here. The best way to appreciate the park is to follow its well-marked hiking trails. Many of these start from parking areas off Ofenpassstrasse, the only highway through the park.

Hotel Il Fuorn ⑤
Built before the national park was established, the Hotel Il Fuorn is one of two places to stay within the park. The other is the Chamanna Cluozza, a hostel with dormitory accommodation.

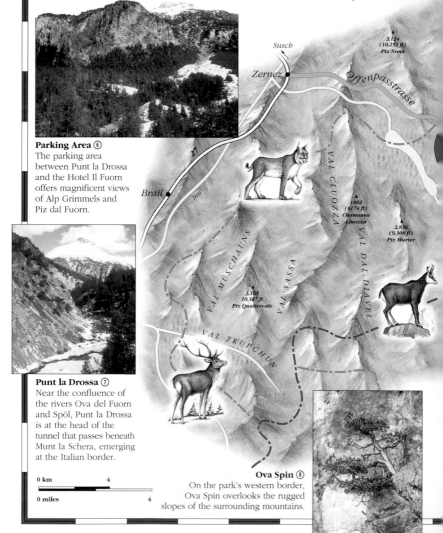

Parking Area ⑥
The parking area between Punt la Drossa and the Hotel Il Fuorn offers magnificent views of Alp Grimmels and Piz dal Fuorn.

Punt la Drossa ⑦
Near the confluence of the rivers Ova del Fuorn and Spöl, Punt la Drossa is at the head of the tunnel that passes beneath Munt la Schera, emerging at the Italian border.

Ova Spin ⑧
On the park's western border, Ova Spin overlooks the rugged slopes of the surrounding mountains.

Susch

Zernez

Brail

Ofenpassstrasse

3,124 (10,253 ft) Piz Nuna

VAL CLUOZZA

1882 (6174 ft) Chamanna Cluozza

2,836 (9,308 ft) Piz Murter

VAL DAL DIAVEL

VAL MÜSCHAUNS

VAL SASSA

3,165 10,387 ft Piz Quattervals

VAL TRUPCHUN

Inn

0 km   4
0 miles   4

Ova dal Fuorn Valley ④
The mountain slopes at lower altitudes are covered with mountain pine.

Scuol

*3,030
(9,944 ft)
Piz della Plattas*

VAL MINGER

VAL FORAZ

VAL DAL BOTSCH

VAL NÜGLIA

...TUR

⑥ ⑤ 28 ④ *3013
Piz Nair* ② ①
③
Il Fuorn
*2,587
(8,491 ft)
Munt la Sachera*

...o del Gallo

Müstair

TIPS FOR DRIVERS

Tour length: 15 km (9 miles).
Stopping-off places: There are several hotels and restaurants in Zernez, and a hotel and hostel within the park.
Other attractions: The Nationalparkhaus in Zernez has a visitor centre. 📧 081 856 13 78.
⏰ Jun–Oct: 8:30am–6pm daily.

Pass dal Fuorn   50 min

Il Fuorn   1 ¼ h
Fcla. Val dal Botsch 3 ½ h
Terasp Fontana   6 ½ h
Minger   5 ¾ h

Alp Buffalora   20 min
Munt la Schera   2 ½ h
Alp la Schera   2 ½ h
Il Fuorn   3 ¼ h

Alp Sprella   3   h
Döss Radond   4 ¼ h
Tschuccai   5 ¼ h
Sta. Maria   6 ¾ h

Alp Buffalora   20 min
Alp la Schera   2 ½ h
Punt la Drossa   3 ¼ h

Buffalora
1968 m

Trail Signboards ③
The park has a total of 80 km (50 miles) of marked hiking trails, and for conservation reasons walkers are forbidden to step off them. The trails are open from June to October.

Eastern Boundary ②
From the park's eastern boundary there are magnificent views of two peaks, Piz Nair to the north and Munt la Schera to the south.

Pass dal Fuorn ①
Breathtaking views of the park and the Ova dal Fuorn valley stretch out below the Pass dal Fuorn (Ofenpass in German).

KEY

▮	Suggested route
▮	Scenic route
=	Other roads
=	River, lake
---	Park boundary
---	National border

Cable car to Corviglia, above St Moritz

St Moritz ㉕

Road map F4. 🏘 5,100.
ℹ️ *Via Maistra 12; 081 837 33 33.*
ⓦ www.stmoritz.ch

ONE OF THE WORLD'S most glamorous winter sports resorts, St Moritz (San Murezzan in Romansh) lies on a sunny terrace on the north shore of the Moritzersee (Lej da San Murezzan). Surrounded by mountains, it offers superb skiing and snowboarding, and is a base for hiking and mountaineering in summer.

Originally a small village whose curative springs had been exploited at least since the Middle Ages, St Moritz began to develop into a winter sports resort in the 19th century. The town has two districts: St Moritz-Bad, the spa area on the southwestern side of the lake, and St Moritz-Dorf, on the northern side, with hotels, restaurants and boutiques.

Although little remains of the original village, St Moritz has two interesting museums. A domed building on Via Somplaz, ten minutes' walk west of St Moritz-Dorf, houses the **Giovanni-Segantini Museum**. This Symbolist painter, who spent the final years of his life in the Upper Engadine, is known for his sensitive Alpine scenes. Many are on display here, including his great triptych entitled *Birth, Life and Death*.

On Via dal Bagn, just below Via Somplaz, is the **Museum Engiadinais**, which is devoted to life in the Engadine and the history of the spa.

🏛 **Giovanni-Segantini Museum**
Via Somplaz 30. ☎ *081 833 44 54.*
🕐 *10am–noon & 3–6pm.* 📷
🏛 **Museum Engiadinais**
Via dal Bagn 39. ☎ *081 833 43 33.*
🕐 *10am–noon & 2–5pm Mon–Fri, 10am–noon Sun.* 📷

Sils ㉖

Road map F4. 🚌 600. ℹ️ *081 838 50 50.* ⓦ www.sils.ch

WITH HOUSES in the traditional style of the Engadine, the charming village of Sils (Segl in Romansh) has a picturesque setting on the north shore of the Silsersee (Lej da Segl).

The village consists of two parts: Sils Baselgia, on the lakeshore, and Sils Maria, to the south. Many writers, painters and musicians have been drawn to Sils. From 1881 to 1889, Sils Maria was the summer residence of the German philosopher Friedrich Nietzsche. The house where he lived, and where he wrote *Also Sprach Zarathustra*, has been converted into a small museum, the **Nietzsche Haus**. The exhibits include photographs of the philosopher and several of his manuscripts.

> IN DIESEM HAUSE WOHNTE
> **FRIEDRICH NIETZSCHE**
> WÄHREND SCHAFFENSREICHER
> SOMMERMONATE 1881-1888

Plaque commemorating Friedrich Nietzsche, in Sils

🏛 **Nietzsche Haus**
☎ *081 826 53 69.* 🕐 *1–5pm Tue–Sun.* 📷

Val Bregaglia ㉗

Road map F4. ℹ️ *Stampa; 081 822 15 55.* ⓦ www.bregaglia.ch

THE WESTERN continuation of the Inn valley culminates at the Maloja Pass (1,815 m/ 5,957 ft), which marks the western boundary of the Engadine. On the western side of the pass a road winds down Val Bregaglia, one of Graubünden's Italian-speaking valleys.

Val Bregaglia, which has many scenic hiking trails and which contains extraordinary rock formations, is popular with mountaineers. It is also dotted with ruined castles and small churches.

The main village in Val Bregaglia is **Vicosoprano**, which has mansions and historic law courts. Further south lies **Stampa**, birthplace of the artists Augusto Giacometti and his son Alberto. Buildings of interest in Stampa include the Casa Granda. This 16th-century palace contains a museum of local history and a display of works by Augusto and Alberto Giacometti.

The charming hamlet of **Soglio**, with narrow alleys, stone houses and *palazzi*, perches on the north side of the valley. The many hiking trails leading out of Soglio follow scenic routes both eastwards up Val Bregaglia and down towards the Italian border.

The hamlet of Soglio, on the north side of Val Bregaglia

One of the Romanesque panels in the Kirche St Martin, Zillis

Zillis ❷❽

Road map F4.
W www.zillis-reischen.ch

I N THE VILLAGE of Zillis (Ziràn in Romansh), on the east bank of the Hinterrhein, stands a small church that contains a remarkable cycle of Romanesque frescoes.

The wooden ceiling of **Kirche St Martin** (Baselgia Sontg Martegn) is covered with 153 square panels, which were painted between 1109 and 1114. While the exterior panels depict an ocean filled with sea monsters, those in the interior show scenes from the life of Christ and of St Martin. Figures of angels symbolizing the four winds fill the corners of the scheme. The history and subject matter of the frescoes, and the methods used to create them, are explained in an exhibition area within the church.

ENVIRONS: About 3 km (2 miles) south of Zillis is the **Via Mala Schlucht**, a 500-m (1,640-ft) canyon carved out by the waters of the Hinterrhein. Steps lead down to the bottom of the canyon.

🏠 **Kirche St Martin**
📞 081 661 10 21.
🕐 Apr–Oct: 8am–6pm; Nov–Mar: 9am–6pm.

San Bernardino Pass ❷❾

Road map E4.
W www.sanbernardino.ch

O N THE GREAT transalpine route running from the Bodensee, in the far northeast of Switzerland, down to Lake Como, in Italy, the San Bernardino is one of Europe's most important mountain passes. It lies at an altitude of 2,065 m (6,777 ft) between the Rheinwald forest to the north and the Valle Mesolcina, in the Italian-speaking region of Switzerland, to the south. Although snow usually blocks the pass from November through to May, the 7-km (4-mile) tunnel beneath it is permanently open.

The village resort of San Bernardino, on the south side of the pass, is a good base for exploring the surrounding mountains. Hiking trails lead up to the summit of Pizzo Uccello (2,724 m/ 8,940 ft), north of the village, and to Lago d'Osso, a lake 2 km (1 mile) to the south.

Mesocco ❸⓪

Road map F4. 🏠 1,200.
W www.mesocco.ch

T HE PICTURESQUE stone houses of Mesocco cluster on the banks of the River Moesa, which runs along the Valle Mesolcina. This valley stretches from the San Bernardino Pass southward to Bellinzona and, although it is in the canton of Graubünden, it has strong cultural links with Ticino.

The **Castello di Misox**, a ruined fortress set on a rocky outcrop above the town, commands a stunning view of the valley and the village of Soazza (see below). Built for the counts of Sax von Misox in the 12th century, the castle was significantly extended in the 15th century and in 1480 it passed into the ownership of the Trivulizio family, from Milan. The slender campanile is a remnant of the castle complex, which was almost completely destroyed in 1526.

At the foot of the castle stands the Romanesque church of **Santa Maria del Castello**. Built in the 12th century, the church was partly remodelled in the 17th. The nave has a coffered ceiling and the walls are decorated with 15th-century murals. These depict St George and the Dragon, St Bernard of Siena, patron saint of Valle Melsocina, and scenes symbolizing the months of the year.

ENVIRONS: About 4 km (3 miles) south of Mesocco is **Soazza**, a village with an attractive 17th-century church. About 15 km (9 miles) south of Soazza is **San Vittore**, where there is an 8th-century chapel. The **Val Calanca**, which runs into Valle Mesolcina, also merits exploration for its beautiful scenery.

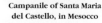

Campanile of Santa Maria del Castello, in Mesocco

CENTRAL SWITZERLAND AND TICINO

T HE CRADLE OF THE SWISS CONFEDERATION *and the birthplace of the legendary hero William Tell, central Switzerland is not only at the geographical hub but also the historical heart of the country. Beyond high mountains to the south lies Italian-speaking Ticino, a canton with its own distinctive culture and Mediterranean orientation.*

Lake Lucerne and the four cantons bordering its eastern and southern shores have a unique place in Swiss history and culture. In 1291, the cantons of Schwyz, Uri and Unterwalden (now divided into the half-cantons of Obwalden and Nidwalden) swore the oath of eternal alliance that led to the formation of the Swiss Confederation. The region is suffused with historic resonance. While Rütli Meadow, on the south shore of Lake Lucerne, is hallowed as the spot where their oath was sworn, the towns of Bürglen and Altdorf, in the canton of Uri, have vivid associations with William Tell. The two other cantons that make up central Switzerland are Luzern, on the west shore of the lake, and Zug, on the north shore.

Schwyz, Uri, Obwalden and Nidwalden are known as the Waldstätte, or Forest Cantons. Central Switzerland is largely Catholic and German-speaking.

Hemmed in by the Alps to the north and bordered on almost all other sides by Italy, Ticino is a geographically, culturally and linguistically separate entity. Long ruled by the dukes of Milan, Ticino was conquered by the Swiss Confederates in the early 16th century but only joined the Confederation as a free canton in 1803. This large canton in the sun-drenched foothills of the southern Alps is Italian-speaking and mostly Catholic, with a lifestyle that is markedly more relaxed than elsewhere in Switzerland.

The Chiesa Collegiata dei SS Pietro e Stefano in Bellinzona

◁ **Sunset on Lake Maggiore, a great lake on the border between Switzerland and Italy**

Exploring Central Switzerland & Ticino

WITH EXCELLENT TRANSPORT facilities and a landscape that matches the classic image of Swiss rural life, central Switzerland is easy to explore. While to the northwest of Lake Lucerne the land is relatively flat, the area to the east and south is more mountainous. Several of the high peaks here have excellent hiking trails, and their summits offer breathtaking views. Towards Andermatt, in the northern foothills of the Alps, the terrain becomes more rugged, culminating in several high mountain passes. The route over the St Gotthard Pass leads down the idyllic wooded valleys of northern Ticino. Further south, beyond Bellinzona, are Lake Maggiore and Lake Lugano, two of southern Ticino's most beautiful natural features.

SEE ALSO

- **Where to Stay** pp257–9.
- **Where to Eat** pp282–3.

SIGHTS AT A GLANCE

Interior detail of the Jesuit church, Luzern

Costumed participants in Fasnacht, Luzern's carnival

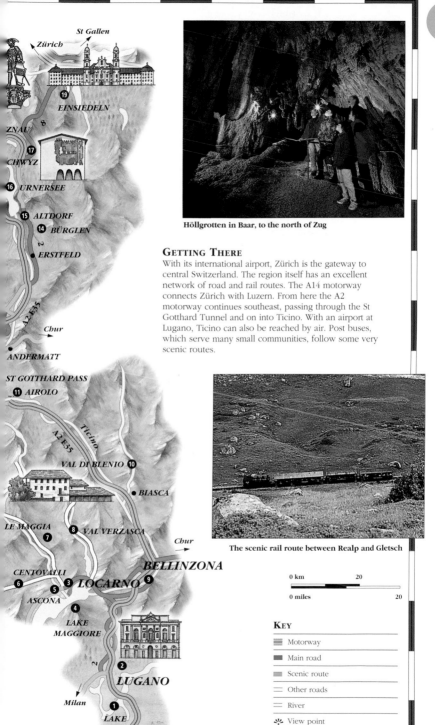

St Gallen

Zürich

⑲ **EINSIEDELN**

ZNAU

8

⑰

CHWYZ

⑯ **URNERSEE**

⑮ **ALTDORF**

⑭ **BÜRGLEN**

● **ERSTFELD**

2

A2 E35

Chur

● **ANDERMATT**

ST GOTTHARD PASS

⑪ **AIROLO**

A2 E35

Ticino

VAL DI BLENIO ⑩

● **BIASCA**

LE MAGGIA
⑦

⑧ **VAL VERZASCA**

Chur

CENTOVALLI

⑥

⑤ ③ **LOCARNO** ⑨

BELLINZONA

ASCONA

④

**LAKE
MAGGIORE**

②

LUGANO

Milan

①

**LAKE
LUGANO**

Milan

Höllgrotten in Baar, to the north of Zug

GETTING THERE

With its international airport, Zürich is the gateway to
central Switzerland. The region itself has an excellent
network of road and rail routes. The A14 motorway
connects Zürich with Luzern. From here the A2
motorway continues southeast, passing through the St
Gotthard Tunnel and on into Ticino. With an airport at
Lugano, Ticino can also be reached by air. Post buses,
which serve many small communities, follow some very
scenic routes.

The scenic rail route between Realp and Gletsch

| 0 km | 20 |
| 0 miles | 20 |

KEY

▬ Motorway

▬ Main road

▬ Scenic route

═ Other roads

═ River

☆ View point

Lake Lugano ①

NESTLING BETWEEN STEEP alpine slopes, this sheltered lake is one of Ticino's most beautiful natural features. Although most of it lies in Swiss territory, its southwestern shore and northeastern branch, and a small central enclave, belong to Italy. The road bridge that crosses the lake leads up to the St Gotthard Tunnel. The best way of exploring Lake Lugano (Lago di Lugano or Ceresio in Italian) is by boat, from Lugano and several other points along the lakeshore. Fine views of the lake can be enjoyed by taking the cable car from Lugano to the summit of mountains flanking the resort.

Lugano
The lakeside resort of Lugano lies in a sheltered bay, with Monte San Salvatore to the south and Monte Brè to the east.

Monte Tamaro
The chapel on the summit of this mountain, north of Lugano, was designed by Mario Botta and decorated by Enzo Cucchi. It was completed in 1996.

★ **Melide**
The main attraction of Melide is the Swissminiatur, a park with 1:25 scale models of Switzerland's most notable buildings and natural features.

Morcote
The small church of Santa Maria del Sasso overlooks Morcote, one of the most attractive hamlets in Ticino.

Lugano

Agno

A2 E35

S 233

Caslano

Tresa

Melide

Figine

Bissc

Brusimpiano

Morcote

Brusino Arsizio

SP61

Porto Ceresio

STAR SIGHTS
★ **Melide**
★ **Monte Brè**

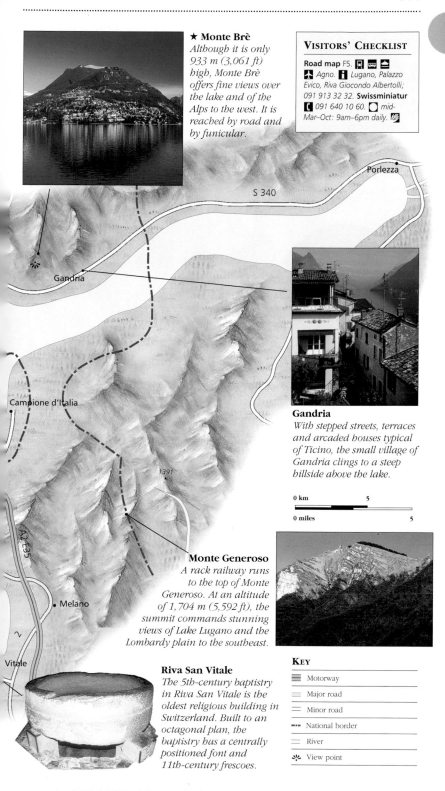

★ Monte Brè

Although it is only 933 m (3,061 ft) high, Monte Brè offers fine views over the lake and of the Alps to the west. It is reached by road and by funicular.

VISITORS' CHECKLIST

Road map F5. 🚆 🚌 🚢
✈ *Agno.* 🛈 *Lugano, Palazzo Evico, Riva Giocondo Albertolli; 091 913 32 32.* **Swissminiatur**
📞 *091 640 10 60.* ◯ *mid-Mar–Oct: 9am–6pm daily.* ♿

Porlezza

S 340

Gandria

Campione d'Italia

1391

A2-E35

Melano

Vitale

Gandria

With stepped streets, terraces and arcaded houses typical of Ticino, the small village of Gandria clings to a steep hillside above the lake.

0 km   5

0 miles   5

Monte Generoso

A rack railway runs to the top of Monte Generoso. At an altitude of 1,704 m (5,592 ft), the summit commands stunning views of Lake Lugano and the Lombardy plain to the southeast.

Riva San Vitale

The 5th-century baptistry in Riva San Vitale is the oldest religious building in Switzerland. Built to an octagonal plan, the baptistry has a centrally positioned font and 11th-century frescoes.

KEY

▭▭▭	Motorway
▭▭	Major road
▭	Minor road
▬▪▬	National border
▭	River
✵	View point

Street-by-Street: Lugano ❷

L YING IN A SHALLOW INLET on the north shore of Lake Lugano, this is the largest town in Ticino and one the canton's great lakeside resorts. Lugano is also a centre of finance and banking. With piazzas, stepped streets and narrow, winding alleys, the Old Town (Centro Storico) has an Italianate character. Its hub is Piazza della Riforma, a square lined with tall shuttered buildings and filled with busy pavement cafés. Palm-fringed promenades line the quays, and the distinctive sugar-loaf outlines of Monte Brè and Monte San Salvatore rise to the east and south.

Palazzo Riva
This 18th-century palace has decorated windows with wrought-iron balconies.

★ **Cattedrale San Lorenzo**
The Renaissance façade contains a rose window depicting the Madonna and Child.

VIA SAN LORENZO

VIA PESSINA

VIA LUVINI

PIAZZA G. MOTTA

VIA MAC

PIAZZA DELLA RIFORMA

VIA GIOCONDO ALBERTOLLI

Piazza della Riforma
Filled with pavement cafés, this spacious square is the social and geographical hub of Lugano's historic centre.

Palazzo Civico
The Neo-Renaissance town hall was built in 1844–5 and features a statue of the Italian architect Domenico Fontana.

STAR SIGHTS

★ **San Lorenzo**

★ **Villa Ciani**

KEY

▬ ▬ ▬ Suggested route

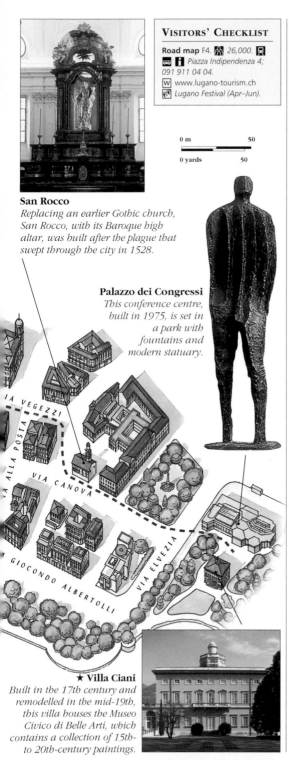

VISITORS' CHECKLIST

Road map F4. 🚶 26,000. 🚆
🚌 ℹ️ *Piazza Indipendenza 4;*
091 911 04 04.
W *www.lugano-tourism.ch*
🎭 *Lugano Festival (Apr–Jun).*

0 m — 50

0 yards — 50

San Rocco
Replacing an earlier Gothic church,
San Rocco, with its Baroque high
altar, was built after the plague that
swept through the city in 1528.

Palazzo dei Congressi
This conference centre,
built in 1975, is set in
a park with
fountains and
modern statuary.

IA VEGEZZI

A ALLA POSTA

VIA CANOVA

GIOCONDO ALBERTOLLI

VIA ELVEZIA

★ Villa Ciani
Built in the 17th century and
remodelled in the mid-19th,
this villa houses the Museo
Civico di Belle Arti, which
contains a collection of 15th-
to 20th-century paintings.

Renaissance frescoes in
Chiesa Santa Maria degli Angioli

🔒 Santa Maria degli Angioli
Piazza Luini 3. 📞 *091 922 01 12.*
This plain 15th-century
church, in a square southwest
of the Piazza della Riforma,
once belonged to a
Franciscan monastery. The
interior is decorated with
Renaissance frescoes by
Bernardino Luini and
Giuseppe Antonio Petrini.
Dating from the first half of
the 16th century, they depict
scenes from the life of Christ.
The sacristy contains a small
display of religious artefacts
from the monastery's treasury.

🏛 Museo d'Arte Moderna
Riva Antonio Caccia 5. 📞 *091 994*
43 70. ◯ *9am–7pm Tue–Sun.* 🎟
Occupying an elegant 18th-
century villa, this museum of
modern art stages temporary
exhibitions of the work of
major painters and sculptors
of the 20th and 21st centuries.
Artists whose work has been
exhibited here include
Francis Bacon, Edvard
Munch, Amedeo Modigliani
and Egon Schiele. The museum
also has a permanent
collection of works by
19th- and 20th-century artists,
including Ticinese painters.

🏛 Museo Cantonale d'Arte
Via Canova 10. 📞 *091 910 47 80.*
◯ *2–5pm Tue, 10am–5pm*
Wed–Sun. 🎟
With a section devoted to the
work of Ticinese artists of the
19th and 20th centuries, this
gallery contains an interesting
display of paintings depicting
local peasant life. Also on
view are paintings by Degas,
Renoir, Turner and Klee, as
well as avant-garde works by
contemporary Swiss artists,
and displays of sculpture and
photography.

Locarno ❸

WITH AN ENCHANTING SETTING at the northern tip of Lake Maggiore, Locarno lies in a wide bay in the shelter of the Lepontine Alps. It is the sunniest of all Swiss towns, and date palm, fig, pomegranate and bougainvillea thrive in its mild climate. During the Middle Ages, Locarno was the centre of a dispute between the bishops of Como and the dukes of Milan, who finally gained control of the town in the 14th century but who lost it to the Swiss Confederates in 1512. The capital of Ticino from 1803 to 1878, Locarno is now a resort that attracts visitors from north of the Alps who come to enjoy its Mediterranean climate.

Promenade Lungolago Giuseppe Motta, fringed with palms

Wall paintings at Castello Visconteo

Exploring Locarno
The old district of Locarno lies west of Piazza Grande, a short distance away from the lakeshore. It is roughly defined by Castello Visconteo, Chiesa San Francesco, Chiesa Sant'Antonio Abate and Chiesa Nuova. To the north of the old district rises the spur on which another church, the Santuario della Madonna del Sasso, is set.

🔒 Chiesa San Francesco
Via Cittadella 20.
Completed in 1572, the church of St Francis stands on the site of a 13th-century Franciscan monastery. The eagle, ox and lamb on its Renaissance façade represent Locarno's aristocrats, ordinary citizens and country-dwellers respectively. The decoration of the interior dates mainly from the 18th century.

♣ Castello Visconteo
Piazza Castello 2. 🔔 *091 756 31 80.*
⏱ *Apr–Oct: 10am–5pm Tue–Thu.* 🈂
The origins of Castello Visconteo go back to the 12th century, when it was built for the Orelli family. In 1342 the castle came into the ownership of the Visconti, a Milanese family, who enlarged it in the

late 15th century. The dovetailed crenellation of the walls and the towers dates from that period. The castle was partly destroyed when the Swiss Confederates seized control of Locarno. The building's surviving wing now houses a museum of history and archaeology. The collection of Roman artefacts is particularly good.

🏛 Palazzo della Conferenza
Via della Pace.
It was in this *palazzo* that the Treaty of Locarno, drawn up between Germany and other European countries in the aftermath of World War I, was ratified in 1925. The terms of the treaty enabled Germany to join the League of Nations in 1926.

🌴 Promenade Lungolago Giuseppe Motta
Lined with palm trees and other Mediterranean plants, this lakeshore promenade

resembles the seafront boulevards of the French Riviera. The promenade leads southwards towards a municipal park and northwards towards a beach and public pool.

🔒 Chiesa di San Vittore
Via Collegiata, Muratta.
The 12th-century Romanesque basilica of San Vittore stands on the site of a 10th-century church in Muratta, east of the train station. The belfry, which was begun in the 16th century but not completed until 1932, has a Renaissance relief of St Victor. The austere interior bears traces of medieval frescoes, and the crypt beneath the presbytery contains columns with carved capitals.

🏛 Piazza Grande
This rectangular paved square is the focus of life in Locarno. Along its north side are 19th-century buildings with arcades of shops, cafés and restaurants. During the International Film Festival, held for ten days in early August, the square becomes an open-air cinema.

Piazza Grande, hub of Locarno's social life

🔒 Chiesa Nuova
Via Cittadella.

This church, also known as Chiesa Santa Maria Assunta, was completed in 1636, and its construction was funded by the architect Christoforo Orelli. It has a splendid Baroque interior, with sumptuous stuccowork and paintings depicting scenes from the life of the Virgin. A large statue of St Christopher graces the west front. The Palazzo Christoforo Orelli, next to the church, now serves as the canon's office.

🏛 Casa Rusca
Piazza Sant' Antonio. **☎** *091 756 31 85.* **○** *10am–5pm Tue–Sun.*

This elegant 18th-century residence, with an arcaded courtyard, houses Locarno's art gallery. With a permanent collection, as well as a progamme of temporary exhibitions, the gallery specializes in the work of modern and contemporary artists, many of whom have donated pieces of their work to the gallery. A highlight of the permanent collection is a display of work by Hans Arp (1886–1966), the Dadaist artist who spent the final years of his life in Locarno.

🔒 Chiesa Sant'Antonio Abate
Via Sant'Antonio.

The Baroque church of St Anthony was completed in 1692 and remodelled in 1863, when the façade and dome were renewed. The high altar, dating from 1740, features a depiction of Christ's deposition from the Cross by G.A.F. Orelli.

🔒 Santuario della Madonna del Sasso
○ *6:30am–7pm daily.*

The pilgrimage church of the Madonna of the Rock overlooks the town from the summit of a wooded spur. Dating from 1596, the church stands on the site of a chapel that was built in 1487 to mark the spot where the Madonna appeared to Bartolomeo da Ivrea, a Franciscan monk. The present church is decorated with frescoes and oil paintings, notable among which is an altarpiece with the *Flight into Egypt* painted by Bramantino in 1522.

VISITORS' CHECKLIST

Road map E5. 🏠 *14,300.* 🚉
🚌 ℹ *Via B. Luini 3; 091 791 00 91.* 🌐 *www.info-locarno.ch; www.maggiore.ch*
🎬 *International Film Festival (early Aug).*

The Santuario della Madonna del Sasso

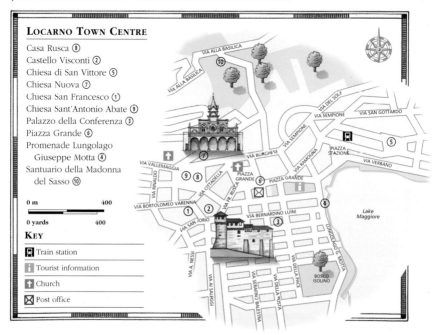

LOCARNO TOWN CENTRE

| 0 m | 400 |
| 0 yards | 400 |

KEY

🚉 Train station

ℹ Tourist information

✝ Church

✉ Post office

Around Lake Maggiore ❹

Only the northern tip of this long, slender lake lies in Switzerland, the remaining portion curving southwards into Italian territory. Some 60 km (40 miles) long and 6 km (4 miles) wide, Lake Maggiore is hemmed in by mountains to the north and south. Sheltered by these mountains, this beautiful lake basks in a Mediterranean climate, and its shores are covered with cork, fig and olive trees. Boats, steamers and hydrofoils cross the lake from Ascona, Locarno and Brissago all the way down to the resorts in its Italian section.

Ascona ⑤
Renowned for its mild climate and beautiful setting, this fashionable resort has attracted many artists.

Ronco ③
Set on a steep mountainside, this small town has beautiful views of the lake and of the Isole di Brissago.

Isole di Brissago ④
These two islands can be reached by boat from Locarno, Ascona and Ronco.

ALBERGO

Brissago ②
This lakeside town is well known for its cigar factory. It is also the burial place of the Italian composer Ruggero Leoncavallo (1858–1919).

Tegna
Domodossola
⑥
⑤
③
④
13
②
①
Gerra Gambarogno
Lake Maggiore
Verbania

Key

- Suggested route
- Scenic route
- Other roads
- River, lake
- View point

Madonna di Ponte ①
This 16th-century Renaissance church stands on the border with Italy. On the high altar is a painting of the Assumption of the Virgin dating from 1569.

TIPS FOR VISITORS

Tour length: 40 km (25 miles).
Stopping-off places:
Ascona and Locarno have the
widest choice of restaurants.
Other attractions: St Pancras,
the larger of the two Isole di
Brissago, has a botanical
garden. ☐ Apr–Oct:
9am–6pm daily. 🖼

Locarno ⑥

The Santuario della Madonna
del Sasso *(see pp214–15)*,
which towers over Locarno,
is accessible on foot or by
funicular.

Magadino ⑦

In summer, organ recitals
take place in Magadino's
Neo-classical parish
church.

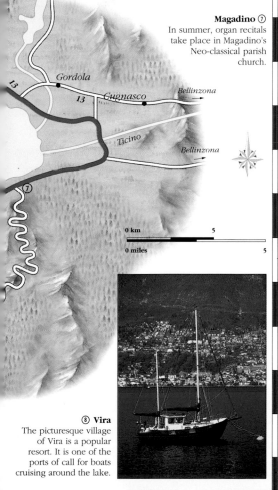

⑧ Vira
The picturesque village
of Vira is a popular
resort. It is one of the
ports of call for boats
cruising around the lake.

**A narrow alley in Ascona's
historic district**

Ascona ⑤

Road map E5. 🏠 *5,000*
🛈 Casa Serodine, Piazza Municipio;
01 791 00 91. ⓦ www.ascona.ch

A SMALL FISHING village for
many centuries, Ascona
rapidly developed in the
19th century, when it became
a fashionable health resort,
attracting writers, painters
and composers. After 1933,
Ascona became a place of
refuge for many German
artists, who were forced to
flee their country in the face
of Nazi persecution.

Ascona's exquisite Old Town
(Centro Storico) is a maze of
narrow cobbled streets lined
with small craft shops and art
galleries. Many of the most
picturesque of Ascona's
historic buildings, the oldest
of which date from the 14th
century, line Contrada
Maggiore. Piazza San Pietro is
dominated by the 16th-century
Chiesa dei SS Pietro e Paolo,
which has an altarpiece
painted by Giovanni Serodine,
a pupil of Caravaggio. Also
notable are the Collegio Papio,
a Renaissance building with
an arcaded courtyard, and
Santa Maria della Misericordia,
a church with 15th-century
frescoes. The Museo Comunale
d'Arte Moderna, in a 16th-
century *palazzo*, contains work
by artists associated with the
town, including Paul Klee and
Hans Arp. Piazza Motta, a
large pedestrianized square
on the lakefront, is lined with
cafés and restaurants.

The village of Lionza, in the Centovalli

Centovalli ❻

Road map E5. W www.centovalli.ch

THE STUNNINGLY beautiful Centovalli (Valley of a Hundred Valleys) is so named for the many side valleys that cut down into it. A railway running from Locarno to Domodossola, in Italy, carries trains on a spectacularly scenic journey up the Centovalli. On this journey of about 40 km (25 miles), the train crosses 79 bridges or viaducts over deep canyons and passes through 24 tunnels. The first part of the journey leads along the vineyard-covered Val Pedemonte. From here the route enters more rugged country, with forests of chestnut trees.

The train stops at several villages along the route. At **Verscio**, 4 km (3 miles) from Locarno, there is a school of circus art, run by the famous Swiss clown Dimitri. About 3 km (2 miles) further up the valley is **Intragna**, where there is a Baroque church. **Palagnedra** has a small Gothic church decorated with 15th-century frescoes.

Valle Maggia ❼

Road map E5. W www.vallemaggia.ch

THIS DEEP VALLEY runs for about 50 km (30 miles) northwest of Ascona up to Cevio. At its lower levels, the valley is wide and covered with vineyards. As it ascends into the high Alps it becomes increasingly rugged, with forests of pine and larch. The valley is also dotted with chalets and villages.

At **Maggia**, the largest village in the valley, is the 15th-century Chiesa Santa Maria delle Grazie. The exterior of this church is unremarkable but the interior is decorated with dazzling 16th- and 17th-century frescoes.

Past **Gliumaglio**, where there are dramatic waterfalls, the road leads further up the valley to **Cevio**. A notable feature of this village is the 17th-century Palazzo Pretorio, its façade featuring the coats of arms of the bailiffs who successively occupied the building. Nearby stands the Palazzo Franzoni (1630), which houses a museum of regional history.

The hamlet of **Mogno** contains the serenely beautiful Chiesa di San Giovanni Battista. Designed by the Ticinese architect Mario Botta and completed in 1996, this extraordinary church is built of local stone, The interior is lined with white marble and grey granite arranged in stripes and chequer patterns. Their effect is enhanced by the play of light entering through the translucent ceiling.

Val Verzasca ❽

Road map E5. W www.ticino-tourism.ch

WASHED BY THE emerald waters of the River Verzasca, Val Verzasca is the smallest of the valleys lying north of Locarno. A gigantic dam near the mouth of the valley has created the Lago di Vogorno, a large artificial lake.

The valley is lined with villages, whose grey stone houses cling to the mountainsides. **Vogorno** has a small church decorated with

Detail of a fresco in the church at Brione-Verzasca

Chiesa di San Giovanni Battista at Mogno, in Valle Maggia

The Ponte dei Salti, a medieval bridge near Lavertezzo, in Val Verzasca

Byzantine frescoes. Near **Lavertezzo**, the river is spanned by the Ponte dei Salti, a medieval double-arched bridge. A modern art trail, running for 4 km long (3 miles) between Lavertezzo and Brione, is lined with works by 34 Italian, Swiss and German sculptors.

At **Brione-Verzasca** is a church whose origins go back to the 13th century. Its façade is decorated with a painting of St Christopher and the interior features 15th-century frescoes. At the head of the valley lies the village of **Sonogno**, with stone houses typical of the Ticino. One of them, Casa Genardini, houses a regional museum.

Bellinzona ❾

See pp220–21.

Val di Blenio ❿

Road map E4.
W www.ticino-tourism.ch

THIS BROAD scenic valley, washed by the River Brenno, leads up to the Lucomagno Pass (1,914 m/6,282 ft). The road up the valley and over the pass leads into Graubünden. Val di Blenio lies in the heart of rural Ticino. It has magnificent scenery and is dotted with picturesque villages.

Biasca, at the foot of the valley, has a Romanesque church with Gothic frescoes. Just north of Biasca is **Malvaglia**. The 16th- to 17th-century church here has a Romanesque tower and its façade features a large painting of St Christopher.

Negrentino is notable for its early Romanesque church of St Ambrose, whose tall square belfry tower can be seen from afar. The interior of the church is decorated with frescoes dating from the 11th to the 16th centuries. **Lottinga** has an interesting museum of regional history. The villages higher up the valley, such as **Olivone**, are good bases for mountain hiking.

Airolo ⓫

Road map E4.
W www.leventinaturismo.ch

LOCATED JUST below the St Gotthard Pass, Airolo lies at the point where the motorway and railway line through the St Gotthard Tunnel emerge. As it is bypassed by these major routes, Airolo is a quiet town and, with several hotels, it is a convenient base for exploring the valley that stretches out below. A plaque in the town

Commemorative plaque in Airolo

commemorates the 177 people who died during the tunnel's construction in the 1880s.

ENVIRONS: Valle Leventina, below Airolo, carries the motorway and main railway line that run from Zürich to Bellinzona and Lugano. The valley is dotted with small towns and villages, many of which have interesting churches. While **Chiggiogna** has a church with 15th-century frescoes, **Chironico** has a 10th-century church with 14th-century frescoes. The 12th-century church in **Giornico** is one of the finest in the Ticino. The interior is decorated with frescoes dating from 1478.

St Gotthard Pass ⓬

Road map E4.
W www.gotthard-hospiz.ch

WITH THE REUSS VALLEY in the canton of Uri to the north, and the Ticino valley to the south, the St Gotthard Pass lies at an altitude of 2,108 m (6,918 ft). It is on the principal route from northern Europe to Italy.

The pass has been used since the 13th century, when a bridge was built across a gorge near Andermatt. It was only in the 19th century, when a 15-km (9-mile) road and rail tunnel was built, that the route began to carry a large volume of traffic. Because of heavy snowfall, the pass is closed in winter, usually from November to April.

The 19th-century hospice on the pass houses the **Museo Nazionale del San Gottardo**. The museum documents the history of the pass and describes the plants and animals of this high Alpine region.

Marked trails lead up to the summit of many of the surrounding peaks, including Pizzo Lucendro, and to mountain terraces from which there are splendid views.

🏛 **Museo Nazionale del San Gottardo**
C 091 869 15 25 ☐ May–Oct: 9am–6pm daily. 🄯

Bellinzona ❾

BECAUSE OF ITS location in a valley on the route over the great Alpine passes, Bellinzona was a fortress town from Roman times. During the Middle Ages, the dukes of Milan built three castles here, enabling them to defend this strategically placed town and control traffic passing through the valley. The Swiss Confederates seized control of Bellinzona in the 16th century, holding the town for 300 years. After gaining its independence in 1803, Bellinzona became the capital of Ticino. Its three castles, Castelgrande, Montebello and Sasso Corbaro, have together been declared a UNESCO World Heritage Site.

Chiesa Collegiata SS Pietro e Stefano

Exploring Bellinzona
The best starting point for an exploration of Bellinzona is Castelgrande, which can be reached by taking a lift located to one side of Piazzella Mario della Valle. Steps from the castle platform wind down to Piazza Collegiata, in the heart of the Old Town, where there are several fine Renaissance buildings. A path east of the piazza leads up to Castello di Montebello. From here, a steep road leads on up to Castello di Sasso Corbaro.

♣ Castelgrande
Museum Storico-Artistico
📞 091 825 13 42.
🕐 10am–6pm daily. 🖋

Set on a high plateau on the west side of the Old Town, Castelgrande is the oldest and also the most impressive of Bellinzona's three castles. In the 12th century, the Roman fortress that already stood on the site was rebuilt and enlarged by the bishops of Como. The castle underwent a further phase of rebuilding after 1242, when Bellinzona was conquered by the dukes of Milan. The fortress was extended on several occasions until the late 15th century.

Today Castelgrande's main features are two square towers, the Torre Bianca (White Tower) and Torre Nera (Black Tower), which are joined by crenellated walls forming inner baileys.

The museum, in the south wing of the castle, documents the history of Bellinzona. Also on display here is a set of 15th-century painted panels from the walls and ceiling of a villa in Bellinzona.

Renaissance arcades around the courtyard of the Palazzo Civico

⛪ Old Town
Bellinzona's Old Town nestles in the wide Ticino valley, in the shadow of its great medieval castles. With Italianate squares, Renaissance buildings, and red cobblestones in its winding alleys, it is a typical Lombard town.

Among Bellinzona's many fine buildings is the Palazzo Civico, an elegant town hall with an arcaded courtyard in the Renaissance style. Other notable buildings are the **Chiesa Santa Maria delle Grazie**, a church with 15th-century frescoes depicting the Passion and Crucifixion, and the **Chiesa di San Rocco**, a Gothic church with a Baroque interior.

On Saturday mornings the Old Town is filled with colourful market stalls heaped with fresh produce, cheeses, bread, wines and local crafts.

♠ Chiesa Collegiata dei SS Pietro e Stefano
This Renaissance monastery church, whose imposing façade is pierced by a rose window, stands at the foot of the ramparts of Castelgrande. Built originally in the Gothic style, it was rebuilt in the first half of the 16th century to plans by Thomas Rodari, the architect of Como's cathedral. The interior, in which the

Firework display over Castelgrande

earlier Gothic arches are preserved, is decorated with elaborate stucco-work and frescoes in a lavish Baroque style. Over the high altar is a depiction of the Crucifixion, painted by Simone Peterzano in 1658.

♣ Castello di Montebello
Museo Archeologico e Civico
[📞] 091 825 13 42. [○] Feb–Dec: 10am–6pm daily. [♿]
Consisting of a 13th-century keep and a 15th-century residential palace surrounded by walls, this fortress is the most complex of Bellinzona's three castles. The crenellated walls linking Castello di Montebello, to the east of the town, and Castelgrande, to the west, created a formidable defence system across the valley.

The museum, in the keep, contains an interesting collection of archaeological artefacts from the vicinity of Bellinzona, as well as weapons and armour.

Doorway, Chiesa dei SS Pietro e Stefano

♣ Castello di Sasso Corbaro
Belvedere al Castello di Sasso Corbaro
[📞] 091 825 59 06. [○] Mar–Dec: 10am–6pm daily. [♿]
Castello di Sasso Corbaro is the most recent of Bellinzona's three fortresses. It was built in 1479 on the orders of the Duke of Milan, after the Swiss had defeated the Milanese at the Battle of Giornico, thus posing an increased threat to Ticino.

The fortress consists of a tall quadrilateral residential tower and square ramparts defended by a corner tower. The fortress is set on an elevated headland on the east side of the town, and commands wide views across the Ticino valley all the way to the northern tip of Lake Maggiore in the southwest (see pp216–17).

The museum, which is in the keep, contains displays illustrating the folk art and traditional crafts of Ticino.

VISITORS' CHECKLIST
Road map E5. [🗺] 17,000. [🚌] [🚆] [ℹ] Palazzo Civico; 091 825 21 31. [W] www.bellinzona.ch [📅] Rabadan (carnival; Feb).

⊞ Villa dei Cedri
Piazza San Biagio. [📞] 091 821 85 20. [○] Summer: 10am–noon & 2–6pm Tue–Sat, 10am 6pm Sun; winter: 10am–noon & 2–5pm Tue–Sun.
Sct in extensive grounds, with a vineyard, this late 19th-century Neo-Renaissance villa is the town's art gallery. Its collection consists of 19th- and 20th-century paintings mainly by Swiss and Italian artists of Ticino and Lombardy. Works by the Swiss Symbolist painter Giovanni Segantini form part of the collection. Also on display is a collection of prints, including examples by Oskar Kokoschka and Alfonse Mucha.

ENVIRONS: Less than 2 km (1 mile) south of Bellinzona is **Ravecchia**. In this town is an attractive Romanesque church, the Chiesa di San Biagio, which is decorated with Gothic frescoes

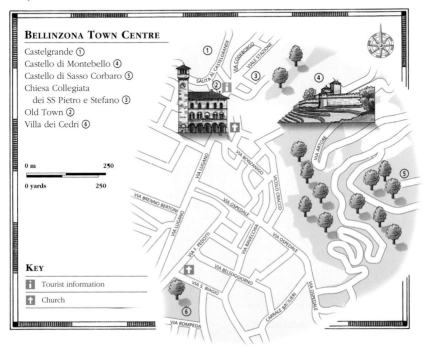

BELLINZONA TOWN CENTRE
Castelgrande ①
Castello di Montebello ④
Castello di Sasso Corbaro ⑤
Chiesa Collegiata
   dei SS Pietro e Stefano ③
Old Town ②
Villa dei Cedri ⑥

0 m   250
0 yards   250

KEY
[ℹ] Tourist information
[✝] Church

Three Passes ⑬

THE CIRCULAR ROUTE over the Uri Alps traverses some of the most spectacular high Alpine scenery in Switzerland. On the route are three mountain passes: the Susten Pass, Grimsel Pass and Furka Pass, each of which mark cantonal borders. A feat of 19th-century engineering, the road twists and turns, makes tightly winding ascents and descents, crosses bridges over dramatically plunging valleys, and passes through tunnels cut into the rock. All along the route are spectacular views of snow-capped mountains, majestic glaciers and beautiful mountain lakes.

Susten Pass ⑤
On the border between the cantons of Bern and Uri, the Susten Pass lies at an altitude of 2,259 m (7,414 ft).

Innertkirchen ⑥
This small town lies at the point where routes leading down from the passes join the road heading north towards Meiringen and Interlaken.

Grimsel Pass ⑦
At an altitude of 2,165 m (7,105 ft), the pass marks the border between the cantons of Bern and Valais. On the pass is the Totensee (Dead Lake).

0 km 5
0 miles 5

Furka Pass ⑧
Lying between the cantons of Valais and Uri, the pass lies at 2,431 m (7,978 ft), with the Bernese and Pennine Alps on either side.

Gadmen

Interlaken

6-11

11

Guttannen

Aare

Arlenbach

Grimselsee

Rhône

Gletsch

Brig

19

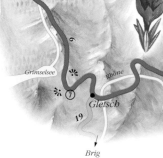

Furkastrasse ⑨
Built in the 1860s, this route over the Furka Pass offers spectacular views of high Alpine scenery. The Glacier Express passes through a tunnel beneath the pass.

Meienreuss Pass ④
Here a bridge spans a deep gorge in the Meien valley. From Wassen, near the foot of the valley, a road leads to Susten.

Tips for Drivers

Tour length: *120 km (75 miles).*
Stopping-off points: *Both Andermatt and Göschenen have small hotels and restaurants.*
Other attractions: *The Handeggfall, between the Grimsel Pass and Guttannen, are impressive waterfalls at the confluence of the Aare and the Arlenbach.*

Wassen ③
The terrace in front of Wassen's Baroque church is a good vantage point for spectacular views of the valley below.

Göschenen ②
This town, at the northern end of the tunnel beneath the St Gotthard Pass, is a good base for hiking in the surrounding mountains.

⑤
11
Meiendörfli
Altdorf
④
③
A2 E35
②
2
Chur
Göscheneralpsee
①
⑩
⑨
Bellinzona

Andermatt ①
A skiing resort in winter and hiking centre in summer, Andermatt lies in the heart of the St Gotthard Massif. Andermatt's church contains a beautiful Gothic font.

Key

- Suggested route
- Scenic route
- Other roads
- River, lake
- View point

Hospental ⑩
Hospental lies at the convergence of roads from the north, south and west. The 13th-century castle that once guarded this crossroads still stands, although it is now in ruins.

Frescoes on the ceiling of the chapel in Bürglen

Bürglen ⑭

Road map E3. 🏛 *3,600.* 🚌

THIS SMALL TOWN at the mouth of the Schächen valley is reputed to be the birthplace of William Tell, hero of Swiss legend. The supposed site of his house is marked by a chapel built in 1582. Its façade and interior are decorated with frescoes illustrating the legend of William Tell. A figure of the hero also graces an 18th-century fountain in the town.

The legend of William Tell and the place it occupies in Swiss culture and national pride are the subject of the displays in the **Tell Museum**. Consisting of chronicles and other documents, as well as paintings, sculptures and other pieces, the exhibits illustrate the legend over the 600 years of its existence.

Also of interest in Bürglen are a 17th-century wooden tavern, the **Adler Inn**, and an early Baroque church with a stucco-decorated interior and a Romanesque tower.

ENVIRONS: At **Riedertal**, 3 km (2 miles) southeast of Bürglen, is a beautiful pilgrimage chapel in the Gothic-Renaissance style. It is decorated with Gothic frescoes and contains a 14th-century Pietà, which is the object of local veneration.

🏛 **Tell Museum**
Postplatz. 📞 *041 870 41 55.*
🌐 *www.tellmuseum.ch* 🔵 *May–Jun: 10–11:30am & 1:30–5pm daily; Jul–Aug: 9:30–5:30pm daily; Sep–Oct: 10–11:30am & 1:30–5pm daily.* 🖼 🗹

Altdorf ⑮

Road map E3. 🏛 *8,000.* 🚌 📱
📱 *Tellspielhaus; 041 872 04 50.*
🌐 *www.altdorf.ch; www.i-uri-ch*
🎭 *Dorffest (1 Aug), Chilbi (Nov).*

THE CAPITAL OF the canton of Uri, Altdorf is supposed to be the town where William Tell shot the apple from his son's head. The **Telldenkmal**, a 19th-century statue of Tell and his son, stands on Rathausplatz. Plays based on the Tell legend are regularly performed in the Tellspielhaus here.

Also of interest in Altdorf is the town's historic arsenal

Entrance to the arsenal in Altdorf

and the **Historisches Museum**, which illustrates the history and traditions of the canton of Uri.

🏛 **Historisches Museum**
Gotthardstrasse 18. 📞 *041 870 19 06.*
🔵 *Dec–Jan: 1:30–5pm Tue–Sun; mid-May–mid-Oct: 10–11:30am & 1:30–5pm Tue–Sun.* 🖼

Urnersee ⑯

Road map E3. 🚌 🚢 📱 *Brunnen, Bahnhofstrasse 32; 041 825 00 40.*
🌐 *www.brunnentourismus.ch*

THE STUNNINGLY beautiful Urnersee forms the southeastern arm of Lake Lucerne. Surrounded on all sides by high, steep-sided mountains, the Urnersee resembles a Norwegian fjord.

On an elevated promontory below Seelisberg, on the west side of the lake, is **Rütli Meadow** (Bergwiese Rütli), where the alliance between the cantons of Uri, Schwyz and Unterwalden was sworn in 1291 *(see p35)*.

The village of **Seedorf**, at the southern extremity of the Urnersee, has a picturesque Gothic-Renaissance castle. It was built in 1556–60 and now houses a small geological museum. **Flüelen**, nearby, is the farthest port of call for the boats that sail across the lake from Luzern.

About 3 km (2 miles) north of Flüelen, on the road to Sisikon, is the **Tellsplate**, a flat rock. According to legend,

WILLIAM TELL

The legendary hero who freed Switzerland from Habsburg oppression, William Tell is supposed to have lived in the 13th century. Having refused to bow to imperial power, Tell was seized by the bailiff Hermann Gessler and, as punishment for his impudence, was ordered to shoot an arrow through an apple balanced on his son's head. Tell shot the apple but, after declaring his intention to kill Gessler, was condemned to prison. During the boat journey across the Urnersee, Tell escaped and later killed Gessler.

Statue of William Tell and his son in Altdorf

The Urnersee, seen from its southern shore

this is where William Tell leapt to freedom during his boat journey across Lake Lucerne, on his way to imprisonment in Hermann Gessler's castle at Küssnacht. Near the rock stands the **Tellskapelle**, a 16th-century chapel that was remodelled in the 19th century.

Brunnen, at the northern extremity of the Urnersee, is one of Lake Lucerne's largest resorts. It commands a sweeping panorama of the Urnersee, with views across the water to Rütli Meadow, on the opposite shore. Brunnen has a small Baroque chapel, the Bundeskapelle, with an altarpiece painted by Justus van Egmont, a pupil of Rubens, in 1642.

Schwyz ⓱

Road map E3. 🏘 14,000. ▦ 🚗
🛈 Bahnhofstrasse 4; 041 810 19 91.
ⓦ www.wbs.ch

THIS QUIET TOWN, capital of the canton of the same name, lies at the foot of the twin peaks of the Mythen. It has immense importance in Swiss history and culture.

The canton of Schwyz gave Switzerland both its name and its flag. Having sworn their mutual allegiance in 1291, the joint forces of Schwyz, Uri and Unterwalden united to defeat the Habsburgs at the Battle of Morgarten (1315). Thereafter they were known collectively as Schwyzers, and Helvetia *(see p35)* became known as Schwyzerland.

The **Bundesbriefmuseum** (Museum of Federal Charters) in Schwyz preserves a number of documents relating to important events in Swiss history. The most highly

prized exhibit is the Charter of Confederation, written on parchment and stamped with the seals of the three Forest Cantons in 1291.

Schwyz's Old Town contains many 17th- and 18th-century buildings. Hauptplatz, the central square, is dominated by Pfarrkirche St Martin, a Baroque church, and by the Rathaus, the 17th-century town hall whose façade features a depiction of the Battle of Morgarten painted in 1891. The **Ital-Reding-Haus**, a mansion built in 1609, contains a suite of rooms with 17th- and 18th-century furnishings and decoration. Nearby is Haus Bethlehem, a wooden house built in 1287.

A former granary dating from 1711 houses the **Forum der Schweizer Geschichte**. This excellent museum of history illustrates daily life in Switzerland from the Middle Ages to the end of the 17th century.

Arms of Uri on the Rathaus in Schwyz

🏛 Bundesbriefmuseum
Bahnhofstrasse 20. 🄲 041 819 20 64. ◔ May–Oct: 9–11:30am, 1:30–5pm Tue–Fri, 9am–5pm Sat–Sun; Nov–Apr: 9–11:30am & 1:30–5pm Tue–Fri, 1:30–5pm Sat–Sun. ⌨

🏛 Ital-Reding-Haus
Rickenbachstrasse 14. 🄲 041 811 45 05. ◔ May–Oct: 2–5pm Tue–Fri, 10am–noon & 2–5pm Sat–Sun. ⌨

🏛 Forum der Schweizer Geschichte
Hofmatt. 🄲 041 819 60 11. ◔ 10am–5pm Tue–Sun.

Vitznau ⓲

Road map E3. 🏘 1,000. 🚌 🚗
🛈 Seestrasse; 041 398 00 35.
ⓦ www.vitznau.ch

BACKED BY THE Rigi massif, this small resort lies in a sheltered bay on the north shore of Lake Lucerne. Besides its watersports facilities, Vitznau's main attraction is as a base from which to hike through the woods and Alpine pastures of the Rigi massif.

Vitznau is also the base station of the oldest rack railway in Europe. It was built in 1871 and leads up to the summit of Rigi-Kulm (1,798 m/5,900 ft), the highest peak in the Rigi massif. The view from this vantage point is breathtaking. Surrounded by the waters of Lake Lucerne, and the Zugersee, the Rigi massif appears to be an island, and in clear weather the distant snow-capped peaks of the Alps are visible in the far southwest.

The northwestern shore of Lake Lucerne, between Vitznau and Weggis

Kloster Einsiedeln ⑲

THE BENEDICTINE ABBEY at Einsiedeln is one of the finest examples of Baroque architecture in the world. Its history goes back to 835, when Meinrad, a monk, chose the spot for his hermitage *(einsiedeln)*. In 934 a monastery was founded on the site. When, according to legend, a miracle occurred during the consecration of the church, the abbey became a place of pilgrimage. The church and monastery were rebuilt from 1704 to 1735, to a lavish Baroque design by Kasper Moosbrugger. Most of the paintings, gilding and stuccowork in the church are by the Bavarian brothers Cosmas Damian and Egid Quirin Asam.

Library
The abbey library is a fine example of the Baroque style. Only a part of the abbey's extensive collection of manuscripts is housed here.

The confessional, a chapel where pilgrims gather to make their confessions, is located in the north wing of the transept.

Interior of the Church
The spacious interior of the church is impressive. The nave is decorated with Baroque frescoes by Cosmas Damian Asam.

Well of Our Lady
As they arrive at the church, pilgrims traditionally drink the water from this well. It is crowned by a statue of the Virgin.

★ Black Madonna
A chapel inside the church contains the statue of a Black Madonna. This 15th-century wooden figure of the Virgin with the infant Jesus is reputed to have miraculous powers.

★ Wall Paintings

The walls, ceiling and domes of the church are covered with frescoes and gilt stuccowork. This extraordinarily rich scheme is typical of the late Baroque style.

Organ

Bedecked with figures of putti playing instruments, the organ occupies a gallery beneath the central dome.

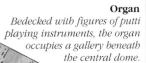

★ Grosser Saal

Lavishly decorated with paintings and stuccowork, the Grosser Saal, or Great Hall, is still used for grand receptions and official ceremonies.

Pulpit

Figures of angels and the symbols of the Four Evangelists decorate the gilt pulpit. It was designed by Egid Quirin Asam and completed in 1726.

STAR FEATURES

★ **Black Madonna**

★ **Grosser Saal**

★ **Wall Paintings**

Lake Lucerne and the towns of Küssnacht am Rigi and Bürgenstock seen from the summit of Pilatus

Zug ⑳

Road map E3. 🏔 *24,000.* 🚉 🚌
🚢 🛈 *Alpenstrasse 14; 041 711
00 78.* W *www.zug-tourismus.ch*

ZUG IS SET on the north-eastern shore of the Zugersee, in the wooded foothills of the Zugerberg. It is the capital of Zug, the smallest and also the richest of all Swiss cantons. Having the lowest taxation in Switzerland, Zug has become the headquarters of many multinational companies.

Substantial parts of the walls, set with towers, still encircle Zug's medieval Old Town. The focal point of the Old Town is Kolinplatz. At the centre of this square is a fountain with a statue of the knight Wolfgang Kolin, a standard-bearer of the Swiss army. Nearby stands the Rathaus, built in 1509. This Gothic building contains a council chamber lined with richly carved wood panelling. Also of interest is

the 15th- to 16th-century Kirche St Oswald, whose portal has figures of the Virgin, St Oswald and St Michael.

The former bailiff's castle houses the **Museum in der Burg**, a museum of local history. Nearby is a 16th-century granary now converted into the Kunsthaus, a gallery of modern art. The **Museum für Urgeschichte** concentrates on prehistory and antiquity.

Cruises on the Zugersee depart from the jetty in the harbour.

🏛 **Museum in der Burg**
Kirchenstrasse 11.
🖀 *041 728 32 97.*
🕐 *2–5pm Tue–Fri,
10am–noon
& 2–5pm Sat–Sun.* 🈂
🏛 **Museum für Urgeschichte**
Hofstrasse 15. 🖀 *041 728 28 80.*
🕐 *2–5pm Tue–Sun.* 🈂

Küssnacht am Rigi ㉑

Road map D3. 🏔 *9,500.* 🚌
🛈 *Unterdorf 1; 041 850 33 30.*
W *www.kuessnacht-tourismus.ch*

THE SMALL TOWN of Küssnacht am Rigi lies at the foot of the Rigi. This massif rises to the east of the Küssnachtersee, the northern arm of Lake Lucerne.

The town is a good base for hiking in the mountains and for exploring Lake Lucerne. It also offers a wide range of sports facilities.

**Poster advertising
winter sports on Rigi**

Buildings of interest in Küssnacht's historic district include the Baroque town hall and the Kirche St Peter und St Paul. Another is the Engel Hotel, a half-timbered building dating from 1552 that has been an inn for over 400 years.

Luzern ㉒

See pp232–3.

Pilatus ㉓

Road map D3. 🛈 *Kriens/Lucerne
Schlossweg 1.* 🖀 *041 329 11 11.*
W *www.pilatus.ch*

THE RUGGED outlines of Pilatus, whose highest peak reaches an altitude of 2,133 m (7,000 ft), rise on the southwestern side of Lake Lucerne. Various

Houses on the waterfront in Zug's medieval Old Town

legends are associated with the mountain. According to one, the body of Pontius Pilate was thrown into a lake on the mountain, and his spirit continues to haunt its heights, unleashing violent storms.

There are several convenient ways of reaching the summit of Pilatus. The first stage is a boat or train ride from Luzern to Alpnachstad, near the foot of Pilatus. From here a rack railway climbs a gradient of 48 per cent, making it the steepest cog railway in the world. From Pilatus-Kulm, the upper station, a walking trail leads up to a viewing platform on one of the mountain's peaks. In good weather it offers views of the Säntis, in the Alpstein, and of the Glarner and Berner Alps. The descent down to Alpnachstad can be made by cable car (which runs only in summer). Another cable car runs from Alpnachstad down to Kriens.

Ibex on the rugged slopes of Pilatus

Hergiswil 24

Road map D3. 👥 5,600. 🚉 🚌
ℹ️ Seestrasse 24; 041 630 12 58
ⓦ www.hergiswil.ch.

THE SMALL LAKESIDE village of Hergiswil, on the rail route from Luzern to Stans, is worth a visit for its glassworks, the Glasi Hergiswil. The factory was established in 1817 and was saved from closure in the late 1970s by the Ticinese glassmaker Roberto Niederer. It now employs about 100 people and is the focus of Hergiswil's life.

The factory is open to visitors, who can watch glassblowers at work. Also on the premises is the **Glasi Museum**, which documents the history of the glassworks, with many photographs and hundreds of different of examples of its glassware.

🏛 **Glasi Museum**
Seestrasse 12. 📞 041 632 32 32.
⏰ 9am–6pm Mon–Fri, 9am–4pm Sat.

Stans 25

Road map D3. 👥 7,300. 🚉 🚌
ℹ️ Bahnhofplatz 4; 041 610 88 33.
ⓦ www.stans.ch

CAPITAL OF THE half-canton of Nidwalden, Stans is a small town on the banks of the River Engelberger Aa. Above the town rises the Stanserhorn (1,900 m/6,236 ft), the summit of which can be reached from Stans by funicular and cable car.

The town's charming historic district revolves around Dorfplatz. This square is dominated by a Baroque parish church, **Pfarrkirche St Peter und St Paul**, with a Romanesque tower, the remains of an earlier church. In the centre of Dorfplatz stands a 19th-century monument to Arnold von Winkelried. A native of Stans, Winkelried became a hero when he sacrificed his life to help his Confederate comrades defeat the Austrians at the Battle of Sempach in 1386.

Also of interest in the town are the Höfli, a medieval turreted house that contains a museum of local history, and the Winkelriedhaus, a late Gothic building that houses a museum of local folk crafts and traditions.

Engelberg 26

Road map D3. 👥 3,400. 🚉 🚌
ℹ️ 041 639 77 77.
ⓦ www.engelberg.ch

WITHIN EASY REACH of both Luzern and Zürich, Engelberg is one of central Switzerland's main mountain resorts. It lies at an altitude of 1,000 m (3,280 ft), at the foot of Titlis, whose rocky peak reaches 3,239 m (10,630 ft).

The village nestles around the **Kloster**, a Benedictine monastery. Founded in the 12th century and rebuilt in the mid-18th, it has an exquisite Rococo church, built in 1735–40. The monastery, and its working cheese dairy, are open to visitors.

Engelberg has about 80 km (50 miles) of skiing pistes and cross-country routes, most of which are suitable for less experienced skiers. It also offers tobogganing and ice-skating facilities. Marked trails in the vicinity lead past small mountain lakes and up to the summits of Titlis, Urirotstock, Schlossberg and Hutstock. There are also many cycling routes and facilities for summer sports such as paragliding. The Rotair cable car, which rotates as it travels so as to give passengers an all-round view, runs from Stand, above Engelberg, over the Titlis glacier.

The Rotair cable car from Engelberg up to Klein Titlis

Luzern ㉒

Cᴇɴᴛʀᴀʟ ꜱᴡɪᴛᴢᴇʀʟᴀɴᴅ'ꜱ ʟᴀʀɢᴇꜱᴛ ᴛᴏᴡɴ, Luzern (Lucerne in French) lies on the western shore of Lake Lucerne. From its origins as a small fishing village, it grew into an important staging point when the St Gotthard Pass was opened in 1220. During the Reformation, Luzern led the Catholic resistance in Switzerland, and was long embroiled in political and religious disputes. Since the 19th century, tourism has underpinned Luzern's economy. Still attracting large numbers of visitors, the town also hosts the renowned Lucerne International Festival of Music.

Chapel Bridge, with the Wasser-turm in the background

Luzern seen from the west, with Mount Rigi in the background

Central Luzern

Luzern is a compact town that is easily explored on foot. The medieval Old Town (see pp234–5) lies on the north bank of the River Reuss and, from the train station on the south bank, it can be reached by crossing the medieval Chapel Bridge. The best view of Luzern is from the towers in the medieval fortifications that encircle the Old Town to the north. Luzern's main shopping districts are on the south bank, southwest of the train station, and in the Old Town, on the north bank.

🏛 KKL

Europaplatz 1.
With its cantilevered roof, the KKL building, or Kultur- und Kongresszentrum Luzern (Luzern Culture and Convention Centre), is a strikingly modernist glass and steel building that juts out over Lake Lucerne. It was designed by the French architect Jean Nouvel and was opened in 1998. The building contains conference halls, concert halls and theatres, and the Kunstmuseum (see below).

🏛 Kunstmuseum

KKL, Europaplatz 1. 🄲 041 226 78 00. ⏰ 10am–5pm Tue & Fri–Sun, 10am–8pm Wed–Thu. 🈶
The collections of the Kunstmuseum are displayed in about 20 rooms on the topmost floor of the KKL building (see above). The gallery has a permanent collection of 18th- and early 20th-century Swiss painting, and also presents a rotating programme of exhibitions of the work of international contemporary artists.

🏛 Rosengart Collection

Pilatusstrasse 10. 🄲 041 220 16 60. ⏰ May–Oct: 10am–6pm daily; Nov–Mar: 11am–5pm daily. 🈶
The Rosengart Collection (Sammlung Rosengart) is a private collection of over 200 modernist paintings that was formed over several decades by the art dealers Siegfried Rosengart and his daughter, Angela. As well as many works by Paul Klee and Pablo Picasso, the collection also includes Impressionist paintings, with canvases by Cézanne and Monet, and work by Chagall, Matisse and Kandinsky.
The Rosengarts also donated the works on display in the Picasso Museum in Luzern (see p236).

♜ Chapel Bridge

This 14th-century covered footbridge spanning the Reuss at an angle formed part of the town's fortifications, protecting it against attack from the direction of the lake. Near the centre of the river, the bridge joins the Wasserturm, an octagonal tower that has served as a lighthouse, a prison and a treasury. In the 17th century, the bridge's roof panels were painted with scenes from the history of Luzern and episodes in the lives of St Leodegar and St Mauritius, martyrs who became the town's patron saints.
The oldest wooden bridge in Europe, Chapel Bridge (Kapellbrücke) has become the symbol of Luzern. It was partly destroyed by fire in 1993 but was rebuilt and most of its paintings either restored or replaced with copies.

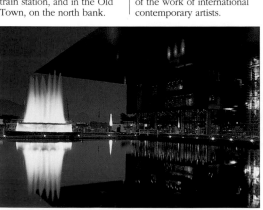

The KKL building, on Luzern's waterfront

◁ **Sonlerto, a typical Alpine village in Val Bavona, Ticino**

⌂ Jesuit Church

A major landmark on the south bank of the Reuss, the great Jesuitenkirche, the Jesuit church of St Francis Xavier, was built in 1666–73, although its onion-domed twin towers were not completed until the 19th century. The Baroque interior is richly decorated with stuccowork and the ceiling paintings depict the apotheosis of St Francis Xavier.

⌂ Franziskanerkirche

Franziskanerplatz.

Dating from about 1270, this Franciscan church is the oldest building in Luzern. It was built in the Gothic style, but has been much altered

Interior of the Franziskanerkirche

over the centuries. The Renaissance choir stalls, 17th-century pulpit and Baroque ceiling paintings are among notable features of the interior.

⌂ Historisches Museum

Pfistergasse 24. **[**] 041 228 54 24. **◯** 10am–5pm Tue–Sun. 🎫

Luzern's history museum occupies the former arsenal, a Renaissance building dating from 1597. It interconnects with the gatehouse leading through to Spreuerbrücke.

The various sections of the museum illustrate the history of the town and canton of Luzern. As well as folk art and religious paintings, there are displays of costumes, crafts and weapons. Of particular interest is a collection of 19th- and early 20th-century posters and packaging for various Swiss products, such as chocolate and powdered milk.

In the adjacent building is the Naturmuseum. Its displays focus on

VISITORS' CHECKLIST

Road map D3. 👥 60,000. 🚉
🚌 ⛴ ℹ *Zentralstrasse 5; 041 227 17 17.* 🔲 *www.luzern.ch*
🎭 *Fasnacht (carnival, early Mar),
Seenachtsfest (Aug),
Lucerne International Music
Festival (mid-Sep).*

various aspects of natural history, most especially zoology, palaeontology and geology.

🌉 Spreuerbrücke

This wooden covered bridge spans the Reuss at the western edge of the Old Town. It was built in 1408 and incorporates a small chapel. The bridge's roof is lined with panels painted by Kaspar Meglinger in 1626–35. Depicting the Dance of Death, they run in sequence from the north bank and culminate with Christ's triumph over Death at the south bank.

The bridge also offers a close view of the Nadelwerk, a 19th-century device to control the river's flow.

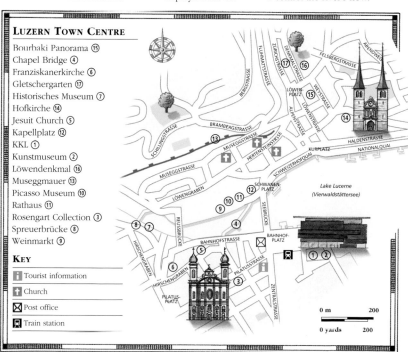

LUZERN TOWN CENTRE

Bourbaki Panorama ⑮
Chapel Bridge ④
Franziskanerkirche ⑥
Gletschergarten ⑰
Historisches Museum ⑦
Hofkirche ⑭
Jesuit Church ⑤
Kapellplatz ⑫
KKL ①
Kunstmuseum ②
Löwendenkmal ⑯
Museggmauer ⑬
Picasso Museum ⑩
Rathaus ⑪
Rosengart Collection ③
Spreuerbrücke ⑧
Weinmarkt ⑨

KEY

ℹ Tourist information

✝ Church

✉ Post office

🚉 Train station

*Lake Lucerne
(Vierwaldstättersee)*

0 m   200
0 yards   200

Street-by-Street: Old Town

L UZERN'S HISTORIC Old Town (Altstadt) is set on a
shallow bend of the Reuss at the point where
the river leaves Lake Lucerne. From the Middle Ages
the town was defended by ramparts on its northern
side and by Chapel Bridge, which spans the river
on its eastern side. The Old Town's ancient layout
survives, and the façades of its fine historic houses,
particularly around Hirschenplatz and along
Weinmarktgasse, are painted with frescoes or
covered with sgraffito decoration. This historic
district of Luzern is also a bustling urban centre,
with plenty of shops, restaurants and cafés.

Alley near Weinmarkt
*The narrow alleys off this
square are lined with tall
houses, some with
colourfully painted shutters.
Many of these houses have
been converted into hotels,
or contain boutiques and
restaurants.*

Weinmarkt
*This central square,
where wine was once
sold, has several fine
houses, many of
which were
guildhalls.*

WEGGISGASSE

EISENGASSE

ROSSLIGASSE

WEINMARKTGASSE

WEINMARKT

KORNMARKT-
PLATZ

UNTER DER EGG

★ Rathaus
*Completed in 1606, the late
Renaissance town hall has an
ornate façade. The main entrance
is flanked by double columns.*

STAR SIGHTS
★ **Chapel Bridge**
★ **Picasso Museum**
★ **Rathaus**

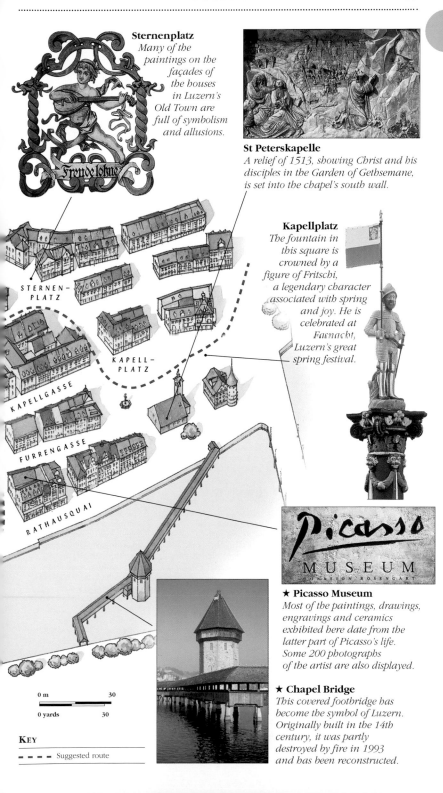

Sternenplatz
Many of the paintings on the façades of the houses in Luzern's Old Town are full of symbolism and allusions.

St Peterskapelle
A relief of 1513, showing Christ and his disciples in the Garden of Gethsemane, is set into the chapel's south wall.

Kapellplatz
The fountain in this square is crowned by a figure of Fritschi, a legendary character associated with spring and joy. He is celebrated at Fasnacht, Luzern's great spring festival.

STERNEN-PLATZ

KAPELL-PLATZ

KAPELLGASSE

FURRENGASSE

RATHAUSQUAI

★ Picasso Museum
Most of the paintings, drawings, engravings and ceramics exhibited here date from the latter part of Picasso's life. Some 200 photographs of the artist are also displayed.

★ Chapel Bridge
This covered footbridge has become the symbol of Luzern. Originally built in the 14th century, it was partly destroyed by fire in 1993 and has been reconstructed.

0 m   30

0 yards   30

KEY

‒ ‒ ‒ Suggested route

Exploring Luzern

ONE OF THE BEST VIEWS over the picturesque squares, churches, chapels and patrician houses of Luzern's Old Town is from the ramparts to the north. A pleasant walk eastwards from the Old Town leads to several other interesting buildings and museums, including the grand Renaissance Hofkirche and the Wagner Museum, dedicated to the Romantic composer. On the lakeshore further east is the fascinating Swiss Transport Museum, one of Luzern's greatest attractions *(see pp238–9)*.

⛪ Weinmarkt

Lined with historic houses, this square is one of the most attractive features of Luzern's Old Town. The Weinmarktbrunnen, a Gothic fountain in the square, is a copy of the original, which now stands in the courtyard of the Ritterscher Palast, on Bahnhofstrasse. The houses around both this square and the adjacent Hirschenplatz have painted façades, ornate doorways and oriel windows. Many were of these buildings were guildhouses.

Detail of fountain in Weinmarkt

🏛 Picasso Museum

Am-Rhyn Haus, Furrengasse 21. 🔲 *041 410 35 33.* ⭕ *Apr–Oct: 10am–6pm daily; Nov–Mar: 11am–4pm daily.* 🌐
The Am-Rhyn Haus, a restored 16th-century mansion, houses a superb collection of late works by Pablo Picasso. They were collected by Siegfried and Angela Rosengart, who also formed the Rosengart Collection *(see p232)*.

Consisting mainly of paintings, drawings, engravings and ceramics, the pieces in the museum illustrate the long friendship that existed between Picasso and the Rosengarts. A series of photographs of Picasso at work taken by the American photographer David Douglas Duncan complement the works on display.

⛪ Rathaus

Kornmarkt 3. 🔲 *041 227 17 17.* ⭕ *by arrangement.*
The present town hall, built in a grand Renaissance style, was completed in 1606. Of the 14th-century town hall that stood on the same site, only a tower remains. The council chamber inside the building is lined with finely carved wood panelling.

⛪ Museggmauer

The Museggmauer, the well-preserved northern section of Luzern's medieval fortifications, runs for about 850 m (930 yd), from the north bank of the Reuss almost to the north shore of Lake Lucerne. The walls are set with nine towers, which were built in the second half of the 14th century. The wall walk commands fine views of the town, the river and the lake.

⛪ Kapellplatz

St Peterskapelle ⭕ *7:30am–6:15pm Mon–Wed, 7:30am–9pm Thu, 7:30am–6:15pm Fri, 7:30am–5pm Sat, 8:30am–8pm Sun.*
This picturesque square buzzes with life, particularly on market days. It takes its name from the Peterskapelle. This 18th-century chapel stands on the site of a 12th-century church, the earliest to be built in Luzern. The chapel contains a 14th-century Gothic crucifix.

Heraldic shield on one of the towers of the Museggmauer

⛪ Hofkirche

St. Leodegarstrasse. ⭕ *daily.*
This collegiate church is a fine example of late Renaissance Swiss architecture. The original church, dating from the 12th century, was almost completely destroyed by fire in 1633. Only the twin towers, with pointed domes, remain and are incorporated into the present building.
  The magnificent interior is decorated in the Renaissance style. Notable features include the high altar, with statues of St Leodegar and St Mauritius, patron saints of Luzern. The altar in the north aisle is graced by a depiction of the Dormition of the Virgin painted in 1500. The church also has elaborate pews, pulpit and font, and a huge organ, built in about 1640.

One of the exhibition rooms at the Picasso Museum

The altar in the north aisle of the Hofkirche

A niche in the north tower frames a moving depiction of Christ in the Garden of Gethsemane.

🏛 Bourbaki Panorama

Löwenplatz 11. 📞 041 412 30 30. ⭘ 9am–6pm daily. ♿

One of the world's few surviving panoramas, this giant circular mural depicts the march of the French army through Switzerland under General Bourbaki, during the Franco-Prussian War (1870–71). In a stone building now housed in a glass shell, it is 112 m (370 ft) long and 10 m (33 ft) high, and was painted by Edouard Castres. Sound effects and a narrative (in several languages, including English) help bring the events depicted to life.

The building also contains a museum, art galleries and a cinema, as well as bars and a restaurant.

🏵 Löwendenkmal

Denkmalstrasse.

This massive figure of a dying lion pierced by a spear is a startling monument to the Swiss Guards of Louis XVI of France. On 10 August 1792, the guards defended the Palais des Tuileries, in Paris, when it was stormed by revolutionaries. Those who survived the attack were arrested and guillotined on the night of 2–3 September.

The Löwen-denkmal, or Lion

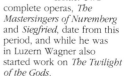

The Löwendenkmal

Monument, was carved out of the sandstone cliff face by the Danish sculptor Bertel Thorwaldsen, and it was unveiled in 1821. Reflected in the waters of a small pond, the monument has great drama and pathos.

🏛 Gletschergarten

Denkmalstrasse 4. 📞 041 410 43 40. ⭘ Apr–Oct: 9am–6pm daily; Nov–Mar: 10am–5pm daily. ♿

In 1872, an unusual discovery was made in the course of building works. Removal of a thin layer of topsoil exposed a rock with 32 large potholes. These were formed by the action of water and stones that fell through crevasses in the overlying glacier.

The Glacier Garden was created to conserve this geological feaure. The rock is protected by a tent, and the geological process that created the potholes is explained in an exhibition in a pavilion nearby. Also on display are a collection of fossils and the reconstruction of an Ice Age hunter's cave. Further exhibits document the history of Luzern.

🏛 Richard Wagner Museum

Richard Wagner-Weg 27. 📞 041 360 23 79. ⭘ mid-Mar–Oct: 10am–noon & 2–5pm. ♿

The German Romantic composer Richard Wagner was a regular visitor to Luzern. It was here that he wrote the third act of his opera *Tristan and Isolde*. Two complete operas, *The Mastersingers of Nuremberg* and *Siegfried*, date from this period, and while he was in Luzern Wagner also started work on *The Twilight of the Gods*.

The tranquil Villa Tribschen where Wagner and his wife and son lived from 1866 to 1872 is devoted to this particularly happy period. Its rooms, with original furniture, are filled with memorabilia of the composer's life, including paintings, letters and musical instruments.

ENVIRONS: The Museum im Bellpark in **Kriens**, 3 km (2 miles) southwest of Luzern and reachable by bus, contains a collection of objects relating to photography, video and the media.

The glass pavilion of the Bourbaki Panorama

Swiss Transport Museum

Almost every mode of mechanized transport, from the earliest bicycle to the latest spacecraft, is displayed and explained at the Swiss Transport Museum (Verkehrshaus der Schweiz) in Luzern. Vintage cars and steam locomotives are part of the sections on road and rail transport, and the section on tourism showcases the ingenuity of rack railways and cable cars. Water transport, aviation and telecommunications are also documented. The section devoted to space travel includes a virtual journey through outer space and among the museum's interactive features is a flight simulator.

★ Benz Three-Wheeler
The German engineer Karl Benz built this three-wheeled, petrol-driven vehicle in 1886. It marked the beginning of motorized transport.

Krokodil
The elongated shape of this electric locomotive led to its being dubbed the Crocodile. Built in 1920, it served the route leading through the St Gotthard Tunnel.

Gotthardmodell
One of the most fascinating of the museum's displays is a model that recreates the rail route through the St Gotthard Tunnel.

Main entrance

STAR EXHIBITS

★ **Aircraft**

★ **Benz Three-Wheeler**

★ **Cosmorama**

KEY

- [ ] Railways
- [ ] Road transport
- [ ] Post
- [ ] Telecommunications
- [ ] Planetarium
- [ ] Space
- [ ] Air transport
- [ ] Water transport & tourism
- [ ] Hans-Erni-Museum
- [ ] IMAX Cinema

Hiflyer
This anchored helium-filled balloon with a gondola for 30 people enables visitors to view Luzern from a height of 150 m (490 ft).

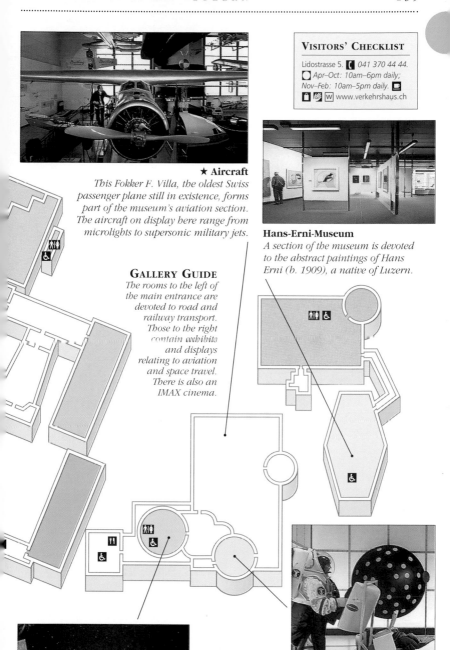

★ Aircraft
This Fokker F. Villa, the oldest Swiss passenger plane still in existence, forms part of the museum's aviation section. The aircraft on display here range from microlights to supersonic military jets.

VISITORS' CHECKLIST

Lidostrasse 5. 041 370 44 44.
Apr–Oct: 10am–6pm daily;
Nov–Feb: 10am–5pm daily.
www.verkehrshaus.ch

Hans-Erni-Museum
A section of the museum is devoted to the abstract paintings of Hans Erni (b. 1909), a native of Luzern.

GALLERY GUIDE
The rooms to the left of the main entrance are devoted to road and railway transport. Those to the right contain exhibits and displays relating to aviation and space travel. There is also an IMAX cinema.

Planetarium
By looking up at a dome representing the night sky, visitors observe the movement of the planets in our galaxy.

★ Cosmorama
As well as space suits and other equipment used by astronauts, the section on space exploration includes Cosmorama, a virtual journey through the asteroid belt.

TRAVELLERS'
NEEDS

WHERE TO STAY

WHETHER YOU ARE looking for a hotel in a city centre, at a leading winter sports resort, on the edge of a beautiful lake or in unspoiled countryside, Switzerland offers accommodation to suit all tastes and budgets. Across all categories and price ranges, Swiss hotels provide high quality and value for money, even though their prices tend to be relatively high. Cheaper options

Hotel sign in Bern

include guesthouses, to be found in some of the country's most attractive towns and villages, or a welcoming mountain inn, where you will be treated to warm Swiss hospitality. For those who enjoy the great outdoors, Switzerland has a host of well-equipped campsites in unforgettable scenery. Many farms also have rooms to let, and even give visitors the opportunity to sleep in barns, on pristine straw.

A grand hotel in Kandersteg, in the Bernese Oberland

CHOOSING A HOTEL

THE BEST SOURCE of information on hotels in Switzerland is **Hôtellerie Suisse**. This organization covers most types of accommodation, from luxury hotels to remote mountain inns. It also grades hotels on a scale of one to five stars, which correspond to certain standards of comfort.

Average prices range from 70 CHF for a double room without a bath in a one-star hotel, to at least 1,200 CHF for a comfortable suite in a five-star establishment. Except in the very cheapest and in the most expensive hotels, prices generally include breakfast, taxes and service. Some hotels, particularly those that are family-run, are not subject to official classification, but they are generally clean and comfortable. While many hotels have restaurants, a *hôtel garni* is an establishment that serves breakfast but no other meals.

In popular resorts, hotel prices are subject to seasonal variations. According to their location, most hotels charge the highest prices during the winter sports season or in July and August, the height of the summer season, although discounts sometimes apply for longer stays. In large towns, where hotels are more likely to rely on a business clientele, prices generally stay constant throughout the year, although special weekend rates are often available.

Hotels in many resorts offer guest cards (*Gästekarte, Kurkarte, carte des visiteurs or tessera di soggiorno*). These cards entitle holders to various discounts ranging from travel in the locality to admission to local museums.

HOTEL CHAINS

MANY HOTELS IN Switzerland belong to international or national chains. The largest international hotel chain is

Best Western, which has over 60 three- and four-star hotels in Switzerland. The **TOP International** hotel chain has over 70 three- to five-star establishments in Switzerland's larger towns and cities and in the country's major holiday resorts. Hotels in this chain offer discounts to holders of the Swiss Pass *(see p301)*.

The **Minotel Suisse** chain is an association of some 110 traditional family-run hotels with a rating of two to four stars. These hotels have restaurants that serve Swiss food and wine. In a less expensive price bracket are **E&G Swiss Budget Hotels**, which has 160 hotels with a one-star to three-star rating. Because they are cheaper, these hotels tend to be off main routes or outside the principal tourist regions but for this reason they offer good value for money. Many are in quiet, uncrowded locations.

The 22 hotels in the **Romantik** group are all independently run establishments in fine historic buildings, such as châteaux. All offer exceptionally high standards of comfort and most are in outstanding locations.

ROOMS/B&B

GUEST HOUSES and private houses advertise rooms for rent with signs reading *Zimmer frei, Chambres à louer* or *affitasi camere*. They are most likely to be found in resorts and in areas frequented by visitors.

The Kulm Hotel Gornergrat, with stunning views of the Matterhorn

Bed and breakfast accommodation is also becoming more widely available in Switzerland. At an average price of 40 CHF per night, both these types of accommodation offer excellent value.

HOSTELS

SWITZERLAND has over 80 hostels, with double rooms, family rooms and dormitories. Prices range from 15 to 25 CHF per night, including breakfast, but there may be an extra charge if you don't bring your own linen. Most hostels have a television room and some serve evening meals.

Hotel sign in Murten

SLEEPING IN STRAW

FROM EARLY MAY until the end of October, many Swiss farms open their barns to visitors, allowing them to sleep on freshly laid straw. Charges per night are no more than about 20 CHF, which usually includes breakfast and the use of a shower. Blankets are sometimes provided, but visitors should bring their own sleeping bags.

Staying on a working farm is another way of experiencing rural Switzerland at first hand. Rooms or apartments can be rented by the night or the week all year round.

MOUNTAIN INNS

PICTURESQUE mountain inns *(Berghausen* or *auberges de montagne)* offer convenient overnight accommodation to hikers. As well as dormitories, many have individual rooms. Most mountain inns also serve hot meals.

CAMPSITES

LIKE ITS HOTELS, Switzerland's campsites are graded on a scale of one to five stars. There are about 450, many in outstandingly beautiful locations. Most campsites are closed in winter, and many of those at higher altitudes are open only for the two or three warmest months of the year. Advance booking is recommended at any time of year.

The Club-Med Hotel in Pontresina, in the Upper Engadine

DIRECTORY

HOTELS

Hôtellerie Suisse
Monbijoustrasse 130, Bern.
☎ 031 370 41 11.
FAX 031 370 44 44.
W www. hotelleriesuisse.ch

HOTEL CHAINS

Best Western Swiss Hotels
Mühlemattstrasse 53, Bern.
☎ 031 378 18 18.
FAX 031 378 18 39.
W www.bestwestern.ch

TOP International Hotels
Seestrasse 129, 8712 Stäfa.
☎ 044 928 27 27.
W www.tophotels.ch

Minotel Suisse
Chemin Renou 2,
1005 Lausanne.
☎ 021 310 08 08.
W www.minotel.ch

E&G Swiss Budget Hotels
Case Postale 160, Route
des Layeux, 1884 Villars.
☎ 024 495 11 11.
W www.rooms.ch

Romantik
☎ +49 (0)69 661 23 4 0.
FAX +49 (0)69 661 23 45 6.
W www.
romantikhotels.com

B&B

Bed and Breakfast
W www.bnb.ch
@ info@bnb.ch

HOSTELS

Swiss Youth Hostels
Schaffhauserstrasse 14,
8042 Zürich.
☎ 044 360 14 14.
FAX 044 360 14 60.
W www.youthhostel.ch

Swiss Backpackers
☎ 044 251 90 15.
W www.backpacker.ch

SLEEPING IN STRAW

Aventure sur la Paille/Abenteuer im Stroh
☎ 024 445 16 31.
W www.
aventure-sur-la-paille.ch;
www.abenteuer-stroh.ch

HOLIDAY FARMS

W www.
bauernhof-ferien.ch

Reka-Ferien
Neuengasse 15. 3001 Bern.
☎ 031 329 66 33.
FAX 031 329 66 01.
W www.reka.ch

CAMPSITES

CampingNET
Grundhaldenstrasse 60,
8303 Bassersdorf.
W www.camping.ch

Verband Schweizer Campings
Bahnhofstrasse 2,
3322 Schönbühl.
☎ 031 852 06 26.
FAX 031 852 06 27.
W www.swisscamps.ch

Choosing a Hotel

THE HOTELS LISTED BELOW have been selected across a wide range of price categories for the excellence of their facilities and location. They are listed by area and the colour-coded thumb tabs correspond to those by which the regions of Switzerland are identified throughout this guide. For a list of restaurants, see pp268–83.

	NUMBER OF ROOMS	RESTAURANT	GARDEN OR TERRACE	SWIMMING POOL	AIR CONDITIONING

BERN

BERN: *Landhaus* Ⓕ
Altenbergstrasse 4, 3013. 【 031 331 41 66. FAX 031 332 69 04.
@ landhaus@spectraweb.ch Ⓦ www. landhausbern.ch
This hotel, a historic building, is in a quiet location near the river and the Bärengraben, a short walk from the city centre. The rooms are pleasant, modern and attractively decorated. 1 🛏 P 🗒

| 10 | ● | ■ | | |

BERN: *National* Ⓕ
Hirschengraben 24, 3011. 【 031 381 19 88. FAX 031 381 68 78.
@ hotel@nationalbern.ch Ⓦ www.nationalbern.ch
A modest family hotel in a historic building near the train station. The rooms are large and characterful, with wood floors and large windows. 🛏 📶 🔒 P 🗒

| 44 | ● | | | |

BERN: *Pension Marthahaus* Ⓕ
Wyttenbachstrasse 22a, 3013. 【 031 332 41 35. FAX 031 333 33 86.
@ info.marthahaus.ch Ⓦ www.marthahaus.ch
An inexpensive guesthouse near the Botanischer Garten, north of the train station. Kitchen for the use of guests. Free Internet access. 1 🛏 📶 🌊 🗒

| 40 | | | | |

BERN: *Waldhorn* Ⓕ
Waldhöheweg 2, 3013. 【 031 332 23 43. FAX 031 332 18 69.
@ hotel@waldhorn.ch Ⓦ www.waldhorn.ch
This modern guesthouse with well-appointed rooms is in a quiet district outside the city centre. Free Internet access. 🛏 TV 📶 🔒 ♿ P 🗒

| 46 | | | | |

BERN: *Allegro Grand Casino Kursaal Bern* ⒻⒻⒻ
Kornhausstrasse 3, 3000. 【 031 339 55 00. FAX 031 339 55 10.
@ allegro@kursaal-bern.ch Ⓦ www.allegro-hotel.ch
A modern hotel in a quiet location, with good views of the city. Facilities include a fitness, relaxation and beauty-treatment centre and a casino. 1 🛏 TV 🌊 📶 Ⓨ 🔒 ♿ P 🗒

| 171 | ● | ■ | | |

BERN: *Bellevue Palace* ⒻⒻⒻⒻ
Kochergasse 3–5, 3001. 【 031 320 45 45. FAX 031 311 47 43.
@ info@bellevue-palace.ch Ⓦ www.bellevue-palace.ch
The terrace of this luxury hotel, a member of the Leading Hotels of the World, offers a fine view of the River Aare and the Alps in the background. Large, comfortable rooms. 1 🛏 TV 📶 🌊 Ⓨ 🔒 🗒 24

| 130 | ● | ■ | | ■ |

BERN: *Innere Enge* ⒻⒻⒻⒻ
Engestrasse 54, 3012. 【 031 309 61 11. FAX 031 309 61 12.
@ info@zghotels.ch Ⓦ www.zghotels.ch
A comfortable hotel in a historic building, set in a park near the city centre. Spacious and well-appointed rooms. 🛏 TV 📶 Ⓨ 🌊 ♿ 🔒 🗒

| 26 | ● | ■ | | ■ |

MITTELLAND, BERNESE OBERLAND AND VALAIS

BIEL/BIENNE: *Metropol* Ⓕ
Dufourstrasse 110, 2502. **Road map** C3. 【 032 344 90 44. FAX 032 344 90 45.
@ info@metropol-biel.ch Ⓦ www.metropol-biel.ch
A comfortable hotel situated in a quiet area. All rooms have Internet access. Good restaurant with terrace. 1 🛏 TV 🌊 📶 🔒 ♿ P 🗒

| 32 | ● | ■ | | |

BRIENZ AM SEE: *Schönegg* Ⓕ
Talstrasse 8, 3855. **Road map** D3. 【 033 951 11 13. FAX 033 951 38 13.
@ info@schoenegg-brienz.ch
A modest but comfortable hotel set away from the main road, overlooking the Brienzersee and the mountains. ◯ *Apr–Oct.* 1 🛏 📶 🌊 P 🔒 ♿ 🗒

| 16 | ● | ■ | | |

	NUMBER OF ROOMS	RESTAURANT	GARDEN OR TERRACE	SWIMMING POOL	AIR CONDITIONING
Price categories are per night for two people occupying a twin room with bath or shower (unless otherwise indicated), with service and tax included. (F) under 150 CHF (Swiss francs) (F)(F) 150–250 CHF (F)(F)(F) 250–350 CHF (F)(F)(F)(F) 350–500 CHF (F)(F)(F)(F)(F) over 500 CHF **RESTAURANT** The hotel has a restaurant that is open to guests as well as non-residents. **GARDEN OR TERRACE** The hotel has a garden or terrace. **SWIMMING POOL** The hotel has a swimming pool. **AIR CONDITIONING** All rooms have air conditioning.					

BRIG: *Ambassador*   (F)

Saflischstrasse 3, 3900. **Road map** D4. 027 922 99 00. **FAX** 027 922 99 09.
@ hotel@ambassador-brig.ch W www.ambassador-brig.ch
A comfortable hotel set in a quiet district of Brig, very near the train station. 1 🛏 TV 🔾 P 🔌 ⚿ ⚯

	31	●	■		

BRIG: *Hotel Victoria*   (F)(F)

Bahnhofstrasse 2, 3900. **Road map** D4. 027 923 15 03. **FAX** 027 924 21 69.
@ hotel_victoria@swissonline.ch W www.minotel.ch
This long-established hotel, opposite the train station, has well-appointed rooms. The restaurant specializes in French cuisine. 1 🛏 TV 🔾 ⓨ P ⚯

	37	●	■		

CRANS-MONTANA: *Primavera*   (F)

Rue de la Gare, 3963. **Road map** C4. 027 481 42 14. **FAX** 027 481 74 14.
@ info@hotelprimavera.ch W www.hotelprimavera.ch
An inexpensive hotel in the centre of Crans-Montana. The rooms are comfortable and well equipped. 1 🛏 TV 🔾 P 🔌 ⚿ ⚯

	32	●	■		

CRANS-MONTANA: *Astor Hotel*   (F)(F)

Rue Pas de L'Ours, 3963. **Road map** C4. 027 480 20 85. **FAX** 027 481 97 18.
@ astor-hotel@rhone.ch W www.demahotels.com
This welcoming, family-run hotel is located near the centre of Crans-Montana, with convenient access to the resort's skiing pistes. 🛏 TV 🔾 ⓨ P ⚿ ⚯

	29	●	■		

CRANS-MONTANA: *Alpina & Savoy*   (F)(F)(F)

3963. **Road map** C4. 027 485 09 00. **FAX** 027 485 09 99.
@ info@alpinasavoy.ch W www.alpina-savoy.ch
A comfortable hotel with modern furnishings. Facilities include fitness rooms, a solarium and a sauna. 1 🛏 TV 🔾 ⓨ P 🔌 ⚿ ⚯

	46	●	■	●	

CRANS-MONTANA: *Aparthotel Helvetia Intergolf*   (F)(F)(F)

Route de la Moubra, 3963. **Road map** C4. 027 485 88 88. **FAX** 027 485 88 99.
@ info@helvetia-intergolf.ch W www.helvetia-intergolf.ch
As well as individual rooms, this modern hotel has 44 self-catering apartments. There is a cosy chalet bar, vegetarian restaurant *(see p269)* and spa facilities. 1 🛏 TV 🔾 ⓨ P 🔌 ⚯

	10	●	■	●	

CRANS-MONTANA: *Royal*   (F)(F)(F)(F)

3963. **Road map** C4. 027 485 95 95. **FAX** 027 485 95 85.
@ info@hotel-royal.ch W www.hotel-royal.ch
Located a few minutes' walk from the resort centre, this attractive and comfortable hotel is near golf courses and ski lifts. The rooms are newly refurbished. 1 🛏 TV 🔾 ⓨ P 🔌 ⚿ ⚯

	54	●	■		

CRANS-MONTANA: *Grand Hotel du Golf*   (F)(F)(F)(F)(F)

Allée Elysée-Bonvin, 3963. **Road map** C4. 027 485 42 42. **FAX** 027 485 42 43.
@ info@grand-hotel-du-golf.ch W www.grand-hotel-du-golf.ch
A luxury hotel, surrounded by a golf course and within easy reach of cross-country skiing routes. Fitness, relaxation and beauty-treatment facilities. 🛏 TV 🔾 ⚡ ⓨ P 🔌 ⚯

	80	●	■		

FIESCH: *Fiescherhof*   (F)

3984. **Road map** D4. 027 971 21 71. **FAX** 027 971 19 85.
@ fiescherhof@rhone.ch W www.rhone.ch/fiescherhof
This hotel is within easy reach of the Aletsch Glacier. The rooms are in a rustic style and the restaurant serves tasty regional dishes. 1 🛏 TV 🔾 🔌 ⚯

	29	●	■		

GRIMSEL PASS: *Grimselblick*   (F)

Grimsel Pass, 3864. **Road map** D4. 027 973 11 77. **FAX** 027 973 14 122.
@ grimselblick@rhone.ch W www.grimselpasshoehe.ch
Located on the heights of the Grimsel Pass, this cosy hotel overlooks the icy Totensee (Dead Lake). The rooms are small, in traditional Alpine wood. There is also a four-poster-bed suite. 1 🛏 TV P ⚯ ● *Nov–Jan.*

	10	●			

For key to symbols see back flap

Price categories are per night for two people occupying a twin room with bath or shower (unless otherwise indicated), with service and tax included.
Ⓕ under 150 CHF (Swiss francs)
ⒻⒻ 150–250 CHF
ⒻⒻⒻ 250–350 CHF
ⒻⒻⒻⒻ 350–500 CHF
ⒻⒻⒻⒻⒻ over 500 CHF

RESTAURANT
The hotel has a restaurant that is open to guests as well as non-residents.

GARDEN OR TERRACE
The hotel has a garden or terrace.

SWIMMING POOL
The hotel has a swimming pool.

AIR CONDITIONING
All rooms have air conditioning.

	NUMBER OF ROOMS	RESTAURANT	GARDEN OR TERRACE	SWIMMING POOL	AIR CONDITIONING
GRINDELWALD: *Best Western Hotel Spinne* ⒻⒻⒻ	44	●	■		
GRINDELWALD: *Eiger* ⒻⒻⒻ	50	●	■		
GRINDELWALD: *Parkhotel Schoenegg* ⒻⒻⒻ	49	●	■	●	■
GRINDELWALD: *Grand Hotel Regina* ⒻⒻⒻⒻ	85	●	■	●	
GSTAAD (SAANEN): *Solsana* ⒻⒻ	60	●	■	●	
GSTAAD: *Bernerhof* ⒻⒻⒻ	45	●	■	●	
GSTAAD: *Gstaad Palace* ⒻⒻⒻⒻ	104	●	■	●	
INTERLAKEN: *Beatus* Ⓕ	9	●	■		
INTERLAKEN: *Hotel du Lac* ⒻⒻ	35	●	■		

GRINDELWALD: *Best Western Hotel Spinne* ⒻⒻⒻ
Hotel Spinne, 3818. **Road map** D4. 033 854 88 88. **FAX** 033 854 88 89.
@ hotel@spinne.ch Ⓦ www.spinne.ch
This comfortable hotel, part of the Best Western chain, is located near the foot of the Eiger. Facilities include a sauna and fitness, relaxation and beauty-treatment centre, and a nightclub. The three restaurants offer a variety of cuisines, including Italian, French and Chinese. 1 🛏 TV 📺 🌊 P 🐾

GRINDELWALD: *Eiger* ⒻⒻⒻ
3818. **Road map** D4. 033 854 31 31. **FAX** 033 854 31 30.
@ hotel@eiger-grindelwald.ch Ⓦ www.eiger-grindelwald.ch
A centrally located hotel with a welcoming atmosphere. The restaurant serves Swiss cuisine. 1 🛏 📺 🌊 P 🐾 🐕 ♿ 🐾

GRINDELWALD: *Parkhotel Schoenegg* ⒻⒻⒻ
3818. **Road map** D4. 033 854 18 18. **FAX** 033 854 18 19.
@ schoenegg@grindelwald.ch Ⓦ www.parkhotelschoenegg.ch
A hotel in a quiet location near the cable-car station to First. Facilities include an indoor swimming pool, jacuzzi, sauna, hammam and solarium. 1 🛏 TV 📺 🌊 P 🐾 🐕 ♿ 🐾

GRINDELWALD: *Grand Hotel Regina* ⒻⒻⒻⒻ
Postfach 120, 3818. **Road map** D4. 033 854 86 00. **FAX** 033 854 86 88.
@ info@grandregina.ch Ⓦ www.grandregina.ch
A luxury hotel in a turreted building opposite the train station. The rooms, with modern furnishings, offer views of the Eiger. Fitness, relaxation and beauty-treatment centre. 1 🛏 TV 📺 🌊 🍽 P 🐾 🐕 ♿ 🐾

GSTAAD (SAANEN): *Solsana* ⒻⒻ
Solsanastrasse, 3792. **Road map** C4. 033 748 94 94. **FAX** 033 748 94 88.
@ solsana@swissonline.ch Ⓦ www.solsana.ch
Run by the Swiss Association for the Blind, this recently refurbished hotel is fully adapted to the needs of disabled people. It has a quiet atmosphere and sunny rooms. ● *early Nov–late Dec.* 1 🛏 TV 📺 🌊 P 🐾 🐕 ♿ 🐾

GSTAAD: *Bernerhof* ⒻⒻⒻ
Bernerhofplatz, 3780. **Road map** C4. 033 748 88 44. **FAX** 033 748 88 40.
@ info@bernerhof-gstaad.ch Ⓦ www.bernerhof.com
This large, centrally located hotel has a pleasant, relaxed ambience. It has a sauna and hammam, family suites and a children's play area.
1 🛏 TV 📺 🍽 P

GSTAAD: *Gstaad Palace* ⒻⒻⒻⒻ
3780. **Road map** C4. 033 748 50 00. **FAX** 033 748 50 05.
@ info@palace.ch Ⓦ www.palace.ch
Located in a turreted castle perched high above Gstaad, this hotel epitomizes Alpine luxury. The rooms are spacious and well appointed, and there is a choice of restaurants. 1 🛏 TV 📺 🍽 P

INTERLAKEN: *Beatus* Ⓕ
Strasse Interlaken-Gunten-Thun, 3800. **Road map** D4.
033 841 16 24. **FAX** 033 841 16 25. @ beatushotel@datacomm.ch
This small, comfortable hotel, part of the E&G Swiss Budget Hotels chain, offers a beautiful view of the Thunersee. The rooms are furnished in rustic Swiss style. 1 🛏 📺 🌊 P 🐾 ♿ 🐾

INTERLAKEN: *Hotel du Lac* ⒻⒻ
Höhenweg 225, 3800. **Road map** D4.
033 822 29 22. **FAX** 033 822 29 15.
@ dulac@bluewin.ch Ⓦ www.bestwestern.ch/dulac
This smart hotel, part of the Best Western Swiss Hotels chain, stands on the bank of the River Aare. The hotel organizes sightseeing excursions for guests. ● *Dec–Feb.* 1 🛏 📺 🌊 P 🐾 🐕 🐾

INTERLAKEN: *Neuhaus* ⓕⓕ 47
Seestrasse 121, 3800. **Road map** D4. ☎ 033 822 82 82. ℻ 033 823 29 91.
@ neuhaus@quicknet.ch Ⓦ www.hotel-neuhaus.ch
One of Interlaken's best mid-range hotels, the Neuhaus is set on
the shores of the Thunersee, in a quiet location just outside the centre.
The rooms in the main building are small but characterful, and the service
is warm and welcoming. ①

INTERLAKEN: *Victoria-Jungfrau* ⓕⓕⓕⓕ 212
Höheweg 41, 3800. **Road map** D4. ☎ 033 828 28 28. ℻ 033 828 28 80.
@ interlaken@victoria-jungfrau.ch Ⓦ www.victoria-jungfrau.ch
The grandest of Interlaken's Alpine palace hotels, the Victoria-Jungfrau
blends glittering opulence and traditional styling. The rooms are large and
immaculate, with perfect mountain views. The hotel has its own spa and
tennis courts. ①

LAUTERBRUNNEN: *Silberhorn* ⓕⓕ 30
3822. **Road map** C4. ☎ 033 856 22 10. ℻ 033 855 42 13.
@ info@silberhorn.com Ⓦ www.silberhorn.com
A delightful family-run hotel in this idyllic village. It has a central
location near the train station and quiet, attractively decorated rooms.
①

LEUKERBAD: *Lindner Hotel* ⓕⓕⓕⓕ 135
Dorfplatz, 3954. **Road map** C4. ☎ 027 470 10 00. ℻ 027 470 10 01.
@ info@lindnerhotels.ch Ⓦ www.lindnerhotels.ch
This very comfortable hotel has small but attractively furnished rooms.
It offers a wide range of spa treatments, and facilities include hot springs,
a fitness, relaxation and beauty-treatment centre and a tennis court.
①

MARTIGNY: *Alpes & Rhône* ⓕⓕ 50
Avenue Grand-St-Bernard 11, 1920. **Road Map** B5
☎ 027 722 17 17. ℻ 027 722 43 00. @ info@alpes-rhone.ch Ⓦ www.alpes-rhone.ch
A mid-range hotel conveniently located in the centre of Martigny.
Although the building's exterior is unremarkable, the rooms within
are comfortable. ①

MÜRREN: *Alpenruh* ⓕⓕ 26
3825. **Road map** C4. ☎ 033 856 88 00. ℻ 033 856 88 88.
@ alpenruh@schilthorn.ch Ⓦ www.schilthorn.ch
Quiet, welcoming, appealing, this is one of the best small Alpine
chalet-style hotels in Switzerland. It is also located very near the
cable-car station and offers stunning views. ①

RIEDERALP: *Golfhotel Riederhof* ⓕⓕ 13
3987. **Road map** D4. ☎ 027 928 64 64. ℻ 027 928 64 74.
@ info@golfhotel-riederhof.ch Ⓦ www.golfhotel-riederhof.ch
This hotel is located near the trail leading to the Aletsch Glacier.
The rooms have south-facing balconies.

SAAS FEE: *Ferieneck Hohnegg* ⓕⓕ 8
3906. **Road map** D5. ☎ 027 957 22 68. ℻ 027 957 12 49.
@ hohnegg@saas-fee.ch Ⓦ www.hohnegg.ch
A quality hotel in an idyllic location, with views of several
high peaks. The public areas and some of the most comfortable rooms
have wood panelling. ● *May & Nov.*

SAAS FEE: *Jägerhof* ⓕⓕⓕ 15
Obere Gasse, 3906. **Road map** D5. ☎ 027 957 13 10. ℻ 027 957 16 55.
@ jaegerhof@smile.ch Ⓦ www.saas-fee.ch/jaegerhof
This quiet, attractive hotel has a fine location on the edge of the
village, within easy reach of the slopes. The rooms are comfortable
and communal facilities include a sauna, jacuzzi and solarium.
①

SAAS FEE: *Ferienart Resort & Spa* ⓕⓕⓕⓕⓕ 83
3906. **Road map** D5. ☎ 027 958 19 00. ℻ 027 958 19 05.
@ info@ferienart.ch Ⓦ www.ferienart.ch
This luxury hotel is decorated in a rustic style and has comfortable,
well-equipped rooms. Its five restaurants offer a choice of different
cuisines. Piano bar, nightclub, fitness and relaxation and beauty-treatment
centre. ● *May.*

For key to symbols see back flap

Price categories are per night for two people occupying a twin room with bath or shower (unless otherwise indicated), with service and tax included.
Ⓕ under 150 CHF (Swiss francs)
ⒻⒻ 150–250 CHF
ⒻⒻⒻ 250–350 CHF
ⒻⒻⒻⒻ 350–500 CHF
ⒻⒻⒻⒻⒻ over 500 CHF

RESTAURANT
The hotel has a restaurant that is open to guests as well as non-residents.

GARDEN OR TERRACE
The hotel has a garden or terrace.

SWIMMING POOL
The hotel has a swimming pool.

AIR CONDITIONING
All rooms have air conditioning.

	NUMBER OF ROOMS	RESTAURANT	GARDEN OR TERRACE	SWIMMING POOL	AIR CONDITIONING
SION: *Europa* ⒻⒻ Rue de l'Envoi 19, 1950. **Road map** C5. ☎ 027 322 24 23. FAX 027 322 25 35. @ hoteleuropa@freesurf.ch Ⓦ www.zghotels.ch Located just outside the centre of the town, this modern hotel offers the best rooms in Sion. It is functional rather than cosy. 🖥 📺 🔼 Ⓨ 🔲 Ⓟ 🗐	65				
SION: *Du Rhône* ⒻⒻ Rue du Scex 10, 1950. **Road map** C5. ☎ 027 322 82 91. FAX 027 323 11 88. @ durhonesion@bestwestern.ch Ⓦ www.bestwestern.ch/durhonesion This is a pleasant, mid-sized hotel in the heart of Sion. The rooms are adequate for the price and the service friendly. ① 🖥 📺 🗐	45				
SOLOTHURN: *Baseltor* ⒻⒻ Hauptgasse 79, 4500. **Road map** C3. ☎ 032 622 34 22. FAX 032 622 18 79. @ baseltor@solnet.ch Ⓦ www.baseltor.ch A charming hotel in the historic centre of the town, this hotel has fresh, modern rooms. Guests on cycle tours are especially welcome. ① 🖥 🗐	9	●			
SOLOTHURN: *Krone* ⒻⒻⒻ Hauptgasse 64, 4500. **Road map** C3. ☎ 032 622 44 12. FAX 032 622 37 24. @ reservation@hotelkrone-solothurn.ch Ⓦ www.hotelkrone-solothurn.ch A traditional hotel, part of the Minotel Suisse chain, located in the Old Town. Some rooms have a view of the cathedral. ① 🖥 🔼 🔳 Ⓟ 🗐	42	●	■		
THUN: *Emmental* ⒻⒻ Bernstrasse 2, 3600. **Road map** C3. ☎ 033 222 01 20. FAX 033 222 01 30. @ welcome@essenundtrinken.ch Ⓦ www.essenundtrinken.ch A recently refurbished hotel in the heart of the Old Town, with a terrace overlooking Schloss Thun, the castle. The rooms are comfortable and well-equipped, with modern furnishings. ① 🖥 📺 Ⓟ 🗐	11	●	■		
VERBIER: *Garbo* ⒻⒻ Rue de Médran, 1936. **Road map** C5. ☎ 027 771 62 72. FAX 027 771 62 71. @ info@hotelgarbo.com Ⓦ www.hotelgarbo.com Located in the centre of Verbier, this small hotel is within easy reach of ski lifts. The rooms are comfortable but simply furnished and the terrace offers magnificent mountain views. ◯ Nov–Apr. 🖥 📺 🔼 Ⓟ 🗐	25	●	■		
VERBIER: *Chalet d'Adrien* ⒻⒻⒻⒻⒻ Route des Creux, 1936. **Road map** C5. ☎ 027 771 62 00. FAX 027 771 62 24. @ info@chalet-adrien.ch Ⓦ www.chalet-adrien.ch This luxury hotel combines the atmosphere of a cosy mountain chalet with the comforts of a modern hotel. It has two restaurants, a cigar bar and a fitness, relaxation and beauty-treatment centre. 🖥 🔼 🏊 🔳 🔲 🗐 🔢	25	●	■		
VISP: *Visperhof* ⒻⒻ Bahnhofstrasse 2, 3930. **Road map** D4. ☎ 027 948 38 00. FAX 027 948 38 01. @ info@visperhof.ch Ⓦ www.visperhof.ch A comfortable, modern hotel located just outside Visp's pedestrianized area. It is a good base for skiing and hiking. ① 🖥 📺 🔼 🏊 Ⓟ 🔳 🗐	35		■		
WENGEN: *Belvedere* ⒻⒻ 3823. **Road map** C4. ☎ 033 856 68 68. FAX 033 856 68 69. @ belvedere@belvedere-wengen.ch Ⓦ www.belvedere-wengen.ch This traditional hotel in Art Nouveau style is set in a peaceful spot above the village. The well-furnished rooms offer panoramic views. ① 🖥 📺 🔼 🗐	62	●	■		
WENGEN: *Regina* ⒻⒻⒻⒻ 3823. **Road map** C4. ☎ 033 856 58 58. FAX 033 856 58 50. @ info@regina.com Ⓦ www.wengen.com/regina Set above the village, this elegant hotel was built in 1894. It offers all the comforts associated with an establishment of its class. ① 🖥 📺 🔼 🗐	90	●	■		

WILDERSWIL: *Luna Motel* — (F) — 29
Hauptstrasse, 3812. **Road map** D4. ☎ *033 822 84 14.* FAX *033 822 84 94.*
@ mail@luna-motel.com W www.luna-motel.com
The newly refurbished rooms of this motel offer a breathtaking view of the Jungfrau massif. Garden with swimming pool. 1 🛏 TV ⚡ P 🔣 🗒

ZERMATT: *Bahnhof* — (F) — 17
3920. **Road map** C5. ☎ *027 967 24 06.* FAX *027 967 72 16.*
@ welcome@hotelbahnhof.com W www.hotelbahnhof.com
A standard, inexpensive hotel in the centre of Zermatt. There are facilities for children, as well as multiple-occupancy rooms. 1 🛏 🗒

ZERMATT: *Kulm Hotel Gornergrat* — (F)(F) — 21
Gornergrat, 3920. ☎ *027 966 64 00.* FAX *027 966 64 04.*
@ gornergrat.kulm@zermatt.ch W www.zermatt.ch
At an altitude of 3,100m (10,000 ft), this hotel claims to be the highest in the Alps. It is located beside the upper station of the Gornergrat railway and offers breathtaking views of the Matterhorn. Although the rooms are rather basic, the hotel has an unforgettable atmosphere. 1 🗒

ZERMATT: *Romantica* — (F)(F) — 15
Chrum 21, 3920. **Road map** C5. ☎ *027 966 26 50.* FAX *027 966 26 55.*
@ romantica.zermatt@reconline.ch W www.reconline.ch/romantica
A small, family-run hotel in the centre of Zermatt, close to the ski lifts. Two historic chalets next to the hotel are also available for rent. 1 🛏 TV 🔼 🗒

ZERMATT: *Riffelalp* — (F)(F)(F)(F) — 63
Riffelalp, 3920. ☎ *027 966 05 55.* FAX *027 966 05 50.*
@ riffelalp@zermatt.ch W www.riffelalp.com
Set in stunning surroundings and offering top-class accommodation, this is one of the most luxurious Alpine resort hotels in Switzerland. It is located near the railway line high above Zermatt, at 2,222 m (7,300 ft).
1 🛏 🔼 🗒

GENEVA

GENEVA: *Hotel At Home* — (F) — 26
16 Rue de Fribourg, 1201. ☎ *022 906 19 00.* FAX *022 738 44 30.*
@ athome@bluewin.ch W www.kis.ch/at-home
This charming small hotel is located north of the city centre, a short distance from Lake Geneva. 1 🛏 TV 🔼 🗒

GENEVA: *Hôtel de la Cloche* — (F) — 8
6 Rue de la Cloche, 1201. ☎ *022 732 94 81.* FAX *022 738 16 12.*
@ hotelcloche@freesurf.ch W www.smpage.ch/cloche
A small, inexpensive hotel in a period building, a short distance from Lake Geneva. Advance booking is recommended. 🛏 🗒

GENEVA: *Hôtel Savoy* — (F)(F) — 50
8 Place Cornavin, 1201. ☎ *022 906 47 00.* FAX *022 906 47 90.*
A classic hotel located near the main train station, not far from Lake Geneva and within easy reach of the city centre.
1 🛏 TV 🔼 Y 🗒

GENEVA: *Auberge D'Hermance* — (F)(F)(F) — 6
12 Rue du Midi, 1248. ☎ *022 751 13 68.* FAX *022 751 16 31.*
@ info@hotel-hermance.ch W www.hotel-hermance.ch
A stylish inn set at the centre of Hermance, a medieval lakeside village about 15 km (9 miles) from Geneva. 1 🛏 TV 🗒

GENEVA: *Hôtel Le Montbrillant* — (F)(F)(F) — 82
2 Rue de Montbrillant, 1201. ☎ *022 733 77 84.* FAX *022 733 25 11.*
@ contact@montbrillant.ch W www.montbrillant.ch
A comfortable hotel in an elegant building very near Lake Geneva. Every room has a different décor. The restaurant serves French and gourmet Swiss cuisine. 1 🛏 TV 🔼 ⚡ Y 🔣 🗒

GENEVA: *Hôtel Beau-Rivage* — (F)(F)(F)(F) — 93
13 Quai du Mont-Blanc, 1201. ☎ *022 716 66 66.* FAX *022 716 60 60.*
@ info@beau-rivage.ch W www.beau-rivage.ch
Established in 1865, this luxury hotel occupies a grand building on the north shore of Lake Geneva. The rooms are large and elaborately decorated. The hotel's restaurants specialize in Thai and French cuisine.
1 🛏 🔼 P 🔣 🗒

For key to symbols see back flap

Price categories are per night for two people occupying a twin room with bath or shower (unless otherwise indicated), with service and tax included.
Ⓕ under 150 CHF (Swiss francs)
ⒻⒻ 150–250 CHF
ⒻⒻⒻ 250–350 CHF
ⒻⒻⒻⒻ 350–500 CHF
ⒻⒻⒻⒻⒻ over 500 CHF

RESTAURANT
The hotel has a restaurant that is open to guests as well as non-residents.

GARDEN OR TERRACE
The hotel has a garden or terrace.

SWIMMING POOL
The hotel has a swimming pool.

AIR CONDITIONING
All rooms have air conditioning.

	Price	Number of Rooms	Restaurant	Garden or Terrace	Swimming Pool	Air Conditioning
GENEVA: *Hotel D'Angleterre*	ⒻⒻⒻⒻ	45	●			■
17 Quai du Mont-Blanc, 1201. ☎ 022 906 55 55. FAX 022 906 55 56. @ angleterre@rchmail.com W www.dangleterre.com A luxury hotel on the north shore of Lake Geneva, with fine views of the lake and of Mont Blanc. Limousine service available.						

WESTERN SWITZERLAND

	Price	Number of Rooms	Restaurant	Garden or Terrace	Swimming Pool	Air Conditioning
AVENCHES: *De la Couronne* 20 Rue Centrale, 1580. **Road map** B3. ☎ 026 675 54 14. FAX 026 675 54 22. @ couronneavenches@vtx.ch W www.lacouronne.ch The smartest small hotel in this little town, very near the Roman amphitheatre.	ⒻⒻ	12	●			
DELÉMONT: *Le Moulin* 1 Rue des Moulins, 2800. **Road map** C2. ☎ & FAX 032 422 12 70. @ aubergedumoulin@mcnet.ch A small hotel in a building typical of the Jura. The restaurant specializes in meat dishes.	Ⓕ	8	●	■		
FRIBOURG: *Hôtel de la Rose* 1 Rue de Morat, 1702. **Road map** B3. ☎ 026 351 01 01. FAX 026 351 01 00. @ info@hoteldelarose.ch W www.hotelrose.com This small hotel occupies a 17th-century building in the Old Town, very near the cathedral. The rooms contain antique furniture.	ⒻⒻ	37	●	■		
FRIBOURG: *Hôtel Duc Berthold* 5 Rue des Bouchers, 1702. **Road map** B3. ☎ 026 350 81 00. FAX 026 350 81 81. @ ducbertholdfribourg@bluewin.ch W www.hotelducberthold.ch A grand hotel in the heart of the Old Town, very near the cathedral. The rooms are large and comfortable.	ⒻⒻ	36	●			
FRIBOURG: *Hôtel du Sauvage* 12 Planche-Supérieure, 1700. **Road map** B3. ☎ 026 347 30 60. FAX 026 347 30 61. @ hotel-sauvage@bluewin.ch W www.hotel-sauvage.ch A charming small hotel in the Old Town, well run with a personal touch.	ⒻⒻⒻ	17	●			
GRUYÈRES: *Hostellerie des Chevaliers* 1663. **Road map** B4. ☎ 026 921 19 33. FAX 026 921 25 52. @ chevaliers@gruyeres-hotels.ch W www.gruyeres-hotel.ch This excellent country hotel has an idyllic location just outside the village. The rooms are grand and comfortable.	ⒻⒻ	34		■		
GRUYÈRES: *Hostellerie St-Georges* 1663. **Road map** B4. ☎ 026 921 83 00. FAX 026 921 83 39. @ hostellerie-st-georges@swissonline.ch W www.st-georges-gruyeres.ch A comfortable establishment in the medieval heart of the town. The rooms are well appointed and the large terrace offers wide views. The restaurant serves French cuisines and local specialities.	ⒻⒻ	14	●	■		
LA CHAUX-DE-FONDS: *Hôtel de la Fleur-de-Lys* 13 Avenue Léopold-Robert, 2300. **Road map** B3. ☎ 032 913 37 31. FAX 032 913 58 51. @ admin@fleur-de-lys.ch W www.fleur-de-lys.ch A pleasant, comfortable hotel in this old watchmaking town. Its main advantage is its central location.	ⒻⒻ	33	●			
LAUSANNE: *Hôtel de l'Ours* 2 Rue du Bugnon, 1005. **Road map** B4. ☎ 021 320 49 71. FAX 021 320 49 73. This comfortable hotel occupies a historic building in the centre of Lausanne. The rooms are well-appointed and the restaurant specializes in Italian cuisine.	Ⓕ	19	●			

LAUSANNE: *Minotel Alagare* (F) 43
14 Rue du Simplon, 1006. **Road map** B4. (021 617 92 52.
FAX 021 617 92 55. @ info@alagare.com W www.alagare.com
A well-equipped hotel with a quiet yet central location, near Lausanne's train station and pedestrianized district. The rooms and communal areas are furnished in a traditional style.

LAUSANNE: *Elite* (F)(F) 33
1 Avenue Sainte-Luce, 1003. **Road map** B4. (021 320 23 61.
FAX 021 320 39 63. @ info@elite-lausanne.ch W www.elite-lausanne.ch
An outstanding mid-range hotel in an unusually tranquil, leafy spot in the town centre. The rooms on the top floor offer superb views of Lake Geneva.

LAUSANNE: *Lausanne Palace & Spa* (F)(F)(F)(F) 152
7–9 Rue du Grand-Chêne, 1002. **Road map** B4. (021 331 31 31. FAX 021 323 25 71.
@ reservation@lausanne-palace.ch W www.lausanne-palace.ch
In a historic building in the town centre, this luxury hotel offers high standards of service and comfort. The best rooms command magnificent views of Lake Geneva and the Alps. Facilities include a fitness, relaxation and beauty-treatment centre.

LES DIABLERETS: *Mon Abri* (F) 25
Route du Pillon, 1865. **Road map** B4.
(024 492 34 81. FAX 024 492 34 82. @ info@monabri.ch W www.monabri.ch
This traditional mountain chalet is richly decorated in rustic Swiss style. There are two bars and a billiards room.

LES DIABLERETS: *Eurotel Victoria* (F)(F)(F) 101
Chemin du Vernex, 1865. **Road map** B4. (024 492 37 21. FAX 024 492 23 71.
@ lesdiablerets@eurotel-victoria.ch W www.eurotel-victoria.ch
A long-established family-run hotel with large, modern, well-appointed rooms, a sauna and a solarium.

MONT-PÈLERIN: *Le Mirador, Kempinski Resort & Spa* (F)(F)(F)(F) 74
5 Chemin du Mirador, 1801. **Road map** B4. (021 925 11 11.
FAX 021 925 11 12. @ mirador@attglobal.net W www.mirador.ch
This is one of Switzerland's finest hotels. The spacious and elegantly furnished rooms have terraces that offer breathtaking views of Lake Geneva and the Alps. Facilities include a fitness, relaxation and beauty-treatment centre and tennis courts.

MONTREUX: *Hôtel Villa Germaine* (F) 9
3 Avenue Collonge, 1820. **Road map** B4.
(021 963 15 28. @ cecileparisi@gve.ch W www.montreux.ch
An inexpensive hotel in a richly decorated Belle Époque villa. Some of the rooms offer views of Lake Geneva and the Alps.

MONTREUX: *Le Montreux Palace* (F)(F)(F)(F) 235
100 Grand'Rue, 1820. **Road map** B4. (021 962 12 12. FAX 021 962 17 17.
@ sales@montreux-palace.com W www.montreux-palace.com
This lakefront palace in the heart of Montreux is perhaps the grandest hotel in Switzerland. Its superbly appointed rooms offer stunning views.

MURTEN/MORAT: *Murtenhof* (F)(F) 20
Rathausgasse 1, 3280. **Road map** B3. (026 672 90 30. FAX 026 672 90 39.
@ info@murtenhof.ch W www.murtenhof.ch
The hotel occupies a large renovated medieval building. It offers a choice of rooms, including suites with circular beds.

MURTEN/MORAT: *Weisses Kreuz* (F)(F) 27
Rathausgasse 31, 3280. **Road map** B3. (026 670 26 41. FAX 026 670 28 66.
@ info@weisses-kreuz.ch W www.weisses-kreuz.ch
A family-run hotel with a central location. While the rooms in the modern wing have views of the lake, those in the older wood-panelled annexe contain antique furnishings.

MURTEN/MORAT: *Le Vieux Manoir au Lac* (F)(F)(F)(F) 30
18 Rue de Lausanne, 3280. **Road map** B3. (026 678 61 61. FAX 026 678 61 62.
@ welcome@vieuxmanoir.ch W www.vieuxmanoir.ch
This hotel occupies a romantic manor house in a tranquil lakeside setting a little way out of the town. It has its own grounds, as well as a private beach and harbour. The restaurant is outstanding.

For key to symbols see back flap

Price categories are per night for two people occupying a twin room with bath or shower (unless otherwise indicated), with service and tax included.
Ⓕ under 150 CHF (Swiss francs)
ⒻⒻ 150–250 CHF
ⒻⒻⒻ 250–350 CHF
ⒻⒻⒻⒻ 350–500 CHF
ⒻⒻⒻⒻⒻ over 500 CHF

RESTAURANT
The hotel has a restaurant that is open to guests as well as non-residents.

GARDEN OR TERRACE
The hotel has a garden or terrace.

SWIMMING POOL
The hotel has a swimming pool.

AIR CONDITIONING
All rooms have air conditioning.

	NUMBER OF ROOMS	RESTAURANT	GARDEN OR TERRACE	SWIMMING POOL	AIR CONDITIONING

NEUCHÂTEL: *La Maison du Prussien* ⒻⒻ — 10, Restaurant ●, Garden or Terrace ■
Au Gor du Vauseyon, 2000. **Road map** B3. 📞 032 730 54 54. **FAX** 032 730 21 43.
@ info@hotel-prussien.ch Ⓦ www.hotel-prussien.ch
A hotel in a restored 18th-century brewery 2 km (1 mile) west of Neuchâtel. It has large rooms and several suites. 1 🛏 TV 🔄 Y P 🌿

NEUCHÂTEL: *Touring au Lac* ⒻⒻ — 51, Restaurant ●, Garden or Terrace ■
1 Place Numa-Droz, 2000. **Road map** B3. 📞 032 725 55 01. **FAX** 032 725 82 43.
@ touring.au.lac@world.com.ch Ⓦ www.touring-au-lac.ch
Decent town-centre hotel, right beside the marina, with plain, compact rooms. 1 🛏 TV 🔄 Y 🔒 🌿

NEUCHÂTEL: *Beau-Rivage* ⒻⒻⒻⒻ — 65, Restaurant ●, Garden or Terrace ■
1 Esplanade du Mont-Blanc, 2001. **Road map** B3.
📞 032 723 15 15. **FAX** 032 723 16 16. Ⓦ www.beau-rivage-hotel.ch
A traditional palace hotel on the lakefront, a short walk from the town centre. The luxurious rooms have fine Alpine views. 1 🛏 TV 🔄 Y 🔒 P 🌿

ST-URSANNE: *La Couronne* Ⓕ — 6, Restaurant ●, Garden or Terrace ■
3 Rue du 23-Juin, 2882. **Road map** C2. 📞 032 461 35 67. **FAX** 032 461 35 77.
@ info@hotelcouronne.ch Ⓦ www.hotelcouronne.ch
This is a small country hotel in a historic building. The restaurants specialize in meat and in fish dishes. 🌿

VEVEY: *Riviera Lodge* Ⓕ — 12
Place du Marché, 1800. **Road map** B4. 📞 021 923 80 40. **FAX** 021 923 80 41.
@ contact@rivieralodge.ch Ⓦ www.rivieralodge.ch
Set on the lakeshore, this is a small hotel in a period villa. Although the rooms are simply furnished and do not have en-suite bathrooms, they offer good value for money. There are also dormitories. 1 📶 P 🌿

YVERDON-LES-BAINS: *Grand Hôtel des Bains* ⒻⒻⒻⒻ — 120, Restaurant ●, Garden or Terrace ■, Swimming Pool ●
22 Avenue des Bains, 1400. **Road map** B3. 📞 024 424 64 64. **FAX** 024 424 64 65.
@ reservation@grandhotelyverdon.ch Ⓦ www.grandhotelyverdon.ch
Set in its own grounds, this is the largest and best spa hotel in Yverdon-les-Bains. The airy rooms are furnished in a modern style. 1 🛏 TV 🔄 Y P 🌿

NORTHERN SWITZERLAND

AARAU: *Aarauerhof* ⒻⒻ — 81, Restaurant ●
Bahnhofstrasse 68, 5001. **Road map** D2. 📞 062 837 83 00. **FAX** 062 837 84 00.
@ bestwestern@aarauerhof.ch Ⓦ www.aarauerhof.ch
A sleek, modern business and conference hotel. Rooms are fairly plain, but the hotel is in a prime central location. 1 🛏 TV 🔄 Y P 🌿

BADEN: *Atrium Hotel Blume* ⒻⒻ — 34, Restaurant ●
Kurplatz 4, 5400. **Road map** D2. 📞 056 222 55 69. **FAX** 056 222 42 98.
@ info@blume-baden.ch Ⓦ www.blume-baden.ch
Located in Baden's spa district, this classic hotel has comfortable, elegantly furnished rooms. Excellent value for money. 🛏 TV 🔄 🌿

BADEN: *Du Parc* ⒻⒻⒻ — 106, Restaurant ●, Garden or Terrace ■
Römerstrasse, 5401. **Road map** D2. 📞 056 203 15 15. **FAX** 056 222 07 93.
@ office@duparc.ch Ⓦ www.duparc.ch
A modern business hotel in a park between the town centre and the spa district. The functional rooms are comfortable. 1 🛏 TV 🔄 Y 🔒 P 🌿

BASEL: *BildungsZentrum 21* ⒻⒻ — 70, Restaurant ●, Garden or Terrace ■
Missionsstrasse 21, 4055. **Road map** C2. 📞 061 260 21 21. **FAX** 061 260 21 22.
@ info@bildungszentrum-21.ch Ⓦ www.bildungszentrum-21.ch
This hotel is set in large private grounds near Basel's historic district. The rooms are comfortable and well appointed. 1 🛏 🔄 P ♿ 🌿

BASEL: *Hotel Au Violon* ⒻⒻ 20
Im Lohnhof 4, 4051. **Road map** C2. 【 *061 269 87 11.* FAX *061 269 87 12.*
@ auviolon@iprolink.ch W www.au-violon.com
This modern hotel occupies a building that was once a prison. Its simple
but tastefully furnished rooms are arranged on two floors, and some look
onto the old town. 1 🚗 TV 🔧 🍴 🏊

BASEL: *Hotel Rochat* ⒻⒻ 50
Petersgraben 23, 4051. **Road map** C2. 【 *061 261 81 40.* FAX *061 261 64 92.*
@ info@hotelrochat.ch W www.hotelrochat.ch
A mid-range hotel in a listed historic building. It is situated in a quiet but
central area of the Old Town. 1 🚗 TV 🔧 🍴 🅿 🛏 🏊

BASEL: *Dorint* ⒻⒻⒻ 171
Schönaustrasse 10, 4058. **Road map** C2. 【 *061 695 70 00.* FAX *061 695 71 00.*
@ info.basbas@dorint.com W www.dorint.com
A modern hotel located near the Messe fairground in Kleinbasel.
It has bright, comfortable rooms and several well-equipped suites.
1 🚗 TV 🔧 🅿 🛏 🏊

BASEL: *Hotel Teufelhof* ⒻⒻⒻ 33
Leonhardsgraben 47–49, 4051. **Road map** C2.
【 *061 261 10 10.* FAX *061 261 10 04.* @ info@teufelhof.com W www.teufelhof.com
The rooms of this acclaimed hotel are decorated by local artists. It is
divided into two sections, the more expensive Kunsthotel, with nine rooms,
and the cheaper Galeriehotel, with 25 rooms. 1 🚗 🔧 🏊 24

BASEL: *Merian am Rhein* ⒻⒻⒻ 63
Rheingasse/Greifengasse 2. **Road map** C2. 【 *061 685 11 11.*
FAX *061 685 11 01.* @ kontakt@merian-hotel.ch W www.merian-hotel.ch
This centrally located hotel has spacious, tastefully furnished rooms
and offers good value for money. It has an excellent fish restaurant.
1 🚗 TV 🔧 🍴 🛏 🅿 🏊

BASEL: *Radisson* ⒻⒻⒻⒻ 205
Steinentorstrasse 25, 4001. **Road map** C2. 【 *061 227 27 27.* FAX *061 227 28 28.*
@ info.basel@radissonsas.com W www.radissonsas.com
A high-class hotel situated in the city centre, near the train station.
The rooms are well appointed and very comfortable.
1 🚗 TV 🔧 🍴 🍴 🛏 🅿 🏊

BASEL: *Drei Könige* ⒻⒻⒻⒻ 88
Blumenrain 8, 4001. **Road map** C2. 【 *061 260 50 50.* FAX *061 260 50 60.*
@ info@drei-koenige-basel.ch W www.drei-koenige-basel.ch
With origins going back to 1026, when it was an inn, this is one of the oldest
hotels in Europe. It is now furnished in the grand 19th-century style, and
some of the rooms overlook the Rhine. 1 🚗 TV 🔧 🍴 🛏 🅿 🏊 24

MURI: *Ochsen* ⒻⒻ 11
Seetalstrasse 16, 5630. **Road map** D2. 【 *056 664 11 83.* FAX *056 664 56 15.*
@ info@ochsen-muri.ch W www.ochsen-muri.ch
A small, well-kept hotel in the heart of the village, with modern rooms
and good service. 1 🚗 TV 🔧 🍴 🛏 🏊

WINTERTHUR: *Hotel Loge* ⒻⒻ 17
Oberer Graben 6, 8402. **Road map** E2. 【 *052 268 12 00.* FAX *052 268 12 33.*
@ info@hotelloge.ch W www.hotelloge.ch
This hotel, an historic building in the centre of the Old Town, has modern,
well-appointed rooms with all facilities. There are three cinemas in the
building. 1 🚗 TV 🔧 🍴 🛏 🏊

WINTERTHUR: *Krone* ⒻⒻ 37
Marktgasse 49, 8401. **Road map** E2. 【 *052 208 18 18.* FAX *052 208 18 20.*
@ info@kronewinterthur.ch W www.kronewinterthur.ch
This hotel occupies a renovated building in the centre of Winterthur.
The rooms are elegantly decorated and the service is excellent.
1 🚗 TV 🔧 🍴 🍴 🛏 🅿 🏊

WINTERTHUR: *Wartmann* ⒻⒻ 72
Rudolfstrasse 15, 8400. **Road map** E2. 【 *052 212 84 21.* FAX *052 213 30 97.*
@ wartmann@wartmann.ch W www.wartmann.ch
A good-quality business hotel near the train station. The rooms are
newly refurbished and the restaurant specializes in vegetarian dishes.
1 🚗 TV 🔧 🍴 🛏 🏊

For key to symbols see back flap

Price categories are per night for two people occupying a twin room with bath or shower (unless otherwise indicated), with service and tax included.
Ⓕ under 150 CHF (Swiss francs)
ⒻⒻ 150–250 CHF
ⒻⒻⒻ 250–350 CHF
ⒻⒻⒻⒻ 350–500 CHF
ⒻⒻⒻⒻⒻ over 500 CHF

RESTAURANT
The hotel has a restaurant that is open to guests as well as non-residents.

GARDEN OR TERRACE
The hotel has a garden or terrace.

SWIMMING POOL
The hotel has a swimming pool.

AIR CONDITIONING
All rooms have air conditioning.

ZÜRICH

	NUMBER OF ROOMS	RESTAURANT	GARDEN OR TERRACE	SWIMMING POOL	AIR CONDITIONING
ZÜRICH: *City Backpacker/Hotel Biber* Ⓕ Niederdorfstrasse 5, 8001. **Road map** E2. 044 251 90 15. FAX 044 251 90 24. @ sleep@citybackpacker.ch W www.city-backpacker.ch Although its rooms are rather small, this hotel gives visitors the opportunity of staying in central Zürich for a relatively small outlay. It is located in the Old Town, just 10 minutes' walk from the train station.	16				
ZÜRICH: *Otter und Wüste Bar* Ⓕ Oberdorfstrasse 7, 8001. **Road map** E2. 044 251 22 07. FAX 044 251 22 75. @ info@wueste.ch W www.wueste.ch Offering excellent value for money, this small hotel attracts many artists and students. The rooms are large and imaginatively furnished. TV ↻ ▨	16		■		
ZÜRICH: *Hotel Lady's First* ⒻⒻⒻ Mainaustrasse 24, 8008. **Road map** E2. 044 380 80 10. FAX 044 380 80 20. @ info@ladysfirst.ch W www.ladysfirst.ch This chic hotel, which opened in 2001, is for women only. The large, airy rooms are smartly decorated. 1 ▤ TV ↻ ▨ Y ▦ ⌧ ▨	28		■		
ZÜRICH: *Rössli* ⒻⒻⒻ Rössligasse 7, 8001. **Road map** E2. 044 256 70 50. FAX 044 256 70 51. @ reception@hotelroessli.ch W www.hotelroessli.ch A comfortable guesthouse in the centre of the Old Town. All the rooms are individually furnished. The suites have their own roof terraces. 1 ▤ ↻ ▨	22				
ZÜRICH: *Dolder Grand Hotel* ⒻⒻⒻⒻⒻ Kurhausstrasse 65, 8032. **Road map** E2. 044 269 30 00. FAX 044 269 30 01. @ reservations@doldergrand.ch W www.doldergrand.ch This luxury hotel occupies a period mansion set in a verdant residential district of Zürich. The rooms are opulently furnished and facilities include a fitness centre, golf course and tennis court. 1 ▤ TV ↻ Y ▨ ▦ P ⌧ ▨	163	●	■		
ZÜRICH: *Hotel Baur Au Lac* ⒻⒻⒻⒻⒻ Talstrasse 1, 8022. **Road map** E2. 044 220 50 20. FAX 044 220 50 44. @ reservation@bauraulac.ch W www.bauraulac.ch This luxury hotel in a park on the edge of the Zürichsee is one of the city's oldest and grandest hotels. The comfortably furnished and well-equipped rooms have peaceful views of the lake. 1 ▤ TV ↻ Y ▦ P ▨	125	●	■		■
ZÜRICH: *Savoy Baur En Ville* ⒻⒻⒻⒻⒻ Am Paradeplatz, 8022. **Road map** E2. 044 215 25 25. FAX 044 215 25 00. @ contact@savoy-baurenville.ch W www.savoy-zurich.ch Occupying a grand six-storey building, this elegant hotel is one of central Zürich's landmarks. The rooms are large and luxuriously furnished. 1 ▤ TV ↻ Y ▦ P ▨	112	●			■

EASTERN SWITZERLAND AND GRAUBÜNDEN

	NUMBER OF ROOMS	RESTAURANT	GARDEN OR TERRACE	SWIMMING POOL	AIR CONDITIONING
APPENZELL: *Adler* ⒻⒻ Adlerplatz, 9050. **Road map** F2. 071 787 13 89. FAX 071 787 13 65. @ info@adlerhotel.ch W www.adlerhotel.ch Located in a central yet quiet district of Appenzell, this hotel occupies a picturesque building in the traditional Appenzeller style. The rooms are newly renovated and well equipped. 1 ▤ TV ↻ ▨	21	●	■		
APPENZELL: *Romantik Hotel Säntis* ⒻⒻ Landesgemeindeplatz, 9050. **Road map** F2. 071 788 11 11. FAX 071 798 11 10. @ romantikhotelsaentis@bluewin.ch W www.romantikhotels.com/appenzell Looking onto the central square, this hotel is in a beautiful old building with a decorated façade. The rooms are decorated in traditional style and the welcome is memorably warm. 1 ▤ TV ↻ Y ▦ P ▨	37	●			

Arosa: *Quellenhof*   Ⓕ   18
Poststrasse, 7050. **Road map** F4. 📞 081 377 17 18. 📠 081 377 48 18.
With its splendid views of the surrounding mountains, this is an
inexpensive yet comfortable family hotel. It is a good base for hiking
and mountain biking. ● *May.* 1 🔒 🔃 🔥 🥗

Arosa: *Waldhotel National*   ⒻⒻ   94
7050. **Road map** F4. 📞 081 378 55 55. 📠 081 378 55 99.
@ info@waldhotel.ch Ⓦ www.waldhotel.ch
Set on a hillside above Arosa, this quiet hotel enjoys a serene
location among tall pine trees. The rooms are tastefully decorated,
and look either onto the forest or the town and the surrounding
mountains. The hotel is also within easy reach of ski lifts and hiking trails.
1 🔒 📺 🔃 🍸 🍴 🔥 🥗

Bad Ragaz: *Grand Hotel Quellenhof*   ⒻⒻⒻⒻ   106
7310. **Road map** F3. 📞 081 303 30 30. 📠 081 303 30 33.
@ reservation@resortragaz.ch Ⓦ www.resortragaz.ch
This vast and opulent hotel is set in a beautiful location, with
stunning views. The facilities, which include a casino, golf course,
thermal spa and fitness, relaxation and beauty-treatment centre, are
equally luxurious. 1 🔒 📺 🍸 🍴 P 🥗

Bad Ragaz: *Hotel Tamina*   ⒻⒻ   44
Am Platz, 7310. **Road map** F3. 📞 081 302 81 51. 📠 081 302 23 08.
@ info@hotel-tamina.ch Ⓦ www.hotel-tamina.ch
A charming hotel furnished in the Art Nouveau style. The rooms
are large and comfortable. The hotel has a smart restaurant and
a brasserie. 🔒 📺 🔃 🍸 P 🔥 🍴 🥗

Chur: *Posthotel*   ⒻⒻ   50
Poststrasse 11, 7002. **Road map** F3. 📞 081 252 68 44. 📠 081 252 01 95.
@ posthotel.chur@bluewin.ch Ⓦ www.comforthotelpost.ch
Located near Chur's pedestrianized district, this standard hotel
offers good value for money. The rooms are comfortable, even though
they are rather small and plainly furnished.
1 🔒 📺 🔃 🍸 🍴 🥗

Chur: *Stern*   ⒻⒻ   46
Reichsgasse 11, 7000. **Road map** F3. 📞 081 258 57 57. 📠 081 258 57 58.
@ info@stern-chur.ch Ⓦ www.stern-chur.ch
With comfortable, well-equipped and modern rooms, the Stern is
one of the best hotels in Chur. It occupies a 17th-century inn at the
entrance to the Old Town. The restaurant specializes in Graubünden
cuisine and offers local wines. 1 🔒 📺 🔃 🍴 🍸 P 🔥 🍴 🥗

Davos Platz: *Bahnhof-Terminus*   Ⓕ   53
Talstrasse 3, 7270. **Road map** F3. 📞 081 414 97 97. 📠 081 414 97 98.
@ hotel@bahnhof-terminus.ch Ⓦ www.bahnhof-terminus.ch
Located opposite the station, this traditional hotel has a friendly
atmosphere and spacious, airy rooms. It has three restaurants,
including a Chinese restaurant, and a bar.
🔒 🔃 📺 🍴 P 🍸 🔥 🍴 🥗

Davos Platz: *Hotel National*   ⒻⒻ   65
Obere Strasse 31, 7270. **Road map** F3. 📞 081 413 60 46. 📠 081 413 16 50.
@ national-davos@bluewin.ch Ⓦ www.national-davos.ch
This comfortable and relaxing hotel is surrounded by trees,
in a quiet part of Davos. Performances of Swiss folk music take place
on some evenings. ● *May & Nov.* 1 🔒 📺 🔃 🍸 🍴 🔥 🍴 🥗

Davos Platz: *Morosani Posthotel Davos*   ⒻⒻ   114
Promenade 42, 7270. **Road map** F3. 📞 081 415 45 00. 📠 081 415 45 01.
@ morosani@posthotel-davos.ch Ⓦ www.posthotel-davos.ch
A traditional hotel consisting of three interlinked buildings.
The lobby is furnished in the regional Engadine style and the rooms
are spacious. 1 🔒 📺 🔃 🍸 P 🔥 🥗

Klosters: *Alte Post*   Ⓕ   10
Aeuja, 7250. **Road map** F3. 📞 081 422 17 16. 📠 081 422 38 07.
@ hotel@post-aeuja.ch
In a quiet yet central part of Klosters, this small and inexpensive hotel
has a family atmosphere. The restaurant offers exceptionally good food.
● *May & Nov.* 🔒 📺 🥗

Price categories are per night for two people occupying a twin room with bath or shower (unless otherwise indicated), with service and tax included.
Ⓕ under 150 CHF (Swiss francs)
ⒻⒻ 150–250 CHF
ⒻⒻⒻ 250–350 CHF
ⒻⒻⒻⒻ 350–500 CHF
ⒻⒻⒻⒻⒻ over 500 CHF

RESTAURANT
The hotel has a restaurant that is open to guests as well as non-residents.

GARDEN OR TERRACE
The hotel has a garden or terrace.

SWIMMING POOL
The hotel has a swimming pool.

AIR CONDITIONING
All rooms have air conditioning.

		Number of Rooms	Restaurant	Garden or Terrace	Swimming Pool	Air Conditioning
KLOSTERS: *Casanna*	Ⓕ	7	●	■		
Landstrasse 171, 7250. **Road map** F3. 📞 081 422 12 29. **FAX** 081 420 20 29. A simple, cosy inn situated just five minutes' walk from Gotschna cable-car station. The restaurant serves inexpensive Swiss and regional dishes. ● *May & Nov.* 1						
KLOSTERS: *Pardenn*	ⒻⒻ	64	●	■	●	
Monbielerstrasse 18, 7250. **Road map** F3. 📞 081 423 20 20. **FAX** 081 423 20 21. @ hotel@pardenn.ch W www.pardenn.ch A traditional hotel in a quiet district just outside the centre of Klosters. The rooms have sunny, south-facing balconies. The restaurant serves light cuisine and vegetarian dishes. ○ *Dec–Apr.* 1						
RAPPERSWIL: *Jakob*	ⒻⒻ	20	●	■		
Hauptplatz 11, 8640. **Road map** E3. 📞 055 220 00 50. **FAX** 055 220 00 55. @ info@jacob-hotel.ch W www.jacob-hotel.ch Established in 1830 and recently renovated, this is an inexpensive hotel with a central location in Rapperswil's old town. The rooms are tastefully but simply furnished. The hotel has a bistro and wine bar.						
SCHAFFHAUSEN: *Parkvilla*	ⒻⒻ	25	●	■		
Parkstrasse 18, 8200. **Road map** E2. 📞 052 625 27 37. **FAX** 052 624 12 53. @ europa.graz@austria-trend.ch W www.hotelgarbo.ch Located on the edge of Schaffhausen's old town, this hotel occupies a stone-clad villa surrounded by beautiful old trees. It has comfortable, stylish rooms and suites.						
SCHAFFHAUSEN: *Fischerzunft*	ⒻⒻⒻ	12	●	■		
Rheinquai 8, 8200. **Road map** E2. 📞 052 632 05 05. **FAX** 052 632 05 13. @ info@fischerzunft.ch W www.fischerzunft.ch Located on the Rhine, a short walk from the town centre, this is the most characterful hotel in Schaffhausen. The rooms are tastefully furnished and the restaurant is excellent.						
SCHWÄGALP: *Schwägalp*	Ⓕ	30	●	■		
9107. **Road map** F3. 📞 071 365 66 00. **FAX** 071 365 66 01. @ contact@saentisbahn.ch W www.saentisbahn.ch Located at the foot of Säntis, near the cable-car station, this mountain hotel occupies a traditional building. The interior is decorated in a rustic style.						
SCUOL: *Crusch Alba*	ⒻⒻ	17	●	■		
Clozza 246, 7550. **Road map** G3. 📞 081 864 11 55. **FAX** 081 864 90 12. @ info@crusch-alba.ch W www.crusch-alba.ch Near the centre of Scuol, this small hotel occupies a building typical of the Engadine. The rooms have ornate wood panelling. The restaurant, in the basement, offers regional specialities.						
ST GALLEN: *Einstein*	ⒻⒻⒻ	65	●			
Berneggstrasse 2, 9001. **Road map** F2. 📞 071 227 55 55. **FAX** 071 227 55 77. @ hotel@einstein.ch W www.einstein.ch A hotel of style and character, in the centre of St Gallen. The rooms are spacious and comfortable.						

ST MORITZ (BAD): *Corvatsch* Ⓕ Ⓕ 26 ● ■
Via Tegiatscha 1, 7500. **Road map** F4. 【 *081 837 57 57*. 𝔽𝔸𝕏 *081 837 57 58*.
@ info@hotel-corvatsch.ch Ⓦ www.hotel-corvatsch.ch
Despite its unremarkable exterior, this hotel in the spa district of
St Moritz is welcoming and comfortable. The well-appointed rooms
have handmade furniture in the Engadine style. The restaurant serves
excellent local dishes.
● *May & Nov.* 🔒 TV 📶 ⛄ 🍸 P 👤 ✦

ST MORITZ (BAD): *Laudinella* Ⓕ Ⓕ Ⓕ 200 ● ■
Via Tegiatscha 17, 7500. **Road map** F4. 【 *081 836 00 00*. 𝔽𝔸𝕏 *081 836 00 01*.
@ info@laudinella.ch Ⓦ www.laudinella.ch
Located in the spa district of St Moritz, this hotel is an exceptionally
good-quality hotel for its price range. The spacious, well-kept rooms have
pine furniture. The hotel runs a variety of art and music courses. It has a
sauna and hammam and four restaurants.
1 🔒 TV 📶 ⛄ P 👤 ✦

ST MORITZ (BAD): *Badrutt's Palace* Ⓕ Ⓕ Ⓕ Ⓕ 180 ● ■ ●
Via Serlas 27, 7500. **Road map** F4. 【 *081 837 10 00*. 𝔽𝔸𝕏 *081 837 29 99*.
@ reservations@badruttspalace.com Ⓦ www.badruttspalace.com
Built in the 19th century, this was one of the first hotels to welcome
visitors who came to St Moritz to enjoy winter sports. Today, this legendary
retreat for royalty, film stars and glitterati offers glamour, opulence and the
finest in Swiss hotel service. 1 🔒 📶 P ✦ 24

STEIN AM RHEIN: *Adler* Ⓕ 25 ● ■
Rathausplatz 2, 8260. **Road map** E2. 【 *052 742 61 61*. 𝔽𝔸𝕏 *052 741 44 40*.
@ hotel-adler@bluewin.ch Ⓦ www.adlersteinamrhein.ch
In a building painted with frescoes, this traditional hotel is set in
the centre of the beautiful medieval town. The rooms are warm and
welcoming, and the restaurant serves regional and French cuisine.
🔒 📶 TV ⛄ P 👤 👤 ✦

STEIN AM RHEIN: *Rheinfels* Ⓕ Ⓕ 17 ● ■
Rhigass 8, 8260. **Road map** E2. 【 *052 741 21 44*. 𝔽𝔸𝕏 *052 741 25 22*.
@ rheinfels@bluewin.ch Ⓦ www.rheinfels.ch
This modest but comfortable hotel occupies a historic inn beside
the Rhine, in the heart of the village. The modernized rooms are cosy
and atmospheric, and there is a pleasant riverside terrace.
1 🔒 TV 📶 🍸 ✦

VADUZ (LIECHTENSTEIN): *Hotel Real* Ⓕ Ⓕ 13 ● ■
Städtle 21, 9490. **Road map** F3. 【 *00 423 232 22 22*. 𝔽𝔸𝕏 *00 423 232 08 91*.
@ real@hotels.li Ⓦ www.hotel-real.li
The best hotel in Liechtenstein's tiny capital, this is a fine traditional
establishment. The rooms are welcoming and the restaurant is renowned
for the quality of its cuisine. 1 🔒 TV 📶 🍸 ✦

CENTRAL SWITZERLAND AND TICINO

ANDERMATT: *Drei Könige & Post* Ⓕ Ⓕ 21 ● ■
Gotthardstrasse 69, 6490. **Road map** E4. 【 *041 887 00 01*. 𝔽𝔸𝕏 *041 887 16 66*.
@ hotel@3koenige.ch Ⓦ www.3koenige.ch
This centrally located hotel has comfortable rooms furnished in a
traditional style. The restaurant serves regional Swiss dishes. Facilities
include a sauna, a fitness, relaxation and beauty-treatment centre and
a golf course. 🔒 TV 🍸 P 👤 ✦

BECKENRIED: *Seehotel Sternen* Ⓕ Ⓕ 41 ● ■
Buochserstrasse 54, 6375. **Road map** D3.
【 *041 624 55 55*. 𝔽𝔸𝕏 *041 624 55 56*.
@ seehotel-sternen@bluewin.ch Ⓦ www.sternen-beckenried.ch
This well-appointed hotel is set among palms on the southern shore
of Lake Lucerne. 🔒 TV 📶 🍸 ⛄ 👤 ✦

BELLINZONA: *Unione* Ⓕ Ⓕ 33 ● ■
1 Via G. Guisan, 6500. **Road map** E5. 【 *091 825 55 77*. 𝔽𝔸𝕏 *091 825 94 60*.
@ info@hotel-unione.ch Ⓦ www.hotel-unione.ch
A standard mid-priced business hotel in a good central location
at the foot of Castelgrande, this is the best place to stay in Bellinzona.
Although the rooms are decorated simply, they are good value.
1 🔒 TV 📶 🍸 ✦

Price categories are per night for two people occupying a twin room with bath or shower (unless otherwise indicated), with service and tax included.
Ⓕ under 150 CHF (Swiss francs)
ⒻⒻ 150–250 CHF
ⒻⒻⒻ 250–350 CHF
ⒻⒻⒻⒻ 350–500 CHF
ⒻⒻⒻⒻⒻ over 500 CHF

RESTAURANT
The hotel has a restaurant that is open to guests as well as non-residents.

GARDEN OR TERRACE
The hotel has a garden or terrace.

SWIMMING POOL
The hotel has a swimming pool.

AIR CONDITIONING
All rooms have air conditioning.

	NUMBER OF ROOMS	RESTAURANT	GARDEN OR TERRACE	SWIMMING POOL	AIR CONDITIONING
BRUNNEN: *Seehotel Waldstätterhof* ⒻⒻⒻ Walstätterquai 6, 6440. **Road map** D3. ☎ 041 825 06 06. FAX 041 825 06 00. @ info@waldstaetterhof.ch Ⓦ www.waldstaetterhof.ch Established in 1870, this grand hotel is set in parkland on the edge of Lake Lucerne. The rooms are large and comfortably furnished, and some have balconies overlooking the lake. Private beach on the lake. ① 🛏 TV 🔁 ⚡ 🍴 🅿 🛁 🌙	105	●	■		
EINSIEDELN: *Sonne* ⒻⒻ Hauptstrasse 82, 8840. **Road map** E3. ☎ 055 412 28 21. FAX 055 412 41 45. @ hotel.sonne@bluewin.ch Ⓦ www.hotel-sonne.ch A hotel with a central location opposite the pilgrimage church. Restaurant and pizzeria. ① 🛏 TV 🔁 🛁 🌙	30	●	■		
ENGELBERG: *Waldegg* ⒻⒻⒻ Schwandstrasse 91, 6390. **Road map** D3. ☎ 041 637 18 22. FAX 041 637 43 21. @ info@waldegg-engelberg.ch Ⓦ www.waldegg-engelberg.ch Set on a sunny terrace above Engelberg, this hotel is a convenient base for hikers. The rooms' south-facing balconies offer views of Titlis. 🛏 TV 🔁 🍴 🛁 🅿 🌙	66	●	■		
KÜSSNACHT AM RIGI: *Du Lac Seehof* ⒻⒻ Seeplatz 6, 6403. **Road map** D3. ☎ 041 850 10 12. FAX 041 850 10 22. @ jtrutmann@bluewin.ch Built in 1854 and recently renovated, this hotel is set on the shore of Lake Lucerne. The restaurant is renowned for its fish dishes. 🛏 🅿 🌙	14	●	■		
LOCARNO: *Hotel Dell'Angelo* ⒻⒻ Viccolo della Motta 1, 6601. **Road map** E5. ☎ 091 751 81 75. FAX 091 751 82 56. @ info@hotel-dell-angelo.ch Ⓦ www.hotel-dell-angelo.ch With simply furnished but comfortable rooms, this hotel in Locarno's old town offers excellent value for money. ① 🛏 TV 🔁 🌙	55	●	■		
LOCARNO: *Belvedere* ⒻⒻⒻ Via ai Monti 44, 6601. **Road map** E5. ☎ 091 751 03 63. FAX 091 751 52 39. @ info@belvedere-locarno.com Ⓦ www.belvedere-locarno.ch This elegant hotel occupies a 17th-century building at the foot of the Belvedere. It has been thoroughly renovated in modern style. All the rooms are south-facing, and some have views of the lake. ① 🛏 🔁 ⚡ 🅿 🛁 🌙	80	●	■		
LOCARNO: *Esplanade* ⒻⒻⒻ Via Delle Vigne 66, 6648. **Road map** E5. ☎ 091 735 85 85. FAX 091 735 85 86. @ reservations@esplanade.ch Ⓦ www.esplanade.ch Set on the summit of a hill, this hotel has stunning views of Lake Maggiore and the Alps. It occupies a Mediterranean-style building, with comfortably furnished rooms. Facilites include a fitness, relaxation and beauty-treatment centre. ① 🛏 TV 🔁 🍴 ⚡ 🛁 🅿 🌙	75	●	■	●	■
LUGANO: *Hotel Zurigo* Ⓕ Corso Pestalozzi 13, 6900. **Road map** E5. ☎ 091 923 43 43. FAX 091 923 92 68. @ hotelzurigolugano@bluewin.ch Ⓦ www.hotelzurigo.ch A well-kept hotel with small but modern rooms. It is located near the lakeshore, within easy reach of the town's commercial centre. ① 🛏 TV 🔁 🅿 🌙	40				■
LUGANO: *Hotel Pestalozzi* ⒻⒻ Piazza Indipendenza 9, 6901. **Road map** E5. ☎ 091 921 46 46. FAX 091 922 20 45. @ pestalo@bluewin.ch Ⓦ www.attuale.com/pestalozzi.html This traditional hotel occupies a period building in central Lugano. The rooms have been refurbished in the Art Nouveau style. ① 🛏 🔁 ⚡ 🌙	55				

LUGANO: *Romantik-Hotel Ticino* ⓕⓕⓕⓕ 25
Piazza Cioccaro 1, 6901. **Road map** E5. (091 922 77 72. FAX 091 923 62 78.
@ romantikhotelticino@ticino.com Ⓦ www.romantikhotels.com/Lugano
Ths smart hotel in central Lugano has modern, tastefully
decorated rooms.

LUGANO: *Splendide Royal* ⓕⓕⓕⓕⓕ 96
Riva A. Caccia 7, 6900. **Road map** E5. (091 985 77 11.
FAX 091 985 77 22. @ info@splendide.ch Ⓦ www.splendide.ch
This long-established and very comfortable hotel is located on
the lakeside, near the town centre. It has a prestigious restaurant,
La Veranda, and a piano bar.

LUZERN: *Gefängnishotel Löwengraben* ⓕⓕ 56
Löwengraben 18, 6004. **Road map** D3. (041 417 12 12. FAX 041 417 12 11.
@ info@loewengraben.ch Ⓦ www.loewengraben.ch
Gefängnis means "jail", and this unusual mid-priced hotel occupies
what was Luzern's town prison from 1862 to 1998. The cells have
been cleverly transformed into small yet comfortable rooms. More
spacious accommodation is, however, available, as the former library,
the visitors' waiting room and the governor's office have also been
converted into rooms.

LUZERN: *Art Deco Hotel Montana* ⓕⓕⓕ 62
Adligenswilerstrasse 22, 6002. **Road map** D3.
(041 419 00 00. FAX 041 419 00 01.
@ info@hotel-montana.ch Ⓦ www.hotel-montana.ch
A superb central hotel in the Art Deco style. Perched above the
lakeshore, it offers stunning views. Service is outstanding and the
rooms are spacious and comfortable.

LUZERN: *Cascada* ⓕⓕⓕ 63
Bundesplatz 18, 6003. **Road map** D3. (041 226 80 88. FAX 041 226 80 00.
@ info@cascada.ch Ⓦ www.cascada.ch
A comfortable hotel, with a central location near Lake Lucerne.
The rooms are tastefully decorated and the restaurant specializes
in Spanish cuisine.

LUZERN: *Wilden Mann* ⓕⓕⓕ 50
Bahnhofstrasse 30, 6000. **Road map** D3.
(041 210 16 66. FAX 041 210 16 29.
@ mail@wilden-mann.ch Ⓦ www.wilden-mann.ch
Tucked away in Luzern's Old Town, this small, romantic hotel dates
from 1517. The rooms are tastefully decorated, and the welcome is warm
and friendly.

LUZERN: *Palace Luzern* ⓕⓕⓕⓕ 168
Haldenstrasse 10, 6002. **Road map** D3.
(041 416 16 16. FAX 041 416 10 00.
@ info@palace-luzern.ch Ⓦ www.palace-luzern.com
One of Luzern's landmarks, this large lakeside palace hotel is a
short walk from the town centre. The rooms are large and splendidly
appointed, and the public areas retain their Belle Epoque style.
The service and facilities are outstanding.

WEGGIS: *Garni-Hotel Frohburg* ⓕⓕ 12
Seestr. 21, 6353. **Road map** D3. (041 392 00 60. FAX 041 392 00 66.
@ Welcome@frohburg.ch Ⓦ www.frohburg.ch
This hotel is set in tranquil, green surroundings on the shore of
Lake Lucerne. All the rooms have balconies with a view of the lake.
The hotel is just 150 m (160 yd) from the jetty, and there is bathing in
summer.

ZUG: *Ochsen* ⓕⓕⓕ 48
Kolinplatz 11, 6301. **Road map** E3. (041 729 32 32. FAX 041 729 32 22.
@ info@ochsen-zug.ch Ⓦ www.ochsen-zug.ch
This hotel, in a fine 16th-century building, stands in a square in the
centre of Zug's Old Town The German poet Goethe (1749–1832)
once stayed here. Although it has been renovated in a rather impersonal
style, the quality of its service and facilities is high.

WHERE TO EAT

Coat of arms on a restaurant in Fribourg

THERE IS A GREAT VARIETY of restaurants in Switzerland, which reflects the country's cultural and regional diversity. While large cities such as Zürich and Geneva have top-class restaurants that serve international cuisine, the great majority of Swiss restaurants are relatively small, family-run concerns. These convivial establishments generally offer wholesome, filling dishes that reflect local rural traditions and that are prepared using local farm produce.

Many lakeside and riverside restaurants all over the country specialize in dishes featuring delicious locally caught fish.

Switzerland also has a great number and variety of small, more informal establishments. While German Switzerland has the *Stübli*, French Switzerland has the *rôtisserie* and *brasserie*. In Ticino the choice ranges from the classic *pizzeria* to the *trattoria* and *osteria*. South of the Alps, you are also likely to dine outdoors, in a sunny town square or informally at a table set outside a *grotto*.

A self-service restaurant in a department store

TYPES OF RESTAURANTS

IN SWITZERLAND, restaurants serving international cuisine are located almost exclusively in Zürich and Geneva, the country's two great cosmopolitan cities. The typical Swiss restaurant, by contrast, is a homely establishment serving a range of local dishes that vary according to the region.

In the German-speaking regions of Switzerland, a restaurant is sometimes called a *Beiz* or *Gasthaus*. Pleasant meals can also be enjoyed in *Kneipe*, which serve a small selection of hot dishes in addition to beer. The rustic *Stübli* often specialize in one type of dish, such as *Rösti*, fondue or *raclette* (see p262).

As well as restaurants, French-speaking regions of Switzerland have *rôtisseries*, which specialize in grilled food. Its more humble version is the *brasserie*, which serves buffet meals at lunchtime, and in the evenings turns into a restaurant with waiter service.

Some wine bars, called *caveaux* in French and *Weinstübli* in German, also serve meals, as do some beer taverns (*Bierstübli*). *Spunte*, or bars in German Switzerland, serve mainly beer. *Bars*, their counterparts in French Switzerland, serve coffee and alcoholic drinks but rarely offer food.

In the Italian-speaking canton of Ticino, one of the most popular and ubiquitous establishments is the *pizzeria*. The typical Italian restaurant is the *trattoria*. An *osteria* offers a smaller choice of dishes. Another simple restaurant is the *grotto*, meaning "cave". In the past this was a niche carved into a rock face, where simple local

dishes, with wine, were served. Today the term signifies a cosy rustic tavern, where meals are usually served outdoors. Ticino is also well-endowed with ice-cream parlours (*gelateria* or *cremeria*).

Inexpensive meals, which are of an excellent quality for the price, are offered in the self-service buffets of chain supermarkets and department stores, including Migros, Coop and Manora. These buffets, with filling soups, freshly made salads, pasta dishes and vegetarian fare, are open all day. Fast-food outlets are most likely to be found only in larger towns.

Smoking in restaurants is widely accepted. Almost none forbids smoking and very few, least of all those in smaller towns and villages, even have separate smoking and non-smoking areas.

The Schneider-Caffè restaurant in Davos

Many restaurants are closed one day a week. This is their "rest day" *(Ruhetag, jour de repos, jour de fermeture* or *giorno de chiusura).*

MEALS

DEPENDING ON the region, breakfast may either be quite substantial or consist simply of a light, appetizing snack. In Ticino, for example, it may consist only of coffee and a croissant. Elsewhere, particularly in German Switzerland, breakfast can be considerably more filling, consisting of muesli, rye bread or crusty bread, salami and cured meats, cheese and eggs, washed down with fruit juice, tea or coffee.

All over Switzerland, lunch is served between noon and 2pm. For many Swiss, this is the main meal of the day and most restaurants offer a hearty dish of the day *(Tagesteller, plat du jour* or *piatto del giorno),* which may consist of more than one course and which is generally excellent value for money.

Evening meals are served between 6:30 and 9pm, depending on the region. The more expensive restaurants, particularly those in large towns, tend to stay open until 10pm or later.

MENUS

IN RESTAURANTS in larger towns, as well as in holiday resorts and areas that attract large numbers of foreign visitors, the menu *(Karte, carte* or *carta)* is written in French or German (or both), and sometimes also in English. A few restaurants have separate menus printed in English. In smaller towns and in rural or remote areas, menus are written in German, French or Italian only.

Menus are often presented with an additional list of seasonal dishes. Almost all establishments display their menus, with prices, outside the premises.

A restaurant with outdoor tables on Zürich's Bahnhofstrasse

Restaurant sign in Thun

PRICES AND TIPPING

RESTAURANT MEALS in Switzerland tend to be relatively expensive. The average price of a dish of the day with salad is 15–20 CHF. A five-course set meal without wine is about 40 CHF. A plate of soup or a salad costs around 6 CHF. The average price of a fondue for two people is about 20 CHF. By contrast, the price of a meal in the self-service restaurant of a department store is typically no more than 10–15 CHF.

The price of a glass of local wine ordered with a meal is 2.50–3.50 CHF. A third of a litre of beer costs roughly the same. The price of a cup of coffee is rarely less than 3 CHF.

Restaurants in the most popular tourist spots or in particularly attractive locations generally charge a little more for their services.

Most restaurants also add a cover charge, which includes bread, per person. At all restaurants a 15 percent service charge is included in the final total. Tipping is therefore officially unnecessary. However, it is still customary to round the bill up, or to add a few francs to the total.

CHILDREN

IN SWITZERLAND, meals out are treated as a family occasion and it is not unusual to see small children in restaurants even late at night. Most restaurants provide high chairs and offer a special children's menu. Many restaurants also have toilets with baby-changing facilities.

VEGETARIANS

ALTHOUGH MEAT features prominently in Swiss cuisine, menus in restaurants usually include a selection of vegetarian dishes, as well as a great variety of vegetables and salads. Restaurants that offer no vegetarian dishes on the menu can sometimes be persuaded to prepare meat-free meals to order.

Interior of the Kornhauskeller in Bern

What to Eat

Swiss CUISINE DRAWS inspiration from its different peoples and cultures, yet it also has its own traditions and great regional diversity. Besides a panoply of cheeses, Swiss menus feature freshwater fish, such as trout and perch, as well as game, pork in various forms, and dried and smoked beef. Whereas fondue is the speciality of French Switzerland, a speciality of German Switzerland is *Rösti*, a patty of grated and fried potatoes. The cuisine of Italian Switzerland is, naturally, dominated by pizza, risotto, polenta and pasta dishes. Cream and chocolate are the main ingredients of delicious cakes and desserts.

Birchermüsli, *invented by Dr Bircher-Benner in the late 19th century, consists of oat-flakes mixed with ground or chopped walnuts, grated apple, and fruits such as strawberries, raspberries or peaches. It is served with milk or yoghurt.*

Gerstensuppe *is a barley soup with vegetables cut into strips and thinly sliced smoked or dried beef. A traditional dish of the Engadine valley, Gerstensuppe has many variations.*

Minestrone *is a tomato-based soup from Ticino. It contains carrots, beans, cauliflower, leeks and pasta and is served with a sprinkling of Sbrinz, a hard Swiss cheese that is similar to Parmesan.*

Käseschnitten *is an hors-d'oeuvre consisting of a slice of bread sprinkled with wine or milk, topped with a thick slice of cheese and toasted under the grill. A slice of ham is sometimes placed between the bread and the cheese.*

Bündner Trockenfleisch *is prime air-dried beef sliced very thin and often served with slices of cheese. It is a speciality of Graubünden.*

Raclette

Pickled onions

Gherkins

Jacket potatoes

Raclette, *roughly translated as "scraped cheese", is prepared by holding a soft cheese over heat and scraping it into a bowl as it melts. It is served with jacket potatoes, pickled onions and gherkins. The dish originated in Valais but is popular throughout Switzerland's Alpine regions.*

FONDUE

This traditional winter dish has many regional variations. It is served very hot, in a heavy pot placed over a small candle. Sharing a fondue, which is never made for fewer than two people, is a convivial occasion. Fondue is eaten by dipping small pieces of bread, held on a long fork, into the pot.

Bread for fondue

Fondue sauce *is usually made with a mixture of Emmental and Gruyère. The cheeses are grated and melted (fondu) in a shallow pot with wine or kirsch.*

Zürcher Geschnetzeltes *is diced veal fried in butter and simmered with onions and mushrooms, with a dash of white wine and cream. This Zürich dish is traditionally served with* Rösti.

Gitzlichüechli *are pieces of kid's meat that are first cooked in a mixture of wine and vegetable stock, then encased in beer pastry and fried. They are a speciality of Appenzell.*

Älplermagrone *is made with equal amounts of cooked noodles and diced cooked potatoes mixed with grated cheese and garnished with fried onion rings. The dish is served with apple sauce.*

Bernerplatte *consists of a selection of several types of meat such as pork knuckle, smoked beef tongue, bacon, chops and Bernese sausages that have been boiled in stock. The cooked meats are served on a large plate with green beans or sauerkraut.*

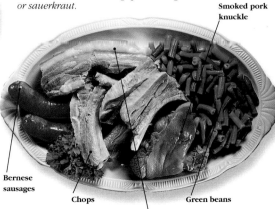

Smoked pork knuckle

Papet vaudois *is a dish consisting of finely sliced leek and diced potato served with hot smoked pork sausage. It is a speciality of the Lake Geneva region.*

Bernese sausages

Chops

Green beans

Filets de perche *are thin strips of filleted perch fried in butter and served with boiled potatoes and slices of fresh lemon. This dish is the greatest speciality of the Lake Geneva region.*

Bacon

CHOCOLATE DESSERTS

The excellent Swiss chocolate, made by traditional methods and containing a large proportion of cocoa solids, is often used in desserts. One of the most popular desserts is a dark chocolate mousse, rich and creamy with a slightly bitter taste.

Engadiner Nusstorte *is a tart consisting of a shortbread case filled with pieces of walnut mixed with caramel and honey.*

Zuger Kirschentorte *is a pastry made of flour and ground hazelnuts soaked in cherry brandy. It is filled with layers of buttercream and is sprinkled with nuts, cherries and icing sugar. It is a speciality of the cherry-growing canton of Zug.*

Chocolate dessert

Swiss Cheeses

SWITZERLAND IS JUSTLY RENOWNED for its cheeses, which range in taste from mild and nutty to rich and spicy. Cheese is a way of life in Switzerland. Thinly sliced, it is eaten for breakfast and is the basic ingredient or garnish of many dishes. It is also tossed into salads and is savoured at lunch or dinner as a delicacy in its own right. Half of Switzerland's milk yield goes into the making of cheese. One of the country's greatest exports, it is also an important part of the Swiss economy.

Poster for Appenzeller cheese

Cheeses in cold storage

ORIGIN OF CHEESE

CATTLE HAVE BEEN raised and pastured in Switzerland since about 2,000 BC. In this mountainous country, expanses of arable land are naturally very limited. By contrast, Switzerland's lush Alpine meadows are ideal for keeping livestock. Milk and milk products formed the basis of the staple diet of Switzerland's mountain-dwellers, and in winter were necessary for their survival.

With the advent of roads, and more importantly of rail-ways, linking the villages of remote mountain regions with the rest of the country, Alpine cheeses found new markets. Cheese-making also spread to the lower valleys.

Until the 15th century, most Swiss cheeses were soft. Hard cheeses gradually became more popular. Being riper, they kept better than soft cheeses, and could therefore be transported over longer distances.

CHEESE PRODUCTION

THE CHEESE-MAKING process involves five basic stages. First the milk is poured into large steel vats and heated to 30–36° C (86–96° F). A starter-culture, a liquid containing bacteria, is added to the milk. This causes the milk to turn sour. With the addition of an enzyme, such as rennet or pepsin, the milk forms a curd, a custard-like substance containing whey. When the curd is heated to 39–54° C (102–130° F), the whey separates from the curd.

Rounds of cheese

The whey is drained off and the curd is salted, packed into moulds and pressed to extract more whey. The curd is then shaped into blocks or circular slabs and left to mature, first in brine, where a rind forms on the cheeses, and later in a cold store, where the cheeses are regularly turned to maintain an even texture and prevent the moisture content from pooling.

The maturing, or ripening, process ranges from a few days to several months, or even years, depending on the type of cheese. The longer the ripening period, the harder the cheese.

The cheese-making season starts in early spring and continues until late autumn, coinciding with the growth of the most nourishing grass. Most Swiss cheeses are produced by small family-run businesses, of which there are about 1,000. Most of them rely on mechanized methods and sophisticated modern equipment. However, in some high Alpine regions, cheeses are still handmade entirely by traditional methods. Such cheeses, known as *Bergkäse*, *Alpkäse*, *fromage des alpes* or *formaggio di alpe*, are highly acclaimed.

Some cheese dairies are open to visitors. Among them are the Appenzeller Schaukäserei in Stein (*see p188*) and La Maison du Gruyère, at Pringy, just outside Gruyères (*see p124*).

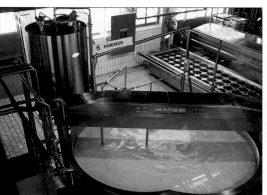

Heating and stirring milk in a vat in a modern cheese factory

TYPES OF CHEESE

THERE ARE MORE than 400 varieties of Swiss cheese, each with its own individual texture, flavour and aroma. Each also reflects German, French or Italian traditions, and is used in different ways: either eaten thinly sliced, made into fondue or *raclette*, or grated onto pasta dishes.

Vacherin Fribourgeois *is a medium-soft cheese produced exclusively in the canton of Fribourg. It is used primarily to make fondue.*

Appenzeller *is a highly aromatic cheese produced in northeastern Switzerland. The length of time it is ripened affects its taste. A black label indicates a well-matured variety, with a strong taste.*

Gruyère *is a hard cheese with a distinctive texture and flavour. Whereas a young Gruyère has a mild flavour, described as* doux, *a highly matured one has an intense flavour and is described as* salé. *Gruyère is made in western Switzerland.*

Tête de Moine, *meaning "monk's head", was first made by monks in the 12th century. Soft and light, it has a strong flavour which is best appreciated when the cheese is cut into slivers. Tête de Moine, also known as Bellelay, is made in the Jura.*

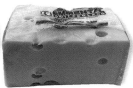

Emmental, *the most popular of all Swiss cheeses, is mild, with a nutty flavour, and large holes. This cheese is made in Emmental and throughout the central lowlands of German-speaking Switzerland. Emmental, which is exported worldwide, is one of the best cheeses to use for making fondue.*

Raclette *has a rich, spicy flavour and, because it melts easily, it is widely used for making the dish known as raclette, hence its name. This is one of the most popular cheeses in Switzerland. Although it originated in Valais, raclette is now made throughout Switzerland.*

Sbrinz *is a dry cheese with an intense flavour, similar to Parmesan. It is grated and sprinkled over dishes, or thinly sliced and served as a dessert cheese. Originating in Brienz, in the Bernese Oberland, Sbrinz is now made throughout central Switzerland. It is matured for up to three years.*

Tilsiter *is a creamy cheese with a delicate flavour. It is named after Swiss émigrés in Tilsit, Prussia, who devised the recipe in the 19th century and returned with it to Switzerland. Tilsiter is now made in eastern Switzerland.*

RETAIL AND EXPORT

SWITZERLAND'S ANNUAL cheese production amounts to 134,000 tonnes, just over half of which is exported. By far the most popular varieties worldwide are Emmental, known as the King of Cheeses, and Gruyère.

Many of Switzerland's cheese dairies have shops where their own cheeses are offered for sale. A wide range of locally produced cheeses, including some of the most highly prized varieties, can also be found on market stalls all over Switzerland.

Some larger towns have specialist cheese shops, which stock the widest range of Swiss cheeses. Supermarkets also sell good-quality cheeses, either pre-packed or cut to order from a chilled counter.

Most Swiss cheeses are made with raw milk, which gives them their distinctive flavour. Those made with pasteurized milk are labelled accordingly. The more mature a cheese, the more expensive it is likely to be.

A variety of cheeses on display in a shop window, Stein am Rhein

What to Drink in Switzerland

Beer mat

Swiss WINES ARE among the finest in Europe but, as they are not exported, they are almost unknown outside their country of origin. The best vineyards are those in the cantons of Valais and Vaud, particularly on the sheltered hillsides around Lake Geneva. Switzerland also has over 100 large and small breweries, which between them produce high-quality dark beers, light ales and lagers, also mostly for domestic consumption. Coffee, sometimes served with cream, and tea, which is usually served black, are popular hot drinks. Unique to Switzerland is Rivella, a soft drink made with whey.

Poster advertising Swiss wines

NON-ALCOHOLIC DRINKS

Rivella, made with whey   **Valser mineral water**   **Caotina, a chocolate drink**

MEALS ARE FREQUENTLY accompanied by still or sparkling mineral water from Switzerland's own mineral springs. The best-known brands include Valser, Henniez, Fontessa, Passugger and Aproz. A popular sweet, fizzy and refreshing drink is Rivella, which is made with whey, a by-product in the cheese-making process *(see p264)*. Three different kinds of Rivella are available: original (with a red label), with a reduced sugar content (a blue label) and with green tea (a green label). Caotina is a smooth, flavoursome chocolate drink.

HOT DRINKS

COFFEE, SERVED IN MANY GUISES, from creamy cappuccino to pungent espresso, is the most popular hot drink in Switzerland. Coffee served with a dash of liqueur or fruit-flavoured vodka is known in German as *Kaffe fertig*, and in Italian as *caffè corretto*. Tea is less widely drunk than coffee but, served ice-cold (as *Eistee*, *thé froid* or *te freddo*), it is particulary refreshing on hot summer days. Mint tea and Alpine herb infusions are also popular. Ovomaltine, a malted powder added to hot milk, and hot chocolate are warming and restorative winter drinks. Ovo Drink is a ready-mixed Ovomaltine and milk drink.

A malted drink, made with hot milk   **Ovomaltine and milk drink**

BEER

Bottled beer from Chur   **Canned lager**   **Bottled beer from Basel**

THE MOST POPULAR TYPE of beer in Switzerland is a light, German-style beer with an alcohol content of 4.2 to 5.5 percent. Strong beers, with a 6 percent alcohol content, include *weizen* (wheat) and *alt* (dark) varieties. Dominant brands include Feldschlösschen, made in the Basel region, Calanda from Chur, Rugenbräu from Interlaken and Cardinal from Fribourg. Draught beer is usually served in measures ranging from 1 to 5 decilitres. The most common are the 3-decilitre *Stange* (about half a pint) and the 2-decilitre *Herrgöttli* (just over a third of a pint).

Label of the dark Calanda beer

WHITE WINE

T HE MOST POPULAR SWISS white wine is the delicate, freshly-scented Fendant from Valais, traditionally served with fondue and *raclette* or drunk as an aperitif. From around Lake Geneva come the well-balanced wines of the Lavaux region, the delicate and refreshing wines of La Côte, and the intensely aromatic wines of the Chablais. This region, as well as Neuchâtel, also produces the light and subtle Chasselas wine, which is served with white meat and cheese and as an aperitif.

Sylvaner, in eastern Switzerland, is also renowned for its white wines. Having a subtle aroma and intense flavour, they are served with fish or asparagus. Chardonnay is produced mainly around Geneva and in Valais. It is served with fish and seafood.

Swiss Blanc from Rheinau Abbey

Pinot Gris from Neuchâtel

Fendant, a Chasselas from Valais

Mont-sur-Rolle Grand Cru de La Côte

RED WINE

T HE FINEST OF ALL Swiss red wines is the subtle Dôle, made from a blend of Gamay and Pinot Noir grapes. This is closely followed by the intensely flavoured pure Pinot Noir wines. Both come from Valais and are ideal with red and white meats and cheese.

The vineyards around Lake Geneva produce the light Salvagnin and Gamay wines, which are often served with red meat and hot hors-d'oeuvres. The Lake Neuchâtel region also produces Gamay, which goes well with poultry, veal and cheese. From eastern Switzerland comes Blauburgunder, a fine accompaniment to poultry. Typical of Ticino is Merlot, a ruby-red wine with a subtle aroma. It is excellent with red meat or risotto.

Wine from the Geneva region

Merlot from Ticino

Pinot Noir from Zürich

Dôle from the Sion region

SPIRITS AND LIQUEURS

A PROPORTION OF THE FRUIT grown in Swiss orchards is used to make a variety of spirits and fruit liqueurs. The most popular spirits include kirsch, made from cherries, and Williams, made from William pears. In the French-speaking regions of Switzerland, *pruneau* is distilled from plums, and in Ticino, *grappa* is distilled from the skins, stalks and pips of grapes. *Betzi*, made in German-speaking regions, is a brandy made from a mixture of fruit. Other Swiss spirits and liqueurs are made from apples, quinces, plums, apricots, cherries, raspberries or herbs. A meal often ends with a glass of brandy, to aid digestion, and a dash of spirits may be added to coffee. Liqueur, such as kirsch, is sometimes added to fondue.

Williamine pear brandy

Grundbacher plum spirit

Grappa from Ticino

Apple spirit from Zug

Choosing a Restaurant

THE RESTAURANTS in this guide have been selected across a wide range of price categories for their good value, exceptional food and/or interesting location. This chart lists the restaurants by region, starting with Bern, and the coloured thumb tabs on the side of each page correspond to those by which the regions of Switzerland are identified throughout this guide.

		CREDIT CARDS	OUTSIDE DINING	SWISS WINES	VEGETARIAN DISHES

BERN					

BERN: *Café Littéraire im Stauffacher* (F)
Ryffligässchen 8, 3011. (031 313 66 66.
w www.stauffacher.ch/litteraire.php
A restaurant and café on the second floor of Stauffacher, a large bookshop.
The menu consists only of vegetarian dishes prepared with organic
produce and includes a wide selection of cheese dishes. A large sunny
terrace is open in summer, and there are smoking and non-smoking areas.
● Sun.
| CREDIT CARDS ■ | OUTSIDE DINING ● | SWISS WINES ■ | VEGETARIAN DISHES ● |

BERN: *Grotto-Ticino-Pizzeria* (F)
Breitenrainplatz 26, 3014. (031 331 96 77. FAX 031 331 72 55.
This rustic restaurant in the city centre serves Italian dishes and specialities
from Ticino, such as polenta, risotto, gnocchi and pork sausage.
| ■ | | ■ | |

BERN: *Vatter* (F)
Bärenplatz 2, 3011. (031 312 51 91. FAX 031 312 53 44. w www.vatter.ch
This restaurant and café in the heart of the Old Town is located above a
shop selling organic produce. The spacious interior has a self-service
counter, with vegetarian and meat dishes prepared with organic produce.
Customers are charged according to the weight of food on their plate.
● Sun.
| ■ | ● | ■ | ● |

BERN: *Brasserie Bärengraben* (F)(F)
Grosse Muristalden 1, 3006. (& FAX 031 313 11 21.
Regional dishes dominate the menu of this small brasserie, which occupies
a former customs house on Nydeggbrücke. The dining room has a simple
décor and a pleasant atmosphere.
| ■ | ● | ■ | ● |

BERN: *Goldener Schlüssel* (F)(F)
Rathausgasse 72, 3011. (031 311 02 16. FAX 031 311 56 88.
@ info@goldener-schluessel.ch w www.goldener-schluessel.ch
In a medieval building reputed to stand exactly 99 steps from the
Zytglogge (Clock Tower), this typical Swiss restaurant serves wholesome,
tasty dishes. It attracts a regular local clientele.
| | ● | ■ | ● |

BERN: *Harmonie* (F)(F)
Hotelgasse 3, 3011. (031 313 11 41. FAX 031 313 11 40.
@ harmonie@harmonie.ch w www.harmonie.ch
This is one of the oldest-established restaurants in Bern, and it has been
run by the same family since 1915. Its principal speciality is fondue.
● Sat–Sun. ⬚ ⬚
| ■ MC V | ● | ■ | ● |

BERN: *Le Beaujolais* (F)(F)
Aarbergergasse 52, 3011. (031 311 48 86. FAX 031 311 48 25.
A restaurant serving French dishes as well as Swiss specialities. It is in a
historic building that has housed a café since the mid-19th century. ⬚ ⬚
| | ● | ■ | |

BERN: *Desperado* (F)(F)
Speichergasse 37, 3011. (031 311 91 93. FAX 031 311 84 80.
w www.desperado.ch
An impressive range of cocktails and authentic Mexican dishes are on offer
in this restaurant and bar in the centre of Bern. The dining room has a
romantic, retro-style décor.
| ■ MC V | | ■ | |

BERN: *Restaurant Altes Tramdepot* (F)(F)
Grosser Muristalden 6, 3006. (031 368 14 15. FAX 031 368 14 16.
w www.altestramdepot.ch
This restaurant occupies a converted tram depot near the Bärengraben. The
menu, which changes regularly, is dominated by international cuisine and
also features dishes cooked in a wok. The terrace, which is open in
summer, offers fine views of the Old Town, across the river. ⬚ ⬚
| ■ | ● | ■ | ● |

Price categories are for a three-course meal for one person, including tax and service but without wine. Ⓕ under 30 CHF (Swiss francs) ⒻⒻ 30–60 CHF ⒻⒻⒻ 60–90 CHF ⒻⒻⒻⒻ 90–120 CHF ⒻⒻⒻⒻⒻ over 120 CHF	**CREDIT CARDS** The restaurant accepts credit cards. **OUTSIDE DINING** Tables outside, on a terrace, in a garden or on a quayside. **SWISS WINES** The restaurant serves Swiss wines. **VEGETARIAN DISHES** Good selection of vegetarian dishes available.		

	CREDIT CARDS	OUTSIDE DINING	SWISS WINES	VEGETARIAN DISHES
BERN: *Restaurant Chindlifrässer Spaghetti Factory* ⒻⒻ Kornhausplatz 7, 3011. 🕽 *031 312 54 55.* FAX *031 312 28 54.* The menu at this Italian restaurant features over 20 different pasta dishes, as well as a large selection of hors-d'oeuvres, salads and ice creams. It has an informal atmosphere and attracts a youthful clientele. 🔧 ⚒	▪			●
BERN: *Restaurant Gourmanderie Moléson* ⒻⒻ Aarbergergasse 24, 3011. 🕽 *031 311 44 63.* FAX *031 312 01 45.* A traditional restaurant specializing in Bernese specialities and the cuisine of the Alsace. The menu features a choice of cheese, meat and vegetarian dishes, all of which are prepared with organic produce. ● *Sat lunchtime, Sun.* 🔧 ⚒			▪	●
BERN: *Schmiedstube* ⒻⒻ Schmiedenplatz 5, 3000. 🕽 *031 311 34 61.* FAX *031 311 52 44.* @ info@schmiedstube.com Ⓦ www.schmiedstube.com A restaurant in a former guild house in the centre of the Old Town. The menu, which changes according to the season, features national and regional dishes. 🔧 ⚒	▪ MC V	●	▪	●
BERN: *Della Casa* ⒻⒻⒻ Schauplatzgasse 16, 3011. 🕽 *031 311 21 42.* FAX *031 311 78 73.* This fine Old Town restaurant serves hearty Bernese fare, including the famous Bernerplatte — an array of meats with sauerkraut and potatoes. The décor is traditional and the service punctilious. ● *Sat; Sun evenings.*	▪		▪	

MITTELLAND, BERNESE OBERLAND AND VALAIS

	CREDIT CARDS	OUTSIDE DINING	SWISS WINES	VEGETARIAN DISHES
BREITEN OB MÖREL: *Taverne* Ⓕ Breitenstrasse 1, 3983. **Road map** D4. 🕽 *027 927 10 22.* FAX *027 927 34 10.* @ taverne@breiten.ch Ⓦ www.breiten.ch/taverne A charming restaurant with an imaginative menu. The tasty and original dishes are based on seasonal produce. ● *November.*	▪	●	▪	●
CRANS-MONTANA: *Crans-Ambassador* ⒻⒻ Avenue du Petit-Signal, 3962. **Road map** C4. 🕽 *027 485 48 48.* FAX *027 485 48 49.* @ info@crans-ambassador.ch Ⓦ www.crans-ambassador.ch Traditional Valais dishes, including *raclette* and fondue, are on offer here. A hot and cold buffet is available on Saturday. Good selection of desserts. ● *First two weeks in Dec.* 🔧 ⚒	▪	●	▪	●
CRANS-MONTANA: *Intergolf* ⒻⒻ Route de la Moubra, 3963. **Road map** C4. 🕽 *027 485 88 88.* FAX *027 485 88 99.* @ info@helvetia-intergolf.ch Ⓦ www.helvetia-intergolf.ch The restaurant of the Aparthotel Helvetia Intergolf *(see p245)*. This cosy, traditional establishment is furnished in the Valais style and serves local dishes. The dining room has spectacular views of the Alps. ◻ *Evenings only.* ● *Mid-Apr–June & Nov–mid-Dec.* 🔧 ⚒	▪	●	▪	●
CRANS-MONTANA: *Primavera* ⒻⒻ Avenue de la Gare, 3962. **Road map** C4. 🕽 *027 481 42 14.* FAX *027 481 74 14.* @ info@hotelprimavera.ch Ⓦ www.hotelprimavera.ch A traditional restaurant serving classic Swiss dishes, with a menu that changes according to the season. It also organizes *raclette* parties. 🔧 ⚒	▪	●	▪	●
GRÄCHEN: *Walliserhof* Ⓕ Dorfplatz, 3925. **Road map** C5. 🕽 *027 956 11 22.* FAX *027 956 29 22.* @ walliserhof@rhone.ch Ⓦ www.hotel-walliserhof.ch Good, traditional dishes served in elegant surroundings are on offer at this restaurant. It occupies a large timber building in the centre of Grächen. 🔧 ⚒	▪	●	▪	●

For key to symbols see back flap

Price categories are for a three-course meal for one person, including tax and service but without wine.
Ⓕ under 30 CHF (Swiss francs)
ⒻⒻ 30–60 CHF
ⒻⒻⒻ 60–90 CHF
ⒻⒻⒻⒻ 90–120 CHF
ⒻⒻⒻⒻⒻ over 120 CHF

CREDIT CARDS
The restaurant accepts credit cards.

OUTSIDE DINING
Tables outside, on a terrace, in a garden or on a quayside.

SWISS WINES
The restaurant serves Swiss wines.

VEGETARIAN DISHES
Good selection of vegetarian dishes available.

	CREDIT CARDS	OUTSIDE DINING	SWISS WINES	VEGETARIAN DISHES

GSTAAD: *Charly's* ⒻⒻ
Promenade, 3780. **Road map** C4. 📞 033 744 15 44. FAX 033 744 94 44.
@ charly-gstaad@bluewin.ch
This is the smartest of the many tearooms and cake shops that line Gstaad's main thoroughfare. It is a popular spot for hot chocolate and pastries, morning coffee or a light meal.

	■		■	●

GSTAAD: *Chesery* ⒻⒻⒻⒻ
Cheseryplatz, 3780. **Road map** C4. 📞 033 744 24 51. FAX 033 744 89 47.
@ chesery@gstaad.ch W www.chesery.ch
The most fashionable meeting-place in Gstaad, this is a very upmarket gourmet restaurant. It was founded in 1962 by the Aga Khan and attracts the resort's wealthiest clientele. The décor is all Alpine wood while the menu is a sophisticated blend of Swiss and international cuisines.
● Mid-Apr–mid-Jun & mid-Oct–mid-Dec. ♿

	■	●	■	●

INTERLAKEN: *El Azteca* ⒻⒻ
Jungfraustrasse 30, 3800. **Road map** D4. 📞 033 822 71 31. FAX 033 822 71 94.
@ hotel-blume@tcnet.ch W www.hotel-blume.ch
An attractive little Mexican restaurant, slightly away from the town centre. It offers a wide range of Mexican dishes and good service. ● Wed; Jan.

	■	●	■	●

INTERLAKEN: *PizPaz* ⒻⒻ
Centralplatz, 3800. **Road map** D4. 📞 033 821 14 28. FAX 033 822 66 16.
A popular, centrally located pizza restaurant that also offers a good range of homemade pastas and other Italian specialities. It is geared primarily to a tourist clientele, and has a pleasant atmosphere.
● Mon

	■	●	■	●

INTERLAKEN: *Schuh* ⒻⒻ
Höheweg 56, 3800. **Road map** D4. 📞 033 822 94 41. FAX 033 822 94 27
@ info@schuh-interlaken.ch W www.schuh-interlaken.ch
A famous Interlaken institution, located on the edge of the Höhematte park, this is an elegant restaurant serving light meals. It is also a refined spot for afternoon tea and cakes, and incorporates a cake shop.

	■	●	■	●

LAUTERBRUNNEN: *Schützen* ⒻⒻ
Dorf, 3822. **Road map** D4. 📞 033 855 30 26. FAX 033 855 29 50.
@ info@hotelschuetzen.com W www.hotelschuetzen.com
This typical Swiss chalet-style hotel next to the tourist office also has a quality restaurant serving hearty Alpine fare and, as a Lauterbrunnen speciality, afternoon tea with freshly made apple strudel. ♿

	■		■	

PORRENTRUY: *Du Jura* ⒻⒻ
1 Rue de la Chaumont, 2900. **Road map** C2. 📞 032 466 17 48.
W www.hotelpizzeriadujura.pagesjaunes.ch
The specialities of this small hotel restaurant are pizzas and pasta dishes. The menu also includes meat and fish dishes.
● Sun.

	■	●	■	●

RIEDERALP: *Derby* Ⓕ
3987. **Road map** D4. 📞 027 927 10 33. FAX 027 927 32 93.
This restaurant occupies a large chalet fronted by a terrace. The décor is rustic and the menu features regional dishes. Live music in the evenings in winter. ● May & Nov. 🚹 ♿

	■	●	■	●

RIEDERALP: *Restaurant Walliser Spycher* ⒻⒻ
Aletschpromenade, 3987. **Road map** D4. 📞 027 927 22 23. FAX 027 927 31 49.
@ info@walliserspycher.ch W www.walliser-spycher.ch
The dining room of this restaurant is decorated in the style of a mountain chalet, with rustic furnishings. As well as Valaisian specialities, the menu features traditional country dishes. ● May & Nov. 🚹 ♿

	■	●	■	●

RIEDERALP: *Tenne*
Art Furrer Resort, 3987. **Road map** D4. 027 928 44 88.
FAX 027 928 44 99. @ art.furrer@rhone.ch W www.artfurrer.ch
This unusual hotel restaurant is arranged on six levels. All the food served
here is prepared entirely with fresh ingredients.
Late May–early June & Oct–Nov.
⒡⒡

SAAS FEE: *Allalin*
3906. **Road map** D5. 027 957 17 71. FAX 027 957 30 71.
@ drehrestaurant@saas-fee.ch W www.drehrestaurant.ch
Revolving 360 degrees every hour, this restaurant offers splendid views of
the high peaks around Saas Fee. The menu features regional cuisine and a
few Italian dishes. Special children's menu.
May–mid-Jun.
⒡⒡

SAAS FEE: *Käsekeller*
3906. **Road map** D5. 027 957 21 20. FAX 027 957 37 30.
@ marba@tic.ch W www.kaese-keller.ch
This restaurant specializes mainly in cheese dishes, including *raclette* and
several varieties of fondue. Steak is also on the menu, and there is a large
selection of local wines. The dining room has rough, whitewashed walls
and simple wooden furniture.
Sun; May & mid-Oct–mid-Nov.
⒡⒡

SCHILTHORN: *Piz Gloria*
At Schilthorn's upper station. **Road map** C4.
033 826 00 07. FAX 033 856 21 31. W www.schilthorn.ch
Perched at 2,970 m (9,750 ft) at the top of this ice-bound peak,
this revolving restaurant is reached by cable car from Stechelberg
and Mürren. The complex was built for the 1969 James Bond film
On Her Majesty's Secret Service. Many hotels in Mürren allow you
to take your breakfast here rather than down below: it is a perk
well worth asking for.
⒡⒡

SION: *Brasserie Lucus*
19 Ruelle du Midi, 1950. **Road map** C5.
027 322 22 82. FAX 027 322 98 82. @ lucus@span.ch
An attractive family-run brasserie with a congenial atmosphere. The
menu concentrates on French cuisine, and specialities include fillet steak,
shrimps and game in season.
⒡

SION: *L'Enclos de Valère*
Rue des Châteaux 18, 1950. **Road map** C5.
027 323 32 30. FAX 027 323 32 03.
A rustic restaurant located on a sunny terrace that commands fine views.
The menu features an international selection of dishes.
Oct–Apr: Sun–Mon.
⒡⒡⒡

SOLOTHURN: *Baseltor*
Hauptgasse 79, 4500. 032 622 34 22.
FAX 32 622 18 79. W www.baseltor.ch
A fine cooperatively run café and restaurant within this charming hotel
in the Old Town. The cuisine is fresh and light, and is based on organic
ingredients from the local market. The atmosphere is warm and pleasant.
Sun lunchtime.
⒡⒡

TÖRBEL: *Bergrestaurant Moosalp*
3923. **Road map** C5. 027 952 14 95. FAX 027 952 29 13.
@ info@moosalp.ch W www.moosalp.ch
The menu at this family-run mountain restaurant includes a choice
of salads as well as delicious Valaisian meat and cheese dishes. *Raclette*
is prepared on an open fire. mid-Oct–mid-Dec & mid-Apr–mid-Jun
(except Easter week).
⒡⒡

VERBIER: *La Marmotte*
Les Planards, 1936. **Road map** C5.
027 771 68 34. FAX 027 771 26 80.
A restaurant in a traditional Alpine chalet with a breathtaking view of
Verbier, the Combins massif and Mont Blanc. *Raclette* and other local
specialities are served here.
May–Jun & Oct–Nov.
⒡⒡

For key to symbols see back flap

<table>
<tr><td colspan="2">

Price categories are for a three-course meal for one person, including tax and service but without wine.

Ⓕ under 30 CHF (Swiss francs)
ⒻⒻ 30–60 CHF
ⒻⒻⒻ 60–90 CHF
ⒻⒻⒻⒻ 90–120 CHF
ⒻⒻⒻⒻⒻ over 120 CHF

</td></tr>
</table>

CREDIT CARDS
The restaurant accepts credit cards.

OUTSIDE DINING
Tables outside, on a terrace, in a garden or on a quayside.

SWISS WINES
The restaurant serves Swiss wines.

VEGETARIAN DISHES
Good selection of vegetarian dishes available.

	CRESIT CARDS	OUTSIDE DINING	SWISS WINES	VEGETARIAN DISHES
VERBIER: *Rosalp* ⒻⒻⒻⒻⒻ Rue de Médran, 1936. **Road map** C5. ☎ 027 771 63 23. **FAX** 027 771 10 59. ⓦ www.rosalp.ch This high-quality restaurant is located in a traditional Alpine chalet. Roland Pierroz, one of the greatest chefs of his generation, uses only natural, fresh ingredients. ● *May–Jun & Sep–mid-Dec.* ⚒ ♿	■	●	■	●
VISP: *Ristorante-Pizzeria Le Bristol* Ⓕ Kantonsstrasse 28, 3930. **Road map** D4. ☎ 027 946 33 23. ⓦ www.blatter.ch/bristol Typical Italian dishes, including a variety of pizzas and pasta dishes, are served here. The spacious dining room has large windows looking onto the street. ● *Mon & 25 Dec–1 Jan.* ⚒ ♿	■	●	■	●
WENGEN: *Da Sina* Ⓕ Dorf, 3823. **Road map** C4. ☎ 033 855 31 72. **FAX** 033 855 30 72. @ sina@wengen.ch ⓦ www.sina.ch An attractive pizza and pasta restaurant in the heart of the village, with a good range of dishes, a good reputation and good service. ● *Mid-Oct–Nov: Wed.*	■		■	●
WILDERSWIL: *La Cabane* ⒻⒻ Obereigasse 19, 3812. **Road map** D4. ☎ 033 822 84 14. **FAX** 033 833 84 94. @ mail@luna-motel.com ⓦ www.luna-motel.com With a magnificent view over the Jungfrau massif, this restaurant serves traditional Swiss dishes, including some memorable desserts. International selection of wines. Barbecues are held on the terrace in summer. ⚒ ♿	■	●	■	●
ZERMATT: *Seilerhaus* ⒻⒻ Bahnhofstrasse, 3920. **Road map** C5. ☎ 027 966 87 39. **FAX** 027 957 87 58. ⓦ www.zermatt.ch/restaurant/seilerhaus A modern restaurant offering a choice of pizzas, hamburgers, salads and grilled dishes. The terrace is heated in winter, and in summer there is live piano music. ⚒ ♿	■	●	■	●
ZERMATT: *Sunnegga* ⒻⒻ 3920. **Road map** C5. ☎ 027 967 73 46. **FAX** 027 967 29 06. @ sunnegga@zermatt.ch ⓦ www.zermatt.ch/restaurant/sunnegga With three dining rooms, the Jagdstübli, Bergstübli and Stübli, this is the largest restaurant in the Zermatt area. It serves traditional Valais dishes and a wide choice of *Rösti* and *Käseschnitten*. ● *May & Nov.*	■	●	■	●
ZERMATT: *Walliserkanne* ⒻⒻ Bahnhofstrasse 32, 3920. **Road map** C5. ☎ 027 966 46 10. **FAX** 027 966 46 11. @ walliserkanne@zermatt.ch ⓦ www.walliserkanne.ch The Walliserkanne has three restaurants. On the ground floor is Il Ristorante, an Italian establishment serving a range of pasta dishes and pizzas cooked in a wood-fired oven. Raclettestube, on the first floor, specializes in *raclette*, and the cosy Pfisterstube at the back of the building serves traditional Valais cuisine, with a choice of meat dishes. ⚒ ♿	■	●	■	●
ZERMATT: *Zum See* ⒻⒻ 3920. **Road map** C5. ☎ 027 967 20 45. **FAX** 027 967 18 73. @ info@zumsee.ch ⓦ www.zumsee.ch A restaurant in a rustic mountain chalet on the route of hiking trails and ski runs leading down to the Furi cable-car station. The menu features traditional regional cuisine and some Italian dishes. Fish is served in season. ● *Mid-Apr–mid-June & mid-Oct–mid-Dec.*	■	●	■	●

GENEVA

GENEVA: *Le Kid*
(F)
99 Boulevard Carl-Vogt, 1205. **Road map** A5. **C** & **FAX** 022 320 44 96.
@ restolekid@hotmail.com W www.restolekid.com
A small, pleasant restaurant near the Plaine de Plainpalais, with a dining
room furnished in rustic style. The menu offers chicken and grilled meat
dishes as well as a good selection of vegetarian dishes.
● *Sun; 25 Dec–1Jan.* 🛉 🛓

GENEVA: *Pizzeria de Paolo*
(F)
3 Rue du Lac, 1207. **Road map** A5. **C** 022 736 30 49.
As well as pizza served straight from the oven, the specialities at this
Italian restaurant include gnocchi and salmon marinated in herbs.
● *24–25 Dec.* 🛉 🛓

GENEVA: *Bleu-Rhône*
(F)(F)
19 Rue du Rhône, 1204. **Road map** A5.
C 022 311 32 00. **FAX** 022 301 20 22.
Traditional dishes from the Geneva region as well as French cuisine
are served at this smart restaurant. Specialities include seafood and
fish. The terrace offers fine views of the Rhône and Lake Geneva.
● *Sun.* 🛉 🛓

GENEVA: *Café Rafael*
(F)(F)
1 Quai Turrettini, 1201. **Road map** A5. **C** 022 909 00 05. **FAX** 022 909 00 10.
W www.mandarinoriental.com
This elegant restaurant in the Hôtel du Rhône serves international
cuisine with a small selection of Asian dishes. The menu also features
seasonal dishes. 🛉 🛓

GENEVA: *Forces Motrices*
(F)(F)
15 Rue de la Coulouvrenière, 1204. **Road map** A5.
C 022 320 03 98. **FAX** 022 735 75 76.
The dining room at this restaurant takes the form of a bistro decorated in
retro style. The menu features Mediterranean dishes, including couscous
and paella, and moussaka. ● *Sun.* 🛉 🛓

GENEVA: *La Veranda*
(F)(F)
20 Rue des Alpes, 1201. **Road map** A5.
C 022 906 97 79. **FAX** 022 906 97 78.
@ international-terminus@swissonline.ch W www.international-terminus.ch
This is the restaurant of the International & Terminus Hotel. It is set in a
garden and is near the train station. It offers traditional Swiss dishes, with a
large selection of salads and many varieties of pizza.

GENEVA: *Le Montbrillant*
(F)(F)
2 Rue Montbrillant, 1201. **Road map** A5. **C** 022 733 77 84. **FAX** 022 733 25 11.
@ contact@montbrillant.ch W www.montbrillant.ch
This restaurant, in a typical Swiss house in the city centre, offers
Swiss and Italian cuisine. On the menu are pastrami, seafood, freshly
caught fish from the lake, and a choice of homemade desserts. Children's
menus are also available. 🛓

GENEVA: *Les Armures*
(F)(F)
1 Puits-St-Pierre, 1204. **Road map** A5.
C 022 310 91 72. **FAX** 022 310 98 46.
@ rest.armures@swissonline.ch W www.hotel-les-armures.ch
This cosy restaurant has a dining room decorated with suits of armour.
The menu includes such typical Swiss dishes as fondue and *raclette*, and
includes some French dishes.

GENEVA: *Pied de Cochon*
(F)(F)
4 Place du Bourg de Four, 1204. **Road map** A5.
C & **FAX** 022 310 47 97. @ hotalp@span.ch W www.pied-de-cochon.ch
A rustic bistro specializing in Swiss and French cuisine. The menu
features many pork dishes, and a selection of vegetarian dishes. 🛓

GENEVA: *Du Parc des Eaux-Vives*
(F)(F)(F)(F)
82 Quai Gustave Ador, 1211. **Road map** A5. **C** 022 849 75 75.
FAX 022 849 75 70. @ info@le-parcdeseauxvives.ch W www.parcdeseauxvives.ch
Gourmet Swiss and French cuisines are the speciality of this elegant
restaurant on the north side of Parc La Grange. The food is exquisitely
cooked and beautifully presented. ● *Mon–Tue.* 🛉 🛓

For key to symbols see back flap

Price categories are for a three-course meal for one person, including tax and service but without wine.
Ⓕ under 30 CHF (Swiss francs)
ⒻⓀ 30–60 CHF
ⒻⒻⒻ 60–90 CHF
ⒻⒻⒻⒻ 90–120 CHF
ⒻⒻⒻⒻⒻ over 120 CHF

CREDIT CARDS
The restaurant accepts credit cards.

OUTSIDE DINING
Tables outside, on a terrace, in a garden or on a quayside.

SWISS WINES
The restaurant serves Swiss wines.

VEGETARIAN DISHES
Good selection of vegetarian dishes available.

	CREDIT CARDS	OUTSIDE DINING	SWISS WINES	VEGETARIAN DISHES
GENEVA: *La Réserve* ⒻⒻⒻⒻ 301 Rue de Lausanne, 1293. **Road map** A5. 022 959 59 59. **FAX** 022 959 59 60. @ info@lareserve.ch W www.lareserve.ch La Réserve comprises two different restaurants. The Tse Fung serves traditional Chinese dishes, and Le Loti specializes in French cuisine with a Mediterranean flavour.	■	●	■	●

WESTERN SWITZERLAND

	CREDIT CARDS	OUTSIDE DINING	SWISS WINES	VEGETARIAN DISHES
BONCOURT: *Lion d'Or* ⒻⒻ 6 Route du Jura, 2926. **Road map** B2. 032 475 52 10. **FAX** 022 475 52 66. @ liondor@bluemail.ch Located in a small village near the border with France, this is the restaurant of a long-established family-run hotel. The menu features regional dishes based on fresh seasonal produce. ● *Mon.*	■	●	■	●
BRENT: *Le Pont de Brent* ⒻⒻⒻⒻⒻ 1817. **Road map** B4. 021 964 52 30. **FAX** 021 964 55 31. @ lrabaey@bluewin.ch W www.lepontdebrent.com Located in a small village above Montreux, Le Pont de Brent is one of Switzerland's top five restaurants. The cuisine is a subtle and sophisticated interpretation of traditional French and French-Swiss country dishes, meticulously prepared and presented. ● *Sun–Mon, 22 Dec–7 Jan & mid-Jul–early Aug.*	■		■	●
CAUX: *Montreux-Vevey-Riviera Panoramique Plein-Roc* ⒻⒻ Rochers-de-Naye, 1824. **Road map** B4. 021 963 74 11. **FAX** 021 963 86 20. Perched on an elevated rocky outcrop, this restaurant commands sweeping views of Lake Geneva and the Alps. ● *Nov–Mar.*	■		■	●
CHAMBESY: *Plage du Reposoir* ⒻⒻ 222 Route de Lausanne, 1292. **Road map** A5. 022 732 42 65. **FAX** 022 731 67 01. @ d.b.reposoir@vtx.ch W www.restaurantreposoir.ch On the north shore of Lake Geneva, between Geneva and Lausanne, this restaurant serves regional and French cuisine, with a large selection of fish and seafood, and a variety of pizzas. The terrace offers views of Mont Blanc. ● *Oct–Apr.* 🏃 ♿	■	●	■	●
CRISSIER: *Hôtel de Ville* ⒻⒻⒻⒻⒻ 1 Rue d'Yverdon, 1023. **Road map** B4. 021 634 05 05. **FAX** 021 634 05 06. @ restaurant.p.rochat@bluewin.ch W www.relaischateaux.ch One of Switzerland's finest, this restaurant occupies the former town hall of Crissier, a small village on the outskirts of Lausanne. It is an idyllic place to enjoy exquisite, classic French-style cuisine, prepared by chef Philippe Rochat. Advance booking recommended. ● *Sun–Mon & mid-Jul–early Aug.*	■		■	●
DELÉMONT: *Café d'Espagne* Ⓕ 2 Rue de Chêtre, 2800. **Road map** C2. 032 423 21 76. **FAX** 032 422 95 85. W www.cafedespagne-jean-mi.ch This family-run café-bistro is located in the centre of Delémont. It serves light dishes based on regional cuisine but with a subtle Spanish influence. ● *Sun–Mon.* 🏃 ♿	■	●	■	●
DELÉMONT: *Du Midi* ⒻⒻ 10 Place de la Gare, 2800. **Road map** C2. 032 422 17 77. **FAX** 032 423 19 89. @ sedem94@bluewin.ch Located opposite the railway station, this restaurant serves mainly regional and French dishes prepared with seasonal produce. ● *Tue evenings & Wed; for three weeks after Easter.*	■	●	■	●

DEVELIER: *Auberge du Cerf*   ⒻⒻ
61 Rue de la Liberté, 2802. **Road map** C2. ☎ *032 422 15 14.* **FAX** *032 423 20 30.*
@ auberge.cerf@bluewin.ch Ⓦ www.chez.com/aubergeducerf
A long-established auberge in an attractive setting of lush green meadows.
The dining room is furnished in a rustic style and the menu includes game
dishes. ● *Wed; late Jul–early Sep.* 🚹 ⓖ

FRIBOURG: *L'Aigle-Noir*   ⒻⒻ
10 Rue des Alpes, 1700. **Road map** B3. ☎ *026 322 49 77.* **FAX** *026 322 49 88.*
@ restaurantaiglenoir@bluewin.ch Ⓦ www.aiglenoir.ch
A restaurant in the town centre, serving Swiss and French cuisine. The
terrace overlooks the river valley. ● *Sun–Mon.* 🚹 ⓖ

FRIBOURG: *Du Gotthard*   ⒻⒻ
18 Rue du Pont-Muré, 1701. **Road map** B3. ☎ *026 322 32 85.*
One of the most celebrated spots in central Fribourg for indulging in the
local speciality: cheese fondue. This is a lovely old-fashioned café-bistro
dating from 1861, with riotous decoration consisting of posters, fairylights
and *objets trouvés*, and a heart-warming atmosphere. Plenty of other Swiss
dishes are also on offer. ● *Jul 2004–Sep 2005.*

FRIBOURG: *Auberge de Zaehringen*   ⒻⒻⒻ
13 Rue de Zaehringen, 1700. **Road map** B3. ☎ *026 322 42 36.* **FAX** *026 322 69 08.*
@ office@auberge-de-zaehringen.ch Ⓦ www.auberge-de-zaehringen.ch
The best restaurant in town, housed in an impressive old patrician
mansion. There are two dining areas: a brasserie, lower-priced and
informal, with a good range of dishes; and a restaurant, higher-priced
and more formal, which concentrates on French-inspired cuisine of a high
order. ● *Sun–Mon*

GRUYÈRES: *Le Chalet*   ⒻⒻ
1663. **Road map** B4. ☎ *026 921 21 54.* **FAX** *026 921 33 13.*
@ chaletgruyeres@bluewin.ch Ⓦ www.gruyeres-hotels.ch/chalet
This charming restaurant occupies a former mill in the medieval town,
near the castle. The specialities here are *raclette* and fondue. However,
the menu also includes grilled dishes. Among the desserts are fruits of the
forest (raspberries and blackberries), served with meringues and locally
made cream.

LA CHAUX-DE-FONDS: *La Pinte Neuchâteloise*   ⒻⒻ
8 Rue Grenier, 2300. **Road map** B3. ☎ *032 913 20 30.*
A wonderfully traditional tavern in the town centre, with an appreciative
local clientele. On offer here are classic Jura dishes, including fondue with
white wine, and specialities such as tripe.

LAUSANNE: *Le Chalet Suisse*   ⒻⒻ
40 Route du Signal, 1018. **Road map** B4. ☎ *021 312 23 12.* **FAX** *021 312 24 01.*
@ chaletsuisse@cdmgroup.ch Ⓦ www.chaletsuisse.ch
This restaurant occupies a classic Swiss chalet in a woodland setting. The
terrace offers a view of Lausanne and Lake Geneva. On the menu are such
classic Swiss specialities as *Rösti*, fondue and *raclette*. Live folk music in
the evenings.

LAUSANNE/OUCHY: *Le Château d'Ouchy*   ⒻⒻⒻ
2 Place du Port, 1006. **Road map** B4. ☎ *021 616 74 51.* **FAX** *021 617 51 37.*
@ info@chateaudouchy.ch Ⓦ www.chateaudouchy.com
This elegant hotel restaurant in the style of a Parisian brasserie is located in
a castle on the shores of Lake Geneva. Diners enjoy a magnificent view of
the lake and the Alps. The menu offers sophisticated French dishes.

LES DIABLERETS: *Les Mazots*   ⒻⒻ
Col de la Croix, 1865. **Road map** B4. ☎ *024 492 10 23.* **FAX** *024 492 10 41.*
@ info@lesmazots.ch Ⓦ www.lesmazots.ch
Les Mazots is the restaurant of the upmarket Hôtel des Diablerets. It serves
traditional cuisine, including *Rösti*, gratin dishes and fondue, as well as
steak and grilled dishes. ● *May & Nov.* 🚹 ⓖ

MONTREUX: *Palais Oriental*   ⒻⒻⒻ
6 Quai Ernest-Ansermet, 1820. **Road map** B4.
☎ *021 963 12 71.* **FAX** *021 963 12 79.* Ⓦ www.palaisoriental.ch
Fabulous Persian restaurant on the waterfront, with a lavish Islamic-style
interior and splendid cuisine, based on Iranian, Moroccan and Lebanese
specialities that is perfectly authentic.

Price categories are for a three-course meal for one person, including tax and service but without wine.
Ⓕ under 30 CHF (Swiss francs)
ⒻⒻ 30–60 CHF
ⒻⒻⒻ 60–90 CHF
ⒻⒻⒻⒻ 90–120 CHF
ⒻⒻⒻⒻⒻ over 120 CHF

CREDIT CARDS
The restaurant accepts credit cards.

OUTSIDE DINING
Tables outside, on a terrace, in a garden or on a quayside.

SWISS WINES
The restaurant serves Swiss wines.

VEGETARIAN DISHES
Good selection of vegetarian dishes available.

	CREDIT CARDS	OUTSIDE DINING	SWISS WINES	VEGETARIAN DISHES

MURTEN/MORAT: *Le Vieux Manoir au Lac*   ⒻⒻⒻⒻ
18 Rue de Lausanne, 3280. **Road map** B3. 📞 026 678 61 61. 📠 026 678 61 67.
@ welcome@vieuxmanoir.ch 🆆 www.vieuxmanoir.ch
This highly acclaimed restaurant occupies a romantic manor house in its own lakeside grounds. The dining room is traditionally styled and the menu offers seasonal cuisine. The wine list is enhanced by Murten's proximity to the top-rated Vully vineyards. ● *Dec–Jan.*

| | ■ | | ■ | ● |

LE NOIRMONT: *Restaurant de la Gare*   ⒻⒻⒻⒻ
2 Rue de la Gare, 2340. **Road map** B2. 📞 032 957 66 33. 📠 032 957 66 34.
@ georges-wenger@swissonline.ch 🆆 www.georges-wenger.ch
In a small village in the Jura, this restaurant has won renown for the fresh, innovative cuisine created by its chef, Georges Wenger. The dining room is traditionally styled, with white tablecloths and drapes, and the menu features dishes prepared with local ingredients. The presentation is superb.
● *Mon–Tue.*

| | ■ | | ■ | ● |

NEUCHÂTEL: *Beau-Rivage*   ⒻⒻ
1 Esplanade du Mont-Blanc, 2001. **Road map** B3. 📞 032 723 15 15.
📠 032 723 16 16. @ reception@beau-rivage-hotel.ch 🆆 www.beau-rivage-hotel.ch
This is the restaurant of the luxury Hôtel Beau-Rivage, which is set directly on the shore of Lake Neuchâtel. The veranda and terrace offer splendid views of the lake and the surrounding mountains. The menu features exquisite French dishes. Large selection of wines. 🚻 ♿

| | ■ | ● | ■ | ● |

NEUCHÂTEL: *Le Cardinal Brasserie*   ⒻⒻ
9 Rue du Seyon, 2000. **Road map** B3. 📞 032 725 12 86.
A popular and utterly authentic old café-brasserie in the Old Town, serving classic fish, seafood and meat dishes in an old-fashioned yet appealing setting. ● *Sun*

| | ■ | | ■ | |

NEUCHÂTEL: *Café des Halles*   ⒻⒻⒻ
4 Rue du Trésor, 2001. **Road map** B3. 📞 032 724 31 41. 📠 032 721 30 84.
@ maison-des-halles@bluewin.ch 🆆 www.maisondeshalles.ch
This fine restaurant occupies a 16th-century building on the Old Town's main square, with tables spilling out onto a lovely terrace. At ground level, the main attraction is delicious pizza cooked in a wood-fired oven. On the upper floor is a more formal dining room serving classic Neuchâtel dishes such as freshly caught perch.

| | ■ | | ■ | ● |

PERLY: *Al Castellino*   ⒻⒻ
278 Route de St-Julien, 1258. **Road map** A5. 📞 022 771 11 98.
📠 022 771 12 03. @ aragnelli@infomaniak.com 🆆 www.alcastellino.com
A family-run restaurant and pizzeria serving Italian and international cuisine. On offer are many fish and meat dishes, as well as a choice of pasta dishes, pizzas and salads. A special children's menu is also available.
🚻 ♿

| | ■ | ● | ■ | ● |

SAIGNELÉGIER: *Café du Soleil*   Ⓕ
14 Rue du Marché-Concours, 2350. **Road map** B2.
📞 032 951 16 88. 📠 032 951 22 95.
An easygoing café-bistro near the station in the centre of this attractive Jura village, with vegetarian options in the restaurant, a programme of live music and exhibitions of the work of local artists and craftworkers. Don't miss the post-prandial glass of Damassine, a delectable plum-based liqueur distilled locally. ● *Mon.*

| | ■ | | ■ | ● |

ST-URSANNE: *La Couronne*   ⒻⒻ
3 Rue du 23 juin, 2882. **Road map** C2. 📞 032 461 35 67. 📠 032 461 35 77.
@ info@hotelcouronne.ch 🆆 www.hotelcouronne.ch
The restaurant of a small family-run hotel, with its own garden. The menu includes regional dishes. ● *Tue–Wed; Oct–Apr.* 🚻 ♿

| | ■ | ● | ■ | ● |

St-Ursanne: *La Demi-Lune*   Ⓕ Ⓕ
2 Rue Basse, 2881. **Road map** C2. 【 032 461 35 31. FAX 032 461 37 87.
@ info@demi-lune.ch W www.demi-lune.ch
This is the restaurant of a small hotel on the river, in the heart of
St Ursanne's historic district. The specialities are dishes made with
homemade pasta. ● *Thu.*

Saint-Ursanne: *Le Boeuf*   Ⓕ Ⓕ
60 Rue du 23-Juin. **Road map** C2. 【 032 461 31 49. FAX 032 461 38 92.
@ hotel.boeuf@bluewin.ch W www.juranet.ch/site/boeuf
Traditional Swiss cuisine and a variety of trout dishes, as well as a choice
of pizzas, are served in this small restaurant. The dining room is furnished
in a rustic style and the atmosphere is friendly and informal.
● *Dec–Jan: Mon.* 🔁 ⒧

Villard-Chamby: *Du Montagnard*   Ⓕ Ⓕ Ⓕ
2 Route du Vallon, 1832. **Road map** B4.
【 021 964 36 84. FAX 021 964 84 49.
Located in a wine-making village outside Montreux, this large restaurant
serves regional and French cuisine, including several varieties of fondue.
Light meals are available on request.
● *Jan–Mar: Mon–Tue.* 🔁 ⒧

Yverdon-les-Bains: *Creperie l'Ange Bleu*   Ⓕ
11 Rue du College, 1400. **Road map** B3. 【 024 426 09 96.
W langebleu.pagesjaunes.ch.
This attractive little creperie has good pancakes, snacks, salads and light
meals at bargain prices. ● *Mon.*

NORTHERN SWITZERLAND

Baden: *Schwyzerhüsli*   Ⓕ Ⓕ
Badstrasse 38, 5401. **Road map** D2. 【 056 222 62 63. FAX 056 222 62 46.
Something of a local institution, this restaurant has two dining areas. While
light meals and traditional local dishes are served in the brasserie, more
substantial dishes are on offer in the Stübli. ● *Sun.*

Basel: *Zem alte Schluuch*   Ⓕ
Greifengasse 6, 4058. **Road map** C2. 【 061 681 88 98.
On offer here, one of the most popular meeting places in Kleinbasel, are
simple, regional dishes, including mouth-watering steaks. Traditionally
brewed beer and Italian-style coffee are also served.

Basel: *Dreiländereck*   Ⓕ Ⓕ
Westquaistrasse 75, 4019. **Road map** C2. 【 061 639 95 40. FAX 061 639 95 49.
@ info@dreilaendereck.ch W www.dreilaendereck.ch
Appropriately for its location on the banks of the Rhine, where the borders
of Switzerland, Germany and France meet, the Dreiländereck serves Swiss,
German and French food. There is a wide choice of fish dishes and
seafood. ● *Christmas & Jan.* 🔁 ⒧

Basel: *Zum Isaak Gastronomie und Kultur*   Ⓕ Ⓕ
Münsterplatz 16, 4051. **Road map** C2. 【 061 261 47 12. FAX 061 261 47 04.
@ info@zum-isaak.ch W www.zum-isaak.ch
Priding itself on its creative cuisine, this restaurant serves sophisticated dishes
prepared with seasonal, organic produce. Fine wines from all over Europe
are also available. The dining room has views of the Münster.
● *Mon.*

Basel: *Gifthüttli*   Ⓕ Ⓕ
Schneidergasse 11, 4051. **Road map** C2. 【 061 261 16 56. FAX 061 261 14 56.
@ info@gifthuettli.ch W www.gifthuettli.ch
In an elegant Art Nouveau dining room, this restaurant offers genuine
regional food and probably the largest choice of cordon bleu cuisine in
Basel. There is a large selection of wines, and meals are served until
10.45pm. ● *Sun.*

Basel: *Gasthof zum Goldenen Sternen*   Ⓕ Ⓕ Ⓕ
St. Alban-Rheinweg 70, 4052. **Road map** C2.
【 061 272 16 66. FAX 061 272 16 67.
@ info@sternen-basel.ch W www.sternen-basel.ch
In an hospitable atmosphere, this restaurant serves numerous specialities,
both from the kitchen and from the cellar. The traditional dishes are
elegantly served. 🔁 ⒧

Price categories are for a three-course meal for one person, including tax and service but without wine.
Ⓕ under 30 CHF (Swiss francs)
ⒻⒻ 30–60 CHF
ⒻⒻⒻ 60–90 CHF
ⒻⒻⒻⒻ 90–120 CHF
ⒻⒻⒻⒻⒻ over 120 CHF

CREDIT CARDS
The restaurant accepts credit cards.

OUTSIDE DINING
Tables outside, on a terrace, in a garden or on a quayside.

SWISS WINES
The restaurant serves Swiss wines.

VEGETARIAN DISHES
Good selection of vegetarian dishes available.

	CREDIT CARDS	OUTSIDE DINING	SWISS WINES	VEGETARIAN DISHES
BASEL: *Kunsthalle* ⒻⒻⒻ Steinenberg 7, 4051. **Road map** C2. 📞 061 272 42 33. ℻ 061 272 42 55. This long-established, high-quality restaurant serves traditional Swiss dishes. Tables are set on the terrace, which is surrounded by greenery.		●	■	
BASEL: *Teufelhof, Bel Etage* ⒻⒻⒻ Leonhardsgraben 478, 4051. **Road map** C2. 📞 061 261 10 10. ℻ 061 261 10 04. @ info@teufelhof.com Ⓦ www.teufelhof.com Sophisticated gourmet dishes, creatively prepared. The menu changes daily and the food is prepared only from the finest fresh ingredients. ● Sun–Mon.	■	●	■	●
KÜSNACHT: *Petermann's Kunststuben* ⒻⒻⒻⒻⒻ Seestrasse 160, 8700. **Road map** E2. 📞 044 910 17 15. ℻ 044 910 04 95. @ petermannskunststuben@bluewin.ch Ⓦ www.grandestables.ch/petermanns Often cited as the best restaurant in Switzerland, this establishment is located in the quiet lakefront town of Küsnacht, a few kilometres south of Zürich. While remaining rooted in classic European styles, the cuisine is highly innovative. ● Sun–Mon, mid-Aug–mid-Sept & two weeks in Feb.	■		■	

ZÜRICH

	CREDIT CARDS	OUTSIDE DINING	SWISS WINES	VEGETARIAN DISHES
ZÜRICH: *Restaurant Britannia Pub* Ⓕ Schaffhauserstrasse 380, 8002. **Road map** E2. 📞 044 312 52 00. This modest but welcoming restaurant has a cosy atmosphere and an English-style interior. As well as international cuisine, over 40 types of beer are on offer here.	■			●
ZÜRICH: *Blumenau* ⒻⒻ Seefeldstrasse 269, 8008. **Road map** E2. 📞 044 381 14 46. ℻ 044 381 24 46. @ mbarfuss@freesurf.ch The restaurant is located in one of the most beautiful districts of Zürich, very near the lake. The comfortable dining room conjures up the elegance of a bygone age, and the menu features a selection of dishes from Graubünden as well as Indian specialities. ● Sat–Sun. 🚻 ♿	■	●	■	●
ZÜRICH: *Canard* ⒻⒻ Seefeldstrasse 25, 8008. **Road map** E2. 📞 044 252 40 77. ℻ 044 252 04 32. A restaurant offering good value for money. The menu always includes two to three satisfying dishes of the day, and one of them is usually vegetarian. 🚻 ♿	■	●	■	●
ZÜRICH: *Crazy Cow Zürich* ⒻⒻ Leonhardstrasse 1, 8001. **Road map** E2. 📞 044 261 40 55. ℻ 044 261 40 59. @ zuerich@crazycow.ch Ⓦ www.crazycow.ch A trendy restaurant with an avant-garde approach. The menu features numerous dishes from various regions of Switzerland, and the dining room is decorated with innovative artwork.	■		■	●
ZÜRICH: *Gasser's Bistro* ⒻⒻ Langensteinenstrasse 2, 8057. **Road map** E2. 📞 043 300 50 03. ℻ 043 300 50 01. @ imw@gassers-bistro.ch Ⓦ www.gassers-bistro.ch A student bistro with a dozen tables, located near Zürich-Irchel University. On offer is a large selection of dishes, including many made with various types of cheese, ham and pepperoni. Open until midnight. ● Sat–Sun.	■		■	●

ZÜRICH: *Helvetia Bar*   ⒻⒻ
Stauffacherquai 1, 8004. **Road map** E2. ☎ 044 242 41 30.
A lakeside bar and restaurant located just five minutes' walk from
Hauptbahnhof. The simply-furnished dining room has a cosy atmosphere,
and the menu features mostly Swiss dishes. At weekends the bar stays
open after midnight. 🚻 ♿

ZÜRICH: *Hiltl*   ⒻⒻ
Sihlstrasse 28, 8001. **Road map** E2.
☎ 044 227 70 00. **FAX** 044 227 70 07.
@ info@hiltl.ch Ⓦ www.hiltl.ch
Opened in 1898, this is probably the oldest vegetarian restaurant in Europe.
The imaginative choice of dishes is complemented by a large selection of
wines. 🚻 ♿

ZÜRICH: *J.O.S.E.F.*   ⒻⒻ
Gasometerstrasse 24, 8005. **Road map** E2.
☎ 044 271 65 95. Ⓦ www.josef.ch
In its price range, this delightful restaurant is probably the best in the
district, and it attracts a large clientele. The menu includes Swiss, Italian
and international cuisine. ● *Sun–Mon.*

ZÜRICH: *King's Cave*   ⒻⒻ
Central 1, 8001. **Road map** E2. ☎ 044 251 55 55.
One of the restaurants in the Central Plaza Hotel. The menu includes
several different cuts of steak served with herb butter. Excellent selection of
wines.

ZÜRICH: *Münsterhof*   ⒻⒻ
Münsterhof 6, 8001. **Road map** E2. ☎ 044 211 43 40. **FAX** 044 211 43 53.
Ⓦ www.muensterhoefli.ch
The choice of good-quality regional dishes served here changes according
to the season. Among the specialities are minced veal and calves' liver with
Rösti. ● *Sun.*

ZÜRICH: *Pinte Vaudoise*   ⒻⒻ
Kruggasse 4, 8001. **Road map** E2. ☎ 044 252 60 09. **FAX** 044 251 23 39.
Swiss cuisine of the highest standard. The menu includes several varieties
of fondue and *raclette*, as well as other dishes. The sausage served with
baby leeks and boiled potatoes is particularly recommended.
● *Sun.*

ZÜRICH: *Bodega Española*   ⒻⒻⒻ
Münstergasse 15, 8001. **Road map** E2.
☎ 044 251 23 10. **FAX** 044 251 22 56.
A very atmospheric Spanish tapas bar and restaurant in the heart of the
Niederdorf district. The menu features many steak and seafood dishes,
although the house speciality is naturally a classic, authentic paella.

ZÜRICH: *Kronenhalle*   ⒻⒻⒻⒻ
Rämistrasse 4, 8001. **Road map** E2. ☎ 044 251 66 69.
Ⓦ www.kronenhalle.com
Located in the heart of the city, this is a true Zürich institution. The menu is
very traditional and features favourite Swiss meat dishes. The dining room
is bedecked with original works of art by such great names as Matisse and
Picasso.

EASTERN SWITZERLAND & GRAUBÜNDEN

APPENZELL: *Appenzell*   ⒻⒻ
Hauptgasse 37, 9050. **Road map** F2.
☎ 071 788 15 15. **FAX** 071 788 15 51.
@ info@hotel-appenzell.ch Ⓦ www.hotel-appenzell.ch
A traditional hotel restaurant with its own pâtisserie, located in the town
centre. The elegantly furnished dining room has a non-smoking area.
🚻 ♿

BAD RAGAZ: *Sardona*   ⒻⒻ
Sarganserstrasse 34, 7310. **Road map** F3.
☎ 081 300 46 42. **FAX** 081 300 46 48.
@ info@sardonaragaz.ch Ⓦ www.sardona.com
On the menu at this gourmet restaurant are hearty meals prepared with
fresh ingredients, as well as many vegetarian dishes. The selection of local
wines is impressive. ● *Wed.*

Price categories are for a three-course meal for one person, including tax and service but without wine.
Ⓕ under 30 CHF (Swiss francs)
ⒻⒻ 30–60 CHF
ⒻⒻⒻ 60–90 CHF
ⒻⒻⒻⒻ 90–120 CHF
ⒻⒻⒻⒻⒻ over 120 CHF

CREDIT CARDS
The restaurant accepts credit cards.

OUTSIDE DINING
Tables outside, on a terrace, in a garden or on a quayside.

SWISS WINES
The restaurant serves Swiss wines.

VEGETARIAN DISHES
Good selection of vegetarian dishes available.

	CREDIT CARDS	OUTSIDE DINING	SWISS WINES	VEGETARIAN DISHES

FALERA: *La Siala* — ⒻⒻ
7153. **Road map** E3. 📞 *081 927 22 22.* FAX *081 927 22 44.*
W www.lasiala.ch
This restaurant is decorated in rustic style, with extensive use of wood. The menu is dominated by regional specialities. From the terrace there are fine views of the mountains.
◻ ● ◻ ●

FEX: *Chesa Pool* — ⒻⒻ
7514. **Road map** F4. 📞 *081 838 59 00.* FAX *081 838 59 01.*
@ chesapool@spin.ch W www.chesapool.ch
This small hotel restaurant is a pleasant 20-minute walk from Sils Maria. It occupies a converted farm building at the base of the peaceful Fex valley. The diverse dishes on the menu are prepared with locally grown organic produce. The wine list includes wines made from organically grown grapes.
● *May & Oct.* 🚻 ♿
◻ ● ◻ ●

GOTTLIEBEN: *Drachenburg und Waaghaus* — ⒻⒻ
Am Schlosspark, 8274. **Road map** E2.
📞 *071 666 74 74.* FAX *071 666 17 09.*
@ info@drachenburg.ch W www.drachenburg.ch
These two hotel restaurants occupy historic buildings on the shore of Bodensee (Lake Constance). While the Drachenburg has an à la carte menu, the Waaghaus specializes in fish dishes. Both restaurants share a waterfront terrace. ● *Drachenburg: Wed–Thu; Jul–Aug;*
Waaghaus: Mon–Tue; mid-Dec–mid-Mar.
◻ ● ◻ ●

KREUZLINGEN: *Bahnhof-Post* — Ⓕ
Nationalstrasse 2, 8280. **Road map** F2. 📞 *071 672 79 72–73.*
FAX *071 672 49 82.* @ hotel-bahnhof-post@swiss-window.ch
This hotel restaurant is located in an enchanting villa very near Bodensee (Lake Constance). The menu features many fish dishes and classic regional cuisine that changes according to season. 🚻 ♿
◻ ● ◻ ●

KREUZLINGEN: *Zum Blauen Haus* — ⒻⒻ
Hauptstrasse 138, 8280. **Road map** F2.
📞 *071 688 24 98.* FAX *071 699 14 06.* W www.blaueshaus.com
This restaurant, in a beautiful half-timbered building, specializes in grilled dishes, including prawns and horsemeat steak. The wine list includes a large selection of regional wines. Live piano music in the evenings.
● *Sun; 2–3 weeks in summer.*
◻ ◻

RAPPERSWIL: *Restaurant Rathaus* — ⒻⒻ
Hauptplatz 1, 8640. **Road map** E3.
📞 *055 210 11 14.* FAX *055 210 11 24.*
As its name implies, this restaurant is located in the Rathaus (town hall). Regional dishes are served here, and there is a summer garden. ♿
◻ ● ◻ ●

RORSCHACH/BODENSEE: *Rosengarten* — Ⓕ
Thurgauerstrasse 22, 9400. **Road map** F2.
📞 *071 841 15 82.* FAX *071 841 15 90.* W www.rosengarten.opd.ch
Modern French cuisine and regional dishes feature on the menu here. The restaurant also has a good wine list, with a large selection of local wines.
◻ ● ◻ ●

SCHAFFHAUSEN (NEUHAUSEN): *Schlössli-Wörth* — ⒻⒻⒻ
Rheinfallquai, 8212. **Road map** E2.
📞 *052 672 24 21.* FAX *052 672 24 30.*
@ info@schloessliwoerth.ch W www.schloessliwoerth.ch
Occupying a historic building, this restaurant is located very near the Rheinfall (*see p182*) and commands a magnificent view of the waterfall's roaring waters. The menu consists of regional dishes, and there is a grill room. ● *Oct–Mar: Wed.*
◻ ● ◻ ●

St Gallen: *Tres Amigos* Ⓕ
Hechtgasse 1, 9004. **Road map** F2. 〖 071 222 25 06.
@ st.gallen@tresamigos.ch Ⓦ www.tresamigos.ch
This Mexican bar and restaurant, with its warm atmosphere and colourful
décor, offers tasty and inexpensive dishes. The menu changes every week.
There is also a large selection of cocktails, including a good choice of
non-alcoholic drinks. ✖ 㐅

St Gallen: *Hörnli* ⒻⒻ
Marktplatz 5, 9000. **Road map** F2.
〖 071 222 66 86. ꜰᴀx 071 222 66 08.
@ info@hoernli.ch Ⓦ www.hoernli.ch
Located on the first floor of an apartment building, this restaurant and beer
bar has a pleasant atmosphere. It specializes in hearty regional cuisine, and
servings are generous.

St Gallen: *Restaurant Benedikt* ⒻⒻ
Bankgasse 12, 9000. **Road map** F2.
〖 071 227 61 00. ꜰᴀx 071 227 61 80.
@ info@benediktrestaurant.bluewin.ch Ⓦ www.hotel-st-gallen.ch
This is the restaurant of the Hotel St Gallen, which is situated at the heart
of the Old Town, near the abbey *(see pp186–7)*. The menu includes
traditional Swiss dishes and modern French cuisine.
● Mon

St Gallen: *Rôtisserie Schoren* ⒻⒻⒻⒻ
Dufourstrasse 150, 9000. **Road map** F2. 〖 071 277 08 51. ꜰᴀx 071 277 58 60.
Ⓦ www.rotisserie-schoren.ch
A restaurant in a beautiful setting outside the city centre. The menu
features meat and fish dishes, and the wine list includes a broad selection
of wines from Switzerland and other countries.
● Sat–Sun.

Stein am Rhein: *Rheingerbe* ⒻⒻ
Schifflände 5, 8260. **Road map** E2.
〖 052 741 29 91.
Located in a converted tannery dating from the early 16th century, this
hotel restaurant specializes in modern cuisine. The menu includes freshly
caught fish. There is a large selection of local wines.
● Dec–Feb: Tue–Wed; Jun–Aug: Wed.

Stein am Rhein: *Sonne* ⒻⒻⒻⒻ
Am Rathausplatz 13, 8260. **Road map** E2.
〖 052 741 21 28. ꜰᴀx 052 741 50 86.
Exquisite food is served in this smart gourmet restaurant. The menu
features a wide choice of fish dishes, with several varieties of locally caught
freshwater fish. ● Tue–Wed.

Vaduz (Liechtenstein): *Real Café Restaurant* ⒻⒻⒻⒻ
Städtle 21, FL-9490. **Road map** F3. 〖 00 423 232 22 22. ꜰᴀx 00 423 232 08 91.
@ real@hotels.li Ⓦ www.hotel-real.li
Small, cosy restaurant locally renowned for its regional dishes. Located
right at the centre of town, in the main street, close to Kunstzentrum. There
is also a summer garden and bar.

Weinfelden: *Gasthaus zum Trauben* ⒻⒻ
8570. **Road map** E2.
〖 071 622 44 44. ꜰᴀx 071 622 44 35.
@ info@trauben-weinfelden.ch Ⓦ www.trauben-weinfelden.ch
This restaurant, a historic building at the centre of Weinfelden, has several
dining rooms, one of which is in the cellar and another a grand hall. On
the menu is a wide choice of dishes, all of them prepared with fresh
regional produce. There is also a huge selection of regional wines. The
garden restaurant at the rear of the building serves light dishes.
● Sun. ✖ 㐅

Zillis: *Viamala* Ⓕ
7432. **Road map** F4.
〖 081 661 10 60. ꜰᴀx 081 630 70 58.
@ info@restaurant-viamala.ch Ⓦ www.viamala.ch
Many local people patronize this homely, traditional restaurant. It has two
dining rooms, one furnished in a modern style and the other decorated in
rustic style. Regional dishes dominate the menu.
● Mon.

Price categories are for a three-course meal for one person, including tax and service but without wine.
F under 30 CHF (Swiss francs)
FF 30–60 CHF
FFF 60–90 CHF
FFFF 90–120 CHF
FFFFF over 120 CHF

CREDIT CARDS
The restaurant accepts credit cards.

OUTSIDE DINING
Tables outside, on a terrace, in a garden or on a quayside.

SWISS WINES
The restaurant serves Swiss wines.

VEGETARIAN CUISINE
Good selection of vegetarian dishes available.

	CREDIT CARDS	OUTSIDE DINING	SWISS WINES	VEGETARIAN CUISINE

CENTRAL SWITZERLAND AND TICINO

ASCONA: *Piazza au Lac* — F
Lungolago Motta 29, 6612. **Road map** E5.
☎ 091 791 11 81. FAX 091 791 27 57.
@ welcome@hotel-piazza-ascona.ch
w www.hotel-piazza-ascona.ch
As well as a variety of pizzas, this small restaurant serves Ticinese and Mediterranean dishes, and delicious homemade ice cream. A generous breakfast buffet is served on the terrace, which overlooks Lake Maggiore.

| | ■ | ● | ■ | ● |

ASCONA: *Al Pontile* — FF
Lungolago Motta 31, 6612. **Road map** E5.
☎ 091 791 46 04. FAX 091 791 90 60.
A cosy, lakeside restaurant with regional Swiss dishes and Italian cuisine. The menu features a wide selection of fish dishes, as well as several delicious pasta and risotto dishes.

| | ■ | ● | ■ | ● |

BECKENRIED: *Panorama Klewenalp* — F
6375. **Road map** D3.
☎ 041 620 29 22. FAX 041 620 60 22.
@ info@klewenalp.ch w www.klewenalp.ch
This restaurant is located near the upper station of the Klewenalp cable car. From the terrace there is a stunning view down over Lake Lucerne. Specialities include meat fondue served with tasty homemade sauces.

| | ■ | ● | ■ | ● |

BELLINZONA: *Ristorante Castelgrande* — FFF
Salita al Castello, 6500. **Road map** E5.
☎ 091 826 23 53. FAX 091 826 23 65.
@ info@castelgrande.ch w www.castelgrande.ch
Housed in one of Bellinzona's three great castles, this fine restaurant has two dining areas. The formal dining room, which is decked out in postmodern style, with tubular steel and black leather, serves gourmet cuisine. The more relaxed, informal *grotto* (Ticinese inn) serves top-quality classic Ticinese dishes such as risottos, pastas and game.
● Mon.

| | ■ | | ■ | ● |

BÜRGENSTOCK: *Hotels und Resort* — FF
6363. **Road map** D3.
☎ 041 612 90 10. FAX 041 612 90 11.
@ information@buergenstock-hotels.ch w www.buergenstock-hotels.ch
This complex comprises three hotels and five restaurants, which between them serve Swiss, French and Italian cuisine. The terraces offer splendid views of Lake Lucerne.
● Nov–mid-Mar.

| | ■ | ● | ■ | ● |

EINSIEDELN: *Klostergarten* — FF
Ilgenweidstrasse 14, 8840. **Road map** E3.
☎ 055 412 11 40. FAX 055 412 81 41.
@ info@klostergarten.ch w www.typoblitz.ch/klostergarten.html
A cosy restaurant in the centre of Einsiedeln, near the abbey *(see p226)*. Regional food is served here, in generous portions.
● Mon.

| | ■ | ● | ■ | ● |

ENGELBERG: *Hotel Bänklialp* — F
Bänklialp, 6390. **Road map** D3.
☎ 041 639 73 73. FAX 041 639 73 74.
@ info@baenklialp.ch w www.baenklialp.ch
A delightful, rustic restaurant attached to this good-quality mid-range hotel. It has a standard menu, offering Swiss mountain staples. Warm, friendly atmosphere and service.

| | ■ | | ■ | ● |

GIORNICO: *Grotto dei Due Ponti* Ⓕ
Road map E5. 【 *091 864 20 30.*
@ info@leventinatourismo.ch Ⓦ www.leventinatourismo.ch
An attractive tavern set on a river island in this quiet Ticinese village, north
of Bellinzona. Meals are served on a shaded terrace. The fare and
the presentation are rustic and simple but quality is high and the
atmosphere exceptional.

KÜSSNACHT AM RIGI: *Zunftstube* ⒻⒻ
Unterdorf 9, 6403. Road map D3. 【 *041 854 33 33.* FAX *041 854 33 34.*
@ info@zumhirschen.ch Ⓦ www.zumhirschen.ch
The restaurant of the family-run Hirschen hotel. On the menu here
is a wide selection of meat and fish dishes, and several good vegetarian
options.

LOCARNO: *Costa Azzura* ⒻⒻ
Via Bastoria 13, 6604. Road map E5.
【 *091 751 38 02.* FAX *091 751 76 77.*
A large selection of international and Swiss dishes is offered at this small,
intimate restaurant. Children are especially welcome.
🚹 ♿

LUGANO: *Colibri* ⒻⒻ
Via Bassone 7, 6974. Road map E5. 【 *091 971 42 42.* FAX *091 971 90 16.*
@ hotel.colibri@swissonline.ch Ⓦ www.montebre.com
Regional dishes and food cooked over an open fire are on the menu
of this restaurant, in a family-run hotel. It is set on the summit of
Monte Brè, and the terrace has breathtaking views of Lake Lugano.
● *Jan–Feb.*

LUGANO: *Ticino* ⒻⒻⒻⒻ
Piazza Cioccaro 1, 6901. Road map E5.
【 *091 922 77 72.* FAX *091 923 62 78.*
@ romantikhotelticino@ticino.com Ⓦ www.romantikhotels.com/lugano
A high-class restaurant in the centre of Lugano, very near the lake.
Besides international fare, the menu includes several delicious
Italian specialities.

LUZERN: *Bamboo Garden* ⒻⒻ
Baselstrasse 31, 6003. Road map D3. 【 *041 240 88 68.* FAX *041 240 88 69.*
@ bestellung@bamboogarden.ch Ⓦ www.bamboogarden.ch
An authentic Oriental establishment, with a sushi bar on the ground floor
and a good Chinese restaurant on the first floor.

LUZERN: *Hofgarten* ⒻⒻ
Stadthofstrasse 14, 6006. Road map D3. 【 *041 410 88 88.* FAX *041 410 83 33.*
The best vegetarian restaurant in Luzern. The dishes here
are prepared with superb fresh ingredients and are stylishly presented in
light, airy surroundings. The buffets are particularly recommended.

LUZERN: *Wirtshaus Galliker* ⒻⒻ
Schützenstrasse 1, 6004. Road map D3. 【 *041 240 10 02.*
This acclaimed traditional restaurant is the best place in Luzern to sample
the celebrated local dish, *Kügelipastete* (veal and mushroom vol-au-vent),
and other meaty specialities. It is famously unpretentious, and is known for
its relaxed and friendly atmosphere. ● *Sun–Mon.*

RIGI KALTBAD: *Bergsonne* ⒻⒻ
6356. Road map D3. 【 *041 399 80 10.* FAX *041 399 80 20.*
@ info@bergsonne.ch Ⓦ www.bergsonne.ch
A hotel restaurant with a magnificent view of the Alps and Lake Lucerne.
The exquisite menu, which offers light dishes and food prepared from the
freshest ingredients, changes according to the season and often reflects the
theme of local food festivals.
● *Mid-Apr–mid-May & mid-Nov–mid-Dec.*

ZUG: *Hecht am See* ⒻⒻ
Fischmarkt 2, 6300. Road map E3. 【 *041 729 81 30.* FAX *041 729 81 47.*
@ hecht-zug@datazug.ch Ⓦ www.hecht.ch
A restaurant located in Zug's historic district, in a lakeside building whose
origins date back to 1435. The speciality here is fish prepared in several
different ways. The restaurant also has an excellent wine cellar, and its
white wines are particularly fine. The elegantly furnished dining room
offers a view of the Zugersee. ● *Thu.*

Sport and Outdoor Activities

A ski-run sign

With snowy mountains and majestic glaciers, green valleys and dense forests, rivers and glistening lakes, Switzerland offers unparalleled opportunities for active holidays. Through the long winter, heavy falls of powdery snow provide superb conditions for skiing, snowboarding and tobogganing. Summer reveals a greener landscape, with some of the best mountaineering, hiking and cycling country anywhere in Europe. Several extreme sports, including canyoning, white-water rafting and bungee-jumping, also have an avid following, as do yachting on the country's largest lakes and canoeing down its wildest rivers. Hot-air ballooning and hang-gliding are experiences that provide serene aerial views of this beautiful country.

A ski station in the Swiss Alps

Winter Sports

Switzerland has over 200 winter sports resorts and almost 50 peaks that exceed altitudes of 4,000m (13,000 ft). The winter sports season starts around the middle of December and continues until just after Easter. The busiest times on the slopes, and the most expensive periods in which to ski, are around New Year and during winter school holidays. However, towards the end of the season prices are much lower and at some resorts discounted ski passes are available.

Most of Switzerland's skiing areas are situated above 2,000m (6,600 ft). However, Zermatt's ski lifts give access to pistes at altitudes as high as 3,900 m (12,800 ft).

Ski pass

The largest Swiss ski resort is Les Portes du Soleil in Valais, which, together with the adjacent areas situated on the French side of the Alps, offers 650 km (400 miles) of ski runs. Other major skiing resorts in Valais include Verbier, Zermatt, Crans-Montana and Saas Fee. One of the largest winter sports areas in eastern Switzerland is Davos-Klosters, with 350 km (220 miles) of pistes. The largest skiing areas in the Bernese Oberland are clustered around Gstaad and in the Jungfrau region (Grindelwald-Wengen-Mürren). The largest resort in western Switzerland is Villars. Other ski areas are in central Switzerland, for example around Engelberg, and in Ticino, around Airolo. Some glaciers, including those near Saas Fee, Les Diablerets, Zermatt, St Moritz and Engelberg, provide opportunities for skiing all year round.

Ski runs are marked with different-coloured stakes according to their level of difficulty. Blue runs are the easiest, and most suitable for beginners, red runs are for intermediate skiers and black for the most experienced. The runs are well maintained and, when necessary, are topped up with artificial snow. Rack railways, funiculars, cable cars and ski lifts transport skiers to the top of the runs.

A one-day adult ski pass costs about 30 CHF in eastern Switzerland, about 60 CHF in St Moritz and Saas Fee and about 72 CHF in Zermatt. A six-day ski pass costs from 100 CHF in Ticino, 200 CHF in Saas Fee and Leukerbad, 300 CHF in Verbier, and about 360 CHF in Zermatt. There is usually no charge for children up to six years of age if they are accompanied by at least one adult. Children up to the age of 16 pay 40–60 percent of the adult price. Resorts also offer various types of ski pass, such as family, senior-citizen or afternoon-only.

The price of a ski pass generally includes travel on a ski-bus or municipal bus.

Almost every Swiss resort also offers superb facilities for snowboarders. There are some exhilarating runs, with chutes, halfpipes and cornices, and several parks.

If you decide to venture off-piste (freeride) you should not do so without checking the avalanche risk beforehand (see p293). It is also advisable to hire a local guide.

Almost all resorts have skiing and snowboarding schools, which provide tuition on an individual or group basis, with day-long and week-long courses. Individual lessons start at about 250 CHF per day. Group lessons cost about 200 CHF per week.

The Swiss Alps also have many marked cross-country skiing routes. Two of the best areas for this pursuit are in and around the Engadine valley, in Graubünden, and in the Goms region of Valais. There are many long sleigh runs. You can also ride sleighs drawn by huskies, or hire snowshoes for long walks across the mountains.

The full range of winter sports equipment can be hired at the resorts, from branches of the **Intersport** or **Swissrent** chains (see p287) and from local hire shops. The cost of hiring skis or a snowboard is about 30 CHF per day (or about 120 CHF for 7 days). Snow-shoes cost about 15 CHF per day (about 60 CHF for 7 days). A sleigh costs from 8 CHF per day (or about 30 CHF for 7 days). It is often possible to return or exchange your equipment at a hire shop in another location if it belongs to the same chain.

In an effort to protect the natural environment and preserve tranquillity, some high mountain towns and villages, including Zermatt, Saas Fee, Wengen and Mürren, have banned motorized transport. Cars must be left at car parks outside the village. Transport into the resorts themselves is then provided by electric carts.

A bobsleigh, designed for racing down ice-covered runs

MOUNTAINEERING AND ROCK-CLIMBING

THE SWISS ALPS offer boundless opportunities for mountaineering and rock-climbing. Two of the world's most challenging peaks are the Matterhorn and the Eiger, suitable only for the most experienced mountaineers. The gentler mountains of the Valais, for example, are more suitable for beginners and intermediate climbers.

However, neither of these sports is for the uninitiated, and should never be attempted without proper clothing and equipment and a qualified guide. Most of the main mountain resorts have mountaineering and rock-climbing schools.

EXTREME SPORTS

SWITZERLAND'S RUGGED terrain also provides excellent conditions for extreme sports. One of the most popular is canyoning, which involves hiking along riverbeds and abseiling down steep rock-faces. Two of best places to experience these thrills are in the canyons near Interlaken, in the Jungfrau region, and near Engelberg, in Obwalden.

From April to September the wild rivers of Graubünden provide ideal conditions for white-water rafting and hydrospeeding, or descending the rapids on rafts. Bungee-jumping and canyon-jumping (in which you leap from a cliff, tied to a line at the waist) are also gaining in popularity.

AERIAL SPORTS

EXHILARATING SPORTS in their own right, hot-air ballooning, paragliding and hang-gliding have the added advantage of providing spectacular aerial views of the Swiss landscape. The international capital of hot-air ballooning is Château d'Oex, in the canton of Vaud.

The best environments for paragliding and hang-gliding are in Graubünden, Valais, the Bernese Oberland and the environs of Lake Geneva and Lake Lucerne.

Paragliding over snow-covered mountains in the Bernese Oberland

Sailing boats moored at a quayside on Lake Geneva

HIKING

Hiking is extremely popular in Switzerland. The country has a network of hiking trails totalling about 65,000 km (40,000 miles) and covering all kinds of terrain, from the relatively flat lowlands to the Alpine glaciers. All trails are well maintained and clearly signed, usually with an indication of the distance and walking time to the next major landmark, village or town.

Yellow direction signs indicate that the trail is relatively easy. Red and white pointers indicate a more demanding trail, and blue signs are reserved for higher and rougher Alpine trails. These may pass over glaciers or snowfields and should not be attempted without a guide and proper equipment.

Whatever the level of difficulty, the correct equipment is essential. Besides a map and sturdy walking boots, hikers should carry warm, waterproof clothing and adequate food and water. Before setting out also check weather forecasts (posted at local tourist offices or mountain guides' bureaux) and avalanche warnings (publicized in Alpine areas).

Hiker in the Swiss Alps

WATER SPORTS

The unpolluted waters of Switzerland's many lakes are ideal for yachting, dinghy sailing, windsurfing, water-skiing and swimming. Most lakeside resorts have water sports centres, where boats and other equipment can be hired. Some also have sailing schools.

With a gentle current and unforgettable scenery, the rivers most suitable for canoeing are the Muota, in the canton of Schwyz, the Doubs, in the Jura, and the more tranquil sections of the Rhine and the Sarine. Infor-mation on canoe-hire companies and canoeing routes is available from local tourist offices.

More adventurous watersports include canyoning and white-water rafting *(see p285)*.

CYCLING

Besides many local routes, Switzerland has nine national cycle trails, which together total 3,300 km (2,000 miles). Demanding varying levels of fitness, these routes are inter-connected and all are excellently signposted.

Mountain biking enthusiasts, or those who simply enjoy downhill bike rides, can take a cable car up to the summit of certain mountains and then ride down their chosen route.

Information on the main Swiss cycle routes, including detailed maps, can be obtained from local tourist offices. Bicycles can be hired from most railway stations and can be carried on most trains *(see p304)*. One-way bicycle hire is also possible.

INLINE SKATING

Many cycling routes and some metalled roads are suitable for inline skating. Switzerland also has three long-distance inline-skating routes, each about 200 km (125 miles) long and often following the shorelines of lakes and the courses of rivers. The routes run from Zürich to Yverdon-les-Bains, from Geneva to Brig and from Schaffhausen to Bad Ragaz.

HEALTH AND FITNESS

Many Swiss hotels, parti-cularly those in spa resorts, offer comprehensive fitness, relaxation and beauty treatments. These hotels are often sited in restful locations on the shore of lakes or in the mountains.

Guests are treated to weight-loss programmes and body peels; there are also stress-relieving massages and reflexology treatments. The thermal pools, hot sulphur springs and brine baths at many Swiss spas are restorative and revitalizing.

A hiking route through a canyon

DIRECTORY

TOURIST OFFICES

**Schweiz Tourismus
(Swiss Tourist
Office)**
📞 0800 100 200 31.
🌐 www.
MySwitzerland.com
Contains information on
all sports and outdoor
activities in Switzerland.

Bernese Oberland
Jungfraustrasse 38,
3800 Interlaken.
📞 033 828 37 47.
FAX 033 828 37 48.
🌐 www.
berneroberland. com

Chablais Tourisme
5 Place Tübingen,
1870 Monthey 2.
📞 024 471 12 12.
FAX 024 471 12 00.
🌐 www.mychablais.com

**Château-d'Oex
Tourisme**
La Place,
1660 Château-d'Oex.
📞 026 924 25 25.
FAX 026 924 25 26.
🌐 www.chateau-doex.ch

Davos Tourismus
Promenade 67, 7270 Davos.
📞 081 415 21 21.
FAX 081 415 21 00.
🌐 www.davos.ch

**Engelberg-Titlis
Tourismus**
Tourist Center,
6390 Engelberg.
📞 041 639 77 77.
FAX 041 639 77 66.
🌐 www.engelberg.ch

**Graubünden
Vacation**
Alexanderstrasse 24,
7001 Chur.
📞 081 254 24 24.
FAX 081 254 24 00.
🌐 www.graubuenden.ch

Jungfrau Winter
Hardestrasse 14,
3800 Interlaken.
📞 033 828 71 11.
FAX 033 828 72 64 .
🌐 www.
jungfraubahnen.ch

Kurverein St Moritz
Via Maistra 12,
7500 St Moritz.
📞 081 837 33 33.
FAX 081 837 33 77.
🌐 www.stmoritz.ch

**Leukerbad
Tourismus**
3954 Leukerbad.
📞 027 472 71 77.
FAX 027 472 71 51.
🌐 www.leukerbad.ch

Valais Tourism
Rue Pré-Fleuri 6,
1951 Sion.
📞 027 327 35 70.
FAX 027 327 35 71.
🌐 www.valaistourism.ch

**Villars Office
du Tourisme**
Rue Centrale,
1884 Villars.
📞 024 495 32 32.
FAX 024 495 27 94.
🌐 www.villars.ch

Zermatt Tourismus
Bahnhofsplatz,
3920 Zermatt.
📞 027 966 81 00.
FAX 027 966 81 01.
🌐 www.zermatt.ch

SKIING &
SNOWBOARDING

Swiss Snowsports
Hühnerhubelstrasse 95,
Postfach 182, 3120 Belp.
📞 031 810 41 11.
FAX 031 810 41 12.
🌐 www.snowsports.ch

Ski equipment hire
🌐 www.swissrent.com
🌐 www.rentasport.ch

MOUNTAINEERING
& ROCK-
CLIMBING

**Schweizer Verband
der Bergsteiger-
schulen**
(Swiss Association of
Mountaineering Schools)
Postfach 141,
6490 Andermatt.
📞 041 872 09 00.
FAX 041 872 09 50.
🌐 www.
bergschule-uri.ch

EXTREME SPORTS

Alpin Center
Haupstrasse 16,
3800 Interlaken.
📞 033 823 02 10.
🌐 www.alpincenter.ch

Swissraft
Obere Jungfraustrasse 72,
3800 Interlaken.
📞 033 823 02 10.
7081 Flims-Waldhaus.
📞 081 911 52 50.
FAX 081 911 30 90.
🌐 www.swissraft.ch

Fun Travel
Garbely Adventure,
3999 Oberwald.
📞 027 973 25 75.
🌐 www.garbely-
adventure.ch

Outventure
Hansmatt 5,
6503 Stansstad.
📞 041 611 14 41.
🌐 www.outventure.ch

**Schweizer
Bergführer
verband**
Hadlaubstrasse 49,
8006 Zürich.
📞 01 360 53 66.
🌐 www.4000plus.ch

Swiss Adventures
3766 Boltigen.
📞 033 773 73 73.
FAX 033 733 73 74.
🌐 www.
swissadventures.ch

Swiss Canyons
📞 078 740 69 96.
🌐 www.
canyoningadventure.ch

AERIAL SPORTS

**Château d'Oex
Tourisme**
📞 026 924 25 25.
FAX 026 924 25 26.
🌐 www.chateau-doex.ch

Scenic Air
PO Box 412, 3800
Interlaken.
📞 033 826 77 17.
FAX 033 823 83 12.
🌐 www.scenicair.ch

HIKING

Eurotrek
Militärstrasse 52,
8021 Zürich.
📞 044 295 59 59.
FAX 044 295 59 58.
🌐 www.eurotrek.ch

**Schweizer
Alpenclub**
Monbijoustrasse 61,
3001 Bern.
📞 031 370 18 18.
FAX 031 370 18 00.
🌐 www.sac-cas.ch

**Schweizer Wander-
wegen SAW**
(Swiss Hiking Federation)
Im Hirsham 49,
4125 Riehen.
📞 061 606 93 40.
FAX 061 606 93 45.
🌐 www.swisshiking.ch

Trekking Team
6652 Tegna.
📞 0848 808 007.
🌐 www.trekking.ch

CYCLING

Cartes Cyclistes
(maps for cyclists)
Postfach, 3360
Herzogenbuchsee.
📞 062 956 56 99.
🌐 www.vcs-ate-ch

Veloland Schweiz
📞 031 307 47 40.
🌐 www.veloland.ch

INLINE SKATING

🌐 www.
swiss-skate-map.ch

HEALTH &
FITNESS

**Espaces Thermaux
Suisses** (Spas)
22 Avenue des Bains,
1400 Yverdon-les-Bains.
📞 024 420 15 21.
FAX 024 423 02 52.
🌐 www.heilbad.org

Swiss Health Hotels
Oberdorfstrasse 53b,
9100 Herisau.
📞 071 350 14 14.
🌐 www.
wohlbefinden.com

SURVIVAL
GUIDE

PRACTICAL INFORMATION

A PRIME TOURIST destination, Switzerland attracts large numbers of visitors, both during the winter sports season and at other times of the year. As tourism is an important part of Switzerland's economy, the country has an excellent tourist infrastructure and a positive attitude towards helping foreign visitors make the most of their stay.

Museums and other places of interest are well-maintained, with helpful

Tourist information sign

information in several languages, usually including English. English is also spoken at all tourist offices, as well as in almost all the larger hotels and major winter sports resorts.

Having one of the most efficiently run and convenient public transport systems in Europe, Switzerland is also a very easy country to travel around in, whether by road or rail, or at a more leisurely pace by boat on Switzerland's larger lakes.

WHEN TO GO

THE BEST TIME of year to visit Switzerland depends on how you plan to spend your time here. The winter sports season runs from mid-December to late spring, peaking just after New Year, when resorts can be very crowded.

Summertime in Switzerland is pleasantly warm, rather than un- comfortably hot. The height of the summer season runs from the beginning of July to the end of August, and prices are then at their highest, accommodation tends to be harder to find, and visitor attractions are at their most crowded.

Spring and autumn are much quieter, and are excellent seasons for exploring the countryside. The mountains are particularly beautiful in spring, when wild flowers start to bloom, and in autumn, when leaves begin to turn. In the countryside, spring and autumn are also the time of year when you are most likely to witness folk festivals.

VISA AND CUSTOMS REGULATIONS

CITIZENS OF the United Kingdom, the Republic of Ireland, the United States, Canada, Australia, New Zealand and South Africa

Information board in Parc Mon Repos, Geneva

need a valid passport to visit Switzerland and Liechtenstein but do not require a visa. However, individual visits are limited to three months, and total visits per year should not exceed six months. Visitors planning a longer stay (to work or study in Switzerland, for example) should contact the Swiss embassy in their own country.

Customs regulations are straightforward. Visitors from Europe may import 2 litres of wine and 1 litre of spirits, and 200 cigarettes or 50 cigars, or 250g of pipe tobacco. Visitors from other countries may import 400 cigarettes, 100 cigars and 500g of pipe tobacco. How- ever, no visitors under the age of 17 may bring alcohol or tobacco into Switzerland.

Visitors may also bring in a variety of items for their own use while in Switzerland, such as camping and sports equip- ment, cameras and laptop computers, and gifts up to a value of 100 CHF.

OPENING HOURS

MOST MUSEUMS and visitor attractions, such as archaeological sites, are open six full days a week. Almost all close on Mondays and some on Tuesdays. Shops, post offices, banks and tourist offices are generally open from Monday to Friday, 8am–6.30pm, and 8am–4pm on Saturday. However, shops in smaller towns and villages may close for lunch and those in smaller towns may be closed on Mondays. In some resorts, shops open for a few hours on Sunday. Shops on station concourses have longer opening hours and are also open on Sundays.

The tourist information centre at the Bärengraben in Bern

◁ **The funicular from Lauterbrunnen to Grütschalp, in the Jungfrau massif**

News kiosk with publications in German, French and Italian

LANGUAGES

GERMAN IS the most widely spoken language in Switzerland, after which are French and Italian. German-speakers, followed by French-speakers, are most likely to speak English as well. Many organizations that have contact with foreign visitors speak English and most tourist offices have English-speaking staff.

Swiss German differs from the standard, or High, German of Germany and Austria. Swiss German *(Schwyzertütsch)*, which has several regional dialects as well as its own syntax and vocabulary, is used in everyday speech and is hardly ever written. High German *(Hochdeutsch)* in Switzerland is primarily a written language, being used for public signs and notices and in the media but also in education and in formal situations such as public speaking.

NEWSPAPERS

SWITZERLAND's national press is dominated by French- and German-language titles. Among the leading dailies are the conservative *Neue Zürcher Zeitung*, the more liberal *Tages- Anzeiger* and the progressive *Le Temps*.

Swiss weeklies include *Die Weltwoche* and *Wochen-zeitung*. The Milanese *Corriere della Sera* has a wide circulation in Ticino.

British and American news-papers, such as the *Times, Guardian, International Herald Tribune* and *USA Today* are sold in large towns and cities and in most major resorts. *The Economist, Time* and *Newsweek* are also available.

TIME

Pillar with news and information

SWITZERLAND IS one hour ahead of Greenwich Mean Time (GMT) in winter and two hours ahead in summer. The Swiss use the 24-hour clock; for example, 7pm is expressed as 19:00. In German *halb* (half) refers to the half-hour before the hour; for example, *halb zwei* means 1:30, not 2:30.

ELECTRICITY

THE CURRENT IN Switzerland is 220v AC. Sockets are of the three-pin type, and they accept the two- or three-pin round-pronged plugs used elsewhere in continental Europe. Although many hotels provide adaptors on request, it can be more con-venient to bring your own. For equipment designed for use in the USA, you will need a transformer.

Personal Security and Health

Logo of Zürich police

WITH EFFICIENT PUBLIC SERVICES and one of the lowest crime rates in the industrialized world, Switzerland is a very safe country for foreign visitors. The Swiss are helpful, polite and welcoming, so that travelling anywhere in their country is a pleasant experience. With a temperate climate, clean water and few natural hazards, Switzerland poses virtually no health risks to visitors. However, those who enjoy the more strenuous outdoor activities, particularly at high altitudes, should be aware of potential dangers.

Patrol car of Geneva police

PERSONAL SAFETY

SWITZERLAND IS one of the safest countries in the world. However, as in most other countries, visitors should be vigilant, particularly when walking in unlit streets late at night, withdrawing cash at an ATM, when travelling on public transport, or when among large crowds of people in public places. Pickpockets in search of wallets and credit cards

Policeman patrolling the streets on a bicycle

sometimes operate in the streets and squares of large towns, and thieves may be on the look-out for opportunities to grab handbags and jewellery from unwary visitors. It is also wise to use hotel safes for valuable items and never to leave valuable items in cars, which should always be left locked. If you intend to stay in hostels, a padlock to make a locker secure can be useful.

Generally, caution and common sense are the best defences, together with an awareness that the greatest danger may be from other visitors rather than from the Swiss themselves. However, if you are the victim of theft, report it at once to the police. Obtaining a police report will also enable you to make an insurance claim. Loss or theft of credit cards should also be reported as soon as possible to the issuing company *(see p294)*.

Women travelling alone are unlikely to experience any problems, wherever they go in Switzerland.

POLICE

THE SWISS ARE scrupulously law-abiding and expect the same of foreign visitors. Simply crossing the street on a red pedestrian light may mean a police caution, and you may even incur a fine. More serious transgressions, such as the possession of drugs, may lead to imprisonment or deportation. At all times, you should carry your passport, which the police will ask to see if they have reason to stop you.

Each of the country's 26 cantons has its own armed police force, as do individual towns and cities. Each canton also has its own laws, although the differences between them are minimal.

HEALTH

NO VACCINATIONS are required for visitors entering Switzerland, except for those who have visited a high-risk region in the two weeks preceding their arrival in the country.

Tap water is safe to drink everywhere in Switzerland, and the water gushing from fountains in towns and villages is also safe, unless otherwise indicated by the words *kein Trinkwasser, eau non potable* or *acqua non potabile*. It is, however, best not to drink from streams and springs, however pure they may appear to be.

Municipal police patrol car

At altitudes over about 3,000 m (10,000 ft), visitors should be aware of the risk of altitude sickness. Aspirin and bed rest may alleviate mild symptoms, which include nausea, headache and fatigue but which usually pass after 48 hours. If symptoms persist, the only effective remedy is to descend to a lower altitude.

Sunstroke is also more likely at high altitudes, where the air is thinner, or where snow or water reflect the sun's

Red Cross rescue helicopter in action in Crans-Montana

rays. To prevent sunstroke, drink plenty of water, wear a hat and sunglasses and use a sunblock with a high UV-protection factor. The best prevention, however, is to limit the amount of time you spend in the sun, especially in the first few days of your stay.

At any time of the year, the weather in the mountains can be very changeable, with cold wind, rain and sudden snow-storms posing the greatest danger. Skiers and hikers should wear several layers of warm clothing, a hat and waterproofs, and carry supplies of high-energy food and water. The best precaution of all is the decision to turn back when weather conditions threaten to deteriorate.

Entrance to a pharmacy in St Gallen

MEDICAL CARE

HEALTHCARE IN Switzerland is entirely private, so that medical treatment of any kind must be paid for. Switzerland has a reciprocal agreement with all EU countries. Collecting form E111, available from post offices in the UK, before you leave will enable you to claim reimbursement should you require medical care. Taking out health insurance before your trip is strongly recommended. This is particularly important if you are planning a skiing, mountaineering or hiking holiday, or intend to practise any extreme sports. Insurance should also cover the cost of helicopter rescue. This is extremely expensive but is often the only means of rescue when someone has suffered serious injury in the mountains.

In case of illness or injury, lists of local doctors can be obtained from the more expensive hotels, the consulate of your own country (see p291) or from tourist information offices (see p287). Almost every hospital (Spital, hôpital, opedale) has a 24-hour accident and emergency department. However, before receiving hospital treatment, you are advised to contact your insurer or your country's embassy (see p291).

PHARMACIES

ALL PHARMACIES (Apotheke, pharmacie or farmacia) are denoted by a sign in the form of a green cross. Pharmacies have helpful and knowledgeable staff who are able to give advice on minor health problems.

Duty pharmacies are open outside normal shopping hours, and their address is posted in the windows of pharmacies that are closed. In larger towns and cities, duty pharmacies stay open round the clock.

EMERGENCIES

IF YOU ARE involved in, or witness, an emergency, immediately call the police by dialling 117, or the ambulance (144), fire brigade (118), road rescue (140) or helicopter rescue service (1414).

An auxiliary services vehicle

If you are asked to sign a police document, do not do so unless you understand its content. Ask to have it translated. If you hold an insurance policy issued in your home country, you should immediately contact the insurer's central office, by ringing the number given on the policy document. Should you need legal assistance, your embassy can offer advice (see p291).

DIRECTORY

EMERGENCIES

Police
📞 117.

Fire Brigade
📞 118.

Ambulance
📞 144.

Road Rescue
📞 140.

Helicopter Rescue
📞 1414.

Note that almost all public telephones are card-operated. There is, however, no charge for calling the emergency numbers given above.

USEFUL NUMBERS

Weather Information
📞 162.

Avalanche Information
📞 187.

Skiing Conditions
📞 120.

Banking and Local Currency

Bureau de change logo

Y OU MAY BRING any amount of currency into Switzerland. Travellers' cheques are the safest way to carry money abroad, but credit and debit cards, both of which can be used to withdraw local currency, are by far the most convenient. The unit of currency both in Switzerland and in Liechtenstein is the Swiss franc (CHF), one of the most stable currencies in the world, and against which global markets are measured.

PAYMENT

A S IT IS NOT a member of the European Union, Switzerland is one of the few European countries that has not adopted the euro as its unit of currency. Generally payment must be therefore be made in Swiss francs or by credit or debit card.

It is worth noting, however, that the ticket offices of SBB, the Swiss federal railway, *(see pp300–01)* may accept payment in euros. Throughout Switzerland euros can often be used at airports and to pay motorway tolls. Some coin-operated telephones also accept euro coins *(see p296)*.

BANKS AND BUREAUX DE CHANGE

M OST BANKS ARE open Monday to Friday from 8.30am to 4.30pm, although in smaller towns they may close from noon to 2pm.

Basler Kantonalbank cash machine

Currency can be exchanged over the counter at banks, or cash withdrawn with a credit or debit card at automatic cash machines (ATMs). Even the banks in small towns have ATMs, and these can of course also be found at all airports and at major railway stations.

Bureaux de change tend to offer slightly better rates of exchange than banks. The least favourable rates are usually those offered by hotels.

CREDIT CARDS

T HE USE OF credit cards is less widespread in Switzerland than in the United Kingdom and United States. Visitors should bear in mind that some shops, hotels and restaurants ask for payment to be made in cash. In general MasterCard and Visa have the widest use in Switzerland, with American Express and Diners Club less widely accepted.

A branch of Crédit Suisse, one of Switzerland's largest banks

TAX-FREE GOODS

V ALUE-ADDED TAX (VAT) is levied at 7.6 percent. Visitors to Switzerland can reclaim sales tax, or VAT, on individual purchases of 400 CHF or more made at a single store. Obtain a VAT refund form at the time of purchase and take the goods out of the country (unopened) within 30 days. The form should be presented to customs when you leave the country. To obtain your refund, either take the form to the refund counter or send it back to the store when you are home. For a fee, **Global Refund**, a Europe-wide refund service, will handle all the paperwork for you.

Banknotes

Swiss banknotes are issued in denominations of 10, 20, 50, 100, 200 and 1,000 francs. The different banknotes are distinguished by their size and colour. The smallest, both in terms of size and value, is the 10-franc note. The largest is the 1,000-franc note.

Currency

THE SWISS UNIT of currency is the Swiss franc, which is abbreviated as CHF and known as *Schweizer Franken* in German, *franc suisse* in French and *franco svizzer* in Italian. The franc is divided into 100 *centimes*, which are known as *Rappen* in German and as *centesimi* in Italian.

Because of the customs union that exists between Switzerland and the principality of Liechtenstein, the Swiss franc is also the official currency of Liechtenstein.

10 francs

20 francs

50 francs

100 francs

200 francs

1,000 francs

5 francs   2 francs   1 franc   50 centimes   20 centimes

10 centimes   5 centimes

Coins

Swiss coins are issued in denominations of 1, 2 and 5 francs, and of 5, 10, 20 and 50 centimes. All Swiss coins are silver-coloured, except the 5-centime coin, which is gold-coloured.

Communications

Swiss post office logo

L IKE THE COUNTRY'S other public services, Switzerland's telephone and postal systems are efficient and reliable. Swisscom's modern public telephones have built-in electronic directories and also built-in facilities for sending faxes, e-mails and text messages. Switzerland's post office, known as Die Post in German, La Poste in French and La Posta in Italian, offers an equally modern and comprehensive mail service, as well as other useful services. Neighbouring Liechtenstein has its own separate telephone and postal systems.

A Swisscom telephone box

Public telephone, with electronic directory and other facilities

TELEPHONES

S WITZERLAND'S principal telecommunications company is Swisscom. It has almost 13,000 public telephones, most of which are located outside post offices and in train stations. Every public telephone has a Tele-guide. This provides access to an electronic directory and also enables users to send an e-mail, fax or text message. Instructions are given in four languages, including English.

Very few public telephones are coin-operated. Those that are accept Swiss francs and euros. The easiest way of using a public telephone is with a pre-paid phonecard, known as a taxcard. Taxcards, in denominations of 5, 10, 20, 50 and 100 CHF, are sold at post offices and train stations and in news kiosks.

Calls within Switzerland are cheapest at weekends, and on weekdays between 5pm and 8am. International calls are cheapest between 9pm and 8am. Inland calls to 0800 numbers are free. Calls from hotels, which set their own phone tariffs, always cost more than from public telephones.

All Swiss telephone numbers now consist of ten digits. This means that you must always include the three-digit area code, even when dialling a local number. The only exception is Zürich, whose existing two-digit area code (01) will be phased out by 2007. All Zürich numbers prefixed by 01 can, however, already be reached by dialling either of the two new area codes for Zürich, which are 043 and 044.

Mobile phones brought in from the US are unlikely to work unless they are tri-band. Mobile phones, known as *Natels* or *Handys*, can be hired at any Swisscom shops, which are found throughout the country.

USING A PHONECARD TELEPHONE

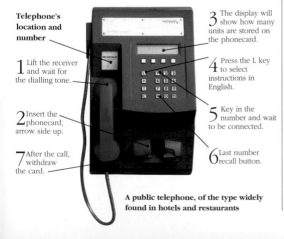

Telephone's location and number

1 Lift the receiver and wait for the dialling tone.

2 Insert the phonecard, arrow side up.

7 After the call, withdraw the card.

3 The display will show how many units are stored on the phonecard.

4 Press the L key to select instructions in English.

5 Key in the number and wait to be connected.

6 Last number recall button.

A public telephone, of the type widely found in hotels and restaurants

Liechtenstein

Liechtenstein has its own telephone company, Telecom FL, and its own postal service, Liechtensteinische Post. It also issues its own postage stamps, which are coveted by collectors.

Swisscom and Telecom FL cards can be used in both countries. Calls from Switzerland to Liechtenstein are treated as international, and you should dial 00, then the country code (423). A call from Liechtenstein to Switzerland is treated as national.

Swiss postage stamps

Postal Services

In large towns post offices are open from 8am to 6.30pm Monday to Friday, and from 8am to noon on Saturdays. In smaller towns, they close between noon and 2pm. In large cities, including Zürich, Geneva, Bern and Basel, post offices situated near railway stations have counters that remain open until 9–10pm. A small extra charge is made for using their services and they do not handle the more complicated transactions, such as money transfers.

Many post offices also have fax machines and automatic cash dispensers (Postomats), where cash can be withdrawn, although you will need a special card to use them.

Postbox in a German-speaking region of Switzerland

Stamps and Mail

Postage stamps are available at post offices, newsagents and hotel reception desks. They can also be purchased from machines, which are located within post offices and also beside some postboxes.

The Swiss postal system operates a two-tier delivery system. Inland letters sent by A-Post are delivered the next day. Those sent by B-Post, which is cheaper, reach their destinations in two to three days. For international letters there are two categories, Prioritaire and Économique. Prioritaire mail is delivered in two to four days within Europe and up to seven days everywhere else. Économique mail is delivered in four to eight days within Europe and up to 12 days elsewhere.

Poste Restante

A convenient way of receiving mail if you are travelling in Switzerland is by using Poste Restante. By this system mail is sent to any post office in the country that you designate, and is kept there until you collect it. Mail should be addressed with your name, the words Poste Restante, the letters CH (for "Switzerland") and the four-digit postcode of the relevant town. A full list of Swiss postcodes is published in phone directories.

Internet

Numerous Internet cafés and special terminals sited in many public places provide easy access to the Internet. Most higher-class hotels offer free access to the

Internet; others charge for the service. At some resorts there are terminals that enable visitors to send virtual postcards by e-mail.

An automatic cash dispenser at a post office

Useful Websites

Yellow Pages (business & services)
w www.gelbeseiten.ch

White Pages (residential subscribers)
w www.weisseseiten.ch

Die Post/La Poste/La Posta
w www.swisspost.ch
www.post.ch

Swisscom
w www.swisscom.ch

Telecom Liechtenstein
w www.telecom.li

Liechtensteinische Post
w www.post.li

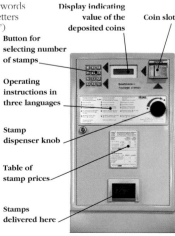

Display indicating value of the deposited coins — Coin slot
Button for selecting number of stamps
Operating instructions in three languages
Stamp dispenser knob
Table of stamp prices
Stamps delivered here
Postage-stamp vending machine

TRAVEL INFORMATION

LYING AT THE crossroads of major European routes, Switzerland has excellent transport connections. With six airports, the country has air links with all major European cities, as well as frequent intercontinental flights.

The country's internal transport system is also highly efficient, pleasant and easy to use, and a panoply of travel passes offer substantial discounts. Complemented

An aircraft of the SWISS fleet

by bus services, the dense rail network covers almost every corner of the country, and also offers visitors some of the best views of Switzerland's dramatic mountain scenery. Well-maintained roads make driving in Switzerland a pleasure and allow motorists either to cover long distances quickly or to explore the country's remoter regions at a more leisurely pace.

Sign indicating Zürich airport

BY AIR FROM THE UK

SEVERAL AIRLINES operate frequent daily direct flights between the United Kingdom and Switzerland. The main carriers are **British Airways** and **SWISS**, the national airline. Several low-cost airlines, including **easyJet** and bmi baby, also operate flights between the United Kingdom and Switzerland.

SWISS provides daily departures from London Heathrow, London City, Birmingham and Manchester to Basel, Zürich and Geneva. The duration of flights between London and any of these destinations is about one and half hours.

Cheaper air fares can usually be obtained if you purchase your plane ticket as part of a package from a tour operator. The London-based Swiss company **Plus Travel**, which specializes in travel to and holidays in Switzerland, can advise on every type of requirement.

BY AIR FROM THE US

DIRECT FLIGHTS between the United States and Switzerland are provided by **SWISS**, **American Airlines** and Delta Air Lines. Flights to Zürich and Geneva depart from New York, Boston,

Atlanta, Miami and Chicago, and from Los Angeles.

The duration of flights is about seven or eight hours from the east coast of the United States, about 10 hours from the Midwest, and about 14 hours from the west coast.

SPECIAL-INTEREST PACKAGES

TOUR OPERATORS both in the United Kingdom and in the United States offer many special-interest package holidays in Switzerland. Most of them revolve around skiing and other winter sports but there are a range of other options, including birdwatching and botanical tours led by specialists, and independent walking or cycling holidays, as well as rail tours and cultural explorations of the country.

SWISS AIRPORTS

SWITZERLAND's three main international airports are Basel, Zürich and Geneva. Both of the latter are connected to the Swiss rail network, which provides a frequent shuttle service to the city centre.

Basel is served by EuroAirport. Split into Swiss and EU sectors, it is located on French territory and also serves Mulhouse (in France) and Freiburg (in Germany). In addition to internal flghts, EuroAirport provides links to several European cities.

Switzerland also has three smaller airports, which provide international flights and a limited number of internal connections. Bern-Belp airport has flights to other destinations in Europe, and Sion airport has connections to Zürich. In winter there are also flights to Sion from London and Amsterdam.

Zürich's Kloten airport, one of the busiest in Switzerland

Zürich's international airport

Lugano's Agno Airport has daily flights to Basel, Bern, Geneva and Zürich and to destinations in Italy.

FLY RAIL BAGGAGE

WHEN FLYING to Switzerland from any airport in the world, you can make use of the convenient **Fly Rail Baggage Service**. From the check-in desk at your home airport, you can send your luggage direct to almost any train station in Switzerland, where you can collect it at your convenience. Some hotels will collect your luggage for you.

To use Fly Rail Baggage you must obtain a special luggage tag from SWISS or a Swiss tourist office. The service costs about £10 ($18) per piece of luggage. It is not, however, available if you are flying with a low-cost airline or any US airline, and bulky items such as bicycles are not carried. As security concerns may also limit the availability of this service, you are advised to check with the airline or your travel agent.

STATION CHECK-IN

IF YOU ARE flying from Switzerland, you can also check your luggage in at any one of 126 Swiss train stations. This costs about 20 CHF per item, or 50 CHF if you are not travelling by train. Your luggage is transported to the airport and loaded onto your flight. You then collect it from the carousel at your destination airport. This service is available for most flights from Geneva and Zürich, and some flights from Basel. It is not, however, available if you are flying with a low-cost airline or any US carrier.

At 50 of the larger train stations in Switzerland you can also check in for your flight (though not more than 24 hours before the flight departure time) and receive a boarding card.

Bus for passenger transfer at Zürich airport

DIRECTORY

British Airways
📞 0845 773 3377 (UK).
📞 1-800-247-9297 (US).
🖳 www.ba.com

SWISS
📞 0845 601 0956 (UK).
📞 1-877 359-7947 (US).
🖳 www.swiss.com

EasyJet
🖳 www.easyjet.com

Plus Travel
📞 020 7734 0383 (UK).
🖳 www.plustravel.co.uk

American Airlines
📞 1-800-433-7300 (US).
🖳 www.aa.com

Fly Rail Baggage & Station Check-in
📞 0900 300 300 (Switzerland).
🖳 www.rail.ch

TOUR OPERATORS

Airtours
📞 0870 241 2567 (UK).
🖳 www.mytravel.co.uk

Alphorn Tours
📞 215 794 5653 (US).

Great Rail Journeys
📞 01904 521 900 (UK).
🖳 www.greatrail.com

Naturetrek
📞 01962 733 051 (UK).
🖳 www.naturetrek.co.uk

Skiers Travel
📞 0870 010 0032 (UK).
🖳 www.skiers-travel.co.uk

AIRPORT	INFORMATION	DISTANCE FROM CITY	JOURNEY TIME BY TAXI	JOURNEY TIME BY PUBLIC TRANSPORT
Basel	📞 061 325 31 11	5 km (3 miles)	20 minutes	Bus: 15 minutes
Bern	📞 031 960 21 11	9 km (6 miles)	30 minutes	Bus: 20 minutes
Geneva	📞 022 717 71 11	5 km (3 miles)	20 minutes	Train: 6 minutes Bus: 20 minutes
Lugano	📞 091 610 11 11	20 km (12 miles)	40 minutes	Bus: 10 minutes
Zürich	📞 043 816 22 11	10 km (6 miles)	25 minutes	Train: 9 minutes

Travelling by Train

Logo of Swiss Federal Railways

THE COMPREHENSIVE Swiss rail network provides an excellent means of transport. Trains are modern, clean and comfortable, and services are frequent and dependably punctual. Because the railway timetable is efficiently integrated with other forms of public transport, connections are very convenient. The train is also one of the best ways to see the country. Special excursions by train and boat enable visitors to enjoy exceptionally beautiful scenery on several routes through mountains and over passes, across lakes and along valleys.

A suburban train

ARRIVING BY TRAIN

THE MOST DIRECT rail route from London to Switzerland is via the Channel Tunnel to Paris Gare du Nord. From here there are several options. From Gare de Lyon, you can catch a TGV (high-speed train) to Geneva, Lausanne, Neuchâtel, Bern or Zürich, or to Sion, Sierre, Visp and Brig at weekends during the summer. From Gare de l'Est ordinary train services run to Basel, and sleeper services run to Zürich and Chur.

The quickest journey (from London to Geneva) takes at least eight hours and, although all these routes are scenic, reaching Switzerland by train from the United Kingdom is not as cheap, quick and convenient as flying *(see pp298–9).*

Switzerland has good links with European high-speed-train networks, among which are Germany's ICE, France's TGV and Italy's Cisalpino. Comprehensive Swiss public transport timetables, including international connections, can be consulted on the website www.rail.ch/timetable.

Board displaying destination codes

Buttons for selecting ticket type

Buttons for selecting destination or PIN number

Slot for inserting banknotes or credit card

Ticket and receipt delivered here

Vending machine for rail tickets

TRAINS

SWITZERLAND'S MAIN train operator is Swiss Federal Railways, or SBB/CFF/FFS (Schweizerische Bundesbahnen/Chemins de Fer Fédéraux/Ferrovie Federali Svizzere). SBB covers almost all the country, and over a dozen smaller operators run certain routes.

Most trains run from 6am to midnight, with hourly services operating between major towns. All trains have smoking and non-smoking, and first- and second-class carriages. Long-distance trains, including Intercity (IC), Eurocity (EC) and Interregio (IR) trains, have restaurant cars and trolleys serving drinks and snacks.

Trains also carry unaccompanied luggage. You can send your luggage ahead from almost any station to another station or bus terminal. This is very useful if you are on the move, and want to spend the day unencumbered by baggage.

TRAVEL PASSES

A GREAT VARIETY of travel passes is available in Switzerland. Offering substantial discounts for rail travel, these passes can also

---

DIRECTORY

SBB Timetable
W www.sbb.ch
C 0900 300 300.

Travel Passes
W www.rail.ch/sts
W www.raileurope.com

SCENIC JOURNEYS

Glacier Express
C 081 288 6104.
W www.rhb.ch

Golden Pass Express
C 021 989 81 81.
W www.goldenpass.ch

Bernina Express
C 081 288 6326.
W www.rhb.ch

William Tell Express
C 041 367 67 67.
W www.lakelucerne.ch

be used on other modes of public transport such as buses, trams, funiculars and boats.

The Swiss Pass allows unlimited rail travel on almost all train, bus and boat services, and on trams and buses in 37 towns. It allows reductions of 25 percent on private railways, funiculars and cable cars. The Swiss Pass is available for periods of 4, 8, 15 or 22 consecutive days.

The Swiss Flexi Pass buys unlimited travel on any 3, 6 or 8 days within a month, and those travelling in groups of two to five receive a 15 percent discount. Further discounts apply to people under the age of 26. The Swiss Transfer Ticket covers one round trip from the Swiss border or any Swiss airport to anywhere in the country. The Swiss Card provides the same plus a 50-percent discount on all other travel. The Family Card allows children up to the age of 16 to travel free if they are accompanied by an adult. Regional passes are also available.

For the full range of passes available for travel in Switzerland visit www.rail.ch/sts. Most national travel passes can be purchased from travel agencies and Swiss tourist offices in your own country.

The concourse of Winterthur railway station

SCENIC JOURNEYS

SPECIAL TRAINS take visitors on panoramic journeys through Switzerland's most spectacular scenery. Some trains have glass-roofed carriages that enable travellers to enjoy views in all directions.

Among the most popular of these rail journeys are the **Glacier Express**, from

Double-decker carriage of an SBB train

St Moritz or Davos over the Oberalp pass to Zermatt; the **Golden Pass Express**, from Montreux over the Brünig Pass to Luzern; the **Bernina Express**, from Davos, Chur or St Moritz over the Bernina Pass and down to Tirano, in Italy; and the **William Tell Express**, which starts with a cruise on Lake Lucerne, then cuts through the St Gotthard tunnel and descends to Lugano.

Tickets for these scenic journeys can be bought at any station. Most require reservation at least 24 hours in advance.

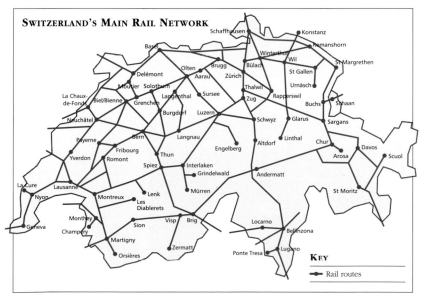

SWITZERLAND'S MAIN RAIL NETWORK

Schaffhausen · Konstanz
Basel · Romanshorn
Winterthur · Wil
Olten · Brugg · Bülach · St Margrethen
Delémont · Aarau · Zürich · St Gallen
Moutier · Solothurn · Thalwil · Urnäsch
La Chaux-de-Fonds · Langenthal · Sursee · Rapperswil
Biel/Bienne · Grenchen · Zug · Buchs · Schaan
Neuchâtel · Burgdorf · Luzern · Schwyz · Glarus · Sargans
Payerne · Bern · Langnau · Altdorf · Chur · Davos
Yverdon · Fribourg · Thun · Engelberg · Linthal · Arosa · Scuol
Romont · Spiez · Interlaken · Andermatt
La Cure · Lausanne · Lenk · Grindelwald · St Moritz
Nyon · Montreux · Mürren
Monthey · Les Diablerets · Visp · Brig · Locarno
Geneva · Champéry · Sion · Bellinzona
Martigny · Zermatt · Ponte Tresa · Lugano
Orsières

KEY

➤ Rail routes

Travelling by Car, Bus, Bicycle and Boat

MOTORWAY LINKS provide swift means of road transport the length and breadth of the country and well-maintained roads link Switzerland's major towns. Scenic routes also lead to high mountain passes and down Alpine valleys. Travelling through Switzerland by car is only one means of exploring the country. A fleet of passenger-carrying post buses traverse spectacular landscape to reach remote Alpine towns and villages. A slower but equally rewarding alternative is to travel by bicycle, using convenient bus and rail links. Switzerland can also be appreciated at a slower pace, by taking a cruise on any of its breathtakingly beautiful lakes.

Multistorey car park in Geneva

Road sign in western Switzerland

ARRIVING BY CAR

FAST CAR-CARRYING train services through the Channel Tunnel and good motorway routes eastwards across France make driving to Switzerland from the United Kingdom a viable alternative to flying. Frequent car ferries also cross the Channel from Dover to Calais and from Hull to Rotterdam or Zeebrugge. From Calais the quickest route is by motorway eastwards through France, entering Switzerland via the A40 to Geneva. From Zeebrugge or Rotterdam, there are fast motorways across Belgium, Luxembourg, France and Germany, from where the A5 leads to Basel. By either route, the journey from the Channel coast to the Swiss border is unlikely to take less than eight hours.

If you drive on French *autoroutes* remember that motorway tolls may add considerably to the cost of your journey.

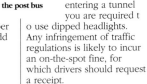
Bus stop sign for the post bus

RULES OF THE ROAD

IN SWITZERLAND, as in the rest of mainland Europe, driving is on the right. Overtaking on the right is prohibited and at junctions priority is given to drivers on the right, except when you are entering a roundabout. Unless road signs indicate otherwise, the speed limit is 120 km/h (75 mph) on motorways, 100 km/h (60 mph) on main highways, and 80 km/h (50 mph) on other roads. In built-up areas it is 50 km/h (30 mph) but can sometimes be as low as 30km/h (20mph).

The driver and passengers of a car must wear seat belts. Children under 12 years old must travel in the back seat, and those under seven must be strapped into a child seat. All vehicles must also carry a breakdown warning triangle. When entering a tunnel you are required t o use dipped headlights. Any infringement of traffic regulations is likely to incur an on-the-spot fine, for which drivers should request a receipt.

The use of mobile phones while driving is considered to be a serious infringement, as is drink-driving. The blood-alcohol content limit is 0.08%. Drivers should also carry their driving licence and the vehicle's registration document, which may be checked by the police.

DRIVING ON MOTORWAYS

TO USE SWISS motorways, which are indicated by green signs, drivers require a disk, or *vignette*. Costing 40 CHF, a *vignette* is valid until the end of January of the following year and can be purchased at border crossings, petrol stations, in post offices and at tourist offices. A *vignette* is also required for motorcycles and trailers. Driving on a motorway without a valid *vignette* incurs a fine.

BP self-service petrol station

DRIVING IN THE ALPS

EQUIPMENT SUCH AS snow tyres or tyre chains is needed for driving in the Alps in winter. Road signs on routes leading into the Alps inform drivers of road conditions ahead and whether passes are closed. The road tunnels beneath the St Gotthard, San Bernardino and Great St Bernard passes are open all year around, and tolls must be paid by vehicles using them. The Lötschberg, Furka, Albula and Vereina tunnels have rail links, and cars are carried on trains.

Most of the country's high Alpine passes are generally open from June until October, although this is subject to weather conditions.

CAR HIRE

ALL THE major international car-hire companies offer services in Switzerland. They have offices in the country's main airports and in the centre of major towns. Local firms usually offer cheaper rates, but for the cheapest deals, which often come in a fly-drive package, it is best to pre-book in your own country. To hire a car in Switzerland, a driver must be over 20 years of age (in some cases 25) and must show a valid driving licence.

A post bus on one of many Alpine routes inaccessible by rail

BUSES AND POST BUSES

IN THE MOUNTAINOUS or more remote regions of Switzerland, some public transport is provided by local buses. Most bus stations are located very near train stations, and bus and rail services are well coordinated, so that bus departures coincide with train arrivals and vice versa.

Alpine routes that are inaccessible by rail are also served by post buses (known as *postautos* or *postcars*), which are yellow and bear the Die Post, La Poste or La Posta logo. As well as carrying mail and passengers, post buses also carry un-accompanied luggage, which is especially convenient for hikers. Some of the routes taken by post buses lead over high passes and through remote and stunningly beautiful mountain scenery.

Sign to a motorway

BICYCLES

SWITZERLAND HAS a remarkably cyclist-friendly infrastructure. Bicycles (which are often called *velos*) can be hired at most train stations (follow signs indicating *Mietvelos*, *Location de Vélos* or *Bici da Noleggiare*), and need not be returned to the same station. Rental information is available from Swiss Federal Railways (*see p301*). Bicycles can also be carried on postbuses and on trains (unless otherwise indicated in the timetables).

Recommended cycle routes are marked by red signs with a white bicycle symbol. Cycling maps for specific areas are obtainable from local tourist offices. Several long-distance cycle routes traverse the country. The North–South Route, for example, runs for 360 km (225 miles) from Basel to Chiasso, in southern Ticino.

To use your own bicycle in Switzerland, you need to buy a *vignette* (costing 5 CHF and obtainable at post offices), which covers road tax and insurance.

A Hertz car-hire office

LAKE CRUISES

TAKING A CRUISE on one of Switzerland's lakes is a relaxing way to explore the country. A fleet of paddle steamers ply Lake Lucerne and many other lakes, and there are scenic cruises of Lake Geneva, Bodensee and Lake Lugano. Most cruises run only from April to October.

All Swiss travel passes are valid for cruises on the lakes, except for Lake Maggiore. The Swiss Boat Pass gives a reduction on many cruises.

Getting Around in Towns

Most swiss towns, particularly the historic districts of larger cities, are compact, making them easy to explore on foot. Some major historic town centres are also pedestrianized, or barred to almost all motorized traffic. To reach outlying attractions, visitors will sometimes need to take buses, trams, suburban trains or in certain cases funiculars. These are all easy to use, especially as tickets and travel passes are valid for every mode of public transport. Taxis are also available, although they are expensive. Bicycles, which can be hired from many rail stations, are an alternative means of getting around. For unforgettable views of Switzerland's great lakeshore towns, visitors should take a boat cruise.

A conducted sightseeing tour of a town centre

TAXIS

Because the swiss public transport system is so efficient, taking a taxi is rarely worth the extra expense. Although they vary from town to town, taxi fares are uniformly high, consisting of a flat rate and an additional charge for every kilometre (just over half a mile) travelled. These charges are higher at night and at weekends.

Taxis can be any colour and are identifiable by a "taxi" sign on the roof. They can be hired from ranks, which are almost always located in front of railway stations. They can also be booked by telephone.

BUSES AND TRAMS

The quickest and easiest way of getting around in towns is by hopping on a bus, trolley-bus or tram. These run at frequent intervals from about 5am until midnight. Night buses run only at

weekends. Inside buses and trams are maps showing the itinerary travelled, and the stops along the route. Each stop is announced by the driver, or by a recording. To request a stop, press the button next to the door. The doors of buses open automatically. Tram doors are opened by passengers pressing a button.

S-BAHN & METRO

Zürich, bern, geneva and other cities are served by S-Bahn, or suburban, trains (known as RER in French). The hubs of these networks are the cities' main stations, from where you can travel not only to the suburbs but to neighbouring towns. Bicycles can be carried on almost all S-Bahn trains. The S-Bahn network map is displayed inside the carriages.

Some towns built on steep cliffs or clinging to hillsides, such as Lausanne and Fribourg, also have funicular railways. Lausanne's funicular trains run from the main train station, in two directions. One line leads up to the town centre, and the other leads down to Ouchy, the suburb on the shores of Lake Geneva. Lausanne is also the only Swiss town to have a metro.

TICKETS

Information on the various types of tickets available is displayed at bus and tram stops. In most towns, the public transport network is divided into zones, and the more zones you intend to traverse the more a ticket will cost. Also, tickets are valid for a limited period, ranging from an hour to a full day or more, and can be used on any mode of transport. In Zürich, for example, one ticket can be used on buses, trams, S-Bahn trains and boats.

There is an automatic ticket machine at every bus and tram stop. The machines accept coins (Swiss francs and sometimes euros) and special cards that are sold in all newsagent kiosks. When you board a bus or tram, you should validate your ticket by stamping it at a machine on board the vehicle. Ticket inspectors (some in uniform) regularly carry out checks. The penalty for travelling without a valid ticket is likely to be 40–60 CHF.

The Swiss Pass and Flexi Pass (see p300) are valid on all modes of public transport in 37 Swiss towns (listed on the ticket). Some towns issue special passes for visitors. The ZürichCard, for example, costs 30 CHF and is valid for three days' travel in the city. It also offers reduced rates

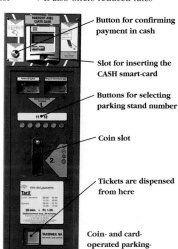

Button for confirming payment in cash

Slot for inserting the CASH smart-card

Buttons for selecting parking stand number

Coin slot

Tickets are dispensed from here

Coin- and card-operated parking-ticket machine

An SBB bus bound for Bülach, in the suburbs of Zürich

for guided tours, entry to certain museums and various other attractions.

PARKING

USING A CAR in town centres can be quite inconvenient. It is far easier to leave your car in an out-of-town car park (signposted P&R, for Park and Ride) and switch to a bus or tram to reach the town centre.

On-street parking and urban car parks are usually very expensive, especially in large towns and cities. Parking bays are colour-coded, or delineated with coloured lines. Those in a White Zone are usually pay-and-display. To use those in a Blue Zone you need a parking disc, which limits the parking time allowed. Discs are available from tourist offices, banks and other points. Bays in a Red Zone allow free parking for 15 hours, and the parking disc must be displayed. Illegal parking is likely to result in a fine. Most parking-ticket machines accept coins but do not accept cards other than CASH, the Swiss smart-card.

Sign for metered car parking

BICYCLES

SWITZERLAND'S zealous anti-pollution and anti-congestion ethic means that the use of bicycles is actively encouraged. Many towns have cycle lanes, filter lights at crossings and ubiquitous cycle racks. Bicycles can be hired at many main railway stations *(see p303)*. Some towns offer free bicycle rental. To hire a bicycle under this scheme, all you need to do is show your passport and pay a deposit of 20–50 CHF, which is refunded when you return the bike. Details can be obtained from local tourist information offices or by visiting www.rentabike.ch.

SIGHTSEEING ON FOOT

MANY OF the oldest and best-preserved town centres have been partly or wholly pedestrianized, restoring their historic atmosphere and making them very pleasant to explore on foot. Suggested itineraries are usually marked with a continuous line or a succession of painted footprints, and major historic buildings and other features of interest along the route have information panels.

The tourist offices in some towns organize guided tours, which are often led by English-speaking guides. Most tourist information offices also provide town maps and helpful information in English.

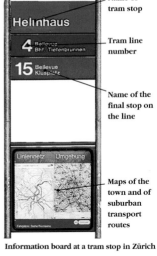

Name of tram stop / Tram line number / Name of the final stop on the line / Maps of the town and of suburban transport routes

Information board at a tram stop in Zürich

FERRIES

FERRY TRIPS can offer quite a different perspective of Switzerland's lakeshore towns. Ferries operate from Zürich, Geneva, Lugano, Locarno, Thun, Luzern and other towns, whose beautiful lakeshore buildings may be seen to their best advantage when viewed from the water.

Most ferry companies run cruises only from early April to the end of October. Among the most scenic trips are those that depart from Zürich and that run along the Limmat and the length of the Zürichsee. Steamer services operate on Lake Geneva and Lake Lucerne. Longer cruises, on Lake Maggiore and Lake Lugano, depart from Locarno and Lugano respectively.

The Swiss Boat Pass gives holders a 50 percent reduction on cruises on 14 lakes. The Swiss Pass *(see p300)* is valid for travel on all lakes except Lake Maggiore. Full details are available from tourist offices.

A tram on Zürich's network

Index

Acknowledgments

DORLING KINDERSLEY and Hachette Livre Polska would like to thank the following people and institutions, whose contributions and assistance have made the preparation of this guide possible.

PUBLISHING MANAGER
Kate Poole

MANAGING EDITORS
Helen Townsend, Jacky Jackson

PUBLISHER
Douglas Amrine

CARTOGRAPHY
Casper Morris

SENIOR DTP DESIGNER
Jason Little

EDITORIAL ASSISTANCE
Anna Freiberger

FACT-CHECKER
Dianne Dicks, Bergli Books

PROOF READER
Stewart Wild

INDEX
Helen Peters

SPECIAL ASSISTANCE
Appenzellerland Tourismus; Artothek, Baud V. Maydell; Bellinzona Turismo; Biel/Bienne Seeland Tourismus; Burgerbibliothek, Bern; Corbis; Enteturistico Lago Maggiore; Furrer Jakob (photograph of beers, p266); Historisches Museum, Basel (Therese Wollmann); Kunsthaus, Zürich (Cécile Brunner); Kunstmuseum, Basel; Kunstmuseum, Bern (Regula Zbinden); Alicja Kusch (photograph of Bomi shop in Klif); André Locher (photographs of Yverdon-les-Bains and Mesocco); Lugano Turismo; Katarzyna and Wojciech Medrzak; Grzegorz Mościbrocki (World of Alcoholic Drinks); Mövenpick Wein, Zug (Brigitte auf der Maur); Musée d'Art et d'Histoire, Geneva (Isabelle Brun-Ilunga, Marc-Antoine Claivaz); Musée d'Art et d'Histoire, Neuchâtel (Marie-Josée Golles); Musée Romain, Avenches (Anne Hochuli-Gysel); Offentliche Kunstsammlung Basel, Kunstmuseum und Museum für Gegenwartskunst (Maria-Theresa Brunner); Schweiz Tourismus, Zürich (Fred Schreiber); Schweizerisches Landesmuseum (Angelica Condrau, Andrea Kunz); Swiss Embassy, Warsaw; Gerry Thönen (photograph of an orchard); Tourist Information Centre, Geneva (Frédéric Monnerat); Verkehrshaus, Luzern (Hans Syfrig, Martin Sigrist); Wistillerie Etter Soehne Ag, Zug (Eveline Etter); Zentralbiliothek, Zürich (Kristin Steiner).

PICTURE CREDITS

t = top; tr = top right; tra = top right above; tl = top left; tlb = top left below; c = centre; cr = centre right; cra = centre right above; crb = centre right below; cl = centre left; cla = centre left above; clb = centre left below; ca = centre above; cb = centre below; b = bottom; bl = bottom left; bla = bottom left above; blb = bottom left below; br = bottom right; bca = bottom centre above.

Every effort has been made to trace the copyright holders, and we apologize in advance for any unintentional omissions. We would be pleased to insert the appropriate acknowledgments in any subsequent edition of this publication.

Works of art have been reproduced with the permission of the following copyright holders: *Davos im Schnee*, 1923, Kunstmuseum Basel © Dr. Wolfgang & Ingeborg Henze-Ketterer, Wichtrach/Bern 147c and Poster (detail) Kirchner Museum Davos © Dr. Wolfgang & Ingeborg Henze-Ketterer, Wichtrach/Bern 191br; *Diego*, 1963-4, Alberto Giacometti ©ADAGP, Paris and DACS, London 2005 – 43c; *Fastnachtsbrunnen*, 1977, Jean Tinguely ©ADAGP Paris and DACS, London 2005; *Schwimmwasserplastik*, 1980, Jean Tinguely ©ADAGP, Paris and DACS, London 2005; *Sheep piece*, 1971-72 (LH627), Henry Moore, this image has been reproduced by kind permission of the Henry Moore Foundation 169t.

Appenzellerland Tourismus: 188b.
Artothek: 54b.
Baud V. Maydell: 92.
Bellinzona Turismo: 220tl.
Biel/Bienne Seeland Tourismus: P. Brisset 16tl.
Burgerbibliothek, Bern: 37b.
Collectif d'enfants: *Le cinema*, ca. 1950, gouache et collage sur papier, 294 x 173.5cm © Collection de l'Art Brut, Lausanne/Photo: Claude Bornand, Lausanne 116bl.
Corbis: O. Alamany & E. Vicens 20d, 21crb, 177b; Paul Almasy 44–5; Roger Antrobus 2–3, 79t; Morton Beebe 84g, 107d; Bettmann 40clb, 40d, 42t, 42b, 43tr, 43bca, 43bl, 84t; Stefano Bianchetti 38bl; Jacques Bock/Sygma 104t; Barnabas Bosshart 60b, 64t, 174g; Christie's Images *Diego*, 1963–4, Alberto Giacometti ©ADAGP, Paris and

DACS, London 2005 – 43ca: Corbis 41crb; Robert Eric/Sygma 105t; Steven E. Frishling 29t; Farrell Grehan 8–9; Historical Picture Archive 40cla, 41c, 45c; Kit Houghton 29c; Dave G. Houser 190b; Pat Jerrold/Papilio 21clb, 21bl; Wolfgang Kaehler 13t, 62t; Mike King 28b; Dimitri Lundt/TempSport 28t; Kelly-Mooney Photography 24tr; Listri Massimo 139t; Francis G. Mayer 38br; Wally McNamee 29b; Richard T. Nowitz 25tr, 158; Gianni Dagli Orti 39b; José F. Poblete 20–21c, 47br, 134; Annie Poole/Papilio 21tl; Christian Sarramon 83b; Leonard de Selva 41b; Ted Spiegel 36t; Ink Swim 41tl, 228c; Tim Thompson 21br; Vittoriano Rastelli 19t; Ruggero Vanni 25cl; Jean Bernard Vernier/Sygma 43crb, 43br, 105b, 106cla, 107t; Scott T. Smith 20cl; Sandro Vanini 25br, 52b, 207b, 214tlb; Pierre Vauthey/Sygma 25cr, 31bl; Patrick Ward 25bl, 30t, 76–7; Werner Forman 141tl; Nik Wheeler 1; Adam Woolfitt 20t.
Enteturistico Lago Maggiore: T. Krueger 214tra.
Historisches Museum Basel: M. Babey 38ca.
Oldrich Karasek: 5t, 68b, 79b.
Piotr Kiedrowski: 106t, 106crb, 107c
Kunsthaus Zürich: 34, 41cra, 170cb, 170b, 171cl, 171crb; *Au-dessus de Paris*, 1968, Marc Chagall ©ADAGP, Paris and DACS, London 2005 – 170t; *Entire City*, 1935–7, Max Ernst ©ADAGP, Paris and DACS, London 2005 – 170ca; *Bird in Space*, 1925, Constantin Brancusi ©ADAGP, Paris and DACS, London 2005 – 171t; *Guitare sur un Gueridon*, 1915, Pablo Picasso ©Succession Picasso/DACS 2005 – 171cra; *Big Torn Campbell's Soup Can (Vegetable Beef)*, 1962, Andy Warhol ©The Andy Warhol Foundation for the Visual Arts, Inc./ARS, NY and DACS, London 2005 – 171b.
Kunstmuseum Basel: 146t, 146clb, 146b, 147ca, 147cb, 147b; *Senecio*, 1922, Paul Klee ©DACS 2005 – 146cra; *Burning Giraffe*, 1936–7, Salvador Dalí ©Salvador Dalí, Gala-Salvador Dalí Foundation, DACS, London 2005 – 147t.
Kunstmuseum Bern: 56t, 56c; Peter Lauri 56b, 57cb; *Ad Parnassum*, 1932, Paul Klee ©DACS 2005 – 57ca; *Eingeschlafene Trinkerin*, 1902, Pablo Picasso ©Succession Picasso/DACS 2005 – 57br; *Moulin de la Galette, Montmartre*, Maurice Utrillo ©ADAGP, Paris and DACS, London 2005 –

57t.
Landesmuseum Zürich: (2003) 35b, 36br, 37t, 37cr, 39t.
André Locher: 128t.
Lugano Turismo: 210t.
Musée d'Art et d'Histoire, Neuchâtel: 40–41c.
Musée d'Art et d'Histoire, Geneva: 102–03: MAH 102t; Jean Marc Yersin 102ca, 102cb, 103cra; Yves Siza 102b, 103clb, 103b; Bettina Jacot-Descombes 103t.
Öffentliche Kunstsammlung, Basel: Martin Bühler 36cl, 38t.
Małgorzata Omilanowska: 4t, 24tl, 24cl, 24cr, 47tr, 47bl, 51b, 53tra, 58c, 58t, 58b, 59tl, 159b, 174b, 175t, 305tr, 305b.
Robert Harding Picture Library: Neil Emmerson 82cb.
Schweizerishes Landesmuseum, Zürich: 4b, 162–3.
Schweiz Tourismus: 111t, 164t, 191t, 191blb; U. Ackermann 18b; D. Brawand 225b; R. Brioschi 172cr; L. Degonda 22t, 119cb; S. Eigstler 21cla; F. Englar 30b, 32b, 101b, 117t, 119bla, 172b, 17li. Giegel 228t; Höllgrotten Baar 209t; P. Maurer 16c, 26t, 232tlb; F. Pfenniger 23b; M. Schmid 15b, 23t, 119t, 225t; H. Schwab 15t, 21crb, 27br, 209b, 228b; C. Sonderegger 16b, 17t, 17b, 19b, 26ca, 26cb, 26bl, 26br, 27tl, 27tr, 27bl, 30c, 31t, 32t, 33t, 119ca, 119tr, 135b, 178, 179, 190t, 208b, 214b, 220b, 229b, 232tra, 232b; W. Storto 215b; Rausser 11t; K. Richter 18t.
Ireneusz Winnicki: 262–3.
Paweł Wroński: 88c, 90b, 116b, 284b, 303b.
Zefa: 288–9; J. Raga 108.
Zentral Bibliothek, Zürich: 36–7c, 38cb.
Andrzej Zygmuntowicz: 262–3.

Jacket: Front - Corbis: John Heaton cr; DK PICTURE LIBRARY: c; GETTY IMAGES: Stone/Siegfried Eigstler main image; Stone/Art Wolfe bl. Back - CORBIS: Richard Klune t; ROBERT HARDING.COM A. Sanders b. Spine - GETTY IMAGES: Stone/Siegfried Eigstler.

All other images © Dorling Kindersley
For further information see www.dkimages.com

DORLING KINDERSLEY SPECIAL EDITIONS

Dorling Kindersley books can be purchased in bulk quantities at discounted prices for use in promotions or as premiums. We are also able to offer special editions and personalized jackets, corporate imprints, and excerpts from all of our books, tailored specifically to meet your own needs.

To find out more, please contact: (in the United Kingdom) – Sarah.Burgess@dk.com or SPECIAL SALES, DORLING KINDERSLEY LIMITED, 80 STRAND, LONDON WC2R 0RL;

(in the United States) – SPECIAL MARKETS DEPARTMENT, DK PUBLISHING, INC., 375 HUDSON STREET, NEW YORK, NEW YORK 10014.

Phrase Book

GERMAN IS the most widely spoken language in Switzerland, followed by French and Italian. Swiss German, which is used in everyday speech, differs from standard High German (see p291). Because it consists of several local dialects, each of which are almost impossible to transcribe, the phrases given below are in High German, with some of the most commonly used expressions in Swiss German marked by an asterisk.

IN EMERGENCY

English	GERMAN	FRENCH	ITALIAN
Help!	Hilfe!	Au secours!	Aiuto!
Stop!	Halt!	Arrêtez!	Alt!
Call a doctor!	Holen Sie einen Artz	Appelez un médecin	Chiami un medico
Call an ambulance!	Holen Sie einen Krankenwagen	Appelez une ambulance	Chiami una ambulanza
Call the police!	Holen Sie die Polizei	Appelez la police	Chiami la polizia
Call the fire brigade!	Holen Sie die Feuerwehr	Appelez les pompiers	Chiami i pompieri
Where is a telephone?	Wo finde ich ein Telefon?	Ou y a-t-il un telephone?	Dov'è il telefono?
Where is the hospital?	Wo finde ich das Krankenhaus?	Ou est l'hôpital?	Dov'è l'ospedale?

COMMUNICATION ESSENTIALS

Yes	Ja	Oui	Si
No	Nein	Non	No
Please	Bitte	S'il vous plaît	Per favore
Thank you	Danke vielmals	Merci	Grazie
Excuse me	Entschuldigen Sie *Äxgüsi	Excusez-moi	Mi scusi
Hello	Grüss Gott *Grüezi	Salut!	Salve!/Ciao!
Goodbye	Auf Widersehen *Ufwiederluege	Au revoir	Arrivederci
Bye!	Tschüss!	Salut!	Ciao!
here	hier	ici	qui
there	dort	là	la
What?	Was?	Quel, quelle?	Quale?
Where?	Wo/Wohin?	Où?	Dove?

USEFUL PHRASES AND WORDS

Where is ...?	Wo befindet sich...?	Où est ...?	Dov'è
Where are ...?	Wo befinden sich...?	Où sont...?	Dove sono?
Do you speak English?	Sprechen Sie Englisch?	Parlez-vous anglais?	Parla inglese?
I understand	Ich verstehe	Je comprends	Capisco
I don't understand	Ich verstehe nicht	Je ne comprends pas	Non capisco
I'm sorry	Es tut mir leid	Je suis désolé	Mi dispiace
big	gross	grand	grande
small	klein	petit	piccolo
open	auf/offen	overt	aperto
closed	zu/geschlossen	fermé	chiuso
left	links	à gauche	a sinistra
right	rechts	à droite	a destra
near	Es ist in der Nähe	près	vicino
far	weit	loin	lontano
up	auf/oben	en haut	su
down	ab/unten	en bas	giù
early	früh	de bonne heure	presto
late	spät	en retard	tardi
entrance	Eingang/Einfahrt	l'entrée	la entrata
exit	Ausgang/Ausfahrt	la sortie	l'uscita
toilet	WC/Toilette	les toilettes/les WCs	il gabinetto

MAKING A TELEPHONE CALL

I'd like to place a long-distance call	Ich möchte ein Fernsgespräch machen	Je voudrais faire un interurbain.	Vorrei fare una interurbana.
I'd like to make a reverse charge call/call collect	Ich möchte ein Rückgespräch machen	Je voudrais faire une communication PCV	Vorrei fare una telefonata a carico del destinatario
I'll try again later	Ich versuche es später noch einmal	Je rapellerai plus tard	Ritelefono più tardi
Can I leave a message?	Kann ich etwas ausrichten?	Est-ce que je peux laisser un message?	Posso lasciare un messaggio?

STAYING IN A HOTEL

Do you have a vacant room?	Haben Sie ein Zimmer frei?	Est-ce que vous avez une chambre libre?	Avete camere libere?
double room	ein Doppelzimmer	une chambre à deux	una camera doppia
twin room	ein Doppelzimmer mit zwei Betten?	une chambre à deux lits	una camera con due letti
single room	ein Einzelzimmer	une chambre à une personne	una camera singola
with a bath/shower	mit Bad/Dusche	avec salle de bains/ douche	con bagno/doccia
How much is the room?	Wievel kostet das Zimmer?	Combien coûte la chambre?	Quanto costa la camera?
Where is the bathroom?	Wo ist das Bad?	Où est la salle de bains?	Dov'è il bagno?
with breakfast	mit Frühstück	avec petit-déjeuner	con prima colazione
with half-board	mit Halbpension	en demi-pension	mezza pensione
dormitory	Schlafsaal	dortoir	ili dormitorio
key	Schlüssel	la clef	la chiave
I have a reservation	Ich habe ein Zimmer reserviert	J'ai fait une réservation	Ho fatto una una prenotazione

SIGHTSEEING

bus	der Bus	l'autobus	el autobus
tram	die Strassenbahn	le tramway	el tram
train	der Zug	le train	il treno
bus station		la gare routière	
train station	der Bahnhof	la gare	la stazione
information (office)	Information	les renseignements	l'informazioni
boat	Boot	le bateau	la barca
(steam) boat	(Dampfer) Schiff	le bateau (à vapeur)	il battello (a vapore)
boat trip	Schiffahrt	la navigation	la navigazione
parking	Parkplatz	la place de stationnement	il parcheggio
car park	Parkhaus	le parking	l'autosilo
(hire) bicycle	Fahrrad/Mietvelo	le vélo (de location)	la bicicletta (a noleggio)
airport	Flughafen	l'aéroport	l'aeroporto
bank	Bank	la banque	il banco
church	Kirche	l'église	la chiesa
cathedral	Dom	la cathédrale	il duomo/la cattedrale
main square	Hauptplatz	la place centrale	la piazza principale
post office	Postamt	le bureau de poste	la posta
tourist office	Verkehrsamt	l'office du tourisme	l'ente turistico

TIME

morning	Vormittag	le matin	la mattina
afternoon	Nachmittag	l'apres-midi	il pomeriggio
evening	Abend	le soir	la sera
in the morning	morgens	le matin	di mattina
in the afternoon	nachmittags	l'après-midi	di pomeriggio
in the evening	abends	le soir	di sera
yesterday	gestern	hier	ieri
today	heute	aujourd'hui	oggi
tomorrow	morgen	demain	domani
Monday	Montag	lundi	lunedi
Tuesday	Dienstag	mardi	martedi
Wednesday	Mittwoch	mercredi	mercoledi
Thursday	Donnerstag	jeudi	giovedi
Friday	Freitag	vendredi	venerdi
Saturday	Samstag/Sonnabend	samedi	sabato
Sunday	Sonntag	dimanche	domenica

SHOPPING

How much does this cost?	Wieviel kostet das?	C'est combien, s'il vous plaît?	Quant'e, per favore?
I would like...	Ich hätte gern...	Je voudrais...	Vorrei...
Do you have...?	Haben Sie...?	Est-ce que vous avez...	Avere...?
expensive	teuer	cher	caro
cheap	billig	pas cher/bon marché	a buon prezzo
bank	Bank	la banque	la banca
book shop	Buchladen	la librairie	la libreria
chemist/pharmacy	Apotheke	la pharmacie	la farmacia
hairdresser	Friseur/Frisör	le coiffeur	il parruchiere
market	Markt	le marché	il mercato
newsagent	Zeitungskiosk	le magasin de journeaux	l'edicola
travel agent	Reisebüro	l'agence de voyages	l'agenzia di viaggi

EATING OUT

Have you got a table for...?	Haben sie einen Tisch für ...?	Avez-vous une table pour...?	Avete una tavola per ...?
The bill/check, please	Zahlen, bitte	L'addition, s'il vous plait	Il conto, per favore
I am a vegetarian	Ich bin Vegetarier	Je suis végétarien(ne)	Sono vegetariano(a)
waitress/waiter	Fräulein/Herr Ober	Madame/Mademoiselle/ Monsieur	cameriera/camariere
menu	die Spiesekarte	le menu/la carte	il menù
wine list	Weinkarte	la carte des vins	la lista dei vini
breakfast	Frühstück	le petit déjeuner	la prima colazione
lunch	Mittagessen	le déjeuner	il pranzo
dinner	Abendessen	le dîner	la cena

MENU DECODER: GERMAN

Ei	egg	Mineralwasser	mineral water
Eis	ice cream	Obst	fresh fruit
Fisch	fish	Pfeffer	pepper
Fleisch	meat	Pommes frites	chips
Garnelen	prawns	Reis	rice
gebacken	baked/fried	Rind	beef
gebraten	roast	Rostbraten	steak
gekocht	boiled	Rotwein	red wine
Gemüse	vegetables	Salz	salt
vom Grill	grilled	Schinken/Speck	ham
Hendle/Hahn/Huhn	chicken	Schlag	cream
Kaffee	coffee	Schokolade	chocolate
Kartoffell/Erdäpfel	potatoes	Schwein	pork
Käse	cheese	Tee	tea
Knödel	dumpling	Wasser	water
Lamm	lamb	Weisswein	white wine
Meeresfrüchte	seafood	Wurst	sausage (fresh)
Milch	milk	Zucker	sugar

MENU DECODER: FRENCH

l'agneau	lamb	grillé	grilled
l'ail	garlic	le homard	lobster
le bifteck/le steak	steak	le jambon	ham
le boeuf	beef	le lait	milk
le canard	duck	les légumes	vegetables
le chocolat	chocolate	l'oeuf	egg
le citron	lemon	le pain	bread
les crevettes	prawns	poché	poached
les crustacées	shellfish	le poivre	pepper
cuit au four	baked	le poisson	fish
l'eau minérale	mineral water	les pommes de terre	potatoes
les escargots	snails	le porc	pork
le frites	chips	le potage	soup
le fromage	cheese	le poulet	chicken
le fruit frais	fresh fruit	le sucre	sugar
les fruits de mer	seafood	le thé	tea
le gâteau	cake	la viande	meat
la glace	ice/ice cream	le vin blanc/rouge	white/red wine

MENU DECODER: ITALIAN

agnello	lamb	lesso	boiled
aglio	garlic	il manzo	beef
al forno	baked	le patate	potatoes
alla griglia	grilled	le patate fritte	chips
arrosto	roast	il pesce	fish
la bistecca	steak	il pollo	chicken
i carciofi	artichikes	il pomodoro	tomato
la carne	meat	il prosciutto cotto/crudo	cooked/cured ham
carne di miale	pork	il riso	rice
la cipolla	onion	la salsiccia	sausage
i contorni	vegetables	i spinaci	spinach
i fagioli	beans	il tè	tea
il fegato	liver	il tonno	tuna
il finocchio	fennel	l'uovo	egg
il formaggio	cheese	vino blanco	white wine
frutti di mare	seafood	vino rosso	red wine
il gelato	ice cream	gli zucchini	courgettes
il latte	milk	la zuppa	soup

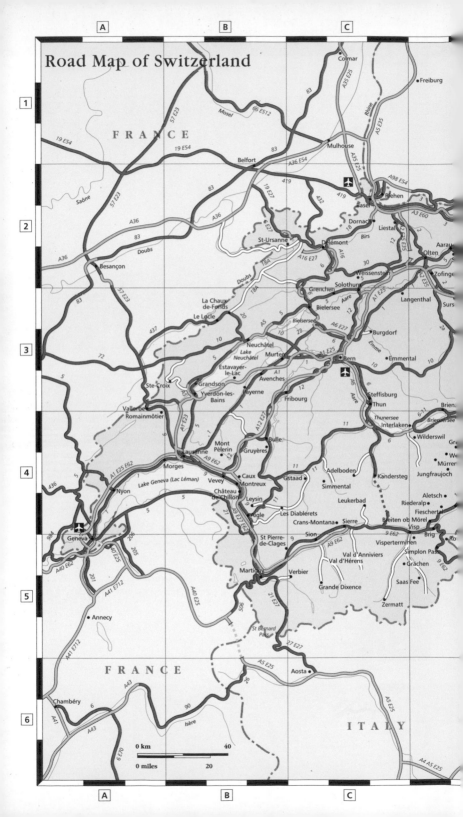

Road Map of Switzerland